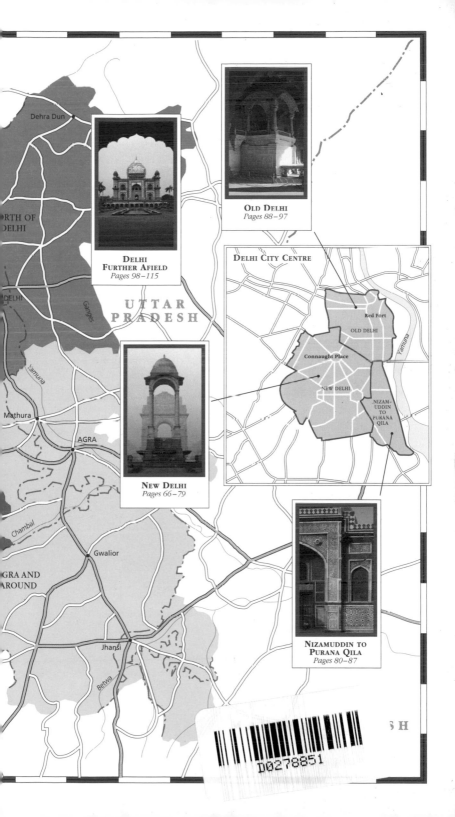

**OLD DELHI**
*Pages 88–97*

**DELHI FURTHER AFIELD**
*Pages 98–115*

**DELHI CITY CENTRE**

Dehra Dun

RTH OF
DELHI

DELHI

**UTTAR PRADESH**

Ganges

Yamuna

Red Fort

OLD DELHI

Connaught Place

NEW DELHI

NIZAM-
UDDIN
TO
PURANA
QILA

Mathura

AGRA

Chambal

Gwalior

GRA AND
AROUND

Jhansi

Betwa

**NEW DELHI**
*Pages 66–79*

**NIZAMUDDIN TO PURANA QILA**
*Pages 80–87*

S H

D0278851

DK TRAVEL GUIDES

# DELHI
## AGRA & JAIPUR

## DORLING KINDERSLEY *TRAVEL GUIDES*

# DELHI
# AGRA & JAIPUR

*Main Contributors:* ANURADHA CHATURVEDI
DHARMENDAR KANWAR & RANJANA SENGUPTA

DK

**DORLING KINDERSLEY**
LONDON • NEW YORK • SYDNEY • DELHI
PARIS • MUNICH • JOHANNESBURG
www.dk.com

# A DORLING KINDERSLEY BOOK

www.dk.com

PROJECT EDITOR Aruna Ghose
ART EDITOR Alpana Khare
EDITORS Ira Pande, Madhulita Mohapatra, Razia Grover
DESIGNERS Anand Naorem, Benu Joshi, Mugdha Sethi
CARTOGRAPHY Uma Bhattacharya
PICTURE EDITOR Radhika Singh

MAIN CONTRIBUTORS
Anuradha Chaturvedi, Dharmendar Kanwar, Partho Datta,
Premola Ghose, Ranjana Sengupta, Subhadra Sengupta

PHOTOGRAPHERS
Aditya Patankar, Amit Pashricha, Dinesh Khanna,
Fredrick & Laurence Arvidsson, Ram Rahman

ILLUSTRATORS
Ajay Sethi, Ampersand, Ashok Sukumaran, Avinash,
Dipankar Bhattacharya, Gautam Trivedi, Mark Warner

Reproduced by Colourscan, Singapore
Text film output by Express Colour Scan, Delhi
Printed and bound by L. Rex Printing Company Limited, China

First published in Great Britain in 2000
by Dorling Kindersley Limited
9 Henrietta Street, London WC2E 8PS

Copyright 2000 © Dorling Kindersley Limited, London

ISBN 0 7513 2744 1

**The information in every
Eyewitness Travel Guide is checked annually**.
Every effort has been made to ensure that this book is as
up-to-date as possible at the time of going to press. Some details,
however, such as telephone numbers, opening hours, prices,
gallery hanging arrangements and travel information are liable to
change. The publishers cannot accept responsibility for any
consequences arising from the use of this book.
We value the views and suggestions of our readers very highly.
Please write to: Senior Managing Editor, Dorling Kindersley Travel
Guides, Dorling Kindersley, 9 Henrietta Street, London WC2E 8PS.
**The external boundaries of India as shown on the maps are
neither correct nor authentic.**

◁ **A view of Taj Mahal from the river**

A bullock-cart and mustard fields

# CONTENTS

## HOW TO USE THIS GUIDE 6

Kishangarh miniature

# INTRODUCING DELHI, AGRA & JAIPUR

A sandstone *jaali*

A traditional *thali*

**Image of the young Krishna**

Humayun's Tomb

# HOW TO USE THIS GUIDE

THIS GUIDE helps you to get the most from your visit to the region. It provides both detailed practical information and expert recommendations. *Introducing Delhi, Agra and Jaipur* maps the region and sets it in its historical and cultural context. The three regional sections, plus *Delhi*, describe important sights, using maps, photographs and illustrations. Features cover topics from music and dance to food and festivals. Restaurant and hotel recommendations can be found in *Travellers' Needs*. The *Survival Guide* has tips on everything from transport to using the telephone, and the *Glossary* explains Indian terms and words.

## DELHI

The city is divided into areas, each with its own chapter. A last chapter, *Further Afield*, covers peripheral sights. All sights are numbered and plotted on the chapter's area map. Information on each sight is easy to locate as it follows the numerical order on the map.

**Sights at a Glance** lists the chapter's sights by category: Mosques and Tombs, Museums and Galleries, Streets and Gardens, Historic Sites, Monuments and Markets.

**Stars** indicate the sights that no visitor should miss.

**All pages** relating to Delhi have red thumb tabs.

**A locator map** shows where you are in relation to other areas of the city centre.

**1 Area Map**
*For easy reference, sights are numbered and located on a map. City centre sights are also marked on the* Delhi Street Finder map *(pages 122–31).*

**2 Street-by-Street Map**
*This gives a bird's-eye view of the key areas in each chapter.*

**A suggested route** for a walk is shown in red.

**3 Detailed information**
*The sights in Delhi are described individually. Useful addresses, telephone numbers, opening hours and other practical information are also provided. The key to the symbols used is on the back flap of the book.*

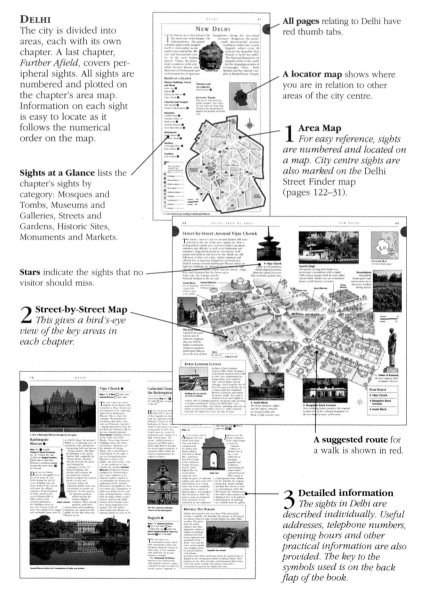

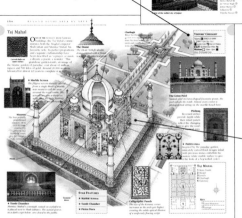

# 1 Introduction

*The landscape, history and character of each region is outlined here, showing how the area has developed over the centuries and what it has to offer to the visitor today.*

## BEYOND DELHI AREA BY AREA

Apart from Delhi, the region has been divided into three areas, each of which has a separate chapter. The most interesting cities, towns and villages, and other places to visit are numbered on a *Pictorial Map*.

# 2 Pictorial Map

*This shows the road network and gives an illustrated overview of the whole region. All interesting places to visit are numbered and there are also useful tips on getting to, and around, the region by car and public transport.*

**Each area** can be quickly identified by its colour coding, shown on the inside front cover.

# 3 Detailed information

*All the important towns and other places to visit are described individually. They are listed in order, following the numbering on the* Pictorial Map. *Within each town or city, there is detailed information on important buildings and other sights.*

**For all top sights,** a Visitors' Checklist provides the practical information you will need to plan your visit.

**Story boxes** explore related topics.

# 4 The region's top sights

*These are given two or more full pages. Historic buildings are dissected to reveal their interiors. The most interesting towns or city centres are shown in a bird's-eye view, with sights picked out and described.*

# Introducing
# Delhi
# Agra & Jaipur

# Putting Delhi, Agra & Jaipur on the Map

THE DELHI, AGRA AND JAIPUR region lies in the heart of North India. It covers an area of about 114,000 sq km (44,000 sq miles) and has a population of over 47 million. Delhi is the capital of India, while Jaipur is the capital of Rajasthan. Agra is a major district headquarters in Uttar Pradesh. Delhi has an international airport. Agra and Jaipur are serviced by domestic flights. The region also has good road and railway connections, with Agra about three hours and Jaipur about four by train from Delhi.

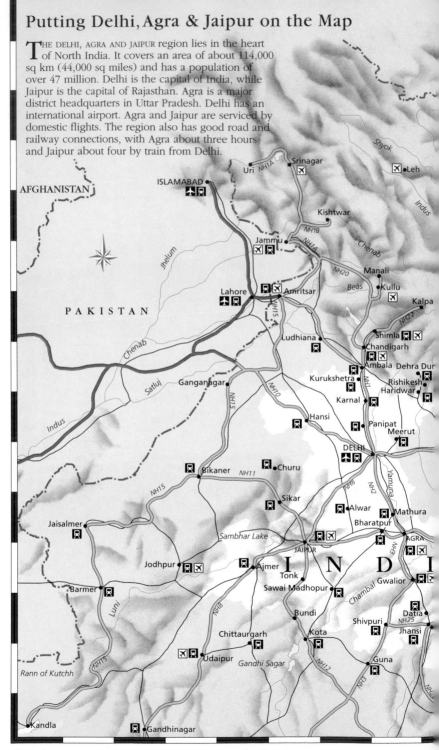

AFGHANISTAN

PAKISTAN

INDIA

Uri
Srinagar
Leh
ISLAMABAD
Kishtwar
Jammu
Manali
Lahore
Amritsar
Kullu
Kalpa
Ludhiana
Shimla
Chandigarh
Ambala
Dehra Dur
Ganganagar
Kurukshetra
Rishikesh
Haridwar
Karnal
Hansi
Panipat
Meerut
DELHI
Bikaner
Churu
Jaisalmer
Sikar
Alwar
Mathura
Bharatpur
Sambhar Lake
AGRA
Jodhpur
Ajmer
JAIPUR
Barmer
Tonk
Gwalior
Sawai Madhopur
Bundi
Shivpuri
Datia
Chittaurgarh
Kota
Jhansi
Udaipur
Gandhi Sagar
Guna
Kandla
Gandhinagar
Rann of Kutchh

Jhelum
Chenab
Satluj
Indus
Beas
Yamuna
Chambal
Luni

NH1A
NH1B
NH20
NH22
NH15
NH10
NH11
NH8
NH2
NH12
NH3
NH25
NH15

◁ **Miniature painting of a Rajput prince, surrounded by female attendants in a garden pavilion**

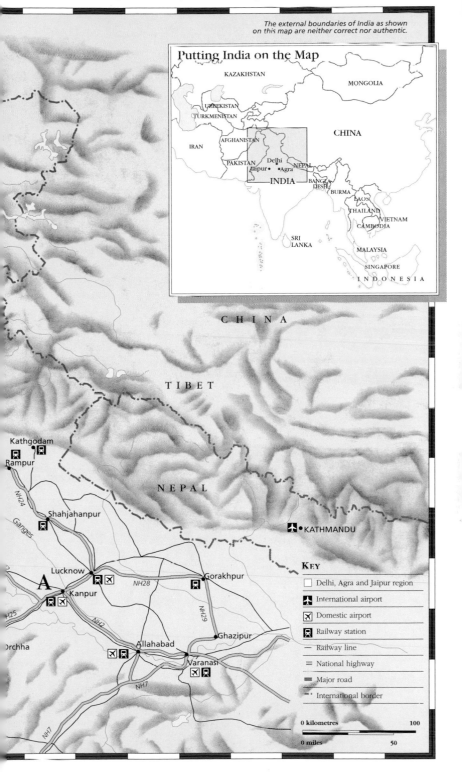

The external boundaries of India as shown
on this map are neither correct nor authentic.

Putting India on the Map

KAZAKHSTAN

MONGOLIA

UZBEKISTAN

TURKMENISTAN

CHINA

IRAN

AFGHANISTAN

PAKISTAN

Delhi

NEPAL

Jaipur • Agra

INDIA

BANGLA
DESH

BURMA

LAOS

THAILAND

VIETNAM

CAMBODIA

SRI
LANKA

MALAYSIA

SINGAPORE

INDONESIA

CHINA

TIBET

Kathgodam

Rampur

NEPAL

Shahjahanpur

KATHMANDU

Ganges

Lucknow

NH24

Gorakhpur

A

Kanpur

NH28

NH25

NH2

NH29

Orchha

Allahabad

Ghazipur

Varanasi

NH7

NH7

KEY

☐ Delhi, Agra and Jaipur region

✈ International airport

✕ Domestic airport

🚉 Railway station

— Railway line

= National highway

━ Major road

-·- International border

0 kilometres                    100

0 miles                    50

# Delhi City Centre and Greater Delhi

Some of Delhi's most impressive buildings can be seen in this area. The sights described in this book are grouped within three areas, each of which can be explored on foot. Vijay Chowk is the vantage point for the grand sweep of Raj buildings grouped on Raisina Hill. To the north, the magnificent Jami Masjid with its busy hive of lanes, was once the heart of the Mughal empire and is still the focus of Old Delhi. The past and present mingle here and yet preserve their own space and identity. To the east, the medieval quarter around the *dargah* of the Sufi Nizamuddin Auliya leads along Mathura Road to the ruined Purana Qila. This ancient site has interesting origins, going back to a distant mythological past.

**Vijay Chowk (see p70), at the base of Raisina Hill, is surrounded by government offices**

**Buddha Jayanti Park (see p104), has been created on the Ridge in northwest Delhi**

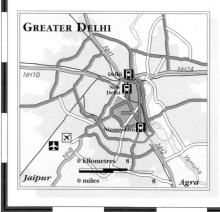

**GREATER DELHI**

NH10   NH1   NH24

Delhi

New Delhi

Nizamuddin

NH8   NH2

Yamuna

*Jaipur*    0 kilometres   8    *Agra*

0 miles   8

## Greater Delhi

*North Delhi houses the university and historic sites associated with the Old City. South Delhi, around the Qutb Minar and Mehrauli, has grown into a busy commercial and residential area.*

MUGHAL GARDENS

RASHTRAPATI BHAVAN

CATHEDRAL CHURCH OF THE REDEMPTION

CHURCH ROAD

PARLIAMENT HOUSE

CENTRAL SECRETARIAT

VIJAY CHOWK   RAJPATH

LAKSHMI NARAYAN MANDIR

CONNAUGHT PLACE

CONNAUGHT CIRCUS

JANTAR MANTAR

National Museum

NEHRU MEMORIAL MUSEUM AND LIBRARY

GANDHI SMRITI

LODI GARDENS

New Delhi

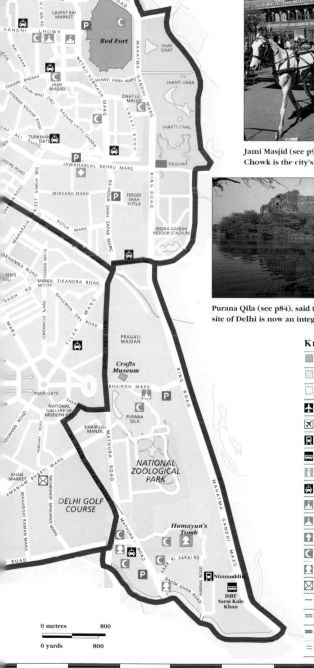

Jami Masjid (see p92) near Chandni
Chowk is the city's main mosque

Purana Qila (see p84), said to be the oldest historical
site of Delhi is now an integral part of the modern city

## KEY

| | |
|---|---|
| ⬛ | Major sight |
| ⬜ | Built-up area |
| ⬜ | Greater Delhi |
| ✈ | International airport |
| ✈ | Domestic airport |
| 🚉 | Railway station |
| 🚌 | Bus station |
| ℹ | Tourist information |
| 🚓 | Police station |
| 🛕 | Temple |
| 🙏 | *Gurudwara* |
| ✝ | Church |
| C | Mosque |
| ⚰ | Tomb |
| ⊠ | Post office |
| — | Railway line |
| ═ | National highway |
| ▬ | Major road |
| = | Minor road |

| | | |
|---|---|---|
| 0 metres | | 800 |
| 0 yards | | 800 |

# A PORTRAIT OF
# DELHI, AGRA & JAIPUR

THE DELHI, AGRA AND JAIPUR REGION *lies at the geographical heart of North India. Its strategic location along the north-south and east-west routes has given it a focal position in Indian history and many great empires have been ruled from here. What we see today is a dynamic blend of the old and the new, a proudly traditional social structure within a modern liberalized economy.*

This landlocked region is enclosed by mountains to the north, the desert and the forested Aravallis to the west. To the east are the agriculturally rich riverine plains, with vast fields of sugarcane, wheat, mustard and lentils. Southwards, these flat plains dramatically metamorphose into the earth pillars of the Chambal ravines, a rugged landscape once inhabited by fierce bandits. Invaders, entering the subcontinent from the mountain passes of the northwestern frontiers, conquered this region centuries earlier and made it their home.

**Ganesha mask**

## THE LEGACY OF THE PAST

The earliest civilization in this region was the Harappan culture in the second millennium BC. However, it was the Aryan settlements in the next millennium that provided the region with its philosophical moorings, epic literature, such as the *Ramayana* and *Mahabharata,* and its early Hindu kingdoms. In the first and second centuries, the area was the centre of a Buddhist empire when the Kushana emperors who ruled from Taxila (now in Pakistan) made Mathura their second capital. After the decline of the great Hindu and

Men in colourful turbans gather at the village square

◁ A young Rajasthani girl at work in a mustard field

Cenotaphs of the Bharatpur kings at Kusum Sarovar near Brindavan

Buddhist empires, powerful Rajput rulers seized control of parts of North India. Many of the magnificent forts from which their feudal kingdoms were ruled can still be seen today.

Religion has always been the cultural link between the epochs, and by the 13th century, Hinduism had been influenced by the Bhakti Movement which stressed the need for a personal god. This resulted in the Krishna cult, centred around Mathura and Brindavan – places associated with the youth of this popular god. Even as the Bhakti Movement flourished, invaders from Afghanistan and Central Asia conquered the north. Delhi, and later Agra, became the capitals of the Muslim sultans. The cross-fertilization of indigenous and Islamic cultures bred a unique hybrid that influenced art, architecture, music and cuisine, reaching its zenith with the Mughals.

The 19th century saw the decline of the Mughal empire and the growing

An open-air village school near Neemrana

power of the British East India Company. In 1858, the East India Company's territories in India were transferred to the British Crown, and the country settled down to a 90-year span of Pax Britannica. The legacy of the British Raj lives on in modern India's administrative and educational systems, and English is today the common language of communication between India's different linguistic regions and states.

In 1947, British rule came to an end and India became an independent nation. Since then, the country has faced the challenge of building industries, and tackling the social problems of illiteracy, poverty and the caste system. As the population of India raced towards one billion, these problems became more pressing. So, in the 1990s, India adopted an open-market economy, adding yet another dimension of change to a land that is constantly on the move.

## PEOPLE AND CULTURE

The capital of India, New Delhi, is known as a city of migrants. After the violent Partition of India and Pakistan in 1947, millions of people, mainly from West Punjab, flocked here in search of a new life. Since then, there has been a continuing influx of people from all over India. The majority of Delhi's 12 million citizens have settled here primarily for economic reasons – the average wage here is twice that of the country as a whole.

This mega-city nevertheless retains a small-town friendliness in its different neighbourhoods. Life still centres around the family, even though the joint family system is breaking down here, as is the case in all big Indian cities. Beyond the family is the larger world of the regional community which plays a significant role in the city's social and cultural life. Diaspora groups very often come together for auspicious occasions such as marriages or festivals, with which the Indian calendar is punctuated.

Its mixed population has made Delhi a resolutely cosmopolitan city where Hindus, Muslims and Christians live side by side. Yet, each community has retained its distinct cultural identity, and the city is less a melting pot than a *thali* (plate) whose offerings may be savoured singly or in interesting combinations.

Different levels of development are evident in Delhi, Agra and Jaipur. But in all three cities, with the liberalized economy bringing in a sudden flood of consumer goods, and cable television channels beaming foreign cultures into their homes, the lifestyles and expectations of the people are rapidly changing.

What makes the region so interesting is that contrasts often exist here in perfect harmony – a bullock cart plods placidly beside the latest luxury car; weather forecasts are made both by satellite imaging and astrological calculations; and jeans-clad youngsters eating pizza in fast food joints are just as much at ease in a sari or *dhoti*, sitting cross-legged on the floor at home, to participate in traditional ceremonies or rituals.

Bullock carts still transport rural goods

A fashion model

A religious procession in Jaipur moves along in traditional splendour

# Landscape and Wildlife

THE DELHI, AGRA AND JAIPUR REGION lies at the heart of Northern India and covers a wide ecological zone, flanked by the Himalayas to the north and the ravines of the River Chambal to the south. To the west are the Aravalli mountain range and the Thar Desert, and to the east stretch the riverine plains watered by the Yamuna and the Chambal. Forests once covered much of this area but, with growing urbanization, have now been reduced to a few pockets around the national parks. These are the habitats of many prized species, like the endangered tiger.

*The peacock, India's national bird*

## INDIAN TREES

The region's rich variety of trees has local species as well as some of recent import. Some are sacred, others are valued for their healing qualities.

*Banyan leaves*

## SUB-HIMALAYAN REGION
The Indian pine *(chir)* and *sal (Shorea robusta)* once formed thick forests that covered this area, but few remain today. However, there are still areas with sufficient forest cover to support a varied wildlife.

## DRY DECIDUOUS FORESTS
This ecological zone covers the arid and semi-arid tracts along the Aravallis. The mixed vegetation of scrub and deciduous trees, comprises acacias, cassia and *dhak (Butea monosperma)*, cacti and wild grasses.

**Indian elephants** *are smaller than the African species and are found on the lower Himalayan slopes. These gentle, intelligent animals are easy to train and domesticate.*

**Sambar**, *India's largest deer, is crowned with impressive antlers.*

**Cheetal**, *the graceful Indian spotted deer, is found in herds in the grassland areas.*

**Tiger**, *the national animal, is now a protected species. Loss of forest cover today has brought it to the brink of extinction.*

**Monkeys** *of two types, the rhesus and the langur, are found here.*

**Crested serpent eagle**, *with its underwing pattern of black and white bands, is a large raptor often seen in the Ranthambhore forests.*

**Ashoka** (Saraca indica), *one of India's five sacred trees, is extolled in Indian literature.*

**Pipal** (Ficus religiosa), *a hardy tree that grows anywhere, is also the sacred Bodhi tree under which the Buddha attained enlightenment in Bodh Gaya.*

**Neem** (Azadirachta indica). *This large, shade-giving tree has an extraordinary range of medicinal, antiseptic and disinfectant properties.*

**Kadamba** (Anthocephalus cadamba) *is a tall majestic tree associated with Krishna and Brindavan.*

## WETLANDS

In the southwest are shallow, inland lakes, marshes and swamps that have been formed from subterranean artesian wells. This is the habitat of otters and a wide variety of resident and migratory birds who feed on fish and aquatic plants.

## RIVERINE AREAS

These lie to the south and east along the Yamuna and Chambal rivers. The southern area is marked by desolate ravines, formed by erosion and covered with tufts of wiry grass, but to the east the rich alluvial plains form a thriving agricultural belt. The rivers support a rich aquatic wildlife.

**Painted stork** *with its black and pink plumage, keeps its long beak immersed in water, probing the sediment at the bottom for food.*

**Gharial** (Gavialis gangeticus) *is a species of crocodile found in the Ganges and its tributaries. It is named after the pitcher-like (ghara) hump on its long, lean snout.*

**Darter or snake bird** *is a bird with dark, glossy plumage. Large flocks can be found in marshy areas, spearing fish with their sharp beaks and then swallowing them.*

**King cobra** *is the world's largest venomous snake. This lethal reptile has a characteristic mark on its hood and is considered to be one of Shiva's sacred creatures.*

# Religions

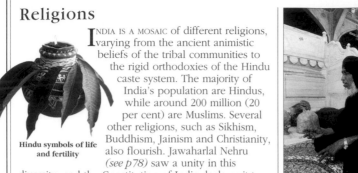

INDIA IS A MOSAIC of different religions, varying from the ancient animistic beliefs of the tribal communities to the rigid orthodoxies of the Hindu caste system. The majority of India's population are Hindus, while around 200 million (20 per cent) are Muslims. Several other religions, such as Sikhism, Buddhism, Jainism and Christianity, also flourish. Jawaharlal Nehru *(see p78)* saw a unity in this diversity, and the Constitution of India declares it to be a secular republic, where the state has no official religion and all faiths can be freely practised.

**Hindu symbols of life and fertility**

**Sufi mystic at a *dargah***

## HINDUISM

THE BEDROCK of Hinduism constitutes the four *Vedas* and the *Upanishads,* which are a holistic compilation of knowledge, philosophy and ethics. Yet, Hinduism is not a religion of the Book, but a way of life that has systematically evolved over the past 5,000 years.

In practice, Hindus worship a huge pantheon of gods and goddesses *(see pp22–3).* Socially, they can be divided into four castes – the upper caste Brahmins (priests), the Kshatriyas (warriors), the Vaishyas (merchants and traders), and the lowest caste, Sudras (workers). The caste system envisioned

**The sacred feet of Vishnu**

society as an organic whole with each part or caste performing a vital function.

The traditional family structure was that of a joint family presided over by its patriarch. This is now fast disappearing in urban areas. Yet, *sanskara,* traditional values, are still instilled into children, and complicated rites mark each stage of orthodox Hindu life. There is also an aspect of Hinduism which shuns idol-worship, and prefers to concentrate on larger philosophical issues. Sadhus, who wear saffron to indicate their retreat from the material world, are its most visible practitioners. They hold a most respected position in Hindu society.

## ISLAM

ISLAM WAS INTRODUCED into Western India in the 8th century by Arab traders, but it gained prominence in the north only after the 12th century, when it was declared the state religion under the medieval Muslim rulers.

Today, Muslims are India's second largest religious community, despite a large exodus to Pakistan after the traumatic Partition of 1947 *(see pp58–9).* Muslims can be broadly divided into two sects, the Sunnis and the Shias. The latter believe that Prophet Mohammed's cousin Ali and his descendents are the true imams. Traditional Muslim education, based on the Koran, is still imparted by the clergy in *madrasas* near mosques, which are central to the entire community. In India, the Friday public prayers, led by the local imam, are only open to men, and nearly all Muslim places of worship follow strict rules of segregation.

Sufism is a less orthodox mystic Islamic order. Its teachings emphasize direct experience of god, and Sufis believe that mystical ecstasy can be attained even through music and dance. Sufi saints like Nizamuddin Auliya *(see p82)* attracted many converts from Hinduism, and the fusion of the two religious traditions led to a flowering of poetry, music and art.

**Matted hair, saffron clothes and ash-smeared bodies mark sadhus**

## SIKHISM

SIKHISM IS a reformist religion founded by Guru Nanak in the 15th century. Violently opposed to idol worship, rituals and the caste system, it believes in a form-less god. The Sikh, with his characteristic turban, is easy to identify. He is supposed to abide by the five "k"s: *kesh* (long hair), *kachha* (underpants), *kirpan* (small sword), *kangha* (comb) and *kara* (bracelet). The Sikhs follow the teachings of ten gurus that are contained in their holy book, the *Adi Granth*, kept in the Golden Temple at Amritsar (Punjab).

Religious persecution by the later Mughals led the tenth guru, Gobind Singh, to reorganize the community in 1699 as a military order called the Khalsa, based on the principles of *sangat* (congregation), *simran* (meditation), *kirtan* (hymn singing), *langar* and *pangat* (sharing and partaking of food in a common kitchen).

**Sikh priest reciting verses from the *Adi Granth***

## CHRISTIANITY

THE RISE OF CHRISTIANITY in this region dates to the late-15th century when Catholic missionaries travelled to India in the wake of Portuguese traders. About this time, Christian Armenian communities also settled in Mughal India, procuring a licence to trade. There is evidence that the

**Church services are often conducted in local dialects**

Mughal emperor Akbar *(see pp52–3)* invited Jesuit priests to religious discussions held in Fatehpur Sikri *(see pp170–71)*. With the coming of the East India Company, Pro-testant missionaries spread across the country, setting up educational institutions and hos-pitals in the 18th and 19th centuries. Many are still run by dedicated workers. They also involved themselves with reform movements and influenced the government to take measures against practices such as *sati (see p48)*. Marriages between Indians and the Europeans who came led to the birth of the Anglo-Indian community. During the Raj *(see pp56-7)*, the railways and many of the subordinate civil services were run by them.

Indian Christians believe that the apostle St Thomas brought the religion to South India in the 1st century AD. Today, church services have been Indianized to a large extent by absorbing some dialects, practices and rituals to make it easier for local worshippers to follow them.

## OTHER RELIGIONS

APART FROM THESE four major groups, India has other smaller though distinct religious communities. **Buddhists** are followers of Gautam Buddha who lived and preached the gospel of non-violence and peace. From India, Buddhism spread to other countries in Asia but, ironically, it has now nearly vanished in the land of its birth. The 14th Dalai Lama, the spiritual leader of the Tibetan Buddhists, now lives in India with his follo-wers in exile and is a widely respected figure. **Jains**, the followers of Mahavira, are a pacific and non-violent community who respect life in every form, and observe rigid fasts and self-denial They are divided into the Svetambaras (dressed in white) and the Digambaras (who shun clothing). The **Parsis** are followers of Zoroaster and came from Persia in the 7th century. A small community, it has nevertheless played a sig-nificant role in Indian industry and is known for its philanthropy. The first **Jews** came to India in about 587 BC and now live mainly in Mumbai and Cochin.

**A golden Buddha statue**

**Jain nuns cover their mouths to avoid swallowing insects**

# The Pantheon of Gods and Goddesses

THE GREAT PANTHEON of Hindu gods and goddesses is a bewildering array, ranging from anthropomorphic symbols and shapes to exotic half-human, half-animal forms. Each god has a personal *vahana* (vehicle) and symbols of power. Although community worship takes place in temples, especially on festivals, for most Hindus, the home with its own shrine and personal deities is where the daily *puja* (prayer) is conducted.

**Lakshmi**, *the goddess of wealth, is also the consort of Vishnu. Her vahana is an owl.*

**Saraswati**, *the goddess of learning and music, is the consort of Brahma and has a swan as her vahana. Seated on a lotus, with a garland of white flowers, she is seen as the embodiment of purity.*

**Shesh Nag** is the hundred-headed leviathan on whose coils Vishnu reclines.

**Narada**, the sage, accompanies Vishnu.

**Ganesha**, remover of obstacles.

**Hanuman**, the monkey god, is a faithful attendant of Lord Rama.

**Vishnu**, the Preserver, floats on Kshirsagar (the sacred ocean), the source of all life.

---

### RELIGIOUS SYMBOLS

**Om**, *a symbol of the primal sound, is recited to start all religious ceremonies.*

**Kamal** *("lotus") is a Vaishnavite symbol for purity.*

**Trishul** *("trident") is a Shaivite symbol of asceticism.*

**Chakra** *("wheel") is a universal symbol of the wheel of life.*

**Shankh** *("conch shell") is a Vaishnavite symbol of the life-giving ocean.*

**Ganesha**, the elephant-headed son of Shiva, is invoked at the start of any auspicious task.

**Hanuman** the monkey god (see p197), is invoked by those in need of courage and fortitude.

**Rama** (right), *the epitome of virtue, was Vishnu's seventh avatara (incarnation), and* **Krishna** (left), *the embodiment of love, was the eighth. Vishnu is said to assume these avataras to save the world from destruction. The last avatara, Kalki, will fashion a new world when this one reaches the end of its time.*

**Brahma** sits on a lotus attached to Vishnu's navel.

**Shiva** lives atop Mount Kailash. The River Ganges flows from his matted locks.

**Nandi**, the bull, is Shiva's vehicle and is always present at Shiva temples.

**Garuda** is Vishnu's vehicle on his travels through the cosmos.

**Parvati** *lives in the Himalayan hills with Shiva. This gentle daughter of the mountains is worshipped in many forms, which collectively represent the Devi (goddess) cult.*

**Durga** *rides a tiger with her deadly arsenal of weapons and destroys evil, in the form of the buffalo-demon Mahishasura. She is the fierce persona of the gentle Parvati.*

## THE HOLY TRINITY

A popular calendar picture depicts the Holy Trinity that comprises Brahma the Creator, Vishnu the Preserver, and Shiva the Destroyer. Vishnu mediates between Brahma and Shiva to preserve life. The world was created when the ocean was churned by the gods and demons *(see p45)* to extract the divine nectar *(amrit)*. The present age (Kaliyuga) is only one stage of the unending cycle of life.

**Kali**, *wearing a garland of skulls, rampages through creation, annihilating evil. Along with Durga, she is the patron goddess of many Rajput clans who lived by the sword.*

# Architecture: A Brief History

IN NORTH INDIA, monumental architecture followed historical and political change. The wide variety of styles that emerged were executed in a distinctly "Indian" way, influenced by climate and local building traditions. Sadly, few buildings before the 12th century survived the ravages of time, war and climate, but the region is rich in medieval remains, of which the Taj Mahal is the centrepiece. An interesting feature is the mingling of Hindu and Islamic styles, which blends the sensuous beauty of temple sculpture with the austere grandeur of Islamic architecture. Gardens, fountains, screened arches and shaded interiors are some features used for keeping buildings cool.

**Carved niche at Agra Fort**

## EARLY INDIAN ARCHITECTURE (UP TO 12TH CENTURY)

The temple was the social and economic focus of a town. Early Hindu temples, built on a square base, follow sacred building rules. The deity lies within the sanctum, and the outer surface is profusely decorated.

**Carved frieze on *shikhara***

***Garbbagriba*,** the womb-like inner sanctum sanctorum.

**Piled stone blocks raise the temple's height**

*Teli ka Mandir (9th century) at Gwalior (see p174) is a rare example of a North Indian temple of that time.*

The ***shikhara*** is a pointed arch that meets over the sanctum.

The ***mandapa*** is a hall in front of the sanctum.

The **entrance** is spanned by a square stone lintel, carved with sacred images.

## SULTANATE ARCHITECTURE (13TH TO 15TH CENTURIES)

Techniques for constructing true arches and domes were learnt by Indian masons from the Muslims after the 12th century. Mortar, another significant technology transfer, made it possible to build high structures. Hindu carving skills added a new element to the Islamic architectural lexicon.

**A sandstone and marble panel**

**Detail of a geometric panel**

**The dome** is crowned with a finial.

**Islamic arches** are often trimmed with a Hindu lotus bud fringe.

**Geometric ornamentation** is an Islamic feature.

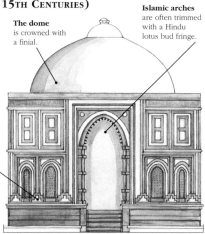

***Alai Darwaza*** *(c.1311) in Delhi, with one of the oldest surviving domes, is one of the gems of early Islamic architecture (see p112).*

## MUGHAL ARCHITECTURE (16TH TO LATE 18TH CENTURIES)

Mughal buildings awe the viewer and assert the exalted status of their imperial patron. Whether built of red sandstone or marble, symmetry, grandeur and landscaping are some common features. Inlay work, decorative *jaalis* and cusped arches give these buildings an ethereal grace that offsets their massive size.

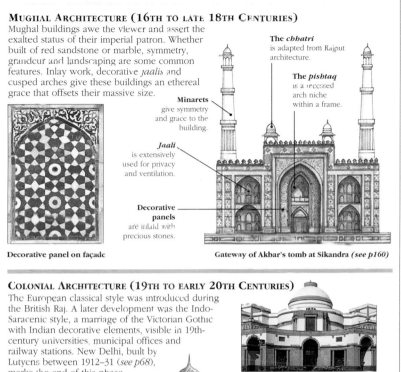

**The *chhatri***
is adapted from Rajput architecture.

**The *pishtaq***
is a recessed arch niche within a frame.

**Minarets**
give symmetry and grace to the building.

***Jaali***
is extensively used for privacy and ventilation.

**Decorative panels**
are inlaid with precious stones.

**Decorative panel on façade**

**Gateway of Akbar's tomb at Sikandra** *(see p160)*

## COLONIAL ARCHITECTURE (19TH TO EARLY 20TH CENTURIES)

The European classical style was introduced during the British Raj. A later development was the Indo-Saracenic style, a marriage of the Victorian Gothic with Indian decorative elements, visible in 19th-century universities, municipal offices and railway stations. New Delhi, built by Lutyens between 1912–31 *(see p68)*, marks the end of this phase.

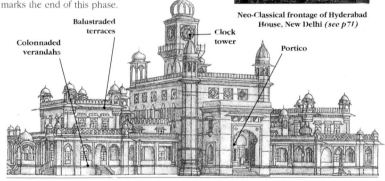

**Neo-Classical frontage of Hyderabad House, New Delhi** *(see p71)*

**Balustraded terraces**

**Clock tower**

**Colonnaded verandahs**

**Portico**

**Ajmer's Mayo College, built in the Indo-Saracenic style in 1875** *(see p219)*

## BUNGALOWS

An architectural legacy of the Raj, originally designed to house Europeans living in remote outposts, bungalows have broad, covered verandahs, a front porch and a balustraded roof. The term

**Government bungalow in New Delhi** *(see p69)*

was a corruption of "Bangla", or Bengal, for its basic structure was derived from the indigenous, Bengali rural hut. Until 1947, few bungalows outside towns had running water or electricity but their high ceilings and shaded interiors kept them dark and cool in summer. However, when Herbert Baker *(see p68)* designed a bungalow for New Delhi's mandarins, its unhappy occupants christened his airless edifice "Baker's Oven".

# Architectural Styles

**Marble podium at Delhi's Jami Masjid**

Some of the country's finest forts and palaces lie in this region. Forts often served both as defensive buildings and as self-sufficient walled cities, built along natural outcrops or near rivers. Palaces were either part of a fort complex or individual royal residences with public and private spaces separated by gardens and courtyards. Later, during the Raj, fortified palaces gave way to stately mansions inspired by European models. The beautiful garden tombs, of which the Taj is the most famous example, were a Mughal innovation. In contrast to these are rural houses that blend into the landscape. These eco-friendly structures, based on instinctive building skills and well-insulated, are both cheap and easy to build.

## FORTS

Most Mughal forts, built of red sandstone with marble trimmings, contained a city complex, with private and public areas and were seats of imperial power. Rajput forts, like Amber *(see pp200–201)* and Gwalior, on the other hand, follow a different plan and their solid bastions were built primarily for self-defence.

**Ramparts** have pierced holes for cannons.

**The *burj*** acted as a watchtower.

**Foundation inscription from the Red Fort**

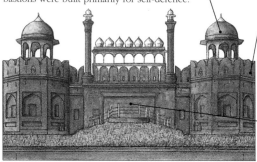

**Lahore Gate** is named after the direction it faced.

**Red Fort at Delhi *(see pp94–5)***

## PALACES

Some of the region's most spectacular palaces date to the 19th century in a style that imitated English stately homes. While, the older, medieval palaces nestle within forts and had separate quarters for men *(mardana)* and women (zenana) with landscaped gardens and private mosques or temples.

**The bangaldar roof** is crowned with decorative spikes.

**A grand flight of steps** leads to the gorgeous interior.

**The simple exterior** conceals a rich interior.

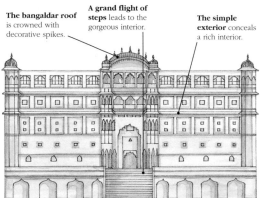

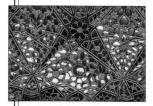

**Detail from a mirrored room**

*Samode Palace, built in the 19th century and now a heritage hotel (see pp232–3), has fabulously gilded and mirrored rooms. It is built in the traditional design but has period furniture rather than the usual cushions and floor coverings used in older palaces.*

## THE GARDEN TOMB

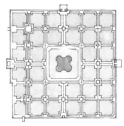

*The* **charbagh** *(see p167) is a terraced garden that surrounds the tomb to give its austere lines a soft focus. The Taj Mahal, set at the edge of one, is the most famous example of this style.*

**The dome** surmounts the central space.

**Arched cloisters** lead to the crypt.

*Humayun's tomb* (see p83) *is one of the earliest Mughal garden tombs, which were set on a raised plinth within a charbagh. Other features include a private mosque and crypts for other royal graves.*

## TRADITIONAL HOUSES

Indian villagers usually live in simple houses made of local material, often mud and thatch. They have cool, shaded interiors and are brightly decorated on the outside. Building materials come from the land and are renewed annually at Diwali (see p37).

**Mud walls** are reinforced with straw and cowdung.

**Thatched roofs** keep the interiors cool and shaded.

**Ritual paintings** brighten mud walls.

**A rural Indian house at Mandawa** *(see p213)*

## HAVELIS

The *haveli*, a multi-storeyed mansion for wealthy merchant families, was usually built around one or more courtyards which formed a focal point for the domestic activity of the joint family. Shekhawati's painted *havelis (see pp212–13)* are examples of this architectural style.

**The terrace** gave an airy overview of the surroundings.

**Covered verandahs** separated living areas into smaller private units.

*Haveli* **of the Bhartiya family, Shekhawati region**

## GLOSSARY OF TERMS

***Baoli*** Underground stepwell, such as Ugrasen's Baoli *(see p76)*.

***Burj*** Residential or fortificatory tower; also bastion.

***Chajja*** Overhanging eaves or cornices to protect buildings from the sun and rain.

***Chhatri*** Open square or octagonal pavilion, literally an umbrella.

**Chhatri**

***Diwan-i-Aam*** Hall of Public Audience.

***Diwan-i-Khas*** Hall of Private Audience.

***Gumbad/gumbaz*** Dome, often crowned with a finial; the term is also used for a mausoleum.

*Gumbad*

***Jharokha*** Overhanging oriel window supported on brackets; some were used for the official appearances of the ruler.

***Masjid*** Mosque.

***Mihrab*** Arched niche facing Mecca in a mosque.

**Jharokha**

***Minar*** Free-standing tower such as the Qutb Minar *(see p112)*.

***Mohalla*** Quarter of town inhabited by members of one caste.

***Namazgah*** Space near mosque for celebration of major Muslim festivals.

***Qila*** Castle, fortress, citadel.

***Sheesh Mahal*** **Minaret** Chamber profusely decorated with mirror mosaic; glass palace.

***Stambha*** Stately pillar, post or column.

***Stupa*** Tumulus, burial or reliquary mound.

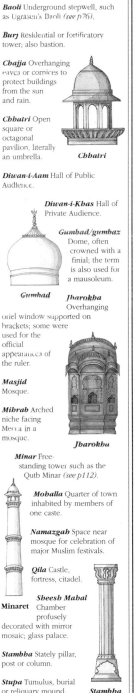

**Stambha**

# Music, Dance and Theatre

INDIA'S PERFORMING ARTS are simultaneously modes of worship and a joyous celebration of life. Music and dance originated in the temples, gradually acquiring a secular, more sensuous character as royal patrons founded individual schools *(gharanas)*. Two prominent classical forms in this region are Kathak and Hindustani music. The artiste creates a mood *(rasa)* which invites the audience to participate in it so as to make the performance a mutually shared experience.

*Sarangi and bow*

*Qawwalis and bhajans are devotional songs that go back to medieval Sufi and Bhakti cults. Sung intensely to arouse mystical ecstasy, they celebrate the power of divine love.*

*Raslila, a folk variation of Kathak, narrates the life of Lord Krishna. Traditionally, the Ramlila (below) and the Raslila featured young boys.*

**Hands** are used in stylized *mudras*, symbolic movements that follow the *Natya Shastra*, a classic treatise on the performing arts.

*Lehenga, a long skirt worn over tight pyjamas, accentuates the swirling movement of the dancer.*

*Ramlila enacts the story of the epic Ramayana in a cycle of ten episodic folk plays during the Dussehra festival (see p37).*

## HINDUSTANI MUSIC

The origins of Hindustani music date to about 3000 BC and the *Sama Veda (see p319)*. The *raga* (melodic mode) and *tala* (rhythmic cycle) are the foundation of Indian classical music, of which the Dhrupad and the Khayal are two major vocal styles. Indian classical music has no formal notational score, giving artistes a wide scope to elaborate the mood of a *raga*, each with its own set of notes. To preserve individuality, knowledge was passed down orally from teacher to pupil through schools called *gharanas*. The Gwalior *gharana (see p174)* is said to be the oldest one in the region.

*Ravi Shankar, one of India's foremost sitar players, introduced classical music to the West.*

*Amjad Ali Khan belongs to a famous family of sarod players, who developed the rabab, a medieval lute from Central Asia, to its present form.*

*Nine* **rasas** *(moods) are mentioned in the 4th-century treatise* Natya Shastra. *From the erotic, comic and pathetic to the odious, marvellous and quiescent, rasa covers every mood and expression, whether in music or painting. This 17th-century* Ragamala *painting (see pp30–31) depicts the mood of the morning* Raga Todi.

BAYADÈRE OF MEWAT.

*Nautch Girl was the pejorative title given to dancing girls in the 19th century when Kathak became mere entertainment.*

**Rapid body movements** keep time with the beat of the accompanying percussionist.

**Ghungroos** are brass bells that aid the rhythmic beat. Foot stamping controls and varies their sound.

**Gorgeous jewellery** and the colour red on the hands and feet make the intricacies of the dance easy to see.

## KATHAK

This North Indian classical dance form, that received lavish patronage in the court of Jaipur, derives from the epic tales *(kathas)* narrated by balladeers. A typical Kathak performance is a blend of complex footwork and facial expressions *(abhinaya)* to enact an episode, often from Krishna's life.

*Bismillah Khan on the* shehnai, *a ceremonial reed pipe of the oboe family that is now also a concert instrument.*

*Zakir Hussain* plays the tabla, *a pair of drums that provide percussion to most music and dance performances.*

*Contemporary theatre draws on classical Sanskrit drama. Avant-garde street plays are popular with fringe and protest theatre groups. The National School of Drama Repertory (see p120) often produces Indian adaptations of classical plays, such as* King Lear, *seen above.*

# Painting

**A bird by Mansur**

TWO DISTINCT SCHOOLS of painting, Rajput and Mughal, emerged in 16th-century North India. The meteoric growth and popularity of miniature painting was due to the introduction of paper as well as the lavish patronage of Muslim and Rajput rulers. The Mughals encouraged Persian miniature painters to settle in India where they came into contact with indigenous traditions. A fusion of the two styles under Akbar, Jahangir and Shah Jahan led to a burst of artistic activity when court painters, such as Mansur, produced folios of birds, flowers, royal portraits and illustrated manuscripts. As Mughal patronage declined in the 18th century, other regional centres of art developed in North India.

*Jain palm leaf manuscripts,
such as this piece (c.1439), use
bright primary colours. Their
large-eyed human figures and
narrative depiction of themes
influenced early Rajput art.*

**Monsters** symbolize the threats to Krishna at birth.

***Early Mughal paintings*** *were
pictorial narratives of historical
events and literary texts. This leaf
from a 16th-century* Babur Nama
*shows Babur crossing the River
Son. Mughal landscapes are
rendered realistically, unlike the
more romantic Rajput allegories.*

**Space** is divided into units, each dealing with a separate episode of the story.

***Rajput paintings***
*are known for their
bright colours and
stylized figures.
Classical texts and
religious figures are
recurrent subjects,
such as this 18th-
century page from the*
Rasikapriya *romance
of the Bundi School.*

**Ragamalas** *are sets
of paintings strung
like a garland, that
depict the mood of
individual ragas
(see p28). This
17th-century Ragini
Dev-Gandhari, an
early morning raga,
has dainty figures
and the delicate
floral border that
was a hallmark of
Mughal paintings.*

*Pahari painting emerged from the hill (pahari) states of the western Himalayas, where many artists went in search of work after the decline of Mughal patronage. Raja Sansar Chand of Kangra, a patron of this style, can be seen in this late 18th-century Pahari painting.*

**Nature** is depicted in metaphorical terms, as in the snake-like ripples of lightning.

**Narrative progression** shows the growth of Krishna from infancy to boyhood.

**Human faces** are drawn in profile and space lacks perspective.

**Colours** and pigments were extracted from precious stones and plants.

*The Company School flourished in the colonial period. This portrait of King Edward VII and Queen Alexandra, attired in Indian clothes and ornaments, was painted by a local artist as a specially commissioned work.*

## RAJPUT MINIATURES

Rajput ateliers were named after their patron courts *(see p215)*, each with a distinctive style, such as this 18th-century Mewar miniature, *Krshna Revealing his Divinity as Visnu to his Parents*. Rajput paintings have a narrative theme – a court episode or a mythological tale. Unlike Mughal paintings, their treatment of space and the natural world is poetic rather than realisitic and evokes a musical mood or *rasa (see p29)*. *Baramasa* (cycle of seasons) and *Ragamala* (garland of *ragas*) paintings are famous examples of this romantic style.

## CONTEMPORARY INDIAN ART

A nationalist poet, musician, philosopher and educationalist, Rabindranath Tagore (d.1943) pioneered the 19th-century Bengal Renaissance art movement, which was a step towards the modernist impulse in Indian art. He drew heavily on the rich mythic content of folk art. Later, Amrita Shergill (d.1940) brought a European style to Indian themes and scenes. Contemporary Indian art evolved from the work of these and other seminal artists. Yet it retained an Indian identity even when experimenting with fashionable European styles. Modern Indian artists have experimented with Tantric symbols, mythology and miniature paintings to produce a vibrant art style which has tried to retain the richness of its folk and classical art forms even as they work with different media and material.

*Head Study,*
**Rabindranath Tagore**

# Indian Design

INDIAN DESIGN HAS EVOLVED out of a very close bond between the artist and his craft, in which the skill of the hand is regarded as a sacred gift, passed down from father to son in an unbroken line. This has ensured a design tradition that is both a living art form as well as a means of fulfilling the everyday needs of the community, be they sacred or functional. Freely enriched by the traditions of other races and cultures, India's artistic heritage is renowned throughout the world for its vibrancy and creativity.

**Mughal flower motif**

*Geometric designs* form the base of traditional decoration.

**Mud** and thatch are regarded as sacred media, being the gift of Mother Earth.

**The rounded shape** of the pot has not changed since 2500 BC.

***Pottery** has a 5,000-year-old history (see pp44–5) making it one of the world's oldest skills. The potter's wheel produces cheap, eco-friendly objects of daily use.*

**The wheel** or *chakra* is regarded as a symbol of the eternal circle of life and death.

**Lime wash** applied on the mud surface adds colour and repels pests.

*The living space is embellished with surface decorations ranging from relief carvings to mirror-work. Whether a mud hut or palace, the Indian home is the origin of most forms of art.*

## COLOUR

The colours of Indian design are taken from nature, with names to match. The five shades of white are lyrically compared to the clouds when the rain is spent, the August moon, conch shell, jasmine flower and the surf of the sea. Indigo, madder and turmeric are valued for their dyes, and the crushed flowers of the flame of the forest *(Butea monosperma)* yield a soft yellow colour still used in rural India for playing Holi *(see p36)*. Each colour has a ritual significance as well: red is associated with weddings and festivals, saffron is the colour of warriors and ascetics, yellow is worn during the spring festival of Vasant, and green in the monsoon. The Indian dyer *(right)* uses plants and roots for extracting colour.

**A dyer at work**

***Animal and flower motifs*** *can be seen everywhere. The most elegant floral patterns were perfected in Mughal and Rajput painting (see pp30–31), while the popular lotus and peacock motifs are inherent to Buddhist and Hindu temple iconography. Worked in a variety of forms these motifs are most visible in textiles, carpets, painting, jewellery, ceramics and zardozi (see p153).*

**The peacock** is a popular symbol of royalty.

**The lotus** is associated grace and purity.

**Paisley** motifs are stylized representations of the mango and cypress.

**The poppy**, the iris, narcissus and tulip are textile motifs inspired by Mughal art.

***Marble inlay*** *can be traced to Mughal pietra dura (see pp156–7). Agra still has families of craftsmen whose ancestors worked at the Mughal court.*

**Precious stones** such as amethyst, lapis, carnelian and jade are inlaid by hand on marble.

**Floral patterns**, inspired by the Islamic paradise garden concept, are common.

## HOME AND FAMILY

The earliest art objects were those needed for everyday life. Emerging from the home and its daily rituals, the shape and form of articles was based on religious symbols which ensured their survival down the ages. With time, sophisticated materials and techniques learnt from royal courts enhanced design consciousness, resulting in a more exclusive range of decorative art

**Wall paintings** are often inspired by nature.

**Flame of the forest**

**Spices**

**Saffron turban for warriors**

**A vermilion-daubed shrine**

***Form and function*** *are equally important in Indian design, endowing even everyday utility objects with beauty. As architectural skills developed over the centuries, basic forms and materials became more sophisticated. This graceful trellised stone window is an example of this change.*

# Popular Culture

**MTV logo**

T<small>HE</small> CONTACT between Indian traditions and a Western global culture has triggered off a spontaneous and vibrant response among both rural and urban societies. The new trends in lifestyle, fashion and entertainment are influenced to some extent by commercial cinema and television. Combining the traditional with the modern, they reflect a change in popular tastes.

**Rangoli** *patterns are a traditional form of renewable art, created daily at entrances to homes. Elaborate designs are seen on auspicious occasions.*

**Statues** *of leaders such as Ambedkar, a champion of the oppressed classes, are a common sight. These colourful but tawdry images made by local sculptors are often installed in public parks.*

**The groom**, accompanied by a young boy, wears a string of flowers *(sehra)*, over his face.

**Plastic products** *are vastly popular throughout India and include toys and decorative items, as well as functional objects of everyday use.*

**The wedding chariot** is an extravagant gilt-plated carriage.

**Signboards** *scream their messages in lurid colours.*

**Street dancers**, *transvestites and eunuchs entertain audiences with bawdy dances.*

**The photographer's tent** *with its fanciful backdrop of exotic locations or film stars, is unique to village fairs.*

**Advertisement on wheels** *ranges from slogans and romantic verse to paintings of film stars and landscapes. Lorries, taxis, even the bicycle of a street vendor selling home-made ice-cream, are gaily painted with tempting messages.*

**Bidis** *are local cigarettes. The different brands have highly whimsical names with lurid wrappings that promote a virile, macho image.*

**Hindi films** *(often called Bollywood offerings) are India's response to Hollywood, especially the spaghetti western. The average formula film is a great mix of themes and emotions – love, violence, comedy, tragedy – generously peppered with song and dance sequences.*

**Rakhi**, *the simple thread tied on the wrist on the festival of Raksha Bandhan (see p39), is today made of imitation gold and silver.*

**Band leaders**, dressed in exotic uniforms, lead the procession.

**Fashion designers**, *models and beauty queens like Aishwarya Rai, Miss World 1997, are cult figures in urban India today.*

## WEDDING PROCESSION

Indian weddings are noisy, colourful affairs. The musical escort of the horse riding bridegroom is a brass band dressed in music hall or Salvation Army style uniforms, complete with braids and epaulettes. Sometimes the groom comes riding a gaudy, gilt-plated chariot, accompanied by an entourage of young relatives dancing to popular tunes from Hindi films. The whole spectacle is a modern day re-enactment of the pomp and pageantry associated with royal wedding processions in the past.

**Popular music** *such as Indipop and Bhangra Rap, popularized by Daler Mehndi and other singers, is a contemporary version of folk music. MTV Asia and Channel V are its main promoters.*

# Festivals in India

**Effigy of Ravana**

INDIANS LOVE CELEBRATIONS. Festivals are both religious and social events, where ritual fasting and joyful feasting often go hand in hand. Hindu festivals usually follow the lunar calendar and both the full moon *(purnima)* and the new moon *(pradosh)* are considered auspicious. Some fairs and festivities are connected to the pantheon of gods and goddesses, others to ancient pastoral, fertility or martial rites. Muslim festivals, too, are determined by the new moon. This means that the dates of festivals vary from year to year.

## SHISHIR (JAN–MAR)

THIS IS the most auspicious period in the Indian calendar. **Lohri** and **Makar Sankranti** follow one another in early January. The former is observed mainly by Punjabis as the height of winter, and the latter, confined to Jaipur, marks the movement of the sun from the equator to the Tropic of Capricorn. The wind usually changes direction on this day and colourful kites fill the sky. **Vasant Panchami**, towards the end of January, is considered the first day of spring. In February, devotees of Shiva observe **Shivaratri**, or the night of his celestial wedding to Parvati. **Holi**, one of the most important Hindu festivals in this region, takes place on a full-moon night, and is celebrated as the end of winter. On the eve of Holi, bonfires are lit and an effigy of the demon Holika is burnt to signify the triumph of good over evil. The next day, people swarm the streets, sprinkling coloured water and powder *(gulal)* on each other. This festival was especially dear to Lord Krishna, and around Mathura *(see p161)* it is played with great abandon.

**Holi colours everyone**

## VASANT (MAR–MAY)

THE HINDU YEAR begins with Vasant (spring). Nine days of fasting *(navaratris)* precede the birth of the hero-god Rama *(see p23)* on **Ramnavami**. During this period, most households prepare special vegetarian foods, which are cooked in *ghee* (clarified butter) without garlic or onions.

The pastoral festival of **Baisakhi** on 13 April heralds the harvest season in North India, and is celebrated with singing and dancing. Later in in the month comes **Shitala Ashtami**, a Rajasthani folk festival to commemorate Shitala Devi, goddess of smallpox and a manifestation of Durga. A religious fair is held at the Chaksu temple *(see p222)* to appease the goddess, and is attended by hundreds of villagers.

Towards the end of April, Shia Muslims observe **Muharram**, a ten-day period of mourning for the martyrdom of the Prophet's grandson, Hazrat Imam Hussain, at Karbala (Iraq). On the tenth and final day, impressive processions of *tazias* (replicas of his tomb) are taken out, followed by drummers and young boys and men dressed in black, who flagellate themselves in a frenzy of religious fervour.

**Holi celebrations in the villages of Brajbhumi, near Mathura**

## GRISHMA (MAY–JUN)

As the heat intensifies, the festival season comes to a halt. Muslims all over India celebrate **Milad-ul-Nabi**, the birthday of the Prophet. The devotees keep night long vigils at mosques, praying or reading from the holy Koran.

## VARSHA (JUL–SEP)

With the monsoon comes **Janmashtami**, the birth of Lord Krishna on a moonless night. Celebrations reach their peak at midnight, while the day is given to fasting. In Brindavan (see p162) and Mathura, pilgrims perform a circumambulation (parikrama) of sacred sites.

Muslim pilgrims at the Urs at Ajmer

Dussehra images being prepared

## SHARAD (SEP–OCT)

This season of festivals begins with **Dussehra**. For ten days, Ramlilas (see p28) are held and fairs organized to celebrate the legend of Rama. These dramatize episodes from the Ramayana: the exile of Rama, his brother Lakshman and wife Sita. Her abduction by the demon-king Ravana of Lanka and the epic battle for her rescue glorifies the monkey god, Hanuman, who helped Rama defeat Ravana and return in triumph to Ayodhya. Huge effigies of Ravana, his brother and son are stuffed with fireworks to be set alight on the last day,

Vijaya Dashami. Dusschra is preceded by the navaratri fasts. Bengalis celebrate this period as **Durga Puja**, when grand marquees (pandals) are erected over images of the goddess Durga.

**Diwali**, or the festival of lights, marks Rama's joyous entry into Ayodhya when the town was lit with lamps to greet him. It also heralds the Hindu New Year when old accounts are closed. Hindus believe that Lakshmi, the goddess of wealth, visits her devotees on that night, so houses are painted, sweets exchanged, and a profusion of melas encourages wild spending on homes and clothes. **Bhai Duj**, two days later, is a family festival in honour of brothers, who give gifts to their sisters.

**Govardhan Puja** or Annakut in both Rajasthan and Mathura commemorates the day Krishna lifted Mount Govardhan on his little finger

Diwali crackers are sold on pavement stalls

to protect the area from a deluge sent by an irate Indra, the god of rain. With the new moon of the season comes the **Urs** at Ajmer. This is the time for one of the biggest Muslim fairs in the subcontinent, held over 13 days at the dargah of the great Sufi saint Moinuddin Chishti (see pp220–21).

## HEMANT (NOV–JAN)

The onset of winter ushers in a number of festivals such as Christmas that are now national celebrations. In Rajasthan, the **Pushkar Fair** (see pp216–17) attracts tourists as well as ordinary pilgrims and herdsmen. On the full moon after Diwali, Sikhs celebrate **Guru Purab**, the birthday of Guru Nanak, the founder of Sikhism. **Id-ul-Fitr** marks the end of Ramadan or Ramzan, the month of fasting for Muslims

Paper kite

commemorating the period when the Prophet received the message of the Koran from Allah. The actual day of celebration varies according to the sighting of the new moon. A special namaaz is held at Delhi's Jami Masjid. This festival is also called Mithi (sweet) Id, as sewian, a delicacy made with sweetened vermicelli, is distributed at all homes.

# DELHI, AGRA & JAIPUR THROUGH THE YEAR

THREE DEFINITE seasons, the
summer, monsoon and
winter, with a brief but
glorious spring and autumn,
span the year in the region.
The calendar is filled with
festivals and fairs celebrated
by each of the diverse religious

Bauhinia
blossom

or local communities. Some follow the
changing seasons and mark pastoral occasions, while others celebrate anniversaries
and events of national importance such as the Republic Day
(see p71). Most cultural shows are
held during the winter.

## SUMMER (MAR–JUN)

FROM MID-MARCH until June
the North Indian plains
experience a hot and dry
summer. The temperatures in
March and April can be mild
and variable, but by May and
June the heat builds up to a
crescendo with the mercury
rising above 40° C (104° F).
This is a signal for many
residents to move to the
Himalayan hill stations.
Those who stay back remain
indoors and only venture
out after sunset. Most
festivities, too, come to a
halt during this period.

**Holi** *(Mar)*. This exuberant
festival of colour marks the
end of winter. In and around
Brindavan *(see p162)* Holi
celebrations last two weeks.

**Elephant Festival** *(Mar)*,
Jaipur. Around Holi, 60
decorated elephants parade
through the streets bearing
revellers who throw colour
at one another. Elephant
polo matches are also held
at Chaugan Stadium.

**Nauchandi Mela**
*(Mar)*, Meerut. Held
around the shrine of a
Muslim saint and a

Procession of Buddhist lamas on Buddha Jayanti

temple, this fair has come to
symbolize Hindu-Muslim
unity. Its origins date to the
late-17th century when local
leaders decided to merge
festivities held concurrently
at both shrines. Today, this is
more a fun-filled carnival
than a religious event.

**Music Festival** *(Mar)*, Delhi.
Well known artistes from all
over the country perform at
this prestigious cultural
event, organized by the Rajiv
Gandhi Foundation and held
at the Siri Fort Auditorium.

**ITC Sangeet Sammelan**
*(Mar)*, Delhi. This important
Hindustani classical music
event, sponsored by a major
Indian industrial
house, attracts all
music-lovers in
the capital.

**Gangaur
Festival**
*(Mar/Apr)*,
Jaipur. For
18 days, new
brides and
young girls wor-
ship Gauri, one of the
manifestations of Parvati, the

Elephant
Festival

consort of Shiva. Bejewelled
images of the goddess are
carried through the city,
escorted by bullock-drawn
chariots, bands of musicians
and women singing hymns.

**Shankarlal Sangeet Sam-
melan** *(Mar/Apr)*, Delhi.
This is the capital's oldest
classical vocal and instru-
mental music festival.

**Baisakhi** *(13 Apr)*. On this
day Gobind Singh, the last
Sikh guru, founded the
Khalsa, the "Holy Army of
the Pure". Gala processions,
dancing and feasting mark
the occasion. It also signals
the onset of summer and the
start of the harvest season.

**Urs** *(Apr)*, Delhi. For three
days devotees of the Sufi
saint Nizamuddin Auliya
*(see p82)* celebrate his birth
anniversary with night-long
qawwalis and a funfair.

**Buddha Jayanti** *(May)*,
Delhi. The Buddha was
born, attained enlightenment
and died on the full moon of
the fourth lunar month.
Prayer meetings are held at
Delhi's Buddha Jayanti Park.

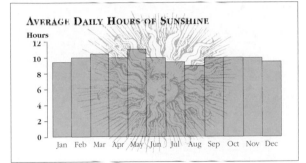

## AVERAGE DAILY HOURS OF SUNSHINE

Hours

Jan Feb Mar Apr May Jun Jul Aug Sep Oct Nov Dec

**Sunshine Chart**
*Ranging from balmy to fiercely hot, North India has sunshine through the year. To those unaccustomed to tropical weather, even the winter afternoons of this region may be uncomfortably warm. Sun hats, dark glasses, sunblock and several glasses a day of mineral water are highly recommended.*

**Summer Theatre Festival**
*(May/Jun)*, Delhi. A theatre festival organized by the National School of Drama.

## MONSOON (JUL–AUG)

JULY, AUGUST and most of September are hot and humid with intermittent showers. All newspapers eagerly report the progress of the southwest monsoon and though rainfall is scanty in the region, this season is celebrated for its magical transformation of the earth.

**Mango Festival** *(early Jul)*, Delhi. Held at the peak of the mango season, over 1,000 varieties of delicious mangoes grown in North India are on view at the Talkatora Stadium.

**National Film Festival** *(Jul)*, Delhi. During this two-weeklong festival, regional films from India that have won awards and have been made by prominent directors, are screened at the large Siri Fort Auditorium.

*Shehnai* player at Teej

**Teej** *(Aug)*, Jaipur. Young girls dressed in green, sing songs and play on specially erected swings. This joyous event venerates Parvati, the goddess of marital harmony. It also heralds the advent of the much awaited monsoon.

**Independence Day** *(15 Aug)*. This is a national

A dancing peacock announces the coming of the monsoon

holiday, commemorating India's freedom from British rule in 1947. The Prime Minister addresses the nation from the ramparts of the historic Red Fort in Delhi.

**Raksha Bandhan** *(full moon in Aug)*. Young girls tie sacred threads *(rakhis)* on their brothers' wrists as a token of love, and receive in exchange, gifts and a promise of everlasting protection.

Independence day celebration

**Janmashtami** *(Aug)*. Krishna's birth is celebrated all over India. In Brindavan, Raslilas are performed, and in Delhi, there are shows of *Krishna Katha*, a dance-drama on the Krishna story.

### NATIONAL HOLIDAYS

**Republic Day** (26 Jan)
**Independence Day** (15 Aug)
**Gandhi Jayanti** (2 Oct)

### PUBLIC HOLIDAYS

**Shivaratri** (Feb)
**Holi** (Feb/Mar)
**Id-ul-Zuha** (Mar)
**Good Friday** (Apr)
**Baisakhi** (13 April)
**Ramnavami** (Apr)
**Mahavir Jayanti** (Apr/May)
**Buddha Jayanti** (May)
**Milad-ul-Nabi** (May/Jun)
**Janmashtami** (Aug)
**Dussehra** (Oct)
**Diwali** (Oct/Nov)
**Guru Purab** (Nov)
**Christmas** (25 Dec)

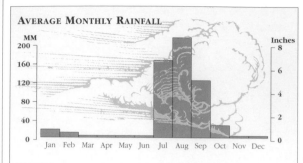

## AVERAGE MONTHLY RAINFALL

Jan Feb Mar Apr May Jun Jul Aug Sep Oct Nov Dec

**Rainfall Chart**
*Apart from local showers, this region receives its rain mostly during the southwest monsoon, which lasts from July to September. The landscape turns lush green but the humidity, sometimes as high as 90 per cent, makes this the wrong season for travelling in the plains of North India.*

## WINTER (OCT–FEB)

THIS IS THE MOST perfect season when the monsoon has cleared the dust haze and the days begin to grow cooler. The onset of winter also marks the sowing of winter crops such as mustard and wheat.

The winter chill is at its worst between mid-December and mid-January, and though temperatures often fall below 3° C (37° F), the days are sunny.

Spring is the main season for weddings, parades, picnics, polo and cricket matches, flower shows and various cultural events.

**Gandhi Jayanti** *(2 Oct)*. Mahatma Gandhi's birthday is widely celebrated as a national holiday.

**Phoolwalon ki Sair** *(early Oct)*. A colourful procession of floral banners and fans from the Jogmaya Temple and the Sufi shrine of Qutbuddin Bakhtiyar Kaki culminates at Jahaz Mahal in Mehrauli *(see pp110–13)*. Music and poetry recitations *(mushairas)* are also held.

**Qutb Festival** *(Oct/Nov)*, Delhi. A feast of Indian classical music and dance, organized by Delhi Tourism, is held against the dramatic backdrop of the Qutb Minar.

**Cricket, the national obsession**

**Dussehra** *(Oct)*. For nine days, episodes from the *Ramayana* depicting Rama's adventures against Ravana are enacted all over the region. The tenth day, Vijaya Dashami, celebrates Rama's defeat of Ravana, and huge effigies of the demon-king, his brother and son are burnt with fireworks. In Delhi, the Shriram Bharatiya Kala Kendra's month-long dance-drama encapsulates the much-loved epic.

**Urs** *(Oct)*, Ajmer. The festival in memory of the Sufi saint Khwaja Moinuddin Chishti attracts thousands of Muslim and Hindu devotees from all over the country.

**Tansen Festival** *(Oct)*, Gwalior. Classical singers pay homage to the most famous of Indian musicians,

**Balloon Mela**

Tansen, who was also the favourite singer at Mughal emperor Akbar's court.

**Diwali** *(Oct/Nov)*. Oil lamps illuminate each home to commemorate Rama's return to Ayodhya after 14 years of exile. Firecrackers are lit and sweets exchanged. During this period every locality holds Diwali *melas*.

**Pushkar Fair** *(Nov)*, Pushkar. Asia's largest camel and cattle fair takes place in this pilgrim town *(see pp216–17)*.

**Kartik Cultural Festival** *(15–21 Nov)*, Ballabhgarh. This festival is held at an 18th-century palace on the Delhi-Mathura Road.

**International Trade Fair** *(14–21 Nov)*, Delhi. Pragati Maidan hosts this major event for Indian industry, exhibiting goods manufactured in India and abroad. Cultural events are also held in the fair grounds.

**Balloon Mela** *(14 Nov)*, Delhi. This festival coincides with Nehru's birthday, celebrated as Children's Day.

**Chrysanthemum Show** *(1st week Dec)*, Delhi. The YWCA organizes a display of magnificent blooms.

**Kathak Utsav** *(Dec)*, Delhi. Exponents of this North Indian dance form enthrall audiences with their artistry.

**Christmas** *(25 Dec)*. A public holiday, Christmas is an occasion for everyone to shop, feast and party.

**Car display at the Trade Fair**

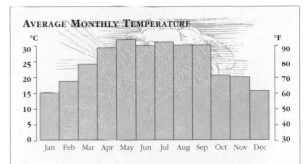

## AVERAGE MONTHLY TEMPERATURE

| °C | | | | | | | | | | | | °F |
|---|---|---|---|---|---|---|---|---|---|---|---|---|
| 30 | | | | | | | | | | | | 90 |
| 25 | | | | | | | | | | | | 80 |
| 20 | | | | | | | | | | | | 70 |
| 15 | | | | | | | | | | | | 60 |
| 10 | | | | | | | | | | | | 50 |
| 5 | | | | | | | | | | | | 40 |
| 0 | | | | | | | | | | | | 30 |
| | Jan | Feb | Mar | Apr | May | Jun | Jul | Aug | Sep | Oct | Nov | Dec |

**Temperature Chart**
*This region is hot and dry throughout the year, barring October to February. The mercury begins to rise from March, and by May heat wave conditions prevail with hot and dusty gusts of the "loo" winds. By the end of June, however, dark clouds signal the onset of monsoon.*

Bagpipers at the Beating Retreat ceremony

**New Year's Eve** *(31 Dec).* All hotels and clubs organize New Year's Eve balls.
**Lohri** *(13 Jan).* Bonfires are lit amidst song and dance to mark the height of winter.
**Makar Sankranti** *(14 Jan),* Jaipur. Kites are flown to celebrate the return of the sun from the equator to the Tropic of Capricorn.
**Republic Day** *(26 Jan).* A national holiday. Pomp and pageantry mark India's birth as an independent republic. In Delhi, a colourful military parade is held at Rajpath.
**Beating Retreat** *(29 Jan),* Delhi. A moving ceremony that recalls the end of the day's battle when armies retreated to their camps. There is a grand display of regimental bands performing against the spectacular backdrop of North and South Blocks. As the sun sets, a bugle sounds the retreat, fireworks are lit and fairy-lights outline the buildings.
**Surajkund Crafts Mela** *(1–14 Feb),* Surajkund. This handicrafts fair is held at an 11th-century historic site on the outskirts of the capital.
**International Yoga Week** *(2–7 Feb),* Rishikesh. Scholars and students from all over the world participate in classes and seminars on the banks of the Ganges.
**Vintage Car Rally** *(Feb),* Delhi. *The Statesman* group of newspapers organizes this event when vintage cars, or the "grand old ladies", are flagged off from Rajpath to embark on a 20-km (12-mile)

race. Their owners often dress up in period costumes.
**Vasant Panchami** *(Feb).* A spring festival when crops ripen and nature is in full bloom. People wear yellow and worship Saraswati.
**Flower Shows** *(Feb).* A number of flower and rose shows are held in Delhi and elsewhere. The Rashtrapati Bhavan's Mughal Gardens are also open to the public.
**Taj Mahotsav** *(18–27 Feb),* Agra. A ten-day cultural fiesta of music and dance in the vicinity of the Taj Mahal.
**Jhansi Festival** *(end Feb),* Jhansi. A five-day arts and crafts extravaganza unfolds against the backdrop of the historic 18th-century fort.
**Shivaratri** *(Feb).* Night-long celebrations mark the marriage of Shiva on the 14th day of a lunar fortnight.
**Kathak Bindadin Mahotsav** *(Feb),* Delhi. A five-day dance festival organized by the Kathak Kendra.
**Dhrupad Festival** *(Feb),* Delhi. Leading exponents of this ancient musical tradition present a series of recitals.

Vintage cars test their strength on an uphill road outside Delhi

# THE HISTORY OF DELHI, AGRA & JAIPUR

NORTH INDIAN SOCIETY sprang from the wide plains of the Indus and Ganges rivers, sites of continuous human settlement since about 2500 BC, when a sophisticated urban culture flourished along the Indus Valley. After 600 BC, powerful monarchies such as the Mauryas, Kushanas and Guptas presided over the rise of Buddhism and Hinduism, two major religions that emerged from North India.

**Statue of the Holy Trinity, Gupta Age**

Overland trade with Central Asia and the Far East invited conquest and settlement as well. Interestingly, "India" is a derivative of Hind, a name given by Arab traders to people who lived across the River Sindhu, or Indus. From 1500 BC on, North India was home to immigrants. These included the Aryans, Greeks and Parthians, Scythians, Huns and Mongols.

An important development took place in AD 1192 when Qutbuddin Aibak displaced the Rajputs from Delhi to found the first major Islamic kingdom in the region. Later, with the coming of the Mughals in 1526, North India underwent a process of social and political change that lasted nearly 300 years, as a vibrant Indo-Islamic cultural fusion took place. Imperial centralization under the Mughals brought peace and prosperity in its wake, while art and architecture scaled new heights of excellence.

The rise of the British East India Company in the 18th century, after the decline of the Mughals, was the start of 200 years of British rule in India. The colonial period, which also marks the political unification of the subcontinent, ended in 1947 when India became an independent republic. Today a mature democracy, India is trying to tackle poverty and illiteracy with economic and political reform in the new millennium.

Dating from 1598, such maps helped the Dutch and English to locate trading bases in India

◁ Royal procession, a mid-19th-century mural in the Moti Mahal, Gwalior

# Early Civilizations

INDIAN CIVILIZATION first flourished between 2500 and 1500 BC in the Harappan settlements along the River Indus. These sophisticated urban settlements, with an underground drainage system and well-laid out streets, were spread over an area much larger than either ancient Egypt or Mesopotamia. The reasons for the decline of this early civilization are still unclear, but by 1500 BC, the Aryans, who had entered India through the passes of the Hindu Kush, had settled down in Northwest India. Sacred texts such as the *Rig Veda* record aspects of their culture. By 600 BC, with the gradual adoption of widespread crop cultivation, several new urban sites had emerged in the Ganges Valley. Many of these were capitals of independent kingdoms, and some cities of that age, such as Mathura, Patna and Varanasi, still exist.

**Mother Goddess icon, Indus Valley**

**EARLY CIVILIZATIONS**

— *Extent of Indus Valley Civilization*

☐ *Extent of Aryan settlements*

**Copper Spearhead** (*c.1500 BC*)
*Copper and bronze implements for farming and hunting were used by the people of the Indus Valley.*

**Burial urn** from a Harappan site.

**Indus Seal (Tree)**
*Over 2,000 steatite seals have been found in the Indus Valley, each with an emblem and a script that has still not been fully deciphered.*

**Platter** (*c.800 BC*)
*A Painted Grey Ware platter from the Ganges Valley area. Austere and functional, such objects were made of baked clay.*

## TIMELINE

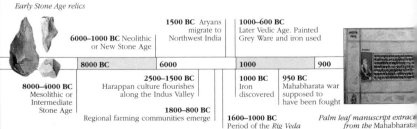

*Early Stone Age relics*

| | 8000 BC | 6000 | 1000 | 900 |
|---|---|---|---|---|
| | **6000–1000 BC** Neolithic or New Stone Age | **1500 BC** Aryans migrate to Northwest India | **1000–600 BC** Later Vedic Age. Painted Grey Ware and iron used | |
| **8000–4000 BC** Mesolithic or Intermediate Stone Age | **2500–1500 BC** Harappan culture flourishes along the Indus Valley | | **1000 BC** Iron discovered | **950 BC** Mahabharata war supposed to have been fought |
| | **1800–800 BC** Regional farming communities emerge | | **1600–1000 BC** Period of the *Rig Veda* | *Palm leaf manuscript extract from the* Mahabharata |

## Beliefs and Ideas

*Sacred Rigvedic hymns, composed by the Aryans in praise of Nature and various gods, were later absorbed into Hinduism. Several Hindu gods and rituals, even the caste system (see p20), can be traced to Aryan beliefs.*

This **toy cart** indicates the use of the wheel.

**Toy animals** testify to the Harappan artisan's skill.

**Baked clay** was used by the Harappans to shape various objects such as this anteater.

**Grain** was stored in wide-mouthed jars.

## HARAPPAN CULTURE

The Indus Valley (or Harappan) Civilization (2500–1500 BC) had an efficient system of government based on trade and a thriving agricultural economy. Worshippers of a mother goddess and trees, they used water for ritual practice. These Harappan artifacts are in the National Museum.

### WHERE TO SEE HARAPPAN ARTIFACTS

**Harappan dice at the National Museum**

The finest collection of Indus Valley artifacts, arranged chronologically, is in New Delhi's National Museum *(see pp 72–3)*. Some archaeological finds, especially Painted Grey Ware from the site of Indraprastha mentioned in the epic *Mahabharata*, are lodged in a small museum in Delhi's Purana Qila itself *(see p84)*. The state museums at Kurukshetra *(see p140)* and Mathura *(see p161)* have a good collection of statues and archaeological finds excavated from this region.

**The Origin of Life**
*An 18th-century painting of a popular Hindu myth that says life was created when the divine nectar (amrit), hidden in the Ocean of Milk, was won by the gods from the demons (see p23).*

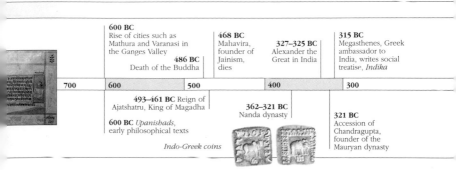

| | 700 | 600 | 500 | 400 | 300 |
|---|---|---|---|---|---|

**600 BC**
Rise of cities such as Mathura and Varanasi in the Ganges Valley

**486 BC** Death of the Buddha

**468 BC** Mahavira, founder of Jainism, dies

**327–325 BC** Alexander the Great in India

**315 BC** Megasthenes, Greek ambassador to India, writes social treatise, *Indika*

**493–461 BC** Reign of Ajatshatru, King of Magadha

**600 BC** *Upanishads*, early philosophical texts

*Indo-Greek coins*

**362–321 BC** Nanda dynasty

**321 BC** Accession of Chandragupta, founder of the Mauryan dynasty

# Ancient Empires

UNDER THE MAURYAN EMPEROR Ashoka, North India saw its first large-scale empire. Contact with Central Asia, which began around 200 BC, determined crucial political alliances after the Mauryas, and by the 1st century AD, the Kushanas from Central Asia had an empire that extended up to the Ganges Valley. This period also saw the rise and spread of Buddhism. In the 4th century, the Gupta kings presided over the flowering of classical Sanskrit at the hands of writers such as Kalidasa. The emergence of the Holy Trinity *(see pp22–3)* and temple worship also date from the Gupta Age.

**Ashokan capital**

**EARLY EMPIRES**

☐ *Mauryan Empire*

— *Kushana Empire*

— *Gupta Empire*

**Buddhism**
*A peaceful, non-violent religion, its message of tolerance and social equality won Buddhism many followers, among them the Mauryan emperor Ashoka. Its rise had a profound impact on social, political and cultural life.*

**Speckled red sandstone** was extensively used in Mathura art.

**The human form,** sensuously carved, has expressive lines. The gold ornaments and elaborate hair styles of the figures reflect the court fashions of the age.

**Ashokan Edict**
*(3rd century BC) Considered valuable historical records, such rock edicts, installed throughout his kingdom, proclaim Ashoka's ethical code* (dhamma) *as well as important events.*

## TIMELINE

| | | | | |
|---|---|---|---|---|
| **273–232 BC** Ashoka's reign | **180–165 BC** Foundation of Indo-Greek empire by Demetrius | | **AD 78–110** Reign of Kushana king Kanishka; Fourth Buddhist Council held in Kashmir | |
| | **260 BC** Battle of Kalinga leads Ashoka to embrace Buddhism | **80 BC** Maues, Shaka king in Northwest India | | *2nd-century Buddhist begging bowl* |

| 200 BC | 100 BC | AD 1 | AD 100 | 200 |
|---|---|---|---|---|

| | **185 BC** Accession of Sungas in Magadha | **165–145 BC** Menander, Indo-Greek king, rules over the northwest | **AD 20–46** Gondophernes, Indo-Parthian king in Taxila; St Thomas comes to South India | **150** Rudradaman, the S king in West India; first Sanskrit inscription on imperishable material d from his reign |
| | *Mauryan sculpture* | | | |

## Kanishka *(AD 78–110)*

*This famous Kushana king came from Central Asia (as the boots and cloak of his headless statue reveal) to control a large part of North India. Another great patron of Buddhism, his reign presided over its spread to China, Central Asia and Afghanistan, along the famous Silk Route.*

**Yakshas** and **yakshis**, male and female nature spirits, as well as the foliage behind them, represent fertility and an abundance of life. Their presence highlights the mood of revelry and fecundity.

**Greek features** like curly hair and sharp noses distinguish Gandhara sculpture.

**Vasantsena,** a courtesan, slumped in a drunken state, is helped to her feet.

### WHERE TO SEE ANCIENT ART

The Government Museum, Mathura *(see p161)* and the National Museum, New Delhi *(see pp72–3)* have fine collections of Mauryan, Kushana, Gupta and Sunga sculptures. The Northern Ridge *(see p103)* and Feroze Shah Kotla *(see p97)* have well-preserved Ashokan pillars

**Sunga pillar, National Museum**

### MATHURA SCHOOL OF ART

Between the 1st and 6th centuries AD, a renowned school of art flourished at Mathura *(see p161)*. Statues of Jain, Buddhist and Hindu divinities, with remarkably expressive faces, were produced along with secular art such as this dramatic 2nd-century Kushana panel, *The Drunken Courtesan.*

### Gandhara Sculpture

*After the 1st century AD, a distinct Hellenistic style first emerged in Gandhara in the northwest. The Buddha was now depicted in a sublime human form, rather than through symbols such as the lotus and chakra, with expressions that recall classical Greek sculpture.*

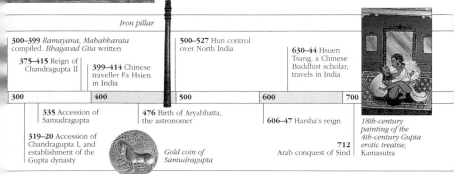

Iron pillar

**300–399** *Ramayana, Mahabharata* compiled. *Bhagavad Gita* written

**375–415** Reign of Chandragupta II

**399–414** Chinese traveller Fa Hsien in India

**500–527** Hun control over North India

**630–44** Hsuen Tsang, a Chinese Buddhist scholar, travels in India

| 300 | 400 | 500 | 600 | 700 |
|-----|-----|-----|-----|-----|

**335** Accession of Samudragupta

**476** Birth of Aryabhatta, the astronomer

**606–47** Harsha's reign

**319–20** Accession of Chandragupta I, and establishment of the Gupta dynasty

*Gold coin of Samudragupta*

**712** Arab conquest of Sind

*18th-century painting of the 4th-century Gupta erotic treatise, Kamasutra*

# Rajput Dynasties

**Rajput shield with sun emblem**

Rajput clans rose to prominence in North India from the late 7th century. Claiming a high caste warrior status *(kshatriya)*, they traced their lineage to the sun and moon to firmly establish their legitimacy, and ruled over North, West and Central India. After losing Delhi and Kannauj to the Muslims, they confined their activities to the western region, now Rajasthan, where rival clans fought for supremacy. Widely renowned for their loyalty and valour, most Rajput clans were welcomed as allies by Mughal rulers.

**LOCATOR MAP**

☐ *Extent of Rajput Kingdoms*

**Prithviraj Chauhan of Ajmer**
*The last Rajput ruler of Delhi, he was defeated in 1192 by Quthuddin Aibak. The Quth Minar and a mosque were built over his citadel, Rai Pithora.*

**Turbans** indicate the home, region and status of a person.

**Pageantry** was a vital part of the Rajput concept of kingship.

**Sacred Beliefs**
*Rajput kings were patrons of Hinduism and worshipped martial gods such as Hanuman (see p197) and Shakti . They were also prolific builders of beautiful temples.*

**Sati Sites**
*Hand imprints mark the sites where women immolated themselves by jumping into their husband's funeral pyre. This cruel practice, called sati, was made illegal in 1829.*

## TIMELINE

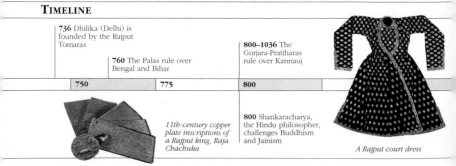

**736** Dhilika (Delhi) is founded by the Rajput Tomaras

**760** The Palas rule over Bengal and Bihar

**800–1036** The Gurjara-Pratiharas rule over Kannauj

| 750 | 775 | 800 |
|-----|-----|-----|

*11th-century copper plate inscriptions of a Rajput king, Raja Chachuka*

**800** Shankaracharya, the Hindu philosopher, challenges Buddhism and Jainism

*A Rajput court dress*

**Rajput Art**
*Rajput rulers were great patrons of architecture and painting. This unusual 18th-century miniature from Jaipur shows Rajput women playing polo (see p195).*

**Man Singh I of Amber**
*This loyal Mughal ally, one of the "nine jewels" (navaratna) of Akbar's court, was among the first Rajputs to befriend the Mughals. Such alliances paved the way for peace in North India and a fusion of Hindu and Islamic cultures, especially in architecture.*

**Palanquins**, such as this fanciful one, were carried by a retinue of clansmen during ceremonial processions.

**The ruler** epitomizes the best of Rajput chivalry and valour.

**Weapons** are an essential part of a Rajput's attire.

## WHERE TO SEE RAJPUT INDIA

Amber *(see pp200–201)* and the jungle fort at Ranthambhore *(see pp 224–5)* are some famous Rajput forts in this region. The museum inside the City Palace, Jaipur *(see pp188–91)* and Alwar *(see p206)* display private collections. The National Museum, New Delhi, also has a wide display of Rajput miniature paintings *(see pp30–31)*, sculpture and jewellery.

**Amber Fort *(see pp200–201)***

## A ROYAL PROCESSION

Rajput princes enjoyed a divine status in the eyes of their clan. Rajputana, literally the land of princes, once had some 21 kingdoms ruled by rival clans which included the Sisodias of Mewar, Kachhawahas of Amber and Jaipur, Rathors of Marwar and Bikaner, Haras of Kota and Bundi, Chauhans of Ajmer, and Bhattis of Jaisalmer.

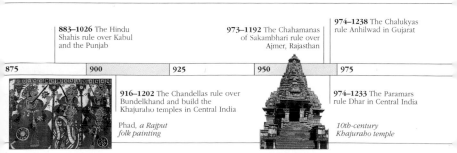

**883–1026** The Hindu Shahis rule over Kabul and the Punjab

**973–1192** The Chahamanas of Sakambhari rule over Ajmer, Rajasthan

**974–1238** The Chalukyas rule Anhilwad in Gujarat

875 | 900 | 925 | 950 | 975

**916–1202** The Chandellas rule over Bundelkhand and build the Khajuraho temples in Central India

Phad, *a Rajput folk painting*

**974–1233** The Paramars rule Dhar in Central India

*10th-century Khajuraho temple*

# The Delhi Sultans

**Astrolabe**

THE FABULOUS WEALTH of India attracted Arab traders and raiders, such as Mahmud of Ghazni. A slave general of Muhammad Ghori, called Qutbuddin Aibak, established himself in North India and founded the Mamluk (Slave) Dynasty. Followed by the Khiljis, Tughlaqs, Sayyids and Lodis, these Muslim rulers, called the Sultans of Delhi, established an empire that survived into the early 16th century and changed the cultural and urban milieu of much of the subcontinent by introducing new technologies and customs.

**COMING OF ISLAM**

— *Empire of Mamluks (1236)*

☐ *Empire of Tughlaqs (1335)*

**Illustrated Koran** *(17th century)*
*The noble Islamic art of calligraphy was introduced by Muslim rulers and used to embellish royal decrees, manuscripts and copies of the Koran, as well as buildings.*

**Ceramic Tiles**
*Jamali Kamali (see p111) has fine examples of this Islamic art.*

**Qutbuddin Aibak** built the first storey of the Qutb Minar and a mosque to proclaim his victory over the Rajputs.

**Quwwat-ul-Islam,** which means "Might of Islam", was the first congregational mosque in Delhi.

***Madrasa* and tomb of Alauddin Khilji**

**Persian Wheel**
*The water wheel came in the wake of Muslim rule. Its simple technology is still used in rural areas to draw underground water for irrigation.*

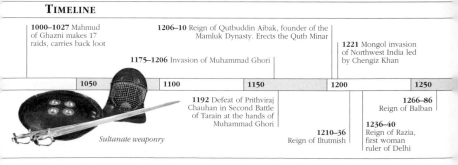

## TIMELINE

**1000–1027** Mahmud of Ghazni makes 17 raids, carries back loot

**1206–10** Reign of Qutbuddin Aibak, founder of the Mamluk Dynasty. Erects the Qutb Minar

**1175–1206** Invasion of Muhammad Ghori

**1221** Mongol invasion of Northwest India led by Chengiz Khan

| 1050 | 1100 | 1150 | 1200 | 1250 |
|------|------|------|------|------|

**1192** Defeat of Prithviraj Chauhan in Second Battle of Tarain at the hands of Muhammad Ghori

**1266–86** Reign of Balban

*Sultanate weaponry*

**1210–36** Reign of Iltutmish

**1236–40** Reign of Razia, first woman ruler of Delhi

**Feroze Shah Tughlaq** added the topmost storeys in 1368.

**Iltutmish**, Qutbuddin's successor, built the second and third storeys.

**Alai Darwaza** was built by Alauddin Khilji in 1311.

**Nizamuddin Auliya**
*Mystic sages called Sufis were among the immigrants from Central Asia. This 17th-century miniature shows Nizamuddin Auliya* (see p82) *with the poet Amir Khusrau. Together, they raised metaphysical love, poetry and music to the level of divine worship.*

## WHERE TO SEE THE DELHI SULTANATE

The Mehrauli area (see pp110–13), Hauz Khas (see p106), Tughlaqabad (see p114), Feroze Shah Kotla (see p97), Purana Qila (see p84) and Lodi Gardens (see p79) show the various architectural styles of the Sultanate. The National Museum (see pp72–3) has a fine collection of artifacts dating to this period.

**Begampuri Masjid** (see p109)

**Music**
*Amir Khusrau, poet and musician, is said to have introduced the multi-stringed* sitar *and the* raga *style to North Indian music.*

## THE QUTB MINAR

In 1192, the first sultan, Qutbuddin Aibak, built the Qutb Minar (see p112) and a mosque to mark his victory over the Rajput rulers. This 19th-century lithograph shows a part of the Qutb complex that was built over the remains of an earlier Rajput citadel at Mehrauli (see pp110–11).

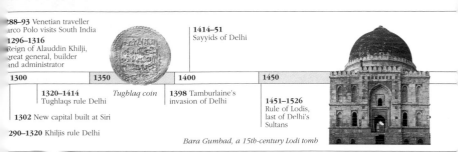

**288–93** Venetian traveller Marco Polo visits South India

**1296–1316** Reign of Alauddin Khilji, great general, builder and administrator

*Tughlaq coin*

**1414–51** Sayyids of Delhi

| 1300 | 1350 | 1400 | 1450 |
|---|---|---|---|

**1320–1414** Tughlaqs rule Delhi

**1398** Tamburlaine's invasion of Delhi

**1451–1526** Rule of Lodis, last of Delhi's Sultans

**1302** New capital built at Siri

**290–1320** Khiljis rule Delhi

*Bara Gumbad, a 15th-century Lodi tomb*

# The Great Mughals

**Mughal cooking vessel**

THE MUGHALS, like the Ottomans of Turkey, the Safavids of Iran and the Tudors of England, were one of the greatest medieval dynasties. For over 200 years they held firm political control over the subcontinent, establishing a stable administrative system and a rich pluralistic culture blending the best of Hindu and Islamic traditions. Great patrons of art and architecture, they also encouraged the translation of Sanskrit texts into Persian. Markets and cities flourished under them, making India famous.

**MUGHAL EMPIRE**

☐ *Mughal Empire at the end of the 17th century*

**Hierarchy** of nobles depended on the rank given by the emperor.

**Buland Darwaza at Fatehpur Sikri**
*Erected to celebrate Akbar's victory over Gujarat in 1572–3, Buland Darwaza (see p173) is part of the great Mughal architectural legacy that still dominates the region.*

**Rajput princes** were often loyal Mughal supporters. Shah Jahan's grandmother was a Rajput princess.

**Mughal Art**
*A ruby-studded ceremonial gold spoon, Jahangir's jade wine cup, a gold enamelled glass hookah base and Mughal miniature paintings (see pp30–31) offer vivid glimpses of their extravagant patronage of art.*

## TIMELINE

**1526** Babur defeats Ibrahim Lodi at Panipat

*Babur, the first Mughal emperor*

**1539** Sher Shah Sur defeats Humayun at Chausa

**1540–55** Sur Sultans rule in Delhi

**1556** Death of Humayun. Accession of his son Akbar

*Jahangir*

**1530** Death of Babur. His son Humayun succeeds him

*Akbar the Great*

**1569** Humayun's Tomb built at Delhi

**1571–85** Fatehpur Sikri built

**1605** Death of Akbar. His son Jahangir succeeds him

| 1525 | 1550 | 1575 | 1600 |

## Order and Symmetry

*The "taming of the land" that took place under the Mughals, whether it was their landscaped gardens or their system of justice and revenue settlement, was founded on this dual principle.*

## WHERE TO SEE MUGHAL INDIA

Fatehpur Sikri *(see pp170–73)* and the Taj Mahal *(see pp154–5)* are among the finest examples of Mughal architecture in this region. The area around Delhi's Red Fort *(see pp94–5)* also has several Mughal relics. Important collections of Mughal art, manuscripts, coins, jewellery, costumes and armoury are housed in both the National Museum, Delhi *(see pp72–3)* and the City Palace Museum, Jaipur *(see pp188–9)*.

**Mughal necklace**

**Shah Jahan** with his son in the foreground receiving a gift from a noble.

**Diwan-i-Khas** was used for special audience with the emperor and his advisors.

**Court robes** and turbans indicated status and religion.

**A railing** separated the imperial circle from lower state officials.

## Military Organization

*All senior administrators (mansabdars) maintained an armed retinue (sawars) and rank (zat) determined salary.*

## SHAH JAHAN'S COURT

The splendour of the Mughal court is illustrated in this 17th-century painting of Shah Jahan among his nobles, grouped in strict hierarchical order round the throne. Mughal emperors, seated in an elevated alcove, used glittering court rituals to display their supreme political position as they took stock of the state affairs from their officials.

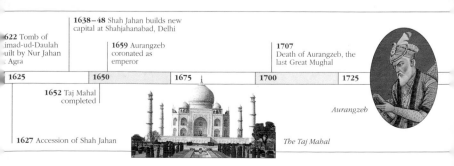

**1622** Tomb of imad-ud-Daulah built by Nur Jahan, Agra

**1638–48** Shah Jahan builds new capital at Shahjahanabad, Delhi

**1659** Aurangzeb coronated as emperor

**1707** Death of Aurangzeb, the last Great Mughal

| 1625 | 1650 | 1675 | 1700 | 1725 |
|------|------|------|------|------|

**1652** Taj Mahal completed

**1627** Accession of Shah Jahan

*Aurangzeb*

*The Taj Mahal*

# European Traders, Colonizers and Mercenaries

CRIPPLED BY THE SACK of Delhi in 1739 by Nadir Shah of Persia, Mughal power declined rapidly. This was exploited by petty rulers, European mercenaries, and the British East India Company, set up in the 1690s to trade in spices and cotton.

**Sahib and mahout** Its commercial success led to the rise of the Company as a political power, which ushered in some social reforms and new power equations. Yet, the social instability engendered by the Company's unpopular trade and political practices erupted in the Indian Mutiny or Great Revolt of 1857.

## THE INDIAN MUTINY OF 1857

☐ *Areas where British administration was disputed*

• *Site of major revolt in 1857*

**British officer** killing a rebel leader at Fatehpur.

## The Decline of the Mughals
*Nadir Shah's plunder of Delhi (see p92) was the signal for the rise of the Jats and Marathas. Suraj Mal Jat (see p166) filled Bharatpur Fort, seen above, with looted Mughal treasures.*

**Sepoys** mutinied against animal grease on bullets as it violated religious taboos.

## Economic Exploitation
*A 19th-century lithograph shows the impoverishment of cotton ginners as cheap English mill-made cloth flooded the Indian market.*

**Indian rebels** led by disgruntled princes ultimately lost the war.

## TIMELINE

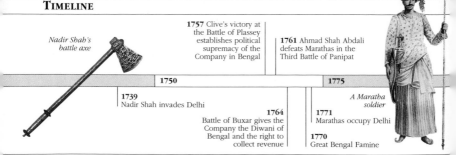

*Nadir Shah's battle axe*

**1757** Clive's victory at the Battle of Plassey establishes political supremacy of the Company in Bengal

**1761** Ahmad Shah Abdali defeats Marathas in the Third Battle of Panipat

**1750**

**1775**

**1739** Nadir Shah invades Delhi

*A Maratha soldier*

**1771** Marathas occupy Delhi

**1764** Battle of Buxar gives the Company the Diwani of Bengal and the right to collect revenue

**1770** Great Bengal Famine

### A Nabob and his Concubines

*A corruption of nawab, this name described officials who made huge fortunes from the East India Company's cotton and spice trade in India. Many adopted the feudal lifestyles of the Indian princes as this 19th-century painting shows.*

**The plains of North India** were the main battle areas.

**Palanquins** transported rebel princes and gentlefolk to the scene of battle.

### Indian Sepoys

*The Company's commercial interests were protected by its military establishment, which employed Indian foot soldiers called sepoys.*

### SEPOYS REBELLING AT FATEHPOOR

This lithograph of a pitched battle during the Mutiny show sepoys and Indian leaders being tackled by the Company's troops. The Indian Mutiny or Great Revolt of 1857 was seen as India's first war of independence from colonial rule by some nationalists as it shook the foundation of the East India Company's rule in India.

### WHERE TO SEE EUROPEAN INDIA

Sardhana *(see p142)* has a cathedral built by Begum Samroo, the Indian wife of Walter Reinhardt, a French mercenary. Meerut's church, where the first shots of the sepoy mutiny were fired, survives in mint condition *(see p142)*. The cantonments in Meerut and Agra, the Agra cemetery *(see p152)* and St James's Church in Delhi *(see p101)* are other sites that go back to the time of the Indian Mutiny.

**Sardhana cathedral *(see p142)***

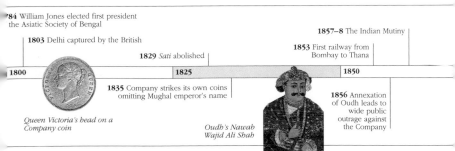

'84 William Jones elected first president the Asiatic Society of Bengal

**1803** Delhi captured by the British

**1829** *Sati* abolished

**1835** Company strikes its own coins omitting Mughal emperor's name

*Queen Victoria's head on a Company coin*

**1853** First railway from Bombay to Thana

**1856** Annexation of Oudh leads to wide public outrage against the Company

**1857–8** The Indian Mutiny

*Oudh's Nawab Wajid Ali Shah*

| 1800 | 1825 | 1850 |

# Pax Britannica

**The Victoria Cross**

THE FOUNDATION OF BRITISH RULE, or the Raj, was laid only after the Indian Mutiny, which truly revealed the unpopularity of the East India Company. An Act of Parliament in 1858 brought its rule to a close and its Indian territories became part of Britain's empire. India was now ruled directly by the Crown through a viceroy. Though the Raj was unabashedly Victorian and conservative, and its *raison d'être* was economic profit and political control, its abiding legacy was the political unification of the subcontinent, and the introduction of modern Western education, a centralized civil administration and judicial system, along with a wide network of railways and postal services.

**BRITISH INDIA**

☐ *British territory, 1858*

**Old Delhi**
is relegated to the background.

**Indian attendants**
in viceregal livery re-enact a Mughal procession.

**The Steel Frame**
*Some 2,000 British officers ruled over a subcontinent of 300 million people. The paternalistic civil service brought order and justice even to remote outposts.*

**Memsahib with her Tailor**
*Despite the climate, the English clung to their own food and dress. Children were sent "home" to study, and a large Indian staff enabled a leisurely lifestyle.*

## TIMELINE

*Lord Canning, the first Viceroy*

**1859** Withdrawal of Doctrine of Lapse, a major cause of the 1857 revolt

**1861** Indian Council Act

*Lord Dalhousie, author of the notorious Doctrine of Lapse (see p319)*

1875

**1858** Victoria proclaims Lord Canning first Viceroy of India

**1876** Victoria proclaims herself Empress of India

**1877** Lytton's Delhi Durbar

**1865** Telegraphic communication is established with Europe

**A Sahib Travelling**
*A vast rail network was set up by the British to facilitate commerce and travel. This lithograph of first-class travel, a privilege of "whites only", is from the 19th century.*

**Raj Cuisine**
*While kababs, curry and rice became a part of British culinary preference, Westernized Indians took to drinking tea and nibbling biscuits. An early 20th-century biscuit tin label reflects this exchange of tastes.*

**Caparisoned elephants**
carry the new rulers.

**Crowds** line the streets to see the grand spectacle.

## WHERE TO SEE BRITISH INDIA

Raisina Hill and the surrounding area *(see pp68–9)*, Agra's St John's College *(see p152)*, Mayo College *(see p219)* in Ajmer are examples of colonial architecture. Delhi's Coronation Park *(see p103)* and the University area *(see p103)* are other sites with a Raj connection.

**Detail of India Gate *(see p71)***

## THE DURBAR, 1903

This painting of Curzon's Delhi Durbar (1903), held to celebrate the coronation of Edward VII, shows a procession winding through the historic streets of Delhi. Held periodically, such assemblies announced both the grandeur and the political might of British rule in India.

**1878**
Vernacular Press Act

**1885**
Indian National Congress founded

**1883–4** Illbert Bill controversy

**1878–80** Second Anglo-Afghan War

*Lord Curzon, Viceroy 1899–1905*

**1899**
Curzon becomes Viceroy

**1905**
Partition of Bengal by Curzon causes national outrage

**1900**

**1904** Ancient Monuments Preservation Act

# The Freedom Movement

**Gandhi's spinning wheel**

THE FOUNDING of the Indian National Congress in 1885 gave Indians a platform from which to demand freedom from foreign rule. Their ideology was provided by Gandhi, whose message of non-violence and economic self-reliance gave them moral confidence, and united castes and communities under a common cause. At first the movement for freedom was ruthlessly suppressed, but by the 1930s it became too large for the British to handle. Finally, weakened by World War II and under growing international pressure, England granted India formal independence in 1947.

**FREEDOM MOVEMENT**

- *Major towns associated with the Freedom Movement*

**Huge crowds** turned out to register their support. Gandhi united castes and communities as never before.

**Khadi**, homespun cloth, was worn as a statement of patriotism.

**Round Table Conference (1931)**
*The British tried to work out a settlement with Gandhi, accompanied by formidable campaigner and poet, Sarojini Naidu.*

**The police** dogged public assemblies, often brutally beating the audience.

**The Cellular Jail, Andaman Islands**
*Hundreds of freedom fighters were shipped here by the British. Many were hanged, some died of diseases such as malaria. Now a national monument, the jail's popular name, Kala Pani ("black waters"), recalls its dark past.*

## TIMELINE

| | | |
|---|---|---|
| *Rabindranath Tagore* | **1913** Rabindranath Tagore wins the Nobel Prize for Literature | **1914** Canada refuses Indians aboard the ship *Kamagata Maru* permission to land |
| **1907** Congress splits at Surat between the moderates and extremists | | **1915** Home Rule League started by Annie Besant |
| | **1910** | **1920** |
| **1906** Muslim League formed at Dacca | **1917** Gandhi takes up the cause of indigo farmers at Champaran, Bihar | |
| **1908** Tilak, a prominent nationalist, sentenced to six years transportation on charges of sedition | **1919** Police fires at unarmed crowd at Jallianwala Bagh in Amritsar, Punjab | |
| | **1920** Non-cooperation Movement launched by Gandhi | |

### New Delhi
*New Delhi was declared the Raj's capital in 1911. This early photo shows Parliament House, then the Legislative Assembly building.*

## WHERE TO SEE THE FREEDOM MOVEMENT

The National Archives *(see p71)* and the Gandhi Smriti *(see p78)* have a permanent exhibition on the Freedom Movement. Panels on this theme are also displayed at the Jawahar Pavilion in Pragati Maidan *(see p85)*. Teen Murti House *(see p78)* offers a view of Nehru's life.

**Gandhi** delivered his powerful message of freedom at public meetings.

### Nehru and Jinnah
*Brilliant lawyers who joined Gandhi's national movement, they enjoyed an iconic status in India and Pakistan after Independence.*

**Gandhi Samadhi, Rajghat** *(see p97)*

### The Partition (1947)
*A huge displacement of people across the borders took place at the division of the subcontinent into India and Pakistan, leading to an eruption of violent communal riots.*

## MAHATMA GANDHI
Called Mahatma ("great spirit"), MK Gandhi returned to India from South Africa in 1915 as a protest against apartheid. He travelled across the subcontinent, launching a moral crusade that encouraged non-violent Civil Disobedience against colonial rule.

**1930–32** Gandhi leads the Dandi Salt March and Civil Disobedience Movement

*Subhash Chandra Bose and members of the Indian National Army*

**1948** Assassination of Mahatma Gandhi

**1940** Muslim League adopts the Pakistan Resolution

**1930**

**1940**

**1942** Quit India Movement

**1939** Resignation of the Congress Ministers

**1947** India attains Independence

*Nehru is sworn in as the first Prime Minister by Lord Mountbatten*

*Bungalow designed for a new capital at Delhi in the 1930s*

# India Today

**Cell-phones are a familiar sight**

INDIA CELEBRATED 50 YEARS of independence in 1997. Nehru, the first prime minister, laid the foundations for a modern nation state with a democratic, secular polity, a strong industrial base and a planned economy, with non-alignment as the keystone of its foreign policy. India's one billion people speak 18 languages, and though many of them are illiterate and unemployed, a vigorous and free press and electoral system ensure that their interests and rights are safe-guarded and well represented. The two major national political parties are the Congress, and the more right-wing Bharatiya Janata Party.

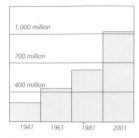

1,000 million

700 million

400 million

1941 1961 1981 2001

**POPULATION FIGURES**

☐ *Growth of population*

**New Delhi**
was built between
1911 and 1933 by
Lutyens and Baker.

**Rural India**
*More than half the country's population lives in its villages. An adult literacy programme is under way to educate the disadvantaged, particularly women.*

**The Nehru Family**
*Jawaharlal Nehru is seen here with his daughter Indira Gandhi (who was not related to Mahatma Gandhi), and her son Rajiv Gandhi. All three were prime ministers of India. Rajiv's Italian-born widow, Sonia, now heads the Congress Party.*

**The Indian flag**
is a tricolour of
saffron, white and
green, with a
*chakra* (wheel) in
the centre.

## TIMELINE

**1952** First General Election

**1953** Mount Everest scaled by Hillary and Tenzing

**1964** Death of Jawaharlal Nehru, first prime minister

**1971** War with Pakistan, birth of Bangladesh

**1977** Janata Party, the first non-Congress coalition, takes power

*Indian flag*

| 1960 | 1965 | 1970 | 1975 | 1980 |
|------|------|------|------|------|

**1955** Bandung Conference on Non-Alignment

**1962** India-China War

**1950** India becomes a Republic

**1966** Indira Gandhi becomes prime minister

**1965** War with Pakistan

**1974** First nuclear test, Pokhran

**1975** Indira Gandhi declares the unpopular Emergency

**1980** Indira Gandhi returns as prime minister

**1982** India sends scientific team to Antarctica

### Cricket
*Introduced by the British, this game is now a national obsession. Sachin Tendulkar, the "little master", is regarded by many as the greatest batsman since Donald Bradman.*

### Industrial Development
*Nehru, the architect of the country's industrial base, hailed factories as the new temples of modern India. India is now a major industrial power with a huge workforce of skilled workers.*

**The Indian Army** is one of the largest in the world.

**South Block** and its twin, North Block, were designed to flank Raisina Hill.

### Protest Rallies
*India's vibrant democracy expresses itself through popular protest (dharna) in which women figure prominently. The Narmada Bachao activists, seen here, have mobilized women and displaced tribal people against the World Bank-funded Narmada Dam.*

### Amartya Sen
*He won the Nobel Prize for Economics in 1998 for his work on development economics, based on studies of India's literacy, population, famine and the status of women.*

## THE REPUBLIC DAY PARADE
A magnificent parade on 26 January celebrates the day when India became a republic in 1950. A colourful flypast, folk dances and floats celebrate its pluralistic society, and the president, as head of the republic, takes the salute at Rajpath.

**1984** Indira Gandhi assassinated, her son Rajiv Gandhi succeeds her as prime minister

**1990** VP Singh becomes prime minister; announcement of reservation for backward classes

**1998** The right-wing Bharatiya Janta Party (BJP) comes to power for the first time

*AB Vajpayee becomes prime minister in 1998*

| 1985 | 1990 | 1995 | 2000 | 2005 |
|---|---|---|---|---|

**1992** Destruction of Babri Masjid in the state of Uttar Pradesh leads to communal riots

**1999** Conflict with Pakistan over Kashmir at Kargil; 13th General Elections re-elect a BJP-led government

**1991** Rajiv Gandhi assassinated; New Liberalization Policy under Prime Minister Narasimha Rao

*A woman casts her vote*

# DELHI
# AREA BY AREA

# Delhi at a Glance

SITUATED ALONG THE YAMUNA RIVER, New Delhi was built by the British in the 1930s and is the youngest of several historic cities that have occupied this site. Now a noisy and chaotic metropolis of 12 million people and a mélange of shanty settlements and smart colonies, it is still dotted with the remains of its interesting past. There are museums and art galleries with impressive collections, and its shops offer a tempting array of handicrafts. Delhi is a major cultural centre of the country with music, dance and art events held throughout the year.

***The Jami Masjid***
(see p92) *is the largest congregational mosque in Asia with lively bazaars in the surrounding lanes.*

***Connaught Place***
(see p76), *was built in the 1930s as the business centre of New Delhi in concentric circles round a central park. Its stately colonnaded corridors contain shops and offices.*

NEW DELHI
*(see pp66–79)*

***Rashtrapati Bhavan*** (see pp68–70) *is the official residence of the President of India. Called Viceroy's House in colonial times, it was designed by Edwin Lutyens and occupies the crest of Raisina Hill. Its forecourt is the venue for colourful state pageantry.*

***The National Museum*** (see pp72–5) *houses the most comprehensive collection of antiquities in the country. This 2nd-century Sunga panel of a grieving woman is part of a stunning section on sculpture from various periods and places.*

| | |
|---|---|
| 0 kilometres | 1 |
| 0 miles | 1 |

◁ **Swirling traffic in the narrow lanes of the old city around Jami Masjid**

OLD DELHI
*(see pp88–97)*

NIZAMUDDIN TO
PURANA QILA
*(see pp80–87)*

**Red Fort** (see pp94–5), *an impressive fort-palace built by Shah Jahan, was the seat of Mughal power. After the Indian Mutiny of 1857, the British converted it into a garrison and it was stripped of many precious treasures.*

**The Crafts Museum** (see pp86–7) *complex offers an insight into India's cultural, craft and rural traditions. The museum exhibits textiles, folk art and objects of everyday use in terracotta, metal and wood.*

**Humayun's Tomb** (see p83) *is where the second Mughal emperor Humayun is buried. This garden tomb with its imposing double dome is considered by many to be the first great Mughal mausoleum in this region.*

# NEW DELHI

THE BRITISH BUILT New Delhi, between 1911 and 1931, to be the showcase of the Empire. On Independence, this grand imperial capital became the official and bureaucratic centre of the new Indian nation. Today, Viceroy's House is the president's residence, and ministers and civil servants live nearby in spacious bungalows along the tree-lined

**Gargoyle**

avenues. Kingsway, the east-west processional avenue leading to India Gate, is now Rajpath, where every 26 January the Republic Day Parade is held (see p71). The National Museum is on Janpath. To the north are Connaught Place, the Birla Mandir and the cultural complex at Mandi House. Despite strict security restrictions, New Delhi is the city's most impressive area.

## SIGHTS AT A GLANCE

**Historic Buildings, Streets and Plazas**
India Gate ❻
Rajpath ❹
Rashtrapati Bhavan ❶
Vijay Chowk ❷

**Churches and Temples**
Lakshmi Narayan Mandir ⓫
Church of Redemption ❸

**Museums**
Gandhi Smriti ⓮
National Gallery of Modern Art ❼
National Museum ❺
Nehru Memorial Museum and Library ⓭

**Monuments**
Jantar Mantar ⓬
Ugrasen's Baoli ❾

**Shops and Markets**
Connaught Place ❿
Khan Market ⓰

**Gardens**
Lodi Gardens ⓯

**Theatres and Art Galleries**
Mandi House Complex ❽

### GETTING THERE
This area is well served by buses and taxis. Once there, the best vistas are from Vijay Chowk.

## KEY

| | |
|---|---|
| ▣ | Street-by-Street map *See pp68–9* |
| 🚉 | Railway station |
| 🚌 | Bus station |
| P | Parking |
| 🚓 | Police station |
| ⊠ | Post office |
| ✚ | Hospital |
| 🛕 | Temple |
| 🛕 | *Gurudwara* |
| ✝ | Church |
| ⚰ | Tomb |

0 metres 750
0 yards 750

◁ **India Gate and the elegant statue canopy designed by Lutyens**

# Street-by-Street: Around Vijay Chowk

THE BARREN, TREELESS GROUNDS around Raisina Hill were selected as the site of the new capital city. Now a well-guarded verdant area, it houses India's president, ministers and officials, as well as its Parliament and ministries. Imperial hierarchical conventions, both spatial and political laid down by the British are still followed, so that even today, Indian ministers and officials live in spacious bungalows on broad tree-shaded avenues around Rashtrapati Bhavan where no high-rise buildings are allowed. From Vijay Chowk, Lutyens's grand central vista lies ahead – large trees and fountains line the lawns of Rajpath up to India Gate, the Canopy and the National Stadium at the far end.

**★ Vijay Chowk**
*A pair of red sandstone obelisk-shaped fountains flank this forecourt that overlooks a grand vista* ②

**North Block**
has an imposing Central Hall which is open to the public.

**Sansad Bhavan** is also known as Parliament House.

**The Iron Gates**
*Copied from a pair Lutyens saw in Chiswick, England, these are held by highly ornamental sandstone gateposts. Rashtrapati Bhavan lies to the west of them.*

KEY

– – – Suggested route

## EDWIN LANDSEER LUTYENS

**Building the Secretariats on rocky scrubland**

Architect Edwin Landseer Lutyens (1869–1944), President of the Royal Academy from 1938 to 1944, was commissioned to design India's new capital in 1911. With Herbert Baker, his colleague, it took him 20 years to build the city in a unique style that combined Western Classicism with Indian decorative motifs. The result is classical in form and English in manner with Neo-Mughal gardens and grand vistas meeting at verdant roundabouts. Delayed by World War I and quarrels between Baker and Lutyens, spiralling costs met by Indian revenues led Mahatma Gandhi to term it a "white elephant". Ironically, the British lived here for only 16 years.

**★ South Block**
*The Prime Minister's Office and the Defence Ministry are located within this block, a high security zone.*

**Sunehri Bagh**
*This gently curving street leads to a picturesque roundabout with a simple 18th-century mosque built by a pir called Sayyid Sahib. Shady trees are a standard feature of all Lutyens's avenues.*

**LOCATOR MAP**
*See Street Finder map 4*

**Roundabout**
*Beautifully landscaped road intersections are a haven for workers during lunch.*

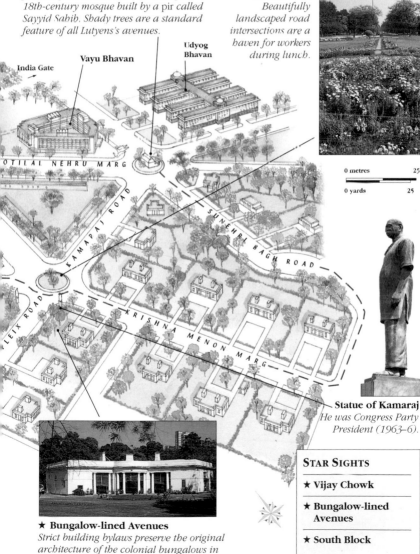

India Gate

**Vayu Bhavan**

**Udyog Bhavan**

OTILAL NEHRU MARG

KAMAPAJ ROAD

SUNEHRI BAGH ROAD

LEIX ROAD

KRISHNA MENON MARG

0 metres 25

0 yards 25

**Statue of Kamaraj**
*He was Congress Party President (1963–6).*

★ **Bungalow-lined Avenues**
*Strict building bylaws preserve the original architecture of the colonial bungalows in the tree-lined avenues of this area.*

**STAR SIGHTS**

★ **Vijay Chowk**

★ **Bungalow-lined Avenues**

★ **South Block**

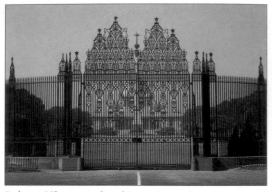

Rashtrapati Bhavan seen through Lutyens's ornate iron gates

## Rashtrapati Bhavan ❶

**Map** 4 E2. **C** *(011) 301 5321.* **●** *to the public. Visit permits can sometimes be obtained from the Deputy Military Secretary to the President of India.* **Change of Guard Ceremony** *Apr–Oct: 8:30am; Nov–Mar: 10:35am Sat.* **Mughal Gardens** ◻ *Feb–Mar.*

Dᴇsɪɢɴᴇᴅ by Edwin Lutyens *(see p68)* to be the focal point of New Delhi during British rule, the house built for the viceroy, which is today the President of India's official residence, stands at the crest of Raisina Hill. This 20th-century architectural masterpiece covers an area of 4.5 acres (2 ha) of land. The cupola of its copper and sandstone dome rises 55 m (180 ft) above the ground.

*Jaipur Column*

Within are courtyards, banqueting halls, state apartments and private living quarters. The *pièce de résistance* is the grand Durbar Hall, where all important Indian state and ceremonial occasions are held. Situated directly beneath the dome and forming the centrepiece of the "H"-shaped building, this circular hall was originally the Throne Room and contains the two gold and crimson thrones Lutyens designed for the viceroy and vicereine. To the west, the beautifully landscaped grounds include the formal **Mughal Gardens**. These terraced gardens with their watercourses and fountains built on three levels, end with Lutyens's "butterfly garden", where the flowers particularly attract butterflies.

## Vijay Chowk ❷

**Map** 4 F2. **N Block** ◻ *9am–6pm Mon–Fri.* **Sansad Bhavan** ◻ *11am–5pm. Visit is subject to Parliament not being in session.*

Tʜᴇ ᴘɪᴀᴢᴢᴀ where Rajpath meets Raisina Hill, known as Vijay Chowk, was planned as a commanding approach to the Viceroy's House. This is where the unforgettable "Beating Retreat" ceremony takes place each year on 29 January *(see p41)*.

Rising impressively from the levelled top of Raisina Hill are the two virtually identical **Secretariat** buildings designed by Herbert Baker and known as the North and South Blocks. These long classical edifices house the Home and Finance ministries and the Ministry of Foreign Affairs. The stately Central Hall of North Block (to the left, if facing Vijay Chowk) is open to the public.

Sited to the north of Vijay Chowk, Baker's circular **Sansad Bhavan** (Parliament House) was a later addition following the Montagu-Chelmsford Reforms of 1919, to house the Legislative Assembly. The Constitution of India was drafted here in the early days of Independence. Today, both the Rajya Sabha (Upper House) and the Lok Sabha (House of the People) meet here when Parliament is in session. The Lok Sabha's often boisterous debates take place in the Central Hall.

Sansad Bhavan (Parliament House), where the Constitution of India was drafted

## Cathedral Church of the Redemption ❸

Church Rd. **Map** 4 F1 ☎ *(011) 301 5396.* ○ *7am–noon; 4–6pm daily.*

Henry Alexander Medd (1892–1977), the architect of this magnificent church, was inspired by Palladio's Church of Il Redentore in Venice, from which it also derives its name. Consecrated in 1931, the cathedral formed an integral element of the plan for the imperial capital complex, and was built as the main Anglican church for senior British officials in New Delhi. Today, it is the diocese of the Bishop of the Church of Northern India. Among the many memorial tablets inside the church, there is one in honour of its architect.

**The Neo-Classical Cathedral Church of the Redemption**

## Rajpath ❹

**Map** 5 A2. **National Archives** ☎ *(011) 338 5000.* ○ *9am–6pm Mon–Fri.* ● *Sat, Sun & public hols.* **Indira Gandhi National Centre for the Arts** ☎ *(011) 338 9216.*

This two-mile-long avenue, used for parades and lined with ornamental canals and fountains along the lawns on either side, is very popular with the residents of Delhi on steamy summer evenings.

The **National Archives**, situated at the intersection with Janpath, houses a major collection of state records and private papers. Opposite is the **Indira Gandhi National Centre for the Arts** (IGNCA) which has an archive of rare manuscripts, and holds national and international exhibitions and symposia.

## National Museum ❺

*See pp72–3.*

## India Gate ❻

**Map** 5 B2.

At the eastern end of Rajpath, the 9 m (30-ft) wide India Gate was built to commemorate the Indian and British soldiers who died in World War I and those who fell in battle in the North-West Frontier Province and the Third Afghan War. An eternal flame burns in memory of unknown soldiers who died in the 1971 Indo-Pakistan war. Facing India Gate is the sandstone canopy where King George V's statue was installed after his death in 1936. The statue is now at Coronation Park *(see p103).* Around India Gate are the stately homes of erstwhile Indian princes, including Hyderabad House where official state banquets are held, and Jaipur, Bikaner, Patiala and Baroda Houses.

**India Gate**

## National Gallery of Modern Art ❼

Jaipur House, near India Gate. **Map** 5 C2. ☎ *(011) 338 2835.* ○ *10am–5pm Tue–Sun.* ● *Mon & public hols.* 🎫 🚻

Jaipur House, the former residence of the Jaipur maharajas, is one of India's largest museums of modern art. Its vast collection includes graphics, paintings and sculptures dating from the mid-19th century to the present day. The galleries display works of British landscape painters such as the Daniells, and early Indian artists such as the Tagores, Jamini Roy, Amrita Shergill and Raja Ravi Verma. Works of contemporary artists such as MF Husain, Ram Kumar, KG Subramanyam and Anjolie Ela Menon are also seen here. Reproductions of paintings are sold at the gallery shop.

### REPUBLIC DAY PARADE

Indians love parades and ever since 1950, when India became a republic, the Republic Day parade on 26 January has always attracted large crowds despite the often chilly weather. The president, the prime minister and other dignitaries watch as soldiers in dashing uniforms from the many regiments and squadrons of the Army, Navy and Air Force march smartly past. Brightly dressed schoolchildren, civil defence services personnel and others quick-step down the grand vistas of Rajpath to the rousing percussion of military bands. Most popular are the Camel Corps and the inventive floats representing each state of the country. A ceremonial fly-past by the Indian Air Force signals the end of the parade.

**Republic Day Parade**

# The National Museum ❺

**F**IVE MILLENNIA OF INDIAN HISTORY can be explored at the National Museum, with a collection of more than 150,000 pieces of Indian art. The nucleus collection of about 1,000 artifacts was sent to London in the winter of 1948–9 for an exhibition at the Royal Academy's Burlington House. After its return, it was housed in the Durbar Hall of Rashtrapati Bhavan until the present building, built of the same beige and pink stone as the imposing new capital, was complete in 1960. The Museum's collection of Indus Valley relics and Central Asian treasures from the Silk Route is considered among the finest in the world.

**Dancing girl from 2500 BC**

**★ Dara Shikoh's Marriage Procession**
*An 18th-century Mughal miniature painting in gold and natural pigments.*

**Gold Tali Pendant**
*Delicately handcrafted, this 19th-century solid gold pendant from South India is part of the ceremonial jewellery displayed in this gallery.*

**The Coins and Indian Scripts Gallery** displays an impressive collection of coins and the evolution of the Indian script.

**Ground floor**

**★ Kubera**
*A rare example of a Hindu god shown as a 2nd-century Kushana (see pp46–7) grandee with marked Central Asian features is among a large collection of Mathura Art.*

**Entran**

## THE SERINDIAN COLLECTION

**Silk painting, 7th–8th century**

Almost 700 years after the Silk Route fell into disuse, Sir Aurel Stein, a British archaeologist, led a series of expeditions (1900–16) to un-cover its treasures. On view at National Museum, Stein's Central Asian collection of the artifacts he found in the Taklamakan Desert has silk paintings, Buddhist manuscripts and valuable records of life along this ancient trade route.

**★ Nataraja**
*This 12th-century Chola statue of the cosmic dance of Lord Shiva is the centrepiece of the museum's South Indian bronzes.*

## Aurangzeb's Sword

*The personal sword of the Mughal emperor Aurangzeb, crafted in 1675 in the Indo-Persian style, has quotations from the Koran inscribed on it.*

## Gold Brocade

*This 19th-century silk wedding sari woven in Varanasi is embellished with motifs in gold thread.*

**Wood carvings** in the form of religious statues, carved doors and lintels are some of the exhibits here.

**Second floor**

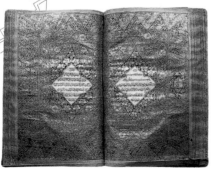

**First floor**

### ★ Illuminated Koran

*A superb example of the elegant Islamic art of calligraphy, this gilded 18th-century Koran is one of a collection that also has a 8th-century Koran in the ancient Kufic script. The latter is among the oldest of its kind in the world.*

### GALLERY GUIDE

*The collection is displayed on three floors, grouped according to theme, epoch and style. The central foyer itself has a display of sculptures from various parts of the country. The museum also has a library and auditorium where film shows and lectures are regularly held. Information on these is published in the newspapers. Information regarding catalogues and souvenirs can be had at the ticket office in the foyer. The display is changed from time to time for variety, and special exhibitions are also mounted.*

### KEY TO FLOORPLAN

- Indus Valley Culture
- Ancient and Medieval Sculpture
- Chola Bronzes
- Buddhist Art
- Tantra Art
- Decorative Arts and Jewellery
- Manuscripts and Miniatures
- Central Asian Antiquities
- Textiles, Arms and Armour, Musical Instruments

### STAR EXHIBITS

- ★ **Dara Shikoh's Marriage Procession**
- ★ **Nataraja**
- ★ **Kubera**
- ★ **Illuminated Koran**

# Exploring the National Museum Collection

**2nd-century Kushana sculpture**

SPREAD OVER THREE FLOORS radiating from an octagonal courtyard, the museum has 30 galleries (some closed for renovation or devoted to temporary exhibitions). The impressive collection includes sculpture, paintings, jewellery, decorative arts and textiles. These represent the finest examples of each style and period from all over the country.

## INDUS VALLEY CULTURE

EXCAVATIONS in the 1920s at Harappa and Mohenjodaro (now in Pakistan) revealed the remains of a sophisticated urban culture that existed between 2500–1500 BC along the Indus Valley *(see pp44–5)*. The museum's collection of relics from these sites is among the finest in the world. Although the Indus copper and bronze instruments are less opulent than the later Mesopotamian and Egyptian ones, other items, such as the figure of a dancing girl and a headless female torso, show enormous artistic skill.

Also on display are soapstone seals, used perhaps by merchants and officials, whose pictographic script remains undeciphered. Particularly notable is the display of Harappan pottery which ranges from functional items such as pots to charming toys, beads, necklaces and weights.

## ANCIENT AND MEDIEVAL SCULPTURE

SIX GALLERIES on the ground floor trace the growth of Indian sculpture over 1,500 years. Among the earliest pieces is a rare terracotta fertility goddess from Mathura dating to the 3rd century BC. From Amaravati in Andhra Pradesh (1st century AD), is a superb sculpted panel depicting its now vanished reliquary mound *(stupa)*. The 2nd-century AD Kushana frieze of Vasantsena, an inebriated courtesan *(see pp46–7)*, is an amusing comment on court life, while the splendid collection of Gandhara art, with its marked Hellenistic style, shows the evolution of the human form in North Indian sculpture after the 1st century. Its delicately draped statues are the first representations of the Buddha in human form. After the great stone-carved Hindu temples and images of the Gupta period (3rd–5th centuries), regional styles emerged in the south and the east. Successive galleries trace sculptural developments of the Pallava, Chalukya and Hoysala dynasties.

## BRONZES

INDIAN BRONZES, executed through the *cire perdue* or "lost wax" process as an alternative to stone temple sculptures, developed in South India under the Chola and Pallava dynasties. Idols made of bronze, an alloy of eight metals with copper as the base, were less weighty than stone and could either be worshipped at home or taken out for festive processions. The gallery's collection covers 600 years (5th–11th centuries). The pride of place belongs to a 10th-century Chola Nataraja, the name given to the Lord of Dance, Shiva. This shows him dancing the Chaturatandava, a classic representation of his cosmic dance of life and death. The circle of flames that surrounds the dancer represents the entire cosmos.

Another 11th-century Chola bronze, *Kaliyamardan Krishna*, is a superb study of the balance and poise of the young Lord Krishna as he dances on the hood of the five-headed serpent, Kaliya, holding his tail in triumph.

*Devi, 15th-century bronze*

## TANTRA ART

TANTRA is the invocation of Shakti or the "female principle". Tantric rites, mainly Shaivite *(see p319)*, are invoked through sexual, mystic and yogic practices. Its complex symbolism is portrayed in paintings, illustrated treatises and votive objects. Examples from Rajasthan, the hill states and Nepal form the gallery's collection.

A 16th-century painting from Jaipur illustrates yogic *asanas* (positions), while Tibetan *thangkas* (silk hangings) are vividly painted with Buddhist figures and motifs, since Mahayana Buddhism, too, has a tantric school which worships the female goddess, Tara.

**2nd-century Jain votive plaque from Mathura**

## DECORATIVE ARTS

THE IMMENSE VARIETY of India's decorative arts fills two adjoining galleries. Even everyday objects, such as a 19th-century silver rosewater sprinkler from Delhi, or a hookah base enamelled in blue and green from 18th-century Rajasthan have individual flourishes.

Court patronage ensured that artists fashioned innumerable *objets d'art* to delight royal whims. Thus, floral arabesques adorn a 17th-century Mughal *degcha* (cooking pot). Daintily carved ivory statues and artifacts and elegant Hyderabad *bidri* ware, delicately inlaid with silver, are also on display.

*Durga Killing Demon Raktabija*, Malwa, c.1640

**An 18th-century bidri ware jewel box**

## JEWELLERY GALLERY

THIS GALLERY has displays dating back to 2500 BC which project the development of the art of the goldsmith in the last 5,000 years. The first showcase represents the ornaments from the Harappan culture, simple terracotta beads as well as gold, silver and faïence work. The star attraction is the museum's royal jewellery, which includes spectacular Mughal and Rajput exhibits, such as a fabulous emerald *sarpech* (turban ornament), *navaratna* (a nine jewel setting) ornaments and stunning antique *meenakari* and *kundan* work *(see p187)*. South Indian ornaments on display are breathtaking items in gold, studded with uncut rubies and diamonds

**Emerald and diamond Mughal sarpech**

## CENTRAL ASIAN ANTIQUITIES

SIR AUREL STEIN'S collection of treasures *(see p72)* discovered from the fabled Silk Route in Chinese Turkestan comprises this invaluable section. Included are paintings on silk (3rd century) and a 10th-century caravan scene on paper from Dunhuang in China that recreate the romance of those times. Fragments of another silk painting, *Ladies in a Garden*, from Astana, show lovely women in elaborate coiffures with impressive gold filigree pins, lounging among blossoms.

## MANUSCRIPTS AND MINIATURES

AMONG THE WEALTH of rare manuscripts in the museum are the *Bustan-e-sadi* (1502), one of the few dated and illustrated manuscripts of pre-Mughal India. Leaves from the 16th-century *Babur Nama*, a biography of the first Mughal emperor, illustrate the style of early Mughal painting. The collection of paintings includes a comprehensive display of Rajput and Mughal miniatures, and a selection of the *Ragamala* series *(see pp30–31)* depicting the mood *(see pp28–9)* of each *raga*. Also on view is a collection of Pahari paintings from the northern hill states.

## TEXTILES, ARMS AND ARMOUR, MUSICAL INSTRUMENTS

THE TEXTILE collection displays a selection of Indian weaving techniques, including the world famous gold and silk brocades of Varanasi from the Mughal period; *ikat* and tie-and-dye from Andhra Pradesh and Gujarat; and 19th-century *kantha* embroidery from Bengal in intricate hemstitch. Also worth noting is a hand-embroidered *rumal* from Golconda dating to 1640.

The Arms and Armour Gallery has the 18th-century painted rhinohide shield of the Rajput king, Maharana Sangram Singh.

The Musical Instruments Gallery has some artifacts that are over 200 years old, including an ivory inlaid *tanpura* (a stringed instrument) from the 18th century. The core collection was donated by Sharan Rani, a famous *sarod* player.

**17th-century jamawar shawl**

## Mandi House Complex ⑧

**Map** 2 D5.
**Triveni Kala Sangam** Tansen Marg.
📞 *(011) 371 8833.* ◷ *9:30am–6pm Mon–Sat.* ● *public hols.* ▯ ▣
**Rabindra Bhavan** Ferozeshah Rd.
📞 *(011) 338 6626.*
**Kamani Auditorium** Copernicus Marg. 📞 *(011) 338 8084.*
**Sri Ram Centre** Safdar Hashmi Marg.
📞 *(011) 371 4307.* ▯ ▣
**National School of Drama** Bhagwan Das Rd. 📞 *(011) 338 9402.*
*For Tickets see Entertainment pp120–21.*

Mᴀɴᴅɪ ʜᴏᴜsᴇ, once the palace of the ruler of a small principality in Himachal Pradesh and today the offices of the state-owned television centre, lends its name to this cultural complex encircling the roundabout.
**Triveni Kala Sangam's** various art galleries hold regular contemporary art exhibitions. A pleasant open air auditorium here stages dance and theatre performances. Well-known artistes and writers can often be glimpsed in the popular café, and there is also a bookshop specializing in Indian arts publications.
The state-sponsored arts complex, **Rabindra Bhavan**, houses the three national academies of literature (Sahitya Akademi), fine arts and sculpture (Lalit Kala Akademi), and the performing arts (Sangeet Natak Akademi) in separate wings. All have libraries and display galleries which also sell reproductions and postcards. The Lalit Kala is the site of the international Triennale exhibition in which painters and sculptors from more than 30 countries participate. Exhibitions of photography, graphics and ceramics are also held here.
**Kamani Auditorium**, the **Sri Ram Centre** and the **National School of Drama** host theatrical, classical music and dance events in their auditoria. The latter two have their own repertory companies which stage plays in Hindi, Urdu and other regional Indian languages.

Ugrasen's Baoli in the heart of New Delhi

## Ugrasen's Baoli ⑨

Off Hailey Rd. **Map** 2 D5.

Tʜɪs sᴛᴇᴘᴡᴇʟʟ *(see p27)* is reached by turning left on Hailey Road into a narrow lane without a signpost just before the Consulate General of Malta. A little way along on the right are the remains of an old stone wall; the *baoli* is behind them and can be entered through a narrow buttressed gateway, usually locked, but the *chowkidar* will open the gate. Considered one of Delhi's finest stepwells, its architectural features suggest a 15th-century date, though popular myth holds that it was built in the 14th century by Raja Ugrasen, an ancestor of the mercantile Aggarwal community, to provide water and shelter for travellers.

**Mirror-work skirts on sale at Janpath**

## Connaught Place ⑩

**Map** 1 C4.
**Shops** ◷ *10:30am–7:30pm Mon–Sat.* ● *Sun & public hols.*

Rᴏʙᴇʀᴛ ᴛᴏʀ ʀᴜssᴇʟʟ, one of New Delhi's architects, designed this imperial plaza named after the Duke of Connaught, an uncle of King George V. Noble Palladian archways and stuccoed colonnades deliberately recalled the very English terraces of Cheltenham and Bath; and when the first shops raised their shutters in 1931, they had names like "Empire Stores" to distinguish them from the local shops selling Indian goods in shopping areas like Gole Market and Chandni Chowk. Today there are as many offices as shops in the central circle, officially renamed Rajiv Chowk. (The outer circle is now Indira Chowk.) The shops are an eclectic mix of travel agencies, banks, outlets for several leading international brands and the ubiquitous gift kiosks. Though Connaught Place has, in recent years, lost out to other local markets, its shaded arcades offer a pleasant atmosphere to stroll in and to browse through the pavement book stalls. There are many restaurants also located here, as well as a number of cinema halls showing the latest Hindi

**Connaught Place, the British-built shopping complex in New Delhi**

The brick and plaster astronomical instruments in Jantar Mantar

potboilers. The central lawns are well kept. Often a venue for street theatre or art shows, they are also frequented by shoeshine boys and self styled "ear cleaners". Other popular shopping centres in the area are the state emporia at Baba Kharak Singh Marg and the stalls along Janpath, especially the Tibetan Market.

## Lakshmi Narayan Mandir ⓫

Mandir Marg. **Map** 1 A4. 📷

THE PROMINENT industrialist BD Birla built this temple dedicated to Lakshmi Narayan in 1938. Mahatma Gandhi attended its first *puja* as this was among the country's first temples that had no caste restrictions. Popularly known as Birla Mandir, it is a fairly typical example of contemporary Indian temple architecture.

Approached by a flight of marble stairs, the main shrine has images of Vishnu and his consort, Lakshmi. It is surmounted by ochre and maroon *shikharas* (temple towers). Subsidiary shrines dedicated to Radha-Krishna, Hanuman, Shiva and Durga *(see pp22–3)* are set around the courtyard. On the walls are inscriptions from Hindu scriptures, often with English translations. They are also decorated with paintings from the *Mahabharata (see p141)* and *Ramayana (see p37)*.

Surrounded by a peaceful park with a pleasant marble pavilion on one side and a large *dharamshala* (resthouse) on the other, this popular temple is a good place to visit as it is spotlessly clean and very well-maintained.

The popular Lakshmi Narayan Mandir

## Jantar Mantar ⓬

Sansad Marg. **Map** 1 C5.

SAWAI JAI SINGH II of Jaipur built this observatory in 1724 when commissioned by the then Mughal emperor Muhammad Shah. A keen astronomer, the maharaja felt that the existing instruments were not accurate enough to calculate the eclipses and planetary positions required to set the timings of his *pujas* and other sacred rituals. To solve the problem he erected five observatories *(see pp192–3)* with instruments that were sufficiently large and fixed to the site to be both exact and not prone to vibration. The instruments are the Samrat Yantra, a right-angled triangle whose hypotenuse is parallel to the earth's axis. This is, in fact, a gigantic sundial, and there are two brick quadrants on either side which measure its shadow. The others are the Jai Prakash Yantra, Jai Singh's invention, which, among other functions, verifies the time of the spring equinox; the Ram Yantra which reads the altitude of the sun; and the Misra Yantra, a group of instruments for a variety of purposes. Today, the observatory lies obsolete, in the centre of a pleasant park, surrounded by high-rises.

The Nehru Memorial Museum and Library at Teen Murti Bhavan

## Nehru Memorial Museum and Library ⓭

Teen Murti Marg. **Map** 4 E3. [C (011) 301 6350. ◯ 9:30am–5:30pm Tue–Sun. ● Mon & public hols. **Nehru Planetarium** [C (011) 301 4504. 🎦 **Shows** 11:30am, 3pm.

JAWAHARLAL NEHRU lived in this house, then called Teen Murti Bhavan, while he was India's first prime minister (1947–64). On his death, the house was converted into a national memorial comprising a museum and a library for research scholars.

Originally the residence of the Commander-in-Chief of British Forces in India and located directly south of Rashtrapati Bhavan, the house was designed by Robert Tor Russell, the architect of Connaught Place and the Eastern and Western Courts on Janpath. Its design follows the established Lutyens-style classicism with a teak panelled interior and vaulted reception rooms. Nehru's bedroom and study, still exactly as he left them, are an austere centre in a grand house. Especially interesting are the bookshelves that line the corridors, containing Nehru's private collection, an eclectic mix of English classics, Left Book Club editions and treatises on the Cold War.

This home has a special place in modern Indian history as it once housed,

not just the incumbent prime minister, but two future ones as well, his daughter, Indira Gandhi, and grandson, Rajiv. Both mother and son were assassinated (see pp60–61).

The extensive grounds are home to the **Nehru Planetarium** and the square, three-arched **Kushak Mahal**, a 14th-century hunting lodge built by the Tughlaq sultan, Feroze Shah (see p97).

On the roundabout, in front of the house, is the memorial known as Teen Murti ("three statues") dedicated to the men of the Indian regiments who died in World War I. It was from this landmark that the house derived its name.

Teen Murti Memorial

## Gandhi Smriti ⓮

Tees January Marg. **Map** 4 F3. [C (011) 301 1480. ◯ 10am–5pm daily. 🚫 [C closed on public hols.

ON 30 JANUARY 1948, at 11am, Nathuram Godse assassinated Mahatma Gandhi as he was going to his daily prayer meeting in the gardens of this house, once the residence of the Birla family (see p77). A simple sandstone pillar marks the spot.

Now a museum commemorating Gandhi's life and final hours, the ambience here reflects Gandhi's philosophy of lofty political principles and down to earth common sense. A series of appealing dioramas made up of dolls in glass cabinets, tell the story of his eventful life through such defining moments as bidding farewell to his parents while going to England and the death of Kasturba, his beloved wife. The rooms where he used to stay when in Delhi are memorably austere and do convey a sense of his history. In the garden, footsteps, cast in red sandstone, lead to the site of his final martyrdom.

The museum complex has shops selling inexpensive editions of Gandhi's writings as well as items made from khadi, the simple homespun cloth he always wore, and which became one of the important symbols of the Freedom Movement (see pp58–9).

## Lodi Gardens ⓯

**Map** 5 M. ☐ *sunrise–sunset daily.*

LODI GARDENS, located in the heart of residential New Delhi, was built at the behest of Lady Willingdon, the Vicereine, in 1936. Originally the site of two villages, their inhabitants were shifted elsewhere and lawns and pathways were laid out around the tombs belonging to the 15th-century Sayyid and Lodi dynasties. Inside, the bridge called **Athpula**, literally "eight piers", near the entrance on South End Road, is said to date from the 17th century. To the west of it are the ramparts of the **tomb of Sikandar Lodi** (r.1489–1517) which enclose an octagonal tomb at the centre of some rather overgrown gardens. Inside it, traces of turquoise tilework and calligraphy are just about visible.

To the south of Sikandar Lodi's Tomb are the **Bara Gumbad** ("big dome") and **Sheesh Gumbad** ("glazed dome"). The names of the nobles buried within have long been forgotten, but the Bara Gumbad is an imposing structure with an attached mosque built in 1494, and a *mehmankhana* (guesthouse). The Sheesh Gumbad derives its name from the glazed turquoise tiles that still cling to its outer walls along with blue calligraphic panels.

Recent research claims that this is Bahlol Lodi's tomb. The **tomb of Muhammad Shah** (r.1434–44), the third ruler of the Sayyid dynasty, is said to be the oldest in the garden. The dome of this octagonal structure is surrounded by *chhatris*, and *jaalis* once filled the spaces between the pillars. The graves inside are said to be that of the sultan himself and some of the most favoured nobles of his court.

Today, with its tree-lined pathways and well-kept lawns and flower beds, the park acts as a "green lung" for the people of Delhi. It is one of the city's most picturesque parks and a favourite haunt of joggers, yoga-enthusiasts and families who come here to picnic on weekends. Vendors selling balloons, ice-creams and snacks from handcarts are popular with children.

**Muhammad Shah's Tomb**

## Khan Market ⓰

Subramaniam Bharti Marg. **Map** 5 B3. **Shops** ☐ *10am–7:30pm Mon–Sat.* ● *Sun & public hols.*

THIS MARKET WAS BUILT in the early 1940s to serve the needs of the British forces living in the hurriedly constructed barracks at Lodi Estate. Its name, Khan Market, is in honour of the prominent Pathan nationalist and social reformer, Dr Khan Sahib, the brother of Khan Abdul Gaffar Khan, the "Frontier Gandhi". Both men were revered for their role for independence among the warlike tribes of the North-West Frontier Province (now in Pakistan).

This popular market is much frequented by Indians and foreigners alike because of the wide range of Indian and Western merchandise on offer. Crockery, clothes and cakes, dog leashes, exotic (for India) vegetables, such as red peppers, avocadoes and asparagus, are just some of the goods available here. There are traditional sari shops, and also Anokhi *(see p266)*, selling blockprinted linen and garments in both Western and Indian style. There are also a number of excellent places to buy shoes, as well as bookshops, such as Bahri & Sons, The Book Shop and Faqir Chand's, one of the oldest shops in the market. Its other charming features are the groceries and the flower shops. A number of fast-food outlets are located here for shoppers in search of a quick snack, and one of Delhi's best delicatessens, Sugar & Spice.

**Athpula, the 17th-century bridge near the entrance to Lodi Gardens on South End Road**

# NIZAMUDDIN TO PURANA QILA

THE NIZAMUDDIN AREA, named after the famous 14th-century Sufi saint, Nizamuddin Auliya, is bisected by Mathura Road and has a clearly visible split personality. East Nizamuddin is the quieter half, with Humayun's Tomb *(see p83)* resting peacefully at the centre of a Persian garden. West Nizamuddin, the old Muslim quarter around the saint's *dargah,* is a lively *basti* which still retains its medieval character. This important pilgrim centre also has the graves of famous poets such as Amir Khusrau and Mirza Ghalib, as well as the tombs of Jahanara, the daughter of Shah Jahan *(see pp154–5),* and the dilettante Muhammad Shah Rangila,

A *jaali* screen

a later Mughal emperor. In this neighbourhood, the medieval and modern co-exist harmoniously. Busy Mathura Road swirls past the Subz Burj with its blue-tiled dome, today a traffic island. Humayun's Tomb and the Sundar Horticulture Nursery is off to the west. Further north is the up-market residential colony of Sundar Nagar with antique shops, Delhi Zoo and Purana Qila, the "old fort", *(see p84).* The crumbling battlements of the fort overlook the Crafts Museum, the small shrine of Matka Pir, a Sufi saint, and the exhibition grounds of Pragati Maidan. To the east stands the Khair-ul-Manazil Mosque, built by Maham Anga in the late 16th century.

## SIGHTS AT A GLANCE

**Historic Site**
Nizamuddin ❶

**Tomb**
*Humayun's Tomb p83* ❷

**Monuments**
Purana Qila ❸
Khair-ul-Manazil Mosque ❹

**Museums**
*Crafts Museum pp86–7* ❺

**Exhibition Grounds**
Pragati Maidan ❻

### KEY

| 🚉 | Railway station |
|---|---|
| 🚌 | Bus station |
| 🅿 | Parking |
| 🛕 | Temple |
| 🕌 | Mosque |
| ⚰ | Tomb |

0 metres 750
0 yards 750

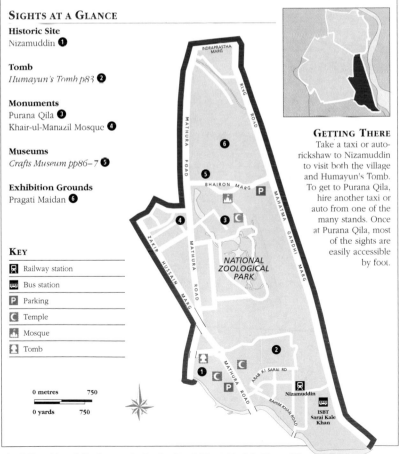

**GETTING THERE**
Take a taxi or auto-rickshaw to Nizamuddin to visit both the village and Humayun's Tomb. To get to Purana Qila, hire another taxi or auto from one of the many stands. Once at Purana Qila, most of the sights are easily accessible by foot.

◁ **Inlaid marble and tiles decorate the façade of Atgah Khan's Tomb in Nizamuddin**

# Nizamuddin Complex ●

West of Mathura Rd. **Map** 6 D5.
**Dargah** ○ *daily.* **Qawwali** *7pm Thurs.* ▧ *Urs (Apr).*

THIS MEDIEVAL settlement, or *basti*, is named after Sheikh Hazrat Nizamuddin Auliya, whose grave and hospice are located here. Nizamuddin belonged to a fraternity of Sufi mystics, the Chishtiyas *(see p319)*, respected for their austerity, piety and disdain for politics and material desires. His daily assemblies drew both the rich and the poor, who believed that he was a "friend of God" and so a master who would intercede on their behalf on Judgement Day. Nizamuddin died in 1325 but his disciples call him a *zinda pir*, a living spirit, who heeds their pleas and alleviates their misery.

**Colourful stalls line the alley leading to Nizamuddin's *dargah***

**Congregational area, Nizamuddin**

The Urs *(see p38)* is held on the anniversary of his birth and death and celebrated by his disciples with qawwalis and offerings of *chadors*.

A winding alley leads to the saint's grave. It is crowded with mendicants and lined with stalls selling flowers and *chadors*, polychrome clocks and prints of Mecca. The main congregational area is a marble pavilion (rebuilt in 1562) where, every Thursday evening, devotees sing devotional songs composed by the celebrated Persian poet, Amir Khusrau (1253–1325). Women are denied entry beyond the outer verandah but may peer through *jaalis* into the small, dark chamber where the saint's grave lies draped with a rose petal-strewn cloth and where imams continuously recite verses from the Koran. The complex also contains the graves of several eminent

disciples, such as Jahanara Begum and Amir Khusrau.

Across the western side of the open courtyard is the red sandstone Jama't Khana Mosque, built in 1325. To its north is a *baoli*, secretly excavated while Tughlaqabad *(see p114)* was being built because Ghiyasuddin Tughlaq had banned all building activities elsewhere. Legend has it that labourers worked here at night with the help of lamps lit, not by oil, but water blessed by Nasiruddin, Nizamuddin's successor *(see p108)*. The early 16th-century tomb of Atgah Khan, Akbar's minister and the husband of one of his wet nurses who was murdered by Adham Khan *(see p113)*, is to the north. An open marble pavilion, the Chaunsath Khamba ("64 pillars"), is close by. Just outside, is an enclosure containing the simple grave of Mirza Ghalib (1786–1869). One of the greatest poets of his time, Ghalib wrote in both Urdu and Persian, and his verses are still recited today. Nearby is the Ghalib Academy, a repository of paintings and manuscripts.

Always crowded, the *basti* preserves with miraculous serenity, the legend of this *pir*, who was called "a king without throne or crown, with kings in need of the dust of his feet" by his disciple, Amir Khusrau.

**Tomb of the famous poet Mirza Ghalib**

## NIZAMUDDIN COMPLEX

One of Delhi's historic necropoli, many of the *pir's* disciples, such as Amir Khusrau and Jahanara Begum, Shah Jahan's favourite daughter, are buried close to their master. Jahanara's epitaph echoes her master's teachings: "Let naught cover my grave save the green grass, for grass well suffices as a covering for the grave of the lowly".

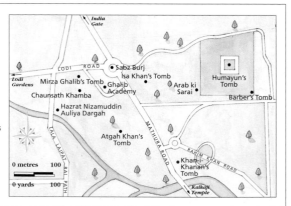

# Humayun's Tomb ❷

**Marble star inlaid on panel**

Humayun, the second Mughal emperor *(see p84)*, is buried in this tomb, the first great example of a Mughal garden tomb and inspiration for several later monuments, such as the incomparable Taj Mahal. Built in 1565 by a Persian architect Mirak Mirza Ghiyas, it was commissioned by Humayun's senior widow, Haji Begum. Often called "a dormitory of the House of Timur", the graves in its chambers include Humayun's wives and Dara Shikoh, Shah Jahan's scholarly son. Also in the complex are the Afsarwala Tomb, the octagonal tomb and mosque of Isa Khan, a noble at Sher Shah's court, and the tomb of Humayun's favourite barber. The Arab ki Sarai housed the Persian masons who built the tomb.

**VISITORS' CHECKLIST**

Off Mathura Rd. **Map** 6 D4.
📞 (011) 462 5275.
🕐 sunrise–sunset daily.
🎫 free on Fri. 📷

**The tomb as seen from the entrance**

**The Dome**
*This imposing white marble double dome is a complete half-sphere, and is surmounted by a finial with a crescent in the Persian style. Later Mughal finials, such as the one at the Taj Mahal, used a lotus.*

**Geometric designs inlaid on panels**

**Jaalis**
*Such fine trellis work in stone later became a signature Mughal feature.*

**The Tomb Chamber**
*The plain white marble sarcophagus stands on a simple black and white marble platform. The grave itself lies in the rather dark, bat-filled basement below.*

**The imposing plinth** is decorated with red sandstone arches and consists of multiple chambers, a departure from the single chamber of previous tombs.

# Purana Qila ❸

Mathura Rd. **Map** 6 D2. 📞 *(011) 460 4260.* ○ *sunrise–sunset daily.* **Son et Lumière** *Sept–Oct & Feb–April: 8:30–9:30pm; Nov–Jan: 7:30– 8:30pm; May–Aug: 9–10pm.* **Tickets**: *from site and the Delhi Tourism office.* 📞 *(011) 331 4229.*

Purana Qila, literally "old fort", stands on an ancient mound. Excavations near its eastern wall reveal that the site has been continuously occupied since 1000 BC. It is also believed to be the place where Indraprastha, the Pandava capital mentioned in the epic, the *Mahabharata (see p141)*, once stood.

It was here that Humayun, the second Mughal emperor, began to construct his city, Dinpanah ("Asylum of Faith"), just four years after his father Babur established the Mughal dynasty in 1526 *(see pp52–3)*. However, his reign was short-lived and, in 1540, he was dispossessed of his kingdom by the ambitious Afghan chieftain, Sher Shah Sur (r.1540–45). When Sher Shah took possession of the citadel, he strengthened its fortifications, added several new structures and renamed it Shergarh. After his death, his successors were defeated by Humayun who recaptured his domains in 1555. Today, of the many palaces, barracks and houses that once existed, only Sher Shah's mosque and the building said to be Humayun's library remain.

The Yamuna once flowed on the fort's eastern side and formed a natural moat: a small lake to the west facing

**Boating outside Purana Qila**

busy Mathura Road is all that remains today. The present entrance, an imposing red sandstone gate on the western wall called the Bara Darwaza, is one of the three principal gates of Shergarh. Its double-storeyed façade, surmounted by *chhatris* and approached by a steep ramp, still displays traces of tiles and carved foliage. Humayun's Gate, on the southern wall, has an inscription bearing Sher Shah's name and the date 950 AH (1543–4). To the north, the Taliqi Darwaza (the so-called "forbidden gate") has carved reliefs, and across the road is the red sandstone Lal Darwaza, or Sher Shah Gate, one of the entrances to the township that grew around the fort.

**Chhatri with decorative tilework**

The single-domed Qal'a-i-Kuhna Mosque, built by Sher Shah in 1541, is an excellent example of a pre-Mughal design. Its prayer hall inside has five elegant arched niches or mihrabs set in its western wall. Marble in shades of red, white and slate is used for the calligraphic inscriptions and marks a transition from Lodi to Mughal architecture. A second storey provided space for female courtiers to pray, while the arched doorway on the left wall, framed by ornate *jharokhas*, was reserved for members of the royal family.

The Sher Mandal stands to the south of the mosque. This double-storeyed octagonal tower of red sandstone was built by Sher Shah and was used as a library by Humayun after he recaptured the fort. The tower is topped by an octagonal *chhatri*, supported by eight pillars and decorated with white marble. Inside, there are remnants of the decorative plasterwork and traces of the stone shelving where, presumably, the emperor's books were placed. This was also the tragic spot where, on 24 January 1556, on hearing the muezzin's call, the devout Humayun hurried to kneel on the stairs, missed his footing and tumbled to his death. His tomb can be seen from the southern gate. Purana Qila flourished as the sixth city of Delhi *(see p107)* and traces of walls still stand in the area.

**Sher Shah's mosque at Purana Qila**

The single dome surmounting the prayer hall at Khair-ul-Manazil

# Khair-ul-Manazil ❹

Mathura Rd. **Map** 5 C2.
◯ sunrise–sunset.

THIS MOSQUE, "the most auspicious of houses", was constructed in 1561 by Akbar's influential wet nurse, Maham Anga, and a courtier, Shiha-bu'd-Din Ahmed Khan. An imposing, double-storeyed red sandstone gateway leads into a large courtyard ringed by cloisters, two storeys high, one of which was used as a *madrasa*. The prayer hall with its five-arched openings is topped by a single dome. Above the central archway, a marble inscription mentions Maham Anga's and Shiha-bu'd-Din's names. Inside, the central mihrab is decorated with bands of blue and green calligraphy. Maham Anga is buried in Mehrauli with her son, Adham Khan *(see p113)*, who was killed by Akbar.

# Crafts Museum ❺

See pp86–7.

# Pragati Maidan ❻

Mathura Rd. **Map** 6 D1. 📞 *(011) 331 4857.* **FAX** *(011) 331 8142.* ◯ *10am–5:30pm daily.* 🎫 📷 🖥 🍴
**Hamsadhwani, Falaknuma** and **Shakuntalam** 📞 *(011) 337 1849.*
**National Science Centre**
◯ *10am–6pm Tue–Sun.* ⬤ *Mon & public hols.* 🎫

INDIA'S LARGEST exhibition centre, covering nearly 150 acres (61 ha), is the venue for exhibitions and trade fairs organized by the India Trade Promotion Organization. The work of some of India's most eminent architects can be seen here. Raj Rewal has designed the Hall of Nations and Industries and Joseph Allen Stein, the World Trade Centre. Among other notable buildings are those by Charles Correa, Achyut Kanvinde and Satish Grover. All the Indian states have pavilions spread across the fair's extensive grounds, linked by 16 km (10 miles) of roads.

Exhibitions are held here throughout the year and cover a range of products from textiles, jewellery, automobiles to mining equipment and food products. Every two years the World Book Fair and the India International Travel and Tourism Show are held, drawing international delegates. Within the grounds are Appu Ghar, a children's amusement park, and the National Science Centre *(see p271)*. Two theatres, the Falaknuma and Shakuntalam, screen a cross-section of Indian and foreign films, while the Hamswadhwani Auditorium is the venue for various cultural events.

A view of Pragati Maidan from Purana Qila

## MATKA PIR

Rows of *matkas* (earthenware pots) line the entrance to the shrine of Matka Pir, a Sufi saint. According to legend, a man and his wife came to the saint to seek his help for the birth of a son. Being poor, they could only offer a humble pot of dal and jaggery. The saint asked them to place the pot in the courtyard and leave the rest to God. A year later, their wish fulfilled, they returned with another pot, a tradition that has continued since then. The pot motif leads all the way up the wide marble stairs to the *dargah*, standing on a ridge overlooking Mathura Road. The saint's powers still attract many pilgrims.

The shrine of the Sufi saint,
Matka Pir

# Crafts Museum ❺

**Wooden doll on toy swing**

FOR CENTURIES, Indian craftsmen, such as potters and weavers, masons and carvers, have created a range of objects of everyday use that are both beautiful and practical. A unique project was started in 1956 to promote indigenous artisans by displaying their work in one place, and by the early 1980s, over 20,000 objects had been collected. This was the core around which grew India's first Crafts Museum.

**Sarota**
*A late 19th-century betel nut cracker from South India.*

★ **Bandhini Odhni**
*This exquisite veil is the work of the Bhansali tribe in Kutch, Gujarat. In tie-and-dye (bandhini), grains are used to set the pattern. Threads are tied around them and the cloth dyed in different colours.*

**Mukhalinga**
*A rare, late 19th-century brass and silver phallic image (linga) with a human face (mukha). Tiny snakes as earrings and the third eye are symbols of Shiva.*

**Amphitheatre**

---

**STAR EXHIBITS**

★ **Bandhini Odhni**

★ **Bhuta Figure**

★ **Charrake**

---

**Crafts Demonstration Area**
*Artisans from all over India set up workshops each month (barring the monsoon) to display their skill to visitors.*

**KEY**

- ☐ Gallery of Aristocratic Arts
- ☐ Gallery of Ritual Arts
- ☐ Gallery of Folk and Tribal Cultures
- ☐ Gallery of Popular Culture
- ☐ Gallery of Textiles
- ☐ Administration Block
- ☐ Temporary Exhibition Gallery
- ☐ Visual Store

### Yashoda and Krishna
*This mid-20th-century plaster cast statuette from South India is an interesting example of popular kitsch, inspired by gods and mythology. It is cheap and easy to reproduce for use as a domestic shrine.*

### ★ Charrake
*These enormous, circular vessels are cast of an alloy known as bell metal. They are still used in Kerala for wedding feasts or at temples for making* payasam *(a type of rice pudding) for devotees during festivals.*

### Madhubani Painting
*A stunning wall painting in natural pigments depicting a wedding scene by Ganga Devi, a famous woman painter of this traditional art form from Bihar in Eastern India.*

### ★ Bhuta Figure
*These life-sized wooden figures were made 200 years ago as part of the Bhuta cult of spirit worship in the southern state of Karnataka.*

Library

Entrance

### GALLERY GUIDE
*The museum's display is spread over two floors of the complex, divided into separate areas by courtyards that also double up as exhibition spaces. A large open area is designated for live art displays by visiting artisans each month, except during the rainy season.*

### The Crafts Museum Shop
*Located on the premises of the Crafts Museum, the shop sells a wide selection of the finest Indian folk crafts and textiles.*

# OLD DELHI

**Detail of a door in Red Fort**

WHAT IS KNOWN as Old Delhi today was originally the Mughal capital of Shahjahanabad, built by Shah Jahan when he moved the imperial court from Agra to Delhi. Construction began in 1638, and ten years later the Red Fort, Jami Masjid, Chandni Chowk and the surrounding residential and mercantile quarters were ready for occupation.

The city was surrounded by a rubble wall pierced by 14 gates of which three, Delhi, Turkman and Ajmeri, survive. An elegant, mannered lifestyle flourished, enriched by the courtiers and merchants, artists and poets who lived in the lanes and quarters, called *galis* and *katras*, of the walled city. In 1739, the Persian freebooter Nadir Shah came to plunder the city of Shahjahanabad and left a bleeding ruin behind him. The final deathblow was, however, dealt when the British troops moved into the Red Fort after the Mutiny of 1857, turning it into a military garrison, while a railway line cut the walled city in half. Yet, the spirit of the place has survived all these vicissitudes and its busy *galis* continue to support a vibrant life. Modernity has brought a new urgency to the pace of the traditional traders who still live and operate from here.

## SIGHTS AT A GLANCE

**Mosques**
Jami Masjid ❶
Zinat-ul Masjid ❻

**Historic Streets and Sites**
Ajmeri Gate ❹
Chandni Chowk ❷
Turkman Gate ❺

**Monuments**
Feroze Shah Kotla ❽
*Red Fort pp94–5* ❸

**Memorial**
Rajghat ❼

### GETTING THERE
The most convenient way to get to Red Fort and Chandni Chowk is by car or auto-rickshaw. You may also join one of the many day tours to the Old City. Once there, explore the area by foot or cycle-rickshaw.

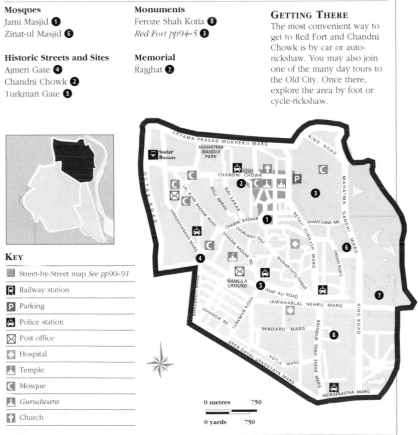

### KEY

| | |
|---|---|
| ▨ | Street-by-Street map *See pp90–91* |
| 🚉 | Railway station |
| P | Parking |
| 🚓 | Police station |
| ⊠ | Post office |
| ✚ | Hospital |
| 🛕 | Temple |
| C | Mosque |
| 🛐 | *Gurudwara* |
| ✝ | Church |

0 metres 750
0 yards 750

◁ **The white marble throne-balcony, Diwan-i-Aam, Red Fort**

# Street-by-Street: Chandni Chowk

NOW A BUSY COMMERCIAL CENTRE, Chandni Chowk was once a grand processional thoroughfare that led from Red Fort to Jami Masjid. When it was laid out in 1648 by Jahanara Begum, Shah Jahan's favourite daughter, a canal ran down the centre of the tree-lined stately avenue. Chandni Chowk, or the "silvery, moonlit square", was then lined with merchants' shops and the grand residences or *havelis* of noblemen.

**Sisganj Gurudwara**
*Guru Tegh Bahadur, the ninth Sikh guru, was beheaded at this site. The gurudwara marks the site of his martyrdom.*

**Sunehri Masjid**
*The "Golden Mosque", with three gilt domes, was built in 1722. On 22 March 1739, Nadir Shah stood on its roof to watch the massacre of Delhi's citizens.*

Fatehpuri Masjid

CHANDNI CHOWK

KINARI BAZAAR

Nai Sarak

DARIBA KAL

**★ Kinari Bazaar**
*Tightly packed stalls sell all manner of glittering gold and silver trimmings such as braids, tinsel garlands and turbans for weddings and festivals.*

CHEL PURI

BAZAAR GULIY

**Karim's**
*Tucked away in a narrow lane to the south of Jami Masjid is Delhi's most authentic Mughlai eatery. Named after a legendary 19th-century chef, the restaurant is now run by his descendants.*

**Shiv Temple**

| STAR SIGHTS |
| --- |
| ★ Jami Masjid |
| ★ Lahore Gate |
| ★ Kinari Bazaar |

**★ Lahore Gate**

*This imposing red sandstone gateway is the main entrance to Red Fort. The Prime Minister addresses the Independence Day rally here.*

**LOCATOR MAP**
*See Street Finder map 2*

**Dariba Kalan**

*Gold and silver ornaments are sold on this lane. Gulab Singh's famous attar shop (see p119) is located here.*

NETAJI SUBHASH MARG

ESPLANADE ROAD

**Charity box at the Bird Hospital**

**★ Jami Masjid**

*India's largest mosque stands on a mound. Its two slender minarets flank three marble domes* ❶

**Govt Girls Senior Secondary School**

**Karim's**

0 metres 25

0 yards 25

**KEY**

– – – Suggested route

Jami Masjid, built by Shah Jahan, is the largest mosque in India

# Jami Masjid ❶

Off Netaji Subhash Marg. **Map** 2 E2.
⬤ for non-Muslims during times of
prayer and after 5pm.

THIS GRAND MOSQUE, built in
1656 by the Emperor Shah
Jahan on a natural rocky
outcrop, took six years and
5,000 workmen to construct
at the cost of nearly a million
rupees. A magnificent flight of
red sandstone steps leads to
the great arched entrances
where, in Aurangzeb's time,
horses were sold and jugglers
performed. Today, sweet-
sellers, shoe-minders and
beggars mill around here. The
huge 28 m (300 ft) square
courtyard accommodates up
to 20,000 people at prayer
times, especially during
Friday prayers and on Id,
when it looks like a sea of
worshippers. Next to the
ablution tank in the centre is
the *dikka* platform where,
before loudspeakers took
over, a second prayer leader

echoed the imam's words and
actions for worshippers too
far from the pulpit.
Three imposing black
and white marble domes
surmount the enormous
prayer hall, and two
minarets frame the
great central arch. From
the top of the southern
minaret, a steep climb of
20 minutes, there are
remarkable views of the
roof-line of Old Delhi
giving way to the high-
rises of New Delhi.
Women require a
male escort to enter
the minaret.

# Chandni Chowk ❷

**Map** 2 D2.

ONCE SHAHJAHANABAD'S most
elegant boulevard, this
wide avenue extending from
Red Fort to Fatehpuri Masjid,
is still the heart of Old Delhi,
where both religious activity

and commerce mix happily
together. All along its length
are shrines sacred to various
communities. The first is the
Digamber Jain Mandir. Next
to it is the Bird Hospital for
sick and wounded birds.
Loud chants, clanging bells
and calls of vendors selling
flowers and vermilion powder
surround the Gauri Shankar
Mandir, dedicated to Shiva
and Parvati, which has a linga
said to be 800 years old. Still
further, close to the Sisganj
Gurudwara, is the Kotwali
(police station), the scene of
British reprisal after 1857
*(see p55)*. Nearly a century
before, another gruesome
spectacle took place
nearby when one
afternoon in 1739, the
Persian chieftain
Nadir Shah stood on
the roof of the Sunehri
Masjid and watched his
men kill nearly 30,000
of Delhi's citizens.
The actual Moonlit
Square (Chandni
Chowk), is the
open space in
front of the very
British Town Hall,
now the Hardayal Library.
Just behind it is the Mahatma
Gandhi Park, which was
called Begum Bagh in Mughal
times. Further down, and
commanding the end of this
charming quarter, stands the
Fatehpuri Masjid, constructed
in 1650 by Fatehpuri Begum,
one of Emperor Shah Jahan's
wives. Nearby are the spice
markets of Khari Baoli.

**Swami Shraddhanand's
statue, Chandni Chowk**

Chandni Chowk, a vibrant centre of commerce and religious activity

# Bazaars of Old Delhi

OLD DELHI'S BAZAARS are legendary. An English visitor to these bazaars over a hundred years ago, wrote in praise of the "Cashmere shawls, gold and silver embroidery, jewellery, enamels and carpets" to be found here. Today, the

**A cycle-rickshaw puller**

great wholesale *katras* of Chandni Chowk and Jami Masjid still retain that souk-like quality. Their narrow streets are lined with shops whose goods spill out onto the pavement; and shopping still means vigorous bargaining for a bewildering array of goods.

*Khari Baoli is Asia's biggest spice market. It spills across this street which derives its name from a stepwell that no longer exists.*

*Katra Neel is reminiscent of Middle Eastern souks. The tiny shops sell a wide variety of textiles, such as brocades from Varanasi, silk, cotton and voile.*

*Kinari Bazaar specializes in tinsel accessories, and attracts trousseau shoppers.*

*Nai Sarak is very popular among students as school and college textbooks and stationery are sold on this street.*

*Chawri Bazaar has every conceivable variety of paper, sold here by weight.*

*Churiwali Gali has garlands of glass bangles strung along rods to match every sari or lehenga. It is popularly called the "lane of bangle-sellers".*

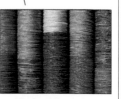

*Dariba Kalan is the jewellers' lane where artisans have worked for over two centuries.*

0 metres 500
0 yards 500

# The Red Fort ❸

A panel in Diwan-i-Aam

**R**ED SANDSTONE BATTLEMENTS give this imperial citadel its name, Red Fort (Lal Qila). Commissioned by Shah Jahan in 1639, it took nine years to build and was the seat of Mughal power until 1857, when the last emperor, Bahadur Shah Zafar, was dethroned and exiled. Lahore Gate, one of fort's six gateways, leads on to the covered bazaar of Chatta Chowk, where brocades and jewels were once sold. Beyond this lies the Naqqar Khana, from where musicians played three times a day.

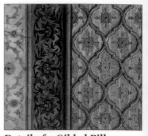

**Detail of a Gilded Pillar**
*The Mughal love of opulence is visible in the lavish use of marble and gold in the fort.*

**Moti Masjid**
*Named after the pearly sheen of its marble, the tiny "pearl mosque" was added by Emperor Aurangzeb in 1659.*

**★ Hamams**
*The royal bath has three enclosures. The first provided hot vapour baths, the second sprayed rose-scented water through sculpted fountains, and the third contained cold water.*

**★ Diwan-i-Aam**
*The emperor gave daily audiences to all his subjects in this 60-pillared hall. The intricately carved throne canopy stands on a platform, while the low marble bench was for the chief minister (wazir).*

| STAR FEATURES |
| --- |
| ★ **Diwan-i-Khas** |
| ★ **Diwan-i-Aam** |
| ★ **Hamams** |

**★ Diwan-i-Khas**
*The legendary Peacock Throne, one of Shah Jahan's seven jewelled thrones, was housed in this exclusive pavilion where the emperor met his most trusted nobles. The walls and pillars were once inlaid with gems and the ceiling was of silver inlaid with precious stones.*

**VISITORS' CHECKLIST**

Chandni Chowk. **Map** 2 D2.
(011) 327 3703.
6am–7pm daily. public hols.
free on Fri.
**Son et Lumière** Apr–Oct: 8pm;
Nov–Mar: 7pm.
**Museum** 10am–5pm. Fri.

**Khas Mahal**
*The royal apartments were divided by the "Stream of Paradise". The emperor's prayer room (Tasbih Khana) was flanked by his sleeping chamber (Khwabgah) and sitting room (Baithak). This overlooked the Yamuna and led to a balcony where he appeared before his subjects at sunrise.*

**Rang Mahal**
*Inside these gilded chambers, once exclusively for women, is an inlaid marble fountain shaped like an open lotus.*

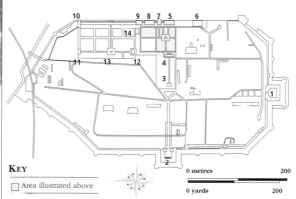

**THE RED FORT**

1 Delhi Gate
2 Lahore Gate
3 Naqqar Khana
4 Diwan-i-Aam
5 Rang Mahal
6 Moti Mahal
7 Khas Mahal
8 Diwan-i-Khas
9 *Hamams*
10 Shah Burj (Tower)
11 Sawan (Pavilion)
12 Bhadon (Pavilion)
13 Zafar Mahal
14 Moti Masjid

**KEY**

☐ Area illustrated above

0 metres 200

0 yards 200

## Ajmeri Gate ❹

Ajmeri Gate Rd. **Map** 1 C3.

THIS IS ONE OF THE 14 gates encircling Shahjahanabad that has survived more than 300 years and today stands in the midst of the city's congested commercial centre. Diagonally opposite Ajmeri Gate is **Ghazi-ud-Din's Tomb** and **Madrasa**. Ghazi-ud-Din Khan was an eminent courtier during the reign of the sixth Mughal emperor Aurangzeb, and his son, Mir Qamar-ud-Din, established the dynasty that ruled the southern state of Hyderabad until Independence in 1947.

The imposing, red sandstone *madrasa* has several arcades and a mosque on its western side. Founded in the late 17th century, this was at one time Delhi's foremost *madrasa* and after 1824 came to be known as the Anglo-Arabic School. English classes were held here, and British teachers also introduced mathematics and science texts to students, which were then translated into Urdu. Ghazi-ud-Din's grave is in a marble enclosure at the mosque's southern end. Athough this complex is surrounded by today's urban congestion, it still performs the noble function it was meant to. The three-domed mosque is in regular use and students crisscross the courtyard, while

**Ghazi-ud-Din's** *madrasa*

striped towels hang from the hostel balconies where glorious silks may once have billowed. Until recently, the esteemed Delhi College, now the Zakir Husain College, was also located on the premises.

A cycle-rickshaw from Ajmeri Gate will take you past tiny shops to the teeming lanes of Lal Kuan Bazaar where the **Zinat Mahal** is situated. Built in 1846, this was the eponymous home of the favourite wife of the last Mughal emperor Bahadur Shah Zafar. Today, it houses a school, lawyers' offices and shops. The original façade was wonderfully carved and arcaded with an oriel window. The beautiful verse by Bahadur Shah Zafar that was inscribed over the arched gateway can still be seen.

## Turkman Gate ❺

Asaf Ali Rd. **Map** 2 D3.

THE SOLID, square-shaped, red sandstone Turkman Gate stands in splendid isolation among the modern high-rise buildings of busy Asaf Ali Road. It marked the southern boundary of Shahjahanabad and was named after a Muslim *pir*, Hazrat Shah Turkman Bayabani, whose 13th-century tomb and *dargah* stand to the east. The serpentine lanes behind the gateway are home to two medieval monuments. **Kalan Masjid** ("black mosque"), in the Bulbulekhan area, was built in 1387 by Khan-i-Jahan Junan Shah, Feroze Shah Tughlaq's prime minister. This is one of the seven mosques he built in Delhi; the others are at Khirkee and Begumpuri *(see p109)*. A short walk away lies, what is believed to be, the **grave of Sultana Razia,** Delhi's only medieval woman ruler *(see pp50–51)*. Her brief reign was bedevilled by revolts and she was killed at Karnal in 1240 while fleeing from Delhi. Her plain rubblestone grave lies open to the sky in a cramped enclosure amidst houses and shops. The aterlier of the last practising craftsman of Delhi's blue pottery, Hazarilal, is situated in the congested alleys of Hauz Suiwalan, located behind Turkman Gate.

**Traffic swirls around the Mughal Turkman Gate**

## Zinat-ul Masjid ❻

Daryaganj. **Map** 2 F3.

Tᴴɪꜱ ᴍᴏꜱQᴜᴇ was built in 1710 by Princess Zinat-un-Nisa Begum, one of Emperor Aurangzeb's daughters. The gracefully proportioned red sandstone mosque has a spacious courtyard built over a series of basement rooms. Its seven-arched prayer hall is surmounted by three domes, with alternating stripes of black and white marble. The locals who worship here have a more lyrical name for it, the Ghata ("Cloud") Mosque because its striped domes simulate the monsoon sky.

Zinat-ul Masjid, also known as the Ghata or "Cloud" Mosque

**Rajghat**

## Rajghat ❼

Mahatma Gandhi Rd. **Map** 2 F3.
⏰ sunrise–sunset daily. **Prayer meetings** 5pm Fri.
**National Gandhi Museum** ☏ (011) 331 1793. ⏰ 9:30am–5:30pm Tue–Sun. ⬤ Mon & public hols.
**Film shows** 4–5pm Sat & Sun.

Rᴀᴊɢʜᴀᴛ, India's most potent symbol of patriotism, is the site of Mahatma Gandhi's cremation. A sombre black granite platform inscribed with his last words He Ram! ("Oh God!") now stands here. The only splash of colour comes from the garlands of orange marigolds draped over it. Devotees sing bhajans and the steady beat of the dholak lends the scene a dolorous melancholy. All visiting heads of state are taken to this samadhi ("memorial") to lay wreaths in memory of the "Father of the Nation". On Gandhi's birthday (2 Oct) and death anniversary (30 Jan), the nation's leaders gather here for prayer meetings.

Just across the road is the **Gandhi National Museum**, crammed with memorabilia connected with Gandhi's life, including his letters and diaries. A framed plaque on the stairs explains his simple philosophy: "Non-violence is the pitting of one's whole soul against the will of the tyrant… it is then possible for a single individual to defy the might of an unjust empire."

## Feroze Shah Kotla ❽

Bahadur Shah Zafar Marg. **Map** 2 F4.

Oɴʟʏ ꜱᴏᴍᴇ ʀᴀᴍᴘᴀʀᴛꜱ and ruined structures remain of Feroze Shah Kotla, the palace complex of Ferozabad, Delhi's fifth city erected by that indefatigable builder, Feroze Shah Tughlaq (see p107). Entry is from the gate next to the Indian Express Building. Towards the very end of the walled enclosure stand the partial ruins of the Jami Masjid. Roofless, with only the rear wall still extant, this was at one time Delhi's largest mosque where as legend says, Tamburlaine, the Mongol conqueror who sacked Delhi in 1398, came to say his Friday prayers. Next to the Jami Masjid is a rubble pyramidal structure topped by one of the Mauryan emperor Ashoka's polished stone pillars (see pp46–7) brought from the Punjab and installed here in 1356 by Feroze Shah. It was from the inscriptions on this pillar that James Prinsep, the Oriental linguist, deciphered the Brahmi script, a forerunner of the modern Devanagari, in 1837.

**Khuni Darwaza** (the "bloodstained gate"), opposite the Indian Express Building, was built by Sher Shah Sur as one of the gates to his city (see p84). This was where Lieutenant Hodson shot Bahadur Shah Zafar's sons after the Mutiny of 1857 was quashed. Across the road is Delhi's main cricket stadium, named after the palace complex, where world-class test matches are held.

**The Ashokan Pillar at Feroze Shah Kotla**

# FURTHER AFIELD

THERE IS MUCH to see and explore beyond the city centre. An undulating wooded area, the Ridge, sweeps across Delhi from the southwest to the north. The north contains the university campus and Civil Lines, an orderly civilian enclave created by the British, and the west houses the army Cantonment. South Delhi, juxtaposed between the old cities of Siri, Jahanpanah and

**Detail, Moth ki Masjid**

Tughlaqabad, is a more recent addition, with many affluent suburbs, smart residential colonies, shops, cinemas and restaurants. Further south, the historic Mehrauli Archaeological Park encompasses 19th-century hunting lodges, tombs, pavilions and the towering Qutb Minar. This picturesque area was the site of Delhi's first city, Qila Rai Pithora built around Lal Kot, a Tomar Rajput fortress.

## SIGHTS AT A GLANCE

**Historic Buildings and Sites**
Chiragh Delhi ⑰
Civil Lines ⑤
Delhi Cantonment ⑩
Delhi University ⑧
Hauz Khas ⑮
Jahanpanah ⑲
Khirkee ⑱
*Mehrauli Archaeological Park pp110–13* ⑳
Old Delhi GPO ②
Siri Fort ⑯
Tughlaqabad ㉓

**Temples, Churches and Mosques**
Baha'i House of Worship ㉕
Kalkaji Temple ㉔
Moth ki Masjid ⑭
St James's Church ①

**Cemeteries**
Nicholson Cemetery ③

**Parks and Gardens**
Northern Ridge ⑦
Qudsia Gardens ④
The Ridge ⑨

**Monuments**
Coronation Memorial ⑥

**Museums**
National Rail Museum ⑪
Sanskriti ㉑

**Tombs**
Safdarjung's Tomb ⑫
Sultan Ghari ㉒

**Markets**
INA Market ⑬

### GETTING THERE
A private car, taxi or auto-rickshaw is the best way of exploring the area. Private tour operators also run coaches to some sites.

| | |
|---|---|
| 0 kilometres | 3 |
| 0 miles | 3 |

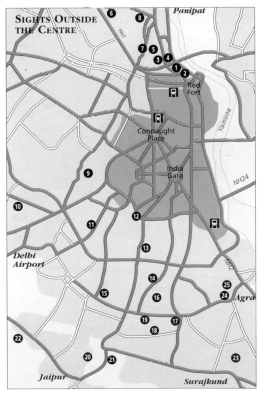

SIGHTS OUTSIDE THE CENTRE

Panipat

Red Fort

Connaught Place

India Gate

NH24

Delhi Airport

Agra

Jaipur

Surajkund

| | |
|---|---|
| ■ | Delhi city centre |
| ▢ | Built-up area |
| ▢ | Greater Delhi |
| 🚉 | Railway station |
| ▬ | Major road |
| ═ | Minor road |

◁ **Safdarjung's Tomb, the last great Mughal garden tomb, was built in the mid-18th century**

# Street-by-Street: Around Kashmiri Gate

A local
bakery sign

**D**ELHI'S KASHMIRI GATE area resonates with memories of 1857. Many of the dramatic events between the months of May and September took place on the short stretch between Kashmiri Gate and the Old Delhi General Post Office (GPO). In the 1920s, this was also a favourite watering hole of the British residents living in nearby Civil Lines. Then the street was lined with smart shops and restaurants, few of which survive now.

**Shop Façades**
*The grand old shops are now shabby and derelict.*

Nicholson Cemetery ❸

### ★ Kashmiri Gate
*The Mughals used to set off from this gate to spend the summer in Kashmir. In 1857, it was the scene of a bitter battle and a plaque on the western side honours "the engineers and miners who died while clearing the gate for British forces on September 14, 1857".*

NICHOLSON RD

**Fakr-ul-Masjid**
*The domes and minarets of this small mosque rise above the rows of shops and offices along this busy street. Local residents come here to worship every Friday.*

RAMLAL CHANDHOK MARG

CHURCH ROAD

LOTHIAN RO

BARA BAZA

0 metres     15

0 yards      15

Old Hindu
College

Old St Stephen's
College

## STAR SIGHTS

★ Kashmiri Gate

★ St James's Church

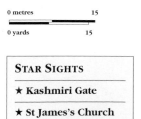

**KEY**

— — — Suggested route

★ **St James's Church**
*Delhi's oldest and
most historic church,
consecrated in 1836,
is an impressive
edifice, painted
yellow and white* ❶

**Northern
Railways Office**
*This Indo-Saracenic
fantasy was once the
residence of the British
Commissioner, William
Fraser, one of Skinner's
closest friends.*

*CHURCH ROAD*

**Delhi College of
Engineering**

**Dara Shikoh's
library**

**Old Delhi GPO** ❷

# St James's Church ❶

Lothian Rd. (011) 296 08 73.
☐ 8am–12 noon; 2–5pm daily.
**Services** 9am Sun.

A TABLET in the church
founded by Colonel James
Skinner explains. "This church
is erected at the sole expense
of Colonel James Skinner" in
fulfilment of a vow made on
the battlefield. Built at the cost
of Rs80,000, the church is in
the shape of a Greek cross,
surmounted by an imposing
eight-leafed dome. The two
stained-glass windows were
installed in the 1860s. Skinner
died at Hansi (see p140). A
marble tablet, in front of the
altar, marks his simple grave.

**The imposing Old Delhi General
Post Office**

# Old Delhi GPO ❷

Lothian Rd. ☐ 9:30am–6pm
Mon–Fri; 9:30am–1pm Sat.

T O THE SOUTH of Kashmiri
Gate is the Old Delhi
General Post Office, an old
fashioned establishment
caught in a time warp. This
stucco-fronted colonial edifice
is significant because it faces
a traffic island on which stand
two structures dating to the
Indian Mutiny of 1857. The
Telegraph Memorial is a
memorial obelisk dedicated to
the officers of the Telegraph
Department. The inscription
on it honours the telegraph
operators, Brendish and
Pilkington, who flashed news
of the Indian Mutiny to the
British garrison at Ambala.
Nearby lies the ruined British
Magazine. It was blown up by
a Captain Willoughby on 11
May 1857 to prevent it from
falling into the hands of the
rebelling sepoys.

## JAMES SKINNER

One of the Empire's most swashbuckling
adventurers, Skinner was the son of a
Scotsman and a Rajput. Rejected by
the British Army because of his mixed
parentage, he raised his own cavalry
regiment, Skinner's Horse, whose
flamboyant yellow uniforms gave rise
to the name Yellow Boys. His troops
fought with distinction and are still part
of the Indian Army. On his death he was
honoured as a Commander of the Order
of the Bath. His descendants still live on
an estate in Mussoorie, Uttar Pradesh.

**James Skinner
(1778–1841)**

**Graves at Nicholson Cemetery**

## Nicholson Cemetery ❸

Lala Hardev Sahai Marg.
◯ 10am–5pm.

IN A RATHER tumbledown walled cemetery named after him, surrounded by brisk traffic and overlooked by the huge Inter State Bus Terminus (ISBT), lies the flamboyant Brigadier General John Nicholson, the British commander. The headstone on his grave, which is to the right of the entrance, records that he "led the assault on Delhi but fell mortally wounded and died 3rd September 1857, aged 35". The surrounding graves belong to others like him who died at the time of the Indian Mutiny, between 10 May and 30 September 1857. The saddest, though, are the tiny graves of children, such as the headless angel mourning over Alfred and Ida Scott's little daughter: "We gave her back to bloom in heaven".

To enter the cemetery, knock on the gate and the *chowkidar* will open it. Though there are no entrance charges, a small tip (10–20 rupees) to the *chowkidar* and a donation to the Church of North India will be welcome.

## Qudsia Gardens ❹

Shamnath Marg. ◯ sunrise–sunset.

QUDSIA BEGUM, the dancing girl who became the wife of Emperor Muhammad Shah (r.1719–48) laid out these gardens in around 1748, and although the Inter State Bus Terminus and the Tourist Park now occupy much of the original site, the imposing gateway still stands. The rest of the present park is more modern with a children's playground and a rather formidable statue of the great Rajput king, Maharana Pratap. North of the gardens is the children's home run by Mother Teresa's Missionaries of Charity, where abandoned children are cared for.

## Civil Lines ❺

Bounded by Shamnath Marg and Mahatma Gandhi Marg.

OLD DELHI's Civil Lines were inhabited by the British civilian population while the Cantonment *(see p104)* was the military enclave. They lived in spacious bungalows, shopped at the Exchange Stores, dined at Maidens Hotel and worshipped at St James's Church. The old "temporary" Secretariat (built in 1912) is also located here on Mahatma Gandhi Marg. This long white building with its two towers, where the Legislative Assembly once sat, now houses the offices of the Delhi Administration. When the British moved into New Delhi, established Indian professional and merchant families settled here. Several old bungalows have been re-developed as modern blocks of flats, yet some areas, such as Rajpur Road, still retain their colonial character.

To the east of Civil Lines, near the Delhi-Chandigarh bypass, is Metcalfe House, a sprawling mansion built in the 1830s by Sir Thomas Metcalfe, Delhi's eccentric British Resident from 1835–53. This house, once the hub of British social life, can be seen from the highway. It is now owned by the Defence Ministry and not open to the public.

**White-plastered façade of the Oberoi Maidens Hotel in the Civil Lines area**

Statues of former viceroys in the Coronation Durbar site

still visible. Feroze Shah also had a large hunting estate here where he built a lodge called Kushak-i-Shikar, a mosque, as well as a double-storeyed mansion, the Pir Ghaib, now in the grounds of the Hindu Rao Hospital (enter the main gate and turn right at the Cardiac Unit). The name, Pir Ghaib, derives from the tale of a resident *pir* who one day, simply vanished (*ghaib*) while meditating at this site. A cenotaph in one of the rooms marks the spot.

# Coronation Memorial **❻**

S of NH1 Bypass. ☐ *sunrise–sunset.*

THIS WAS THE SITE of the Royal Durbar held in 1911 to proclaim the accession of George V as King Emperor of India. A red sandstone obelisk records that the King Emperor proclaimed his coronation to the "governors, princes and peoples of India" (in that order) and "received their dutiful homage". He also announced the transfer of the capital from Calcutta to Delhi and two days later laid the foundation stones for the new city (*see pp68–9*). On 12 December 1911, more than 100,000 people thronged the site where the King Emperor and Queen Empress sat beneath a golden dome mounted on a crimson canopy. Today, the site is a flat, dusty and forlorn spot, and ranged round in a pathetic semi-circle are statues of former viceroys, evicted from their perches in the city to make way for later Indian leaders. These include Lords Hardinge and Willingdon (distinguished for their role in the construction of New Delhi).
Towering over them all, is the 22 m (73 ft) statue of the King Emperor himself, draped in his Durbar robes, which was removed from the canopy at India Gate (*see p71*) and installed here in the 1960s.

**Coronation Memorial**

# The Northern Ridge **❼**

Rani Jhansi Rd, Ridge Rd, Magazine Rd. ☐ *sunrise–sunset.*

THE NORTHERN END of the Ridge is a forested park cut through by Ridge Road and Rani Jhansi Road with the small clearing of Bara Hindu Rao in the middle. This area still resounds with memories of 1857. It was round Flagstaff Tower, to the far north, that British women and children took shelter before they were evacuated to Karnal near Panipat (*see p140*).
The Mutiny Memorial (known locally as Ajitgarh), at the southern end, is a red sandstone, Victorian Gothic spire built by the British to commemorate "the soldiers, British and native ... who were killed" in 1857 and lists separately, the names of those who died. At the entrance is a plaque, dated 1972, which points out: "The enemy of the in-scriptions were those who fought bravely for national liberation in 1857". There are pano-ramic views of Old Delhi from the platform at the base of the tower. Nearby is a 3rd-century Ashokan Pillar, one of the two Feroze Shah Tughlaq (*see p97*) brought from Meerut in 1356. Faint inscriptions in Brahmi, extolling the virtues of practising *dhamma* (the Buddhist Way of Truth), are

**St Stephen's College**

# Delhi University **❽**

Vishwavidyalaya Marg.

THE UNIVERSITY area runs parallel to the Northern Ridge, and colleges dot the vast campus. Arguably the most attractive of these is St Stephen's College, designed by Walter George in 1938. With its long corridors built in quartzite and its well-kept gardens, it has some deliber-ately cultivated Oxbridge associations. At one time this was one of India's premier institutions, with renowned scholars such as the historian Percival Spear on its staff. The office of the Vice Chancellor was once the guesthouse for British officials. It was here, in what is now the registrar's office, that the young Lord Louis Mountbatten proposed to, and was accepted by, Edwina Ashley. A plaque celebrates the event. They eventually became India's last viceroy and vicereine.

The image of the Buddha installed at Buddha Jayanti Park

# The Ridge ❾

Upper Ridge Rd. ◯ *sunrise–sunset.*

DELHI'S RIDGE, the last outcrop of the Aravalli Hills extending northwards from Rajasthan, runs from southwest to northeast. The area was originally developed by Feroze Shah Tughlaq, some 600 years ago as his hunting resort. He erected many lodges, the ruins of which can still be seen here and towards the northern end of the Ridge *(see p103).* This green belt of undulating, rocky terrain is covered by dense scrub forest consisting mainly of laburnum *(Cassia fistula),* kikar *(Acacia arabica)* and flame of the forest *(Butea monosperma)* trees, interspersed with bright splashes of bougainvillea.

A large portion in the southwest is now the **Buddha Jayanti Park**, a peaceful, well-manicured enclave, criss-crossed with paved paths. Pipal *(Ficus religiosa)* trees abound, and on a small ornamental island is a simple sandstone pavilion shading the large gilt-covered statue of the Buddha, installed by the 16th Dalai Lama in October 1993. An inscription nearby quotes the Dalai Lama: "Human beings have the capacity to bequeathe to future generations a world that is truly human". Every May, Buddhist monks and devotees celebrate Buddha Jayanti *(see p38)* here.

# Delhi Cantonment ❿

Bounded by NH8, MG Rd and Sadar Bazaar Marg. **St Martin's Church** Church Rd. 🎫 *(011) 569 4632.* **War Graves Cemetery** Brar Square. 🎫 *(011) 569 1958.* ◯ *8am–5pm daily.*

THE CANTONMENT in Delhi was planned by John Begg and built by the Military Works Department in the 1930s. With its straight roads, neat, whitewashed walls, well-clipped hedges, parade ground and shooting-range, it epitomizes the quint-essential spit and polish of the military.

The garrison **Church of St Martin's**, probably the most original modern church in India, was designed by Lutyens's close associate, Arthur Gordon Shoosmith (1888–1974). Consecrated in 1931 and built from three and a half million bricks, it rises straight-walled with small,

A memorial tablet

recessed windows and a 39 m (128 ft) tower, the lines between the bricks being the only ornamentation. Within is a stark classical interior with a plaque in honour of the architect and a haunting tablet in memory of the three children of Private Spier who died within days of each other at Abbottabad (now in Pakistan) in 1938. If the church is locked, contact the Presbyter-in-Charge who lives in the adjacent cottage.

A short distance from Dhaula Kuan Circle is the **War Graves Cemetery** where lie the Commonwealth soldiers and airmen who died on the Eastern Front in World War II. A monument at the entrance proudly declares: "Their Name Liveth Ever-more". The graves are set in neat rows with matching headstones; only the regi-mental insignia and biblical texts are different. Every Remembrance Day (11 Nov), wreaths are laid at the Memorial Column, followed by a short prayer.

# The National Rail Museum ⓫

Chanakyapuri. 🎫 *(011) 688 1816.* ◯ *9:30am–5pm Tue–Sun.* ● *1:30–2:30pm & public hols.* 🎥 *extra for video and train rides.* 📷

INDIA'S RAILWAY NETWORK gives rise to astonishing statistics. It has a route length of 63,360 km (39,370 miles) and tracks that cover 108,513 km (67,427 miles). There are about 7,150 stations, 12,600 passenger trains, and 1,350 goods trains

The War Graves Cemetery

that run every day. The railways employ 1.6 million people, while 13 million passengers travel by train each day and eat 6 million meals through the journey.

This museum encapsulates the history of Indian railways. Steam locomotive enthusiasts will appreciate the collection that traces the development of the Indian railways from 1849, when the first 34 km (21 miles) of railway between Bombay (now Mumbai) and Kalyan was planned. The wealth of memorabilia on display inside includes the skull of an elephant which collided with a mail train at Golkara in 1894, and a realistic model of an 1868 first-class passenger coach with separate compartments for accompanying servants. Outside, are several retired steam locomotives built in Manchester, Glasgow and Darlington in the late 19th century, and the splendid salon that carried the Prince of Wales (later King Edward VII) on his travels during the 1876 Royal Durbar.

A "toy train" offers rides around the compound, and the shop sells model loco-motives, ranging from Rs1,000 to 3,000.

## Safdarjung's Tomb ⑫

Aurobindo Marg. ◯ *sunrise–sunset.* ◙ ◙ *extra charges for video photography.* ◖ *(011) 301 7293.*

THIS IS THE LAST of Delhi's garden tombs and was built in 1754 for Safdarjung, the powerful prime minister of Muhammad Shah, the emperor between 1719–48. Marble allegedly was stripped from the tomb of Abdur Rahim Khan-i-Khanan in Nizamuddin *(see p82)* to construct this rather florid example of late Mughal architecture. Approached by an ornate gateway, the top storey of which houses the Archaeological Survey of India's library, the tomb, with its exaggerated onion-shaped dome, stands in a *charbagh* cut by water channels. Its red and buff stone façade is extensively ornamented with well-preserved plaster carving and the central chamber itself is unusually light and airy with some fine stone inlay work set into the floor.

**A well-stocked shop at INA Market**

## INA Market ⑬

Aurobindo Marg. **Shops** ◻ *9am–9pm Tue–Sun.* ● *Mon.*

THIS LIVELY BAZAAR retains all the trappings of a tradi-tional Indian market but also sells imported foodstuffs such as cheese, pasta and exotic varieties of seafood. The stalls are crammed together under a ramshackle roof, mostly corrugated iron and oilcloth. Shops selling stainless steel utensils, spices, ready-made garments, live chickens and tiny restaurants offering Indian fast food, co-exist cheek by jowl. Ingredients for regional Indian cuisine, such as South Indian *sambhar* (curry) powder, Bengali spices or massive red chillies from Kashmir are also available. Great pots of Punjabi pickles, made from cauliflower, carrots, radish and mustard seeds are sold by weight. Diplomats, out-of-town shoppers and locals all patronize this market for its reasonable prices and variety of products.

The name derives from Indian National Airports, as people working at nearby Safdarjung Aerodrome lived in the adjacent colony. The aerodrome, further down Aurobindo Marg, was built in the 1930s. During World War II, it was the headquarters of the South Eastern Command Air Wing. It now houses offices of the Ministry of Civil Aviation and the Delhi Gliding Club. Indian Airlines also has a 24-hour booking office here *(see p293).*

**A steam engine at the National Rail Museum**

## CANTONMENT TOWNS

After the 1860s, over 170 cantonments (pronounced "cantoonment") were built on the outskirts of major towns to impress Indians with the seriousness of British military might. Each was a self-contained world, with symmetrical rows of barracks, finely graded bungalows, clubs and regimental messes, bazaars, hospitals and churches. Military hierarchies, too, were rigidly followed. Even after Independence, the military is mostly stationed in cantonment areas.

**Indian cavalry officer, pre-World War II**

## Moth ki Masjid ⓮

South Extension, Part II.

BUILT IN 1505 by Miyan Bhuwa, Sikander Lodi's prime minister, the design of this graceful red sandstone structure with its five-arched, three-domed prayer hall was developed further in later Mughal mosques. Over the central arch is a fine *jharokha* with traces of the original plaster decoration. The red sandstone gateway and the ornate decorations on the mosque's façade are also noteworthy. It is said that Sikander Lodi gave Miyan Bhuwa a *moth* (lentil seed) which reaped him such rich returns that he was able to endow this mosque. Sadly, he annoyed Sikander's successor, Ibrahim Lodi (r.1517–26), who had him put to death.

**Detail of Moth ki Masjid**

## Hauz Khas ⓯

W of Aurobindo Marg.

BEYOND THE BOUTIQUES, art galleries and restaurants that have taken over the former village of Hauz Khas, are the medieval monuments from Feroze Shah Tughlaq's reign. In 1352, the sultan constructed a number of buildings on the banks of Hauz Khas, the large tank (now dry) excavated by Alauddin Khilji for his city of Siri *(see p108)*. Contemporary accounts claim that Feroze Shah was a prolific builder, and during his 37-year reign he constructed an astounding 40 mosques, 200 towns, 100 public baths and about 30 reservoirs.

Among the buildings here are a *madrasa*, Feroze Shah's tomb and the ruins of a small mosque at the extreme north of the complex. The double storeyed *madrasa* was built so that the tank and lower storey were at the same level, while the upper floor was at ground level. Refreshing breezes across the water must have once cooled the theological discussions held there by scholars. The low domes, colonnades and *jharokhas* relieve the severity of its façade, while plaster carvings and deep niches for books embellish the interior. The *chhatris* in the entrance forecourt are said to cover the teachers' burial mounds. The tomb of Feroze Shah lies at one end of the *madrasa*. Wine-red painted plaster calligraphy decorates the interior of the austere tomb.

The complex is best viewed in the afternoon when sunlight filters through the *jaalis* carved into the linteled archway, to cover the graves of the sultan, his sons and grandson with delicate star-shaped shadows.

East of Hauz Khas, off Aurobindo Marg, is a small rubble-built tapering structure called **Chor Minar** ("tower of thieves") with a staircase, now locked, leading to the top. This dates to the 14th-century Khilji period and its walls, pockmarked with holes, are said to have held the severed heads of thieves to deter others from crime.

Close by, to the northwest, is the **Nili Masjid** ("blue mosque"), named after the blue tiles above its *chhajja*. The inscription on the central of its three arches reveals that it was built in 1505 by one Kasumbhil, the nurse of the son of the governor of Delhi. Nearby is an Idgah, whose remaining long wall is carved with 11 mihrabs and an inscription proclaiming that it was built in 1404–5 by Iqbal Khan, a Tughlaq noble.

**The double-storeyed *madrasa* at Hauz Khas**

# Early Capitals of Delhi

Delhi's famous "seven cities" range from the 12th-century Qila Rai Pithora, built by Prithviraj Chauhan *(see p48)*, to the imperial Shahjahanabad, constructed in the 17th century. Each of these cities comprised the settlements that grew around the forts and palaces erected by powerful sultans with territorial

**Purana Qila**

ambitions. As the Sultanate was consolidated, the rulers moved their capitals from those defensively situated in the rocky outcrops of the Aravallis, northwards towards the open plains by the banks of the Yamuna. Today, Delhi is an amalgam of medieval citadels, palaces, tombs and mosques, and a spreading, modern concrete jungle.

*Ferozabad, stretching north from Hauz Khas to the banks of the Yamuna, is Delhi's fifth city built by Feroze Shah Tughlaq (r.1351–88).*

Shahjahanabad

Ferozabad

New Delhi

Purana Qila

**Shahjahanabad** *was Delhi's seventh city, built between 1638 and 1649 by Shah Jahan who shifted the Mughal capital here from Agra (see pp150–51).*

**Siri**, *Delhi's second city can still be seen near the Siri Fort Auditorium and the adjacent village of Shahpur Jat (see p108). The once prosperous city of Siri was built by Alauddin Khilji in 1303.*

**Purana Qila**, *the citadel (see p84) of Delhi's sixth city, was built by Humayun. It was captured and occupied by the Afghan chieftain, Sher Shah Sur (r.1540–45) who called it Shergarh.*

Siri

Jahanpanah

Qila Rai Pithora

Tughlaqabad

**Jahanpanah** *was built by Muhammad-bin-Tughlaq (r.1325–51) as a walled enclosure to link Qila Rai Pithora and Siri. The ruined battlements of Delhi's fourth city stand near Chiragh (see p108).*

*Qila Rai Pithora was the first of Delhi's seven cities, built by the Chauhans in about 1180. In 1192, it was captured by Qutbuddin Aibak who established his capital here (see pp110–11).*

**Tughlaqabad**, *a dramatic fortress (see p114) on the foothills of the Aravallis, was Delhi's third city built during Ghiyasuddin Tughlaq's four-year reign (1321–5).*

**Ruins of Siri, Delhi's second city built by Alauddin Khilji**

## Siri Fort 🔟

Siri Fort Rd. **Siri Fort Auditorium**
📞 (011) 649 3370.

SOME CRUMBLING ramparts are all that remain of Alauddin Khilji's 14th-century city of Siri *(see p107)*. The ruins of mosques and tombs can be found in the adjoining village of Shahpur Jat, today a shopper's paradise with many up-market boutiques, offices and a few art galleries. Siri Fort is commonly associated with the Siri Fort Auditorium which regularly hosts concerts and film festivals. It is directly adjacent to the Asian Games Village complex where there are speciality restaurants serving Indian, Chinese and Mexican cuisine.

## Chiragh Delhi 🔟

Bordered by Outer Ring Rd & LB Shastri Marg.

THE DARGAH of the Sufi saint Nasiruddin Mahmud (died 1356), who succeeded Hazrat Nizamuddin Auliya *(see p82)* as spiritual leader of the Chishti sect, lies in the once secluded village of Chiragh Delhi. This saint, known as Raushan Chiragh-i-Dehlvi ("illuminated lamp of Delhi"), was buried here and the village that grew around his tomb was named after him. Muhammad-bin-Tughlaq, the sultan at that time, built the original village walls in the 14th century.

The shrine itself is small and should be approached on foot through the narrow, congested village lanes, past rows of tailoring establishments (including one specializing in *burqas*) and shops selling varieties of *mithai* ("sweetmeats"), *chadors*, flower garlands and other religious offerings. Some ruined *havelis*, which must have once been very beautiful, also line the street. A huge arched doorway leads to the *dargah*, a quieter and simpler shrine than that of Hazrat Nizamuddin. Shaded by trees, the tomb is set in a 12-pillared square chamber, enclosed by *jaali* screens and surmounted by a large plastered dome rising from an octagonal drum. Small domed turrets stand at the four corners. The roof inside has been embellished with fine painted plaster carvings set with mirrors, clearly a recent addition. Within the enclosure are several smaller mosques and halls, added over the years for religious discourses.

At the far end from the gateway is a partially ruined tomb that is locally claimed to be that of Bahlol Lodi (r.1451–88), the founder of the Lodi dynasty. The *chhajja* has collapsed, but the square chamber is still surmounted by five domes, the central being the largest. The arches have engraved inscriptions.

**Women devotees worshipping at Chiragh Delhi**

Covered corridors with arches in the Begumpuri Mosque provided relief from the summer heat

## Khirkee 🔞

N of Press Enclave Marg.

THE VILLAGE adjacent to Chiragh Delhi is called "Khirkee" after the huge mosque built by Feroze Shah Tughlaq's prime minister, Khan-i-Jahan Junan Shah *(see p96)*. In the mid-14th century. Standing today in a declivity and surrounded by village houses, is the unusual two-storeyed Khirkee ("windows") Mosque. It has a sombre fortress-like appearance with bastions on all four corners, and its severe façade is broken by rows of arched windows that are covered by portcullis-like *jaalis* which give the mosque its name. Built on a high plinth, flights of stairs lead up to imposing gateways on the north, south and east sides. The inner courtyard is partly covered, its roof supported by monolithic stone pillars, and crowned by nine sets of nine small domes. Only four courtyards remain open to the sky. This was the first example of this type of mosque design. But the division of open space by pillars

**Detail of an arched window with *jaali***

was found unsuitable for large congregations, so this design was never repeated.

**Satpula** ("seven-arches"), the dam and stone weir built by Muhammad bin-Tughlaq in 1326, is located a few metres down the same road. It formed part of the reservoir used for irrigation, and the grooves, meant for sliding the shutters that regulate the flow of water, can still be seen on the seven arches. The weir also formed a portion of the fortified wall enclosing the city of Jahanpanah *(see p107)*. Its upper storey was used during Muhammad-bin-Tughlaq's time as a *madrasa*.

**The fortress-like Khirkee Mosque**

## Jahanpanah 🔞

S of Panchsheel Park.

IN THE HEART of Jahanpanah, Muhammad-bin-Tughlaq's capital, stands **Begumpuri Mosque**, also built by Khan-i-Jahan Junan Shah. (When asking for directions, it is advisable to specifically ask for the old mosque, as a new one is located nearby.) Built on a high plinth with massive, typically Tughlaq walls, the mosque has a single imposing doorway at the head of a flight of stairs leading into the vast rectangular courtyard surrounded by arched cloisters, surmounted by 44 small domes. The prayer hall has 24 arched openings, the central one surmounted by a large dome. It is said that in times of need, this mosque also functioned as a treasury, granary and meeting place.

Nearby, to the north, is the palace of **Bijay Mandal**, a derelict, brooding octagonal structure rising from a high plinth. It is worth climbing the broken stone-cut stairs to the upper platform to get a sense of its size. According to the famed 14th-century Arab traveller, Ibn Batuta, it was from these very bastions that Muhammad-bin-Tughlaq held public audience and reviewed his troops. Later, in the early 16th century, the palace is believed to have been used as a residence by Sheikh Hasan Tahir, a much revered saint who visited Delhi during the reign of Sikandar Lodi. Panoramic views of the city of Delhi, extending from the Qutb Minar to Humayun's Tomb and beyond, can be seen from its upper platform.

# Mehrauli Archaeological Park ⑳

**Dargah Qutb Sahib**
*This 13th-century* dargah *is still a pilgrim point.*

*Chhatri* **outside Jamali-Kamali**

**B**EST KNOWN FOR the Qutb Minar, a World Heritage monument, Mehrauli was built over Rajput territories known as Lal Kot and Qila Rai Pithora. In 1193, Qutbuddin Aibak made this the centre of the Sultanate of Delhi and by the 13th century a small village, Mehrauli, had grown around the shrine of the Sufi saint, Qutb Sahib. Later, Mughal princes came to Mehrauli to hunt and some 19th-century British officials built weekend houses here, attracted by its orchards, ponds and abundant game *(shikar)*. It is still a popular weekend retreat for Delhi's rich and famous.

**Zafar Mahal** is a palace named after the *nom de plume* of the last Mughal emperor, Bahadur Shah Zafar.

**Mehrauli village**

**Hauz-i-Shamsi** is a large reservoir built in 1230 by Iltutmish, who is supposed to have been guided to this site by the Prophet in a dream.

**★ Jahaz Mahal**
*Venue of the Phoolwalon ki Sair (see p40), this square pleasure pavilion, built during the Lodi era (1451–1526), seems to float on the Hauz-i-Shamsi tank.*

**Jharna** (waterfall) was so-called because after the monsoon, water from the Hauz-i-Shamsi would flow over an embankment into a garden.

**Bagichi Masjid**

**Madhi Masjid**
*Surrounded by bastions and a high wall, this fortress-like mosque has a large open courtyard and a three-arched, profusely ornamented prayer hall.*

**STAR FEATURES**

★ **Qutb Minar**

★ **Jamali-Kamali Mosque and Tomb**

★ **Jahaz Mahal**

### Adham Khan's Tomb
*Built by Akbar in the 16th century, this was rescued from decay by Curzon (see pp56–7).*

### ★ Qutb Minar
*The Qutb (Arabic for pole or axis) area saw the advent of Islamic rule in India. The world's highest single tower, this is the focus of an early Islamic complex (see p112).*

| 0 metres | 250 |
|---|---|
| 0 yards | 250 |

Dilkusha

New Delhi

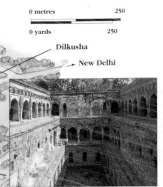

### Rajon ki Bain
*This dramatic three-storeyed stepwell was also called Sukhi Baoli (dry well). Nearby is the five-storeyed Gandhak ki Baoli, named after its strong sulphur (gandhak) smell. These baolis once supplied fresh water to the area.*

### Balban's Tomb
*Balban's 13th-century tomb lies in a square rubble-built chamber, open to the sky.*

### ★ Jamali-Kamali Mosque and Tomb
*The tomb of Jamali (the court poet during the late Lodi and early Mughal age) is inscribed with some of his verses. Its well-preserved interior has coloured tiles and richly decorated painted plasterwork. The grave of the unknown "Kamali" is probably an alliterative corruption of Jamali.*

# The Qutb Complex

**Floral motif**

THE QUTB MINAR TOWERS over this historic area where Qutbuddin Aibak laid the foundation of the Delhi Sultanate *(see pp50–51)*. In 1193, he built the Quwwat-ul-Islam ("the might of Islam") Mosque and the Qutb Minar to announce the advent of the Muslim sultans. Later, Iltutmish, Alauddin Khilji and Feroze Shah Tughlaq added other buildings, bringing in a new architectural style *(see p24)*. The fusion of decorative Hindu panels and Islamic domes and arches shows the mingling of two cultures.

**Iron Pillar**
*This 4th-century pillar, originally made as a flagstaff in Vishnu's honour, is a tribute to ancient Indian metallurgy.*

**Iltutmish's Tomb**

**Alauddin Khilji's Tomb**

**Qutb Minar**
*The five-storeyed Victory Tower started by Qutbuddin Aibak was completed by his successor, Iltutmish.*

**Carved Panels**
*Panels, carved with inscriptions from the Koran, embellish the gateway.*

**Alai Darwaza**
*This gateway to the complex, erected in 1311 by Alauddin Khilji, is one of the earliest buildings in India to employ the Islamic principles of arched construction (see p24).*

**Imam Zamin's Tomb**

Dargah Qutb Sahib, shrine of the Sufi saint Qutbuddin Bakhtiyar "Kaki"

### Iltutmish's Tomb
*Built in 1235 by Iltutmish himself, its dome has vanished. The interior is carved with geometric and calligraphic patterns.*

**To Entrance**

## Quwwat-ul-Islam Mosque
*Hindu motifs, such as tasselled ropes and bells, are clearly visible on the carved pillars of this mosque.*

### Exploring Mehrauli
Clustered round the *dargah* of Qutb Sahib, Mehrauli became a sylvan retreat for the later Mughals and top officials of the East India Company. Its medieval bazaar survives despite its recent conversion into boutiques and cafés, popular with Delhi's "smart set".

**Medallion with calligraphy**

### 🔳 Dargah Qutb Sahib
In the heart of the Mehrauli bazaar, lies the *dargah* of a Sufi saint called Qutbuddin Bakhtiyar or "Kaki", after the small sugared cakes *(kaki)* he was fed when he fasted. It has been rebuilt several times since his death in 1235, so that today many mosques, tanks and chambers surround it, among them the lovely Moti Masjid ("pearl mosque") built in 1709. A domed marble pavilion contains his grave, which women may only view through the marble *jaalis*. A royal necropolis in the same area has the graves of some later Mughal kings, such as Bahadur Shah I (1707–12) and Akbar II (1806–36). The *dargah* and the Jogmaya Temple are the starting point for the Phoolwalon ki Sair *(see p40)*, the procession of flower-sellers which began in the 1720s as a floral tribute to the Mughal emperor. Revived by Nehru after 1947, it is now an important cultural event.

### 🔳 Adham Khan's Tomb
Near the bus terminus, at the approach to Mehrauli village, is an imposing, single-domed structure standing on a high platform. This is believed to be the last of the octagonal tombs built in Delhi and its shaded colonnades are much favoured by local youth for their siestas. Adham Khan, the son of Akbar's wet nurse, Maham Anga *(see p85)*, was considered a foster-brother of the emperor. In 1562, Adham Khan killed a rival, Atgah Khan, the husband of another wet nurse *(see p82)*. A furious Akbar ordered Adham Khan's execution, but was so moved by the death of his mother, Maham Anga, 40 days later, that he had a tomb built for both mother and son.

By far the largest building here, the tomb is locally known as the *bhulbhulaiyan* (maze) because of the narrow passages concealed within its walls. In the 1800s, the British used the tomb as a rest-house, police station and residence for minor officials.

A corridor in Adham Khan's Tomb

**Sanskriti Museum**

## Sanskriti ㉑

Anandgram, Mehrauli-Gurgaon Rd.
📞 (011) 650 1125. ⏰ 10am–5pm
Tue–Sun. ⬤ Mon & public hols.

THIS UNUSUAL MUSEUM is set amidst beautifully land-scaped spacious grounds where exhibits are displayed both in the garden and in specially constructed rural huts. The collection, too, is equally unusual. It is devoted to traditional objects of everyday use, exquisitely crafted by the unknown, unsung, rural artisan. OP Jain, whose personal collections gave birth to this museum, has donated exquisite combs, nutcrackers, lamps, foot-scrubbers and kitchenware. Terracotta objects from all over India are also on display. The pots are especially dazzling, particularly as their production techniques have not changed for centuries.

## Sultan Ghari ㉒

Off Mahipalpur-Mehrauli Rd.

SULTAN GHARI was the first Islamic tomb to be built in Delhi and among the earliest in India. The Slave king, Iltutmish erected this tomb in 1231 for his eldest son and heir, Nasiruddin Muhammad, who was killed in battle. Today, its fortress-like exterior appears out of place in the midst of one of Delhi's largest residential complexes, Vasant Kunj. Inside is a raised courtyard, and the tomb itself is an octagonal platform, forming the roof of the crypt (*ghar*) below. Like many monuments of this early medieval period, Sultan Ghari was constructed from pillars and stones taken from temples nearby. Fragments of these are visible in the surround-ing colonnades, which may have once housed a *madrasa*. The mihrab on the west side has some fine calligraphic decoration and, interestingly, there is a marble *yonipatta*, the base of a Shiva linga (*see p319*) embedded in the floor.

The tomb, located on the road from Andheria More to Delhi Airport, is reached after turning left from the Spinal Injuries Centre and taking the next left after that.

## Tughlaqabad ㉓

Off Mehrauli-Badarpur Rd.

THIS SPECTACULAR fortress, built by Ghiyasuddin Tughlaq (*see p107*), was com-pleted in just four years. The quality of its construction was influenced by building techniques in Multan where Ghiyasuddin had served as governor. It was so sturdy that the rubble-built walls clinging to the shape of the hill, survive intact all along the 6.5 km (4 mile) perimeter. To the right of the main entrance is the citadel from which rise the ruins of the Vijay Mandal ("tower of victory"). To the left is a rectangular area where arches are all that remain of a complex of palaces and halls. Beyond these, houses were once laid out in a neat grid pattern.

**Ghiyasuddin Tughlaq's Tomb**

Legend has it that when Ghiyasuddin tried to prevent the building of the *baoli* at Hazrat Nizamuddin Auliya's *dargah* (*see p82*), the saint cursed him by saying that one day only jackals and the Gujjar tribe would inhabit his capital. Perhaps the saint forgot to add tourists and monkeys to that list!

A good view of the fort and of the adjoining smaller one of Adilabad is possible from

**The crumbling ramparts of Tughlaqabad Fort**

The lotus-domed Baha'i House of Worship, one of Delhi's most spectacular sights

the walls. Adilabad was built by Muhammad-bin-Tughlaq (r.1325–51), who is believed to have killed his father Ghiyasuddin by contriving to have a gateway collapse on him. They are both buried in Ghiyasuddin's Tomb, joined to the Tughlaqabad Fort by a causeway that crossed the dammed waters of a lake.

The tomb was the first in India to be built with sloping walls, a design that was repeated in all subsequent Tughlaq architecture. Its severe red sandstone walls, relieved by white marble inlay, are surmounted by a white marble dome. The red sandstone *kalasha* (urn) which crowns it and the lintel spanning the arched opening decorated with a lotus bud fringe, are both influenced by Hindu architecture.

## Kalkaji Temple ㉔

Nehru Place. ⛩ *Navaratri (Mar–Apr & Sep–Oct).*

THIS TEMPLE is a good place to see Hinduism in bustling, popular practice. It is approached through a narrow winding alley, lined with stalls selling laminated religious prints, bangles, *sindur* (vermilion powder) and fruit, while devotional hymns blast from rival cassette stalls. The 12-domed temple, with a heavily decorated pillared pavilion, was built in the mid-18th century on an older site by Raja Kedarnath, prime minister of Emperor Akbar II. Thereafter, many contemporary additions, financed by rich merchants, have been made. The goddess Kali or Kalka, draped in silks, sits under silver umbrellas and a marble canopy. Legend has it that a farmer, on discovering that his cow regularly offered her milk to the goddess, built this temple in her name.

## Baha'i House of Worship ㉕

Bahapur, Kalkaji. 📞 *(011) 644 4029.* ⏱ *Apr–Sep: 9am–7pm; Oct–Mar: 9:30am–5:30pm Tue–Sun.* ● *Mon & public hols.* **Prayer services** *10am, noon, 3pm & 5pm.*

JUST OPPOSITE the Kalkaji Temple is the Baha'i House of Worship, a world where silence and order prevails. The arresting shape of its unfurling 27-petalled white marble lotus has given it its more popular name, the Lotus Temple. The edifice, circled by nine pools and 27 acres (92 ha) of green manicured lawns, is one of Delhi's most innovative modern structures.

The Baha'i sect originated in Persia and this temple was designed by Iranian architect, Fariburz Sahba. Construction began in 1980 and was completed in 1986. Inside, the lofty auditorium can seat 1,300 and all are welcome to meditate there and attend the daily 15-minute services. The temple looks spectacular after dark when the lighting gives the marble panels a luminous, ethereal quality.

**Inside view of Kalkaji Temple**

# Day Trips from Delhi

**I**F YOU WANT A BREAK from the hustle and bustle of Delhi and wish to explore the surrounding countryside, there are several interesting sights to visit, all within a 50-km (30-mile) radius of the city. The lake at Sultanpur is a haven for migratory birds in winter, and in Pataudi is a beautiful palace which belongs to its cricket-loving nawabs, now open to tourists. Surajkund, with its vast medieval reservoir, is the venue of a popular crafts fair held every February. All these excursions take about eight hours. Since they are not particularly easy to reach by public transport, it is best to hire a car and driver for the day, which can be organized by your hotel or local taxi rank and is relatively inexpensive.

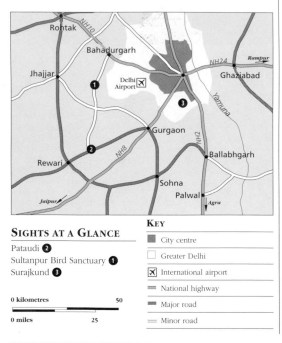

## SIGHTS AT A GLANCE

Pataudi **2**
Sultanpur Bird Sanctuary **1**
Surajkund **3**

0 kilometres            50

0 miles            25

### KEY

▦ City centre

☐ Greater Delhi

✗ International airport

▬ National highway

▬ Major road

═ Minor road

## Sultanpur Bird Sanctuary **1**

46 km (27 miles) W of Delhi.
**ℹ** *Haryana Tourism, Chanderlok Building, Janpath, Delhi (011) 332 4911.* ◯ *sunrise–sunset daily.* 🔲 📷
🚫 ✗

**T**HIS SANCTUARY, a two-hour drive from Delhi, has been developed around a low-lying marshy area that is dry in summer, but fills up during the monsoon to form a shallow lake *(jheel)*. Sultanpur is at its best in the winter when this shallow sheet of water provides a haven for migratory birds.

Several pleasant walks, including a paved pathway which runs around the small lake, allow one to explore the 35-km (22-mile) area, while the many hides or *machans*, mounted on stilts, provide a good view of the birdlife on the lake. The Sarus crane, the world's tallest flying bird, breeds in the mud spits covered with reeds that rise above the waters. Often, on late winter evenings, large, noisy flocks of demoiselle cranes descend on the lake. The other birds that visit the lake include egrets, herons, kingfishers, pelicans and painted storks.

The rolling tree-shaded lawns, home to herds of friendly deer, have beautifully sited picnic spots. The sanctuary shop has a good selection of books and posters on Indian birdlife.

Sultanpur is home to a variety of deer and many migratory birds

## Pataudi ❷

60 km (37 miles) S of Delhi.
**Ibrahim Kothi** *Advance reservations are essential.* *(011) 301 3549.*

THE TWO-AND-A-HALF hour drive to Pataudi is a pleasant one, particularly after crossing Gurgaon when the road runs through open wheat fields and occasional villages. Pataudi, a typical North Indian town with a tangle of narrow lanes and a congested bazaar, is famous for its cricket-playing nawabs who claim descent from a 16th-century Afghan noble.

The old palace, built about 200 years ago, is now derelict, but still retains its romantic charm. The new palace, known as **Ibrahim Kothi**, was built in 1939. The elegant white, double-storeyed building, set amidst 10 acres (4 ha) of flowering gardens, has deep, pillared verandahs and is surmounted by a small dome. The well-maintained interior includes polished parquet floors, pink Venetian chandeliers and chintz furnishings. The walls are lined with portraits and sepia photographs of the present nawab's ancestors. One is of his father as a member of the famous "bodyline" English cricket team which toured Australia in the 1930s.

A section of the palace has now been refurbished and opened as a hotel for tourists who want to spend a relaxed holiday in royal splendour.

**Elegant interior of Ibrahim Kothi**

**Ibrahim Kothi at Pataudi**

### SURAJKUND CRAFTS MELA

For two weeks in early February, Surajkund comes alive with the sounds and colours of one of India's largest arts and crafts fair. Craftsmen and artisans from every part of the country sell their wares at a specially created village, under thatched canopies decorated with *rangoli*. Here, mirrorwork from Gujarat, painted puppets from Jaipur, fanciful bell-metal beasts from Orissa and Madhubani paintings from Bihar can be found at a wide range of prices. There are balloon sellers and food stalls to give the *mela* a carnival air, while folk dancers and musicians in colourful costumes weave in and out of the crowds. The evenings, given over to folk theatre, dance and music performances, attract huge crowds.

**Performances by folk singers are held at the Surajkund Crafts Mela**

## Surajkund ❸

21 km (13 miles) S of Delhi.
*Haryana Tourism, Chanderlok Building, Janpath, Delhi (011) 332 4911.*

KING SURAJPAL of the Rajput Tomar dynasty *(see p48)*, hero of many legends, built this reservoir some time in the late 10th or early 11th century. An embankment of stone terraces was built round a pool which trapped rain water running down from the hills. A sun temple is thought to have stood on the western side. Tomar Rajputs trace their descent from the sun, hence the name: *suraj* (sun) *kund* (pool). Today, the embankment is more or less intact, though there is no trace of the temple and the pool itself is none too clean. The nearby artificial lake is picturesque and is best enjoyed from the paddle or rowing boats on hire. You might even glimpse a pale green water snake swimming alongside.

About 2 km (1.5 miles) to the west is **Anangpur Dam** built by the Tomar king, Anangpal. A rather impressive quartzite stone stucture, it blocks a narrow ravine to create an artificial lake. The dam is reached on foot, but it is an extremely brambly and rocky walk and best avoided in the rainy weather.

This area is a popular picnic spot for Delhi's residents. Haryana Tourism and the Delhi Transport Corporation run special daily buses to Surajkund during the annual crafts *mela* *(see p41)*.

# SHOPPING IN DELHI

THE HALLMARK of shopping in Delhi is the bewildering variety of styles, merchandise and markets. Besides Connaught Place, almost every residential colony boasts a market. Old, established shops and bazaars co-exist happily with glitzy, high-end boutiques and department stores and one can buy

**Logo of Dastkar**

anything from seasonal vegetables, fruits and traditional handicrafts to designer clothes and the latest imported electronic items. Be prepared to bargain where required, even a small success will make your shopping spree in Delhi a complete and satisfying experience. For practical information, see page 264.

## SHOPS AND MARKETS

NEW DELHI'S main shopping centres are in Connaught Place and Janpath where the Central Cottage Industries offers an exciting and varied range of textiles, jewellery and souvenirs at fixed and reasonable prices. Indian handicrafts and handlooms are available at the state emporia on Baba Kharak Singh Marg, Dilli Haat and the Crafts Museum Shop *(see pp86–7)*. In the north is Chandni Chowk *(see p93)*, the traditional market, while to the south are Khan Market, Sundar Nagar and Santushti. The old urban villages of Hauz Khas, Shahpur Jat and Mehrauli have trendy boutiques where shoppers rub shoulders with loitering cows. The South Extension, Lajpat Nagar and Sarojini Nagar markets are popular with local shoppers. The five-star hotels, too, have shopping arcades that sell carefully-selected goods.

**Silver fruit bowl**

## ANTIQUES, CARPETS AND SHAWLS

GENUINE ANTIQUES are rare to come by and cannot be taken out of the country unless certified by the ASI *(see p279)*. However, hotel shops, Sundar Nagar and the **Crafts Museum Shop** stock excellent reproductions of miniature paintings, woodcarving and bronzes made by artisans today. Contemporary silverware is available at **Cooke & Kelvy** and **Frazer & Haws**. For Afghan and Kashmiri carpets and shawls, such as the paisley jamawar and pashmina, the best outlets are **Cottage Industries** and **Khazana**.

## JEWELLERY

SUPERB PIECES of traditional jewellery, such as *kundan* and *meenakari*, are available at **Bharany's**. The best places for silver jewellery are Dariba Kalan, in Chandni Chowk, and Sundar Nagar market.

**Poster displaying a selection of cotton *dhurries* from Fabindia**

## TEXTILES AND QUILTS

INDIAN SILKS AND COTTON are famous throughout the world. Cottage Industries and the state emporia have a good selection of textiles from different parts of India. **Fabindia**, **The Shop** and **Anokhi** are fine places to shop for good quality readymade garments, linen and light cotton quilts, while **Shyam Ahuja** sells *dhurries* and linen. Designer accessories such as Abraham & Thakore scarves are available at **Tulsi** and **Ogaan**.

## LEATHER

LEATHER GOODS, in particular shoes and bags, are found in most major shopping areas. For quality handmade shoes and jackets, the Chinese-owned outlets such as **John Brothers**, still set the standards for comfort and durability. For trendier goods there is **Hyde Out**, a miniscule shop that is quite chaotically piled high with bags and footwear.

**The Chor Bazaar, held on Sundays outside the Red Fort**

## HANDICRAFTS AND GIFTS

INDIAN HANDICRAFTS are available at the state emporia, the Crafts Museum Shop, **Dastkar** and **Dilli Haat** on Aurobindro Marg. **Tibet House** has *thangkas*, carpets, woollen shawls and jackets. **The Neemrana Shop**, Tulsi *(see Textiles)* and **Good Earth** have a good selection of gift items, such as candles, hand-made paper and artifacts in ceramics, wood and metal.

Embroidered textiles sold on Janpath

## BOOKS, MUSIC AND NEWSPAPERS

EVERY LOCAL MARKET has stalls selling newspapers, magazines, music cassettes and bestsellers. The largest number of books and music shops are in South Extension and Khan Market. **The Book Shop**, **Bookworm** and **Timeless Book Gallery** stock a wide variety of books by international publishing houses. **Motilal Banarasidas** in Old Delhi specializes in books on Indology. Every Sunday, a bazaar selling old and second-hand books is held on the pavements of Daryaganj where one can pick up interesting bargains.

## SPECIALITY SHOPS

IN CHANDNI CHOWK's Dariba Kalan is **Gulab Singh Johari Mul**, a marvellous old-fashioned shop where one can test Indian perfumes from cut-glass bottles. Their attar soaps are also worth buying. Herbal cosmetics by **Shahnaz Herbal** and **Biotique** are found at most chemists, and Ogaan *(see Textiles)* also stocks herbal products.

Spices and fresh seasonal fruit are found at INA Market while **Sugar & Spice** and Steak House stock a variety of cheese, cold cuts and other delicious food stuffs. Indian tea, from the gardens of Assam, is sold in a small shop in Kaka Nagar Market (near the Oberoi Hotel (on Zakir Hussain Marg), Khan Market and at **Aapki Pasand**.

---

### DIRECTORY

#### ANTIQUES

**Cooke & Kelvy**
Janpath. **Map** 1 C5.
(011) 372 1081.

**Cottage Industries**
Janpath. **Map** 1 C5.
(011) 332 0439.

**Crafts Museum Shop**
Pragati Maidan.
**Map** 6 D2.
(011) 337 1269.

**Frazer & Haws**
Green Park.
(011) 651 1666.

**Khazana**
Taj Mansingh. **Map** 5 B3.
(011) 302 6162.

#### JEWELLERY

**Bharany's**
Sundar Nagar Market.
**Map** 6 D3.
(011) 461 8528.

#### TEXTILES

**Anokhi**
Khan Market. **Map** 5 B3.
(011) 460 3423.

**Fabindia**
Greater Kailash I.
(011) 621 1032.

**Ogaan**
Hauz Khas Village.
(011) 685 3849.

**Shyam Ahuja**
Santushti. **Map** 4 E4.
(011) 467 0112.

**The Shop**
Connaught Place.
**Map** 1 C5.
(011) 374 6050.

**Tulsi**
Santushti. **Map** 4 E4.
(011) 687 0339.

#### LEATHER

**Hyde Out**
Khan Market. **Map** 5 B3.
(011) 462 2100.

**John Brothers**
B Block, Connaught Place.
**Map** 1 C4.
(011) 335 2812.

#### HANDICRAFTS AND GIFTS

**Dastkar**
45–B, Shahpur Jat.
(011) 649 5920.

**Good Earth**
Ambavata, Mehrauli.
(011) 685 6466.

**The Neemrana Shop**
F–580, Lado Sarai.
(011) 685 8539.

**Tibet House**
Lodi Rd. **Map** 5 B5.
(011) 461 1515.

#### BOOKS AND MUSIC

**Motilal Banarasidas**
Jawahar Nagar.
(011) 391 1985.

**The Bookshop**
Khan Market.
**Map** 5 B3.
(011) 469 7102.

**The Bookworm**
B Block, Connaught Place.
**Map** 1 C4.
(011) 332 2260.

**Timeless Book Gallery**
South Extension Part I.
(011) 463 2903.

#### SPECIALITY SHOPS

**Aapki Pasand**
15, Netaji Subhash Marg.
**Map** 2 E3.
(011) 326 0373.

**Gulab Singh Johri Mul**
Dariba Kalan, Chandni Chowk. **Map** 2 E2.
(011) 327 1345.

**Sugar & Spice**
Khan Market.
**Map** 5 B3.
(011) 462 8504.

# ENTERTAINMENT IN DELHI

Delhi, as the capital of India, has a rich and varied cultural life, mainly because the government has, over the last 50 years, consciously promoted a revival of traditional art forms. As a result, dancers, musicians and folk artistes from all over India deem it an honour to perform here before discerning audiences. Although Delhi is

Logo of the International Film Festival of India

still a culturally conservative city, jazz, theatre and rock concerts are frequent, and there are several good bars and discotheques.

The city's cultural calendar livens up between October and March when the season is in full swing. The number of events multiply as all major festivals of music, dance, theatre and cinema are held at this time.

India International Centre, Delhi

## ENTERTAINMENT GUIDES AND TICKETS

All newspapers list the day's entertainment on their engagements page. Other useful sources of information on events, restaurants, sports and related activities are the weekly *Delhi Diary* and in monthly magazines such as *City Scan* and *First City*.

At several venues in the city, such as the India International Centre *(see Lectures and Discussions)*, there is free entry. At others, such as the Indian Council for Cultural Relations, it is by invitation. Tickets for selected music and dance festivals and theatre, however, are advertised and sold at certain bookshops or at the box office.

## MUSIC AND DANCE

Delhi is the best place to experience the range and richness of classical dance and music. Performances by the best exponents of the

major dance styles of Bharata Natyam, Kathak, Odissi and Kathakali take place in the high season. The same is true of concerts of Hindustani and Carnatic music, the two major streams of classical music. During the season, shows are held mainly at **Siri Fort Auditorium** and **Kamani**. Some venues, such as **Triveni Kala Sangam** and the **India Habitat Centre,** have performances all the year round. The state-run **Indian Council for Cultural Relations** also organizes

City magazines

shows at Azad Bhavan and the FICCI auditorium.

Colourful folk dances from all over India can be seen during the annual Trade Fair at **Pragati Maidan** *(see p85).*

## THEATRE

The main theatre repertory company is the **National School of Drama** which presents plays in its own open air auditorium and at Kamani Auditorium near by. In 1999, the company began a National Theatre Festival, to be held every May–Jun. Its performances are in Hindi and Urdu and include works by contemporary Indian and Western playwrights.

Several amateur theatre groups perform in both Hindi and English, contributing to a hectic theatre season in the winter. The main venues are **Shri Ram Centre,** Kamani, and the India Habitat Centre *(see Music and Dance).*

## FILMS

Delhi plays host to an international film festival which is held in the January of every even year at the Siri Fort complex. Tickets can be obtained from the box-office. Other film festivals, organized by the Directorate of Film Festivals, are held here as well. These are mainly regional Indian cinema and foreign films that are not usually screened on the commercial circuit. Documentary films, presenting the works of up-and-coming filmmakers, are screened at the India International Centre, **Max Mueller Bhavan** and the **British Council**. Many foreign cultural centres, like the Alliance Française and the **French Cultural Centre** also have regular film shows.

Popular Indian and foreign films are screened at the many cinema halls dotted all

Shubha Mudgal, a well-known classical singer

over the city. Among the better equipped halls are **PVR Anupam**, **Priya** and **Chanakya**. All daily newspapers carry details of film shows. The tickets should be bought in advance as cinema, both Indian and foreign, continues to be a major form of popular entertainment.

## EXHIBITIONS

IN THE PAST FIVE YEARS the number of art galleries has grown in response to an increased interest in contemporary Indian art. Regular exhibitions present the work of painters, sculptors and photographers. Certain well known galleries such as **Art Heritage** and others located at Triveni Kala Sangam, **Art Today**, India Habitat Centre, India International Centre and Max Mueller Bhavan are in

the city centre. Others, such as **Vadehra Art Gallery**, are in South Delhi. The **National Gallery of Modern Art** *(see p71)* and the **National Museum** *(see pp72–5)* both organize major exhibitions.

## LECTURES AND DISCUSSIONS

LECTURES, DISCUSSIONS and seminars covering a wide range of subjects, such as international and current affairs, wildlife and ecology, mountaineering and Indian culture are regularly held at the **India International Centre**. These are announced in the daily newspapers and are open to all. Other venues where such programmes are held are the **Indira Gandhi National Centre of the Arts** (IGNCA), British Council and the India Habitat Centre.

A popular bar in a five-star hotel

## NIGHTLIFE

DELHI'S NIGHTLIFE is becoming livelier by the minute. The five-star hotels house most of the better bars and discotheques, such as **Club Lounge**, **Djinns**, **Jazz Bar**, **Patiala Peg** and others. These are popular with the young crowd, especially on Saturday nights. Clubs are open only to their registered members.

# DELHI STREET FINDER

**D**ELHI IS A confusing city to get around. New Delhi and the adjoining Nizamuddin to Purana Qila area are fairly well marked out, whereas Old Delhi is a maze of narrow lanes *(gullies)* and bylanes. The city has extended far beyond the main city centre, in keeping with its burgeoning population, and the vast complexes of residential housing add to the confusion of getting around. Navigating the city's roads and streets *(margs)* is challenging. Signposts are often hard to find and most of the names have changed in recent years or are known by more than one name. Connaught Place is now officially Rajiv Gandhi Chowk, Connaught Circus is Indira Gandhi Chowk and Sansad Marg is also known as Parliament Street. The Street Finder covers the city centre area and lists the major sights, hotels, restaurants, shops and entertainment venues. The Further Afield map is on page 99 and covers the area north, west and south of the city centre.

**Ashokan lions**

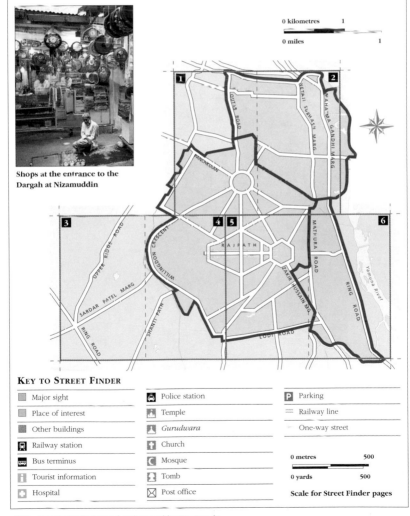

**Shops at the entrance to the Dargah at Nizamuddin**

0 kilometres 1

0 miles 1

## KEY TO STREET FINDER

| | | |
|---|---|---|
| Major sight | Police station | P Parking |
| Place of interest | Temple | Railway line |
| Other buildings | *Gurudwara* | One-way street |
| Railway station | Church | |
| Bus terminus | Mosque | 0 metres 500 |
| Tourist information | Tomb | 0 yards 500 |
| Hospital | Post office | **Scale for Street Finder pages** |

◁ **The President's Bodyguard at the Republic Day Parade**

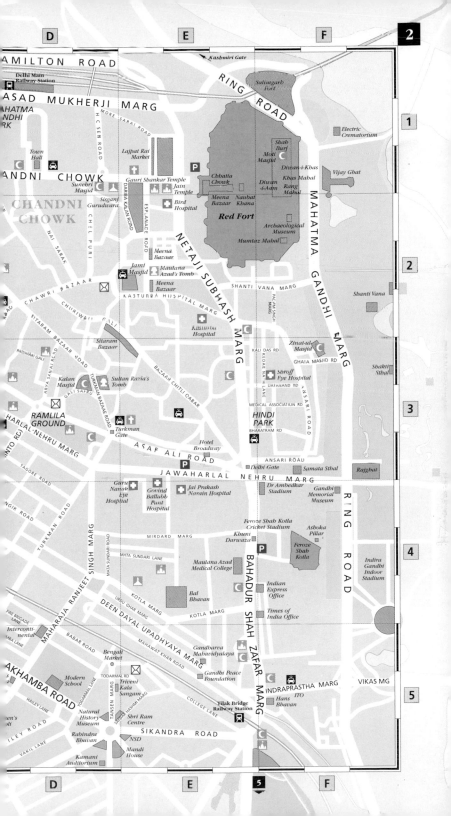

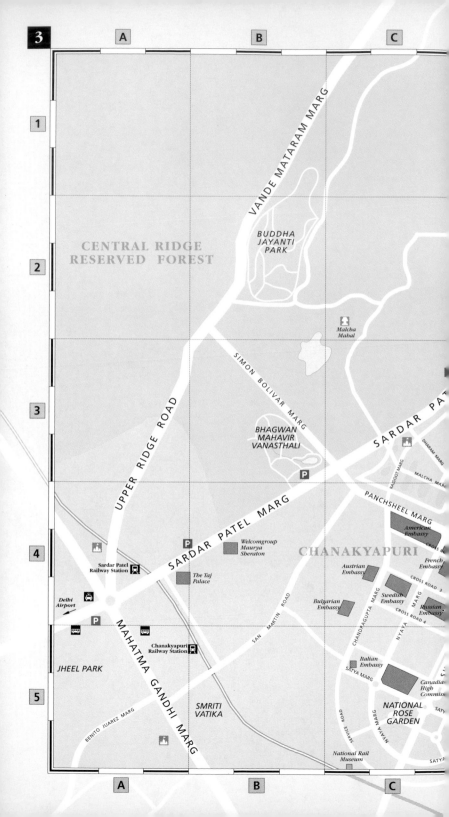

A  B  C

1

2

CENTRAL RIDGE
RESERVED FOREST

VANDE MATARAM MARG

*BUDDHA
JAYANTI
PARK*

*Malcha
Mahal*

3

SIMON BOLIVAR MARG

UPPER RIDGE ROAD

*BHAGWAN
MAHAVIR
VANASTHALI*

SARDAR PAT

SARDAR PA

DHARAM MARG

RADOOJI MARG

MALCHA MARG

PANCHSHEEL MARG

P

4

SARDAR PATEL MARG

*Welcomgroup
Maurya
Sheraton*

CHANAKYAPURI

*American
Embassy*

CROSS R

P

*Sardar Patel
Railway Station*

*The Taj
Palace*

*Austrian
Embassy*

*French
Embassy*

CROSS ROAD 3

*Delhi
Airport*

SAN MARTIN ROAD

*Bulgarian
Embassy*

*Swedish
Embassy*

*Russian
Embassy*

CROSS ROAD 4

CHANDRAGUPTA MARG

N Y A Y A   M A R G

P

5

MAHATMA GANDHI MARG

*Chanakyapuri
Railway Station*

*JHEEL PARK*

*Italian
Embassy*

SATYA MARG

*Canadian
High
Commiss*

*SMRITI
VATIKA*

*NATIONAL
ROSE
GARDEN*

SATY

BENITO JUAREZ MARG

SERVICE ROAD

NAYA MARG

*National Rail
Museum*

SATYP

A  B  C

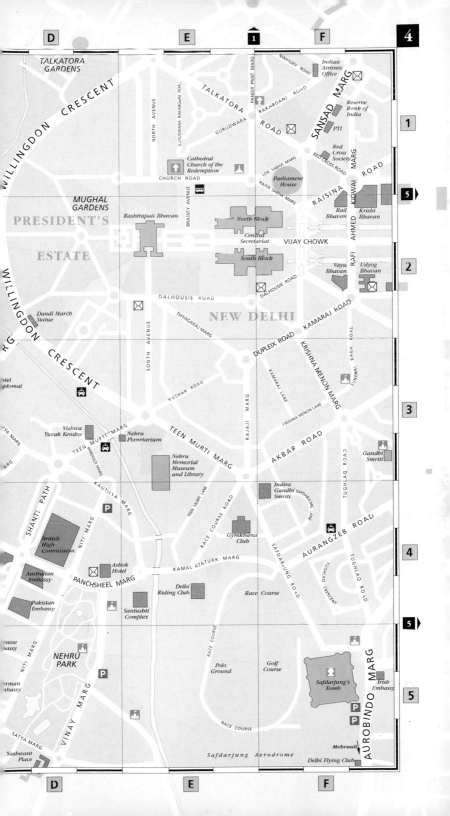

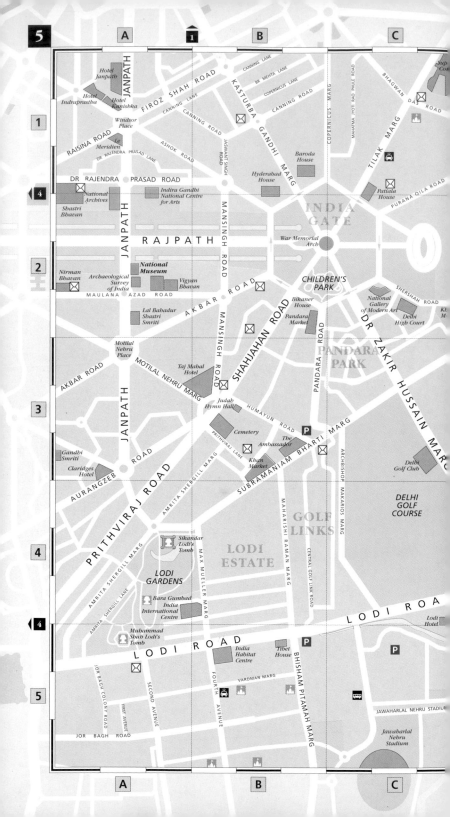

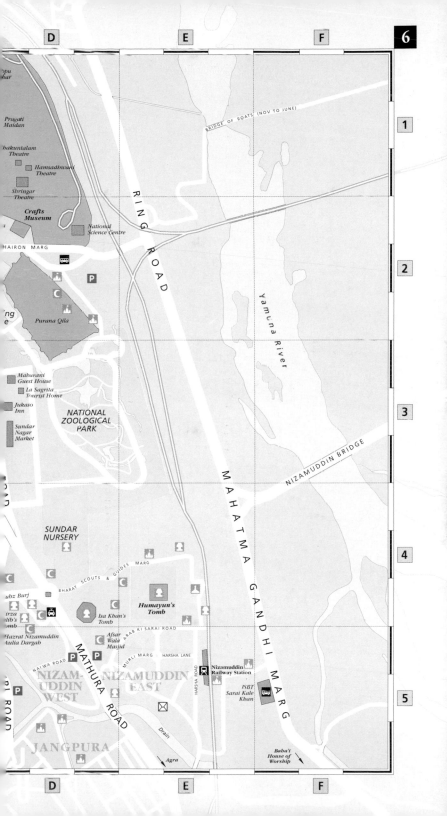

**D** **E** **F**

1

2

3

4

5

*Pragati Maidan*

*Shakuntalam Theatre*

*Hamsadhwani Theatre*

*Shringar Theatre*

**Crafts Museum**

*National Science Centre*

HAIRON MARG

*Purana Qila*

RING ROAD

BRIDGE OF BOATS (NOV TO JUNE)

Yamuna River

NIZAMUDDIN BRIDGE

*Maharani Guest House*

*La Sagrita Tourist Home*

*Jukaso Inn*

*Sundar Nagar Market*

**NATIONAL ZOOLOGICAL PARK**

**SUNDAR NURSERY**

MAHATMA GANDHI MARG

BHARAT SCOUTS & GUIDES MARG

*Subz Burj*

*Mirza Ghalib's Tomb*

**Humayun's Tomb**

*Isa Khan's Tomb*

*Hazrat Nizamuddin Aulia Dargah*

*Afsar Wala Masjid*

ARAB KI SARAI ROAD

NAI WA ROAD

MATHURA ROAD

**NIZAM-UDDIN WEST**

**NIZAMUDDIN EAST**

MURLI MARG

HARSHA LANE

HARSHA ROAD

**Nizamuddin Railway Station**

**ISBT Sarai Kale Khan**

**JANGPURA**

*Drain*

*Agra*

*Baba'i House of Worship*

# Street Finder Index

# BEYOND DELHI AREA BY AREA

# Beyond Delhi at a Glance

Inlaid panel

THE REGION beyond Delhi is bounded by the snow-capped Himalayas in the north and the ravines of the River Chambal in the south. The rich alluvial plains of the Ganges and Yamuna lie at its heart, and to the west are the Aravalli Range and Thar Desert. The Rajputs and Mughals enriched the area with architectural gems of which the finest are in and around Agra and Jaipur. Mighty fortresses, luxurious palaces, mosques, tombs and temples are what draw tourists to the Delhi, Agra and Jaipur region. Away from the cities are wildlife sanctuaries, and to the north are rivers, ideal for white-water rafting and adventure sports.

**Alwar** (see pp206–7), a former princely state, is dominated by a large hilltop fort, at the base of which lie elegant palaces, cenotaphs and gardens. Alwar is also a convenient base to explore forgotten forts and cities in and around the Sariska National Park.

**Ajmer** (see pp218–19) is best known for the shrine of the Sufi saint Khwaja Moinuddin Chishti and the ancient and stately Adhai Din ka Jhopra. The pilgrim city of Pushkar, where the annual camel fair is held, is a short distance away.

DELHI

JAIPUR AND ENVIRONS
(See pp178–225)

**Jaipur** (see pp182–99), was built by Sawai Jai Singh II in the early 1700s. In 1949 it became the capital of Rajasthan. A popular tourist destination, it is visited for its historic palaces, observatory, hilltop forts, palace-hotels and tempting markets.

0 kilometres 100

0 miles 50

◁ **Royal cenotaphs outside Jaipur**

***Haridwar*** (see p144), *one of North India's holiest cities, stands on the banks of the Ganges as it descends to the plains. The Kumbh Mela is held here every 12 years.*

**NORTH OF DELHI**
*(See pp136–45)*

***Roorkee*** (see p143), *a small town on the way to Haridwar, lies in the heart of a rich horticultural belt. Its famous Engineering College, established in 1847, is housed in an elegant colonial building.*

**AGRA AND AROUND**
*(See pp146–77)*

***Agra*** (see pp150–59), *the imperial Mughal capital during the 16th and 17th centuries, is best known for the Taj Mahal, built by Shah Jahan for his favourite wife, Mumtaz Mahal. Other Mughal monuments can be seen within and outside the city.*

***Orchha*** (see pp176–7), *the early capital of the Bundela kings, is picturesquely situated on the banks of the Betwa. Their temples, palaces and cenotaphs are architectural gems.*

# NORTH OF DELHI

LYING BETWEEN THE GANGES AND YAMUNA RIVERS, *this agriculturally prosperous region is believed to be the cradle of Indian civilization. Its historical and mythological past extends from the ancient brick cities of the Indus Valley and the early Aryan settlements to the later Muslim and European forts and cities. Each culture has enriched the region and given it its remarkable diversity.*

This vast plain, from about the second millennium on, has remained one of India's most densely populated areas. As time went on, ancient fortified city states developed into medieval walled towns which contained prosperous agricultural lands and flourishing markets. Many of these are today important industrial centres. Since the area had such a diverse history, its architectural remains are an eclectic mixture of styles so that ancient brick structures, Mughal monuments and colonial churches rub shoulders with modern factories.

To the north are the pilgrim towns of Haridwar and Rishikesh, where the Ganges, India's most holy river, enters the plains. With the splendid backdrop of the Shivalik Hills, this area, rich in flora and fauna, offers exciting places for adventure sports such as white-water rafting.

To most Indians, however, this is the sacred territory of the *Mahabharata (see p141),* where gods and epic heroes fought a legendary battle at Kurukshetra and where Krishna *(see pp162–3)* expounded the famous *Bhagavad Gita.* The development of ideas that led to the later compilation of the *Vedas* and *Upanishads,* the bedrock of Hindu philosophy and ethics, are believed to have taken place here as well. Panipat, the site of three decisive battles that changed the history of North India, lies close by.

To the northeast and northwest lie the now forgotten towns of Narnaul, Hansi and Sardhana, associated with the medieval Tughlaq and Sur dynasties, and European freebooters and nabobs such as Skinner, Reinhardt and his wife, Begum Samroo. Meerut, the epicentre of the Indian Mutiny, is now a busy market and trading centre.

Roadside stalls selling religious paraphernalia are a common sight outside temples

◁ The famous Har-ki-Pauri ghat at Haridwar, seen from the Ganga Temple

# Exploring North of Delhi

BEYOND DELHI, the landscape changes dramatically. The way to Haridwar, at the foothills of the Himalayas, is lined with mango and litchi orchards. The canal network around Roorkee sustains an agriculturally prosperous rural region. On the other hand, the busy Grand Trunk Road that leads beyond Panipat and Kurukshetra all the way to the Punjab, has always been an important artery of trade and commerce. Rolling fields of paddy and wheat are dotted with electricity pylons that service this important industrial belt. Yet the odd *kos minar* and medieval fort recall another age when this was the scene of important battles and the road to the north.

St Andrew's Church at Roorkee

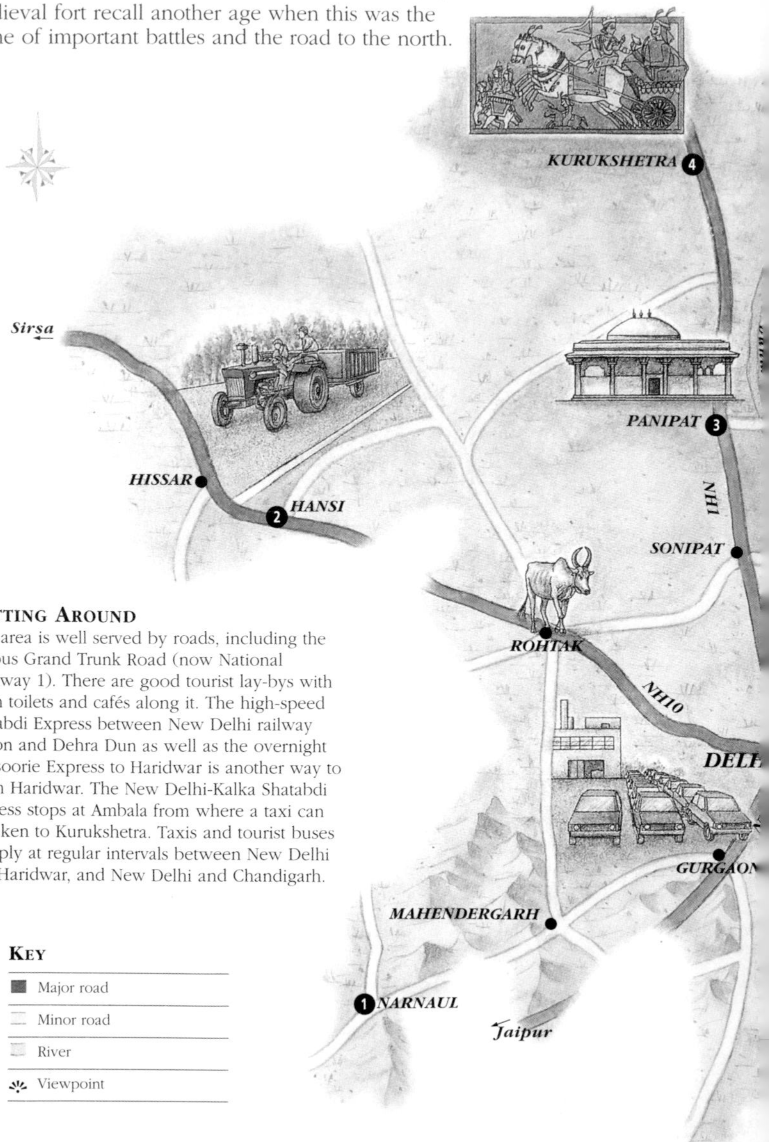

KURUKSHETRA ❹

*Sirsa* ←

PANIPAT ❸

HISSAR

❷ HANSI

SONIPAT

## GETTING AROUND

This area is well served by roads, including the famous Grand Trunk Road (now National Highway 1). There are good tourist lay-bys with clean toilets and cafés along it. The high-speed Shatabdi Express between New Delhi railway station and Dehra Dun as well as the overnight Mussoorie Express to Haridwar is another way to reach Haridwar. The New Delhi-Kalka Shatabdi Express stops at Ambala from where a taxi can be taken to Kurukshetra. Taxis and tourist buses also ply at regular intervals between New Delhi and Haridwar, and New Delhi and Chandigarh.

ROHTAK

NH10

DELH

GURGAON

MAHENDERGARH

## KEY

| | |
|---|---|
| ▪ | Major road |
| ▫ | Minor road |
| ▫ | River |
| �◌ | Viewpoint |

❶ NARNAUL

*Jaipur*

Grazing sheep tended by Gujjar tribesmen near Panipat

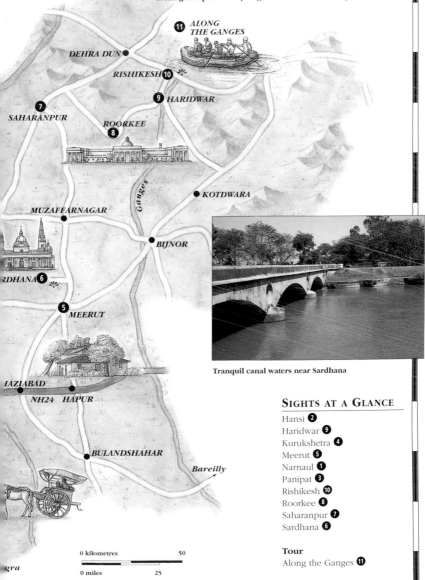

**11** ALONG THE GANGES

DEHRA DUN

RISHIKESH **10**

**9** HARIDWAR

**7**
SAHARANPUR

ROORKEE **8**

KOTDWARA

MUZAFFARNAGAR

Ganges

BIJNOR

RDHANA **6**

**5** MEERUT

IAZIABAD
NH24 HAPUR

BULANDSHAHAR

Bareilly

gra

Tranquil canal waters near Sardhana

0 kilometres    50

0 miles    25

## SIGHTS AT A GLANCE

Hansi **2**
Haridwar **9**
Kurukshetra **4**
Meerut **5**
Narnaul **1**
Panipat **3**
Rishikesh **10**
Roorkee **8**
Saharanpur **7**
Sardhana **6**

### Tour
Along the Ganges **11**

## Narnaul ❶

Narnaul district. 132 km (82 miles) W
of Delhi. **Road map** C3.

**B**ELIEVED to have been
founded by the Pandava
Sahdev, the town of Narnaul
is historically significant as the
birthplace of the great ruler
Sher Shah Sur *(see p84)*
whose grandfather, Ibrahim
Shah Sur, is buried here in a
magnificent Afghan-style
mausoleum. The Jal Mahal
("water palace"), situated in
what was once an artificial
lake built by Shah Quli Khan
in 1591, is a Mughal-style
structure; so is the Birbal ka
Chatta, with its projecting
balconies and pavilions. In
the town's old section are
some magnificent, but neglec-
ted *havelis* with murals in the
Shekhawati style *(see p212)*.

## Hansi ❷

Narnaul district. 137 km (85 miles) W
of Delhi. **Road map** C2.

**T**HIS NONDESCRIPT TOWN is
associated with two
soldiers of fortune. At
the end of the 18th
century, the Irish
adventurer, George
Thomas, repaired the
city's defensive wall,
remodelled the
ruined fort and
made it his head-
quarters. Some 30
years later, Colonel
James Skinner *(see
p101)* of Skinner's Horse,
built a large mansion (now
derelict) here where he spent
his last years. The town is
scattered with monuments
dating to the 12th century,
including the shrine called
Char Qutbs, a Sufi *dargah* of
the Chishtiya order, and the
19th-century tomb of Begum
Skinner, one of Skinner's 12
Indian wives.

**ENVIRONS**: Hissar, 26 km (16
miles) west of Hansi, was the
favourite retreat of Feroze
Shah Tughlaq *(see p97)*. He
built many palaces and forts
here, now in ruins. An oddity
from that time is an edifice
called the Jahaz, so named as
it resembles a ship *(jahaz)*.

Qalandar Shah's *dargah* at Panipat, built 700 years ago

**Memorial of the Third
Battle of Panipat**

## Panipat ❸

Panipat district. 85 km (53 miles) N of
Delhi on NH1. **Road map** C2. 🎏 *Urs
of Qalander Shah (Jan–Feb)*.

**O**N THE FLAT, DUSTY PLAINS of
Panipat, three decisive
battles were fought that
changed the course of Indian
history. The Mughal empire
*(see pp52–3)* was established
in 1526 after Babur defeated
the Delhi sultan, Ibrahim
Lodi, and was consolidated 30
years later when his grandson
Akbar triumphed over
Sher Shah's general in
1556. Finally, in 1761,
the Marathas, the Mughal
emperor's military arm,
were routed by Afghan
invader, Ahmad Shah
Abdali, paving the
way for the British
*(see pp54–5)*.
Today, Panipat is a
busy town well
known for its
furnishing fabrics and carpets.
The 700-year-old Sufi *dargah*
of Qalandar Shah is situated
here. On its outskirts are *kos
minars* (milestones) indicating
that Panipat was part of the
Grand Trunk Road *(see p160)*.

**Sacred tank at Kurukshetra**

## Kurukshetra ❹

Kurukshetra district.175 km (109
miles) N of Delhi on NH1. **Road map**
C1. 🎏 *Gita Jayanti (Nov–Dec)*.

**L**INKED WITH 360 legendary
sites of the *Mahabharata*,
this strategic plain was ruled
by the Kuru tribe in the later
Vedic period. The 18-day epic
battle between the Pandavas
and Kauravas was fought on
this "field of righteousness".
The town of Kurukshetra is
also the start of a pilgrimage
circuit of 128 km (80 miles)
undertaken during the solar
eclipse and at Gita Jayanti in
November or December,
when lighted clay lamps are
set afloat on the sacred waters
of the tanks during a ceremony called the *deepdan*.
   The main bathing tanks are
the Brahmasar, with a small
temple on an island, and the
smaller, more sacred Sannahit
Sarovar, lined with ghats and
temples. Hindus believe that a
dip here during the solar
eclipse is very sacred for it is
when the twin planets, the
malefic Rahu and Ketu, try to
swallow the sun to spread
terror in the world. However,
the sun defeats their machi-
nations, so, after a holy dip,
pilgrims donate food equal to
their body weight as thanksgiving. The last solar eclipse
of the 20th century occurred
in August 1999, and the next,
the first of the new millennium, is due on 31 May 2003.
   The Krishna Museum and
Gita Research Centre in the
town has a large collection
that brings out the pervasive-
ness of the Krishna cult in
Indian art down the ages.

# The Mahabharata

Considered an inexhaustible fund of knowledge and ideas, the *Mahabharata* is about an eponymous battle between the Pandavas and Kauravas. Said to be first narrated by a sage, Ved Vyas, the epic was written down only between the 6th and 7th centuries BC. Eight times the length of the *Iliad* and *Odyssey* put together, the subtle moral subtext of its legends and stories codifies notions of theology and statecraft that inspired rulers down the ages.

The *Bhagavad Gita,* a later insertion of 700 stanzas, records the sermon

***Ganjifa* card of Arjuna**

that was given by the divine charioteer, Lord Krishna, to the Pandava prince Arjuna on the epic battlefield of Kurukshetra. It extols the virtues of performing one's moral duty without seeking reward, and condones the use of violence against injustice. Its philosophy of righteous living and the importance of one's *dharma* (duty, calling) continues to guide the lives of millions of Indians. A few years ago, a television serial on the *Mahabharata* became so popular that life came to a virtual standstill when it was transmitted.

**The battle** is an allegory for the war between right and wrong. The epic's didactic tone made it an authoritative manual on moral rules and righteous conduct.

**Folk art** often uses the epic as a theme. This *patachitra* from Eastern India is used as a visual aid by minstrels, while *ganjifa* playing cards similarly use Arjuna as the icon for a king.

**Krishna** is seen as the divine charioteer who steers the mind (chariot) and five senses (the five horses that pull Arjuna's chariot) to follow the right path through life.

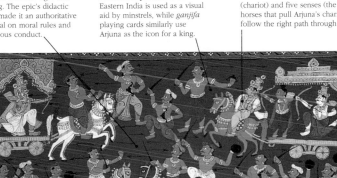

## THE BATTLE OF THE MAHABHARATA AT KURUKSHETRA

The kingdom of Hastinapur and Queen Draupadi were lost by the five Pandavas when their evil cousins, the Kauravas, tricked them in a game of dice. After a long exile, the Pandavas, though outnumbered by the hundred Kauravas, were led by Krishna to victory in the Battle of the Mahabharata.

*Arjuna, the skilled archer, shoots the eye of a fish reflected in water. This act won him the hand of Draupadi and the envy of the Kaurava princes.*

*Lord Krishna gives the sermon of the Gita to Arjuna on the battlefield of Kurukshetra. As the charioteer of the Pandavas in the war, this god plays a crucial role in the epic.*

**A cantonment house in Meerut**

# Meerut ❺

Meerut district. 72 km (44 miles) NE
of Delhi on NH24. **Road map** D2.
🏛 *3,447,912.* 🚉 *Mon.*
🎪 *Nauchandi Mela (Mar).*

AN IMPORTANT commercial
and administrative town,
Meerut is better known as the
place where the sepoys first
mutinied on 10 May 1857
igniting the Indian Mutiny
*(see pp54–5).* Today, this
bustling town swirls around
architectural monuments
dating to the 11th and 12th
centuries, such as the Jami
Masjid (1019), Salar Masa-ud
Ghazi's *maqbara* (1194), the
tomb of Makhdum Shah
Wilayat and the *maqbara* of
Shah Pir (1628). Meerut's
colonial heritage is, however,
preserved in its manicured
cantonment to the north of
the old city. This is one of the
country's best-planned
cantonments with a broad,
tree-lined mall or main road

and colonial bungalows *(see
p25)* with sprawling gardens
along its length. The
cantonment's Neo-Classical St
John's Church (1821), where
British residents had gathered
for refuge when the revolt
broke out, was the scene of a
bloody massacre that fateful
May day. Memorial tablets
with their names and histories
lie inside. The old Central Jail,
associated with the worst
excesses of the Mutiny and its
aftermath, is now converted
to a public park.

# Sardhana ❻

Meerut district. 85 km (57 miles) NE
of Delhi. **Road map** D2. 🎪 *Feast of
Our Lady of Graces (2nd Sun of Nov).*
📷 *(to Cathedral)* 🚻

SURROUNDED BY a network of
canals, Sardhana's history
is inextricably linked with two
flamboyant European adventurers, Walter Reinhardt and

George Thomas, who had
come to India to seek their
fortunes in the mid-18th
century *(see pp54–5).*

Reinhardt deserted the
French army in 1750 and
organized a band of fierce,
well-trained mercenaries who
fought for various local chiefs.
Called "Sombre" or "Samroo"
for his swarthy complexion,
he settled in Sardhana on
land gifted by Najaf Khan, a
nobleman of Delhi. Reinhardt
was succeeded by his wife,
Begum Samroo, a formidable
and wily lady who converted
to Catholicism in 1781. She
was known throughout the
region as the only Roman
Catholic "queen" in India, as
she led her husband's troops
until her death in 1836. Her
military skills, matched by her
piety and philanthropy, made
her popular with the locals,
who still respect her memory.

Begum Samroo's palace, the
grand Dilkusha Kothi, with its
impressive hallway, is situated
within a garden of almost 75
acres (30 ha). It now houses a
charity school and orphanage.
The Cathedral nearby has a
white marble altar inlaid with
semi-precious stones and a
Carrara marble monument to
the Begum sculpted by Tado-
lini of Rome. Now raised to
the status of a basilica, this is
still an important centre for
Catholics. Both the palace
and cathedral, built between
1822 and 1834 in a hybrid
colonial style, reflect the spirit
of that adventurous era.

**The classical façade of Dilkusha Kothi at Sardhana**

## Saharanpur ❼

Saharanpur district. 165 km (103 miles) NE of Delhi on NH24. **Road map** D1. 🏯 *2,309,029*.

SAHARANPUR was founded in 1340 during the reign of Muhammad-bin-Tughlaq *(see p107)*. During the Mughal period it was a popular summer resort for nobles attracted by its cool climate and plentiful game. Many of the gardens that were laid out 200 years ago, such as the Company Bagh in the centre of town, were transformed into nurseries and botanical gardens in the 19th century, laying the foundation for the town's eventual growth into an important horticultural centre. Today, Saharanpur is one of North India's largest producers of luscious mangoes, while the sprawling Government Botanical Gardens, on its outskirts, is an important centre for research on the medicinal properties of plants.

Within the old city, highly skilled artisans craft items of intricately carved furniture, ornamental screens, panels and trays brass-inlaid with intricate geometric and floral designs. Some of the finest examples of Saharanpur's woodcraft can be seen in St Thomas's Church. Also of interest are the old Jami Masjid (1530), Zabita Khan's Mosque (1779) and the old Rohilla Fort in Nawabganj.

**Stone lion at the head of the aqueduct in Roorkee**

## Roorkee ❽

Haridwar district. 198 km (123 miles) from Delhi on Delhi-Haridwar Rd. **Road map** D1. 🏯 *Roorkee Flower Show (Mar)*.

AN IMPORTANT university and cantonment town, this was originally a sleepy village on the banks of the Solani River. It gained importance when the Ganga Canal Workshop was set up in 1843 as part of the massive Ganga Canal Irrigation Project. This transformed the surrounding arid region into the highly productive agricultural area of today. To the north of the town is a magnificent brick aqueduct, marked with two enormous stone lions. It was considered a major engineering feat of the 19th century, and carries the water of the Ganga Canal over the Solani River. The Thomson Civil Engineering College (now the University of Roorkee) was established in 1847 and is the oldest technical institution in the country. The pleasantly sited campus, located within extensive wooded areas, has several important research institutions. Some of the structures from the colonial period are exceptional, such as the Church of St John the Baptist (1852), with beautiful stained-glass windows. The town is also renowned for high quality replicas of 18th- and 19th-century engineering and survey equipment.

**Interior of the Roorkee University**

### MANGO

The mango or *aam* is the best-loved fruit of the country. The Mughal emperor Babur called it the "finest fruit of Hindostan." Hundreds of varieties, with exotic names and pedigrees, are available from May to July, before the monsoon arrives. Savoured most for the sweet pulp of the ripe fruit, the raw mango is also valued for its medicinal properties, as well as its sharp tang, and is made into pickles and chutneys eaten through the year. The popular design motif of the paisley is derived from the shape of its fruit, and mango leaves, considered auspicious, are used as buntings at festive occasions.

*Langra* **mangoes**

**Saharanpur's Botanical Gardens, a repository of rare plants**

**Pilgrims taking a dip in the holy Ganges at Haridwar**

A good way to experience Haridwar's ambience, which has changed little since ancient times, is to stroll along the riverside bazaar, lined with stalls full of ritual paraphernalia – small mounds of vermilion powder, coconuts wrapped in red and gold cloth, and brass idols. The most popular items with the pilgrims, however, are the jars and canisters sold here. These are used to carry back water from the Ganges (*Gangajal*), a vital part of Hindu worship which, the faithful believe, remains ever fresh.

## Haridwar ❾

Haridwar district. 214 km (133 miles) N of Delhi. **Road map** D1. 🚶 1,125,000. ℹ *Regional Tourism Office, Rahi Motel (0133) 42 7370.* 🚉 *Railway Rd.* 🎎 *Kumbh Mela (every 12 years; Feb–Mar); Ardh Kumbha Mela (every 6 years; Feb–Mar); Haridwar Festival (Oct); Dusshera (Oct–Nov).*

T HE GANGES, India's holiest river, descends from the Himalayas to the plains at Haridwar. This gives the town such a unique status that a pilgrimage to Haridwar is every devout Hindu's dream.

Remarkably bare of ancient monuments, Haridwar's most famous "sight" and a constant point of reference is the Ganges and its numerous bathing ghats, tanks and temples. These bustling sites

**Chotiwala, a popular restaurant**

of ritual Hindu practices, performed by pilgrims for the salvation of their ancestors and for their own expiation, demonstrate their deep faith in the power of the river. The main ghat, Har-ki-Pauri, is named after a supposed imprint of Vishnu's feet there. Hundreds attend the daily evening *aarti* at this ghat, when leaf boats are filled with flowers, lit with lamps and set adrift on the Ganges. Further south, a ropeway connects the town to the Mansa Devi Temple across the river with a panoramic view of Haridwar. South of the town, the famous Gurukul Kangri University is renowned as a centre of Vedic knowledge, where students are taught in the traditional oral style. It also has a section displaying archaeological exhibits.

## Rishikesh ❿

Haridwar district. 238 km (148 miles) N of Delhi. **Road map** D1. 🚶 82,000. ℹ *UP Tourist Bureau, Railway Station Rd (01364) 30 209.* 🎎 *International Yoga Week (Feb).*

T HIS TWIN CITY of Haridwar, situated at the confluence of the Chandrabhaga and the Ganges, is the start of the holy Char Dham pilgrim route to the Himalayas. Muni-ki-Reti (literally "sand of the sages"), lies upstream from the Triveni Ghat and is believed to be a blessed site since ancient sages meditated here. It has several famous ashrams, such as the Sivanand, Purnanand and Shanti Kunj ashrams, which offer courses to those interested in India's ancient knowledge systems. Maharishi Mahesh Yogi, a cult figure during the 1960s, when the Beatles were his followers, also has an ashram here.

## KUMBH MELA

According to Hindu mythology, four drops of the immortal nectar (*amrit*) wrested by the gods from the demons, spilled over Haridwar, Allahabad, Ujjain and Nasik. A Kumbh Mela is held once every 12 years by rotation at these venues in Magh (Feb–Mar), when the sun transits from Pisces to Aries, and when Jupiter is in the sign of Aquarius (Kumbh in Hindu astrology). Hindus believe that they can imbibe the immortal *amrit* and wash away their sins by bathing in the Ganges at this propitious time. The *mela* is regarded as the largest congregation of human beings in one place anywhere in the world, when millions come for a holy dip, and to attend the seminars, discourses and debates held in the camps of leading Hindu sages and theologians. Haridwar's last Kumbh Mela, held in 1997, attracted over ten million people. A smaller celebration, called the Ardh Kumbh (half-Kumbh), is held every six years.

**Pilgrims thronging the ghats at the Kumbh Mela**

# River Tour along the Ganges ⑪

FROM OCTOBER TO MAY, the Ganges, swollen by the monsoon rains of the upper catchment areas, becomes a torrent gushing over the rocky boulders as it hurtles out of the mountains to the plains. This is the time when a few stretches of rapids, where the flow is rough but safe, become a popular circuit for enthusiasts of white-water rafting (see p275). Only organized tours, run by certified experts are allowed. For the less adventurous, a driving tour offers a panorama of this valley of the sages whose ashrams nestle in the surrounding forests along the holy river.

**The Ganges flows serenely through a forested valley**

**Kaudiyala ①**
The starting point of the river tour, it has scenic camp sites on the river bank.

**Marine Drive ②**
An early camp site named after a Bombay promenade famous for its view.

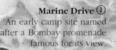

*Devaprayag*

*The Wall*

*Three Blind Mice*

*Golf Course*

**Shivpuri ③**
The beautiful Glass House on the Ganges (see p239) offers a spectacular view of the river and the surrounding countryside.

**Brahmapuri ④**
The location of an ashram, one of many along the Ganges.

**Lakshman Jhula ⑤**
A modern suspension bridge replaced the old rope bridge in 1929. This leads to the quieter east bank of Rishikesh where most ashrams are situated.

**Rishikesh ⑥**
An ancient spiritual centre, Rishikesh is serenely located on the banks of the Ganges amid lush, wooded hills.

## KEY

| | |
|---|---|
| ▬ | Tour route |
| ═ | Roads |
| ≈ | River |
| ☆ | Viewpoint |
| ◪ | Rapids |
| Ⓐ | Camping |

### TIPS FOR RIVER RAFTERS

**Length:** 36 km (22 miles).
**Stopping-off points:** White-water rafting can be done in leisurely stages, over two days, with a night halt at the Kaudiyala Camp. Stopover points are provided at Marine Drive, Shivpuri and Brahmapuri. However, a shorter tour of the same stretch can also be covered in one day.

0 kilometres 10

0 miles 5

# AGRA AND AROUND

GRA WAS THE IMPERIAL CAPITAL *of the Mughal court during the 16th and 17th centuries before it was shifted to Delhi. The Mughals were prolific builders and nowhere is this more evident than in the picturesque riverine region along the Yamuna which is the backdrop for its palaces, tombs, forts and gardens. Three of these, the Taj Mahal, the Agra Fort and Akbar's abandoned capital of Fatehpur Sikri, have been declared World Heritage Sites by UNESCO.*

The imperial Mughal highway which still runs along the Yamuna between Delhi and Agra is a link to the region's historical past. The rich pastoral and agricultural land around Brindavan, the supposed homeland of Krishna *(see p163),* was the main axis of the Mughal empire. The outer fringes of this area, formed by Mathura, Bharatpur and Deeg, have wetlands that attract many rare migratory birds, such as the Siberian crane, who come each winter to the World Heritage Site of the Keoladeo Ghana National Park.

As one goes further west and south, the greens and gold of the Yamuna lands give way to the scrub and ravines along the River Chambal. This is the centre of the subcontinent: hot, dusty and vast. These awesome ravines were the preferred habitat of robbers, dacoits and bandits. After the decline of the Mughals, some of the more ambitious bandits declared themselves Rajput Bundela kings and built for themselves small kingdoms with magnificent fortresses in this harsh area. Their unique architecture, that is a happy amalgam of traditional Hindu with Muslim building, can be seen in Datia and Orchha.

Itinerant poets and musicians in this area still sing of daring kings and queens such as Laxmibai, the Rani of Jhansi. Her spirited resistance to the British forces during the Indian Mutiny of 1857, made her a popular icon during the Freedom Movement. Close by lies Gwalior. This important princely state has a magnificent fort that goes back to the 3rd century, and splendid palaces built by its Scindia rulers.

The three-domed mosque to the west of the Taj Mahal

◁ Ablution tank in the *namazgah* of Fatehpur Sikri's Jami Masjid

# Exploring Agra and Around

AGRA LIES IN THE CENTRE of a rich and varied cultural territory. At one end of this region are the pastoral fields around Yamuna, and at the other, the stark and awesome ravines of the Chambal River. Between these two rivers are a number of towns, monuments and sanctuaries, making this one of the most popular travel circuits in North India. In mythology, Mathura was the sacred territory of Krishna *(see p163)* while in history, it was the centre of an important Buddhist kingdom, and the imperial Mughal highway ran through it. Later, Jat and Rajput Bundela kings built forts and palaces in nearby Bharatpur, Deeg, Jhansi, Datia and Orchha. Thus, this region contains some of the best examples of Indian art and architecture, while the riverine wetlands around Bharatpur provide a natural habitat for a range of wildlife and migratory birds.

*Delhi*

*Jaipur*

BRINDAVA
BRAJBHUMI 5
GOVARDHAN
6
DEEG
BHARATPUR 7
8
KEOLAD

11
BARI

*Chamba*

SHIVPU

*Guna*

Cows have a sacred status in Krishna's territory

A Mughal *kos minar* on the Grand Trunk Road

## KEY

- Major road
- Minor road
- River
- Viewpoint

0 kilometres      50

0 miles      25

**Temples and bathing ghats line the Yamuna at Mathura**

## SEE ALSO

- **Where to Stay** pp238–43
- **Where to Eat** pp260–61

## GETTING AROUND

The best way to explore this region is by car. The National Highway (NH2) which runs from Delhi to Agra goes through Mathura. A network of smaller roads links the region beyond Mathura and Brindavan. Except in patches, particularly after the monsoon, these are generally in a good condition. Once in Mathura, a boat trip along the Yamuna is a good way to see the ghats. The Keoladeo Ghana Sanctuary provides tourists with cycle-rickshaws and guides on payment. The area is also well serviced by trains, including the high speed Shatabdi Express, which goes from Delhi to Bhopal via Gwalior and Jhansi and the Taj Express between Delhi and Agra. Several trains pass through Jhansi from where easy car trips can be made to Datia and Orchha. Agra and Gwalior also have domestic airports.

## SIGHTS AT A GLANCE

# Agra ❶

**Detail of *jaali*, Musamman Burj**

**A**GRA was the imperial Mughal capital during the 16th and 17th centuries. It was from here that the emperors, Akbar, Jahangir and Shah Jahan, governed their vast empire. The city flourished under their patronage, attracting artisans from Persia and Central Asia, and also from other parts of India, who built luxurious forts, mausoleums and gardens. Agra's strategic location on the banks of the Yamuna as well as on the Grand Trunk Road linking eastern India with the west, made it a trading station, visited by merchants and travellers from all over the world. With the decline of the Mughals, Agra was captured by the Jats, the Marathas, and finally the British.

**A riverside view of the Jahangiri Mahal**

## 🏛 Agra Fort

⏰ *6am–6pm daily.* 📷 *free on Fri.*
📽 **Son et Lumière** *7:30pm daily.*

Situated on the west bank of the Yamuna, Agra Fort was built by Akbar between 1565 and 1573. Its imposing red sandstone ramparts form a crescent along the riverfront, and encompass an enormous complex of courtly buildings, ranging in style from the early eclectisim of Akbar to the sublime simplicity of Shah Jahan. The barracks to the north are 19th-century British additions. A deep moat, once filled with water from the Yamuna, surrounds the fort.

The impressive Amar Singh Gate to the south leads into the fort. To its right is the so-called Jahangiri Mahal, the only major palace in the fort that dates to Akbar's reign. This complex arrangement of halls, courtyards and galleries with dungeons below was the zenana or main harem

building. In front of Jahangir Mahal is a large marble pool which, as legend says, in Nur Jahan's time used to be filled with thousands of rose petals so that the empress could bathe in its scented waters.

Along the riverfront are the Khas Mahal, an elegant marble hall with an exuberantly painted ceiling, characteristic of Shah Jahan's style of architecture, and the two golden pavilions with typical *bangaldar* roofs *(see p319)*. These pavilions were supposedly associated with the princesses Jahanara and Roshanara, and have narrow niches where jewels could be concealed. Facing them is Anguri Bagh ("grape garden") with its lily-pools and candle-niches. The Sheesh Mahal and royal baths are to the

**Musamman Burj**

northeast near the gloriously inlaid Musamman Burj, the double-storeyed octagonal tower with clear views of the Taj. This was where Shah Jahan, imprisoned by his son Aurangzeb, spent the last years of his life. Mina Masjid ("gem mosque"), probably the smallest in the world and the emperor's private mosque, is nearby. To the side of Musamman Burj is the Diwan-i-Khas, a lavishly decorated open hall where the emperor met his court. Two thrones, in white marble and black slate, were placed on the terrace for the emperor to watch elephant fights below. Opposite is the Machchhi Bhavan ("fish house"), once a magnificent water palace. To its west is the Diwan-i-Aam, an arcaded hall within a large courtyard. Its throne-alcove of inlaid marble provided a sumptuous setting for the fabled Peacock Throne. To the northwest is the Nagina Masjid ("jewel mosque") built by Shah Jahan for his harem, and the Moti Masjid ("pearl mosque").

Beyond is the Meena Bazaar, the fort's shopping centre, overlooked by a fine marble balcony where, according to legend, the beautiful Mumtaz Mahal first met Shah Jahan. The bazaar street led directly to Delhi Gate, the original entrance, and to the Jami Masjid in the old city. Both the gate and bazaar street are now closed to the general public.

**Colonnaded arches of the  Diwan-i-Aam**

**Jami Masjid, built by Shah Jahan's favourite daughter Jahanara**

## VISITORS' CHECKLIST

Agra district. 223 km (139 miles)
SE of Delhi. **Road map** D3.
🚍 1,120,000. ✈ Kheria 16 km
(10 miles). 🚊 Agra Cantonment
(0562) 36 4244; Raja ki Mandi
(0562) 35 4477. 🚌 Idgah
(0562) 36 6588. ℹ UPTDC 64
Taj Rd, (0562) 36 0517; ITDC 191
Mall Rd, (0562) 36 3959.
🎪 Kailash Fair (Aug–Sep).

### 🄲 Jami Masjid
⭘ daily.

A magnificently proportioned building in the heart of the medieval town, the "Friday Mosque" was sponsored by Shah Jahan's favourite daughter, Jahanara Begum, who also commissioned a number of other buildings and gardens, including the canal that once ran down Chandni Chowk in Delhi *(see pp90–91)*. Built in 1648, the mosque's sandstone and marble domes with their distinctive zigzag chevron pattern dominate this section of the town. The eastern courtyard wing was demolished by the British in 1857 *(see pp54–5)*. Of interest are the tank with its *shahi chirag* ("royal stove") for heating water within the courtyard, and the separate prayer chamber for ladies.

**A detail of the minaret**

**ENVIRONS:** The area around Jami Masjid was a vibrant meeting place, famous for its kabab houses and lively bazaars. A stroll or rickshaw ride through the captivating network of narrow alleys can be a rewarding experience, offering glimpses of a close-knit way of life reminiscent of Mughal Agra. This is also the city's crafts and trade centre where a staggering array of products such as jewellery, *zari* embroidery, *dhurries*, dried fruit, sweets, shoes and kites are available.

Some of the main bazaars are Johri Bazaar, Kinari Bazaar, Kaserat Bazaar and Kashmiri Bazaar. The quieter back lanes such as Panni Gali have many fine buildings with decorative upper storeys and imposing gateways leading into secluded courtyards where the thriving workshops of master craftsmen still exist.

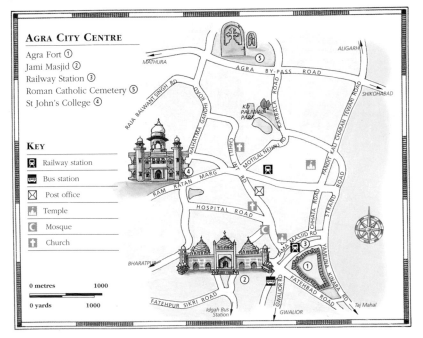

## AGRA CITY CENTRE

Agra Fort ①
Jami Masjid ②
Railway Station ③
Roman Catholic Cemetery ⑤
St John's College ④

### KEY

🚉 Railway station
🚌 Bus station
⊠ Post office
🛕 Temple
🄲 Mosque
✝ Church

0 metres 1000
0 yards 1000

# Exploring Agra: The Outer Sights

A *pietra dura* motif

**A**GRA'S EUROPEAN LEGACY dates to the reign of Akbar, when the first Jesuit missionaries from Portuguese-governed Goa, visited his court to participate in religious debates. This marked the advent of Christianity in North India and paved the way for future European traffic in the region. In the 18th and 19th centuries this was a great cosmopolitan centre where priests and scholars, merchants and mercenaries employed by the Scindias of Gwalior *(see p174)*, lived, traded or set up schools, colleges and impressive churches.

The monument in memory of John Hessing

Auto-rickshaws parked outside the Fort Railway Station

### ☷ Fort Railway Station
🄲 *(0562) 36 9590.*
This memorable colonial building was constructed in 1891 as a stopping-off point for colonial tourists visiting Agra's monuments. The octagonal bazaar *chowk* that originally connected the Delhi Gate and Agra Fort to the old city and the Jami Masjid was demolished and the many-towered station with its French château-style slate roofed platforms was built in its place. This is still one of Agra's most frequently-used stations, the other two are located in the cantonment and at Raja ki Mandi.

### ☷ St John's College
NH2 (Drummond Rd/Mahatma Gandhi Rd). 🄲 *35 5147.*
St John's College, started by the Church Missionary Society, has been described as "an astounding mixture of the antiquarian, the scholarly and the symbolic". It consists of a group of red sandstone buildings, including a hall and library, arranged around a quadrangle, all designed in a quasi-Fatehpur Sikri style by Sir Samuel Swinton Jacob *(see p194)*. The building was inaugurated in 1914 by the viceroy, Lord Hardinge, and it remains one of the region's highly lauded institutions.

### ✝ Roman Catholic Cemetery
Opp Civil Courts. ◯ *daily.*
Towards the north of the town is the Roman Catholic Cemetery, the oldest European graveyard in North India. It was established in the 17th century by an Armenian merchant, Khoja Mortenepus, on a piece of land purchased from the church as the burial ground for Agra's large Armenian trading community.

A number of Islamic-style gravestones, with inscriptions in Armenian, survive today, and include the graves of the cannon expert, Shah Nazar Khan, and Khoja Mortenepus himself. The cemetery also contains tombs of European missionaries, traders, and adventurers such as Walter Reinhardt *(see p140)*.

One of the oldest tombs belongs to the English merchant, John Mildenhall (1614), envoy of Elizabeth I, who arrived at the Mughal court in 1603 seeking permission to trade. Other interesting graves include those of the Venetian doctor,

St John's College, designed by Sir Samuel Swinton Jacob

**St George's Church in Agra Cantonment**

Bernardino Maffi, and Geronimo Veroneo (once wrongly regarded by some as the architect of the Taj).

Near the chapel is the tall obelisk marking the grave of the four children of General Perron, French commander of Scindia's forces. Another Frenchman, a member of the Bourbon family and kinsman of Henry IV of France, is also buried at this site.

The largest and most impressive grave is that of John Hessing (1803) who first ventured out East as a soldier with the Dutch East India Company at Kandy (Sri Lanka). He came to India in 1763 and joined the service of the Nizam of Hyderabad in the South before moving northwards to be a mercenary with the Scindia's forces. His red sandstone tombstone, interestingly modelled on the lines of the Taj Mahal, was built by a local architect.

One of the tombs, in memory of Father Santos, is enclosed by a trellis frame where Hindus and Muslims tie threads, praying for the fulfillment of their wishes.

To its south, on Wazirpura Road, is the **Roman Catholic Cathedral**, constructed in the 18th century at the expense of Walter Reinhardt. An old, derelict church from Akbar's time stands next to it.

### 🏛 Cantonment
Bounded by Mahatma Gandhi Rd, Grand Parade Rd and the Mall Rd.

The pleasant, tree-shaded army cantonment area, with its own railway station and orderly avenues has many interesting public buildings

churches, cemeteries and bungalows in a medley of styles dating from the British days. **St George's Church** (1826), a yellow ochre plastered building, visible even from the Taj, is a typical example of the North Indian cantonment style of architecture. JT Boileau, the architect, also built the Christ Church in Shimla.

**Havelock Memorial Church** (1873) constructed in a "trim Classical style" commemorates one of the British generals of the 1857 mutiny. **Queen Mary's Library** and the **Central Post Office** are other buildings in the area.

Structures such as the **Agra Club**, once the hub of British cantonment social life, and the hybrid Indo-Saracenic government Circuit House which used to accommodate officials of the Raj, are also located in the cantonment.

### 🏛 Firoz Khan Khwajasara's Tomb
5 of Agra, on Gwalior Rd.
🕐 daily.

A signpost on the Gwalior Road indicates the turning to this unusual 17th-century octagonal tomb, standing on the edge of a lake. This is where Firoz Khan, natural-born eunuch and custodian of Shah Jahan's palace harem, is buried. The red sandstone structure stands on a high plinth and has a gateway attached to the main building. Steps lead to the upper storey where a central pavilion containing the cenotaph is located. Highly stylized stone carvings decorate the surface. Interestingly, unlike other buildings of the period, there is an absence of calligraphic inscriptions. If the tomb is closed, the *chowkidar* from the village will open the gate.

**The central pavilion where Firoz Khan is buried**

### GOLD THREAD AND BEAD ZARDOZI

Agra's flourishing local craft tradition of elaborate gold thread and bead embroidery is known as *zardozi*. This technique was Central Asian in origin and came to the region with the Mughal emperors. Local craftsmen in the old city added further refinements to create garments and accessories for the Imperial court. However, with the decline of court patronage, the skill languished and almost vanished. It owes its recent revival to encouragement from contemporary fashion designers. The delicate stitches and complicated patterns in genuine gold thread and coloured beads are now widely used for both traditional and contemporary garments and accessories, including shawls and scarves, bags and shoes.

**Detail of a *zari*-embroidered textile**

# Taj Mahal

**Carved dado on outer niches**

ONE OF THE WORLD'S most famous buildings, the Taj Mahal commemorates both the Mughal emperor Shah Jahan, and Mumtaz Mahal, his favourite wife. Its perfect proportions and exquisite craftsmanship have been described as "a prayer, a vision, a dream, a poem, a wonder." This grandiose garden-tomb, an image of the Islamic garden of paradise, cost nearly 41 million rupees and 500 kilos of gold. Around 20,000 workers laboured for almost 22 years to complete it in 1653.

**The Dome**
*The 44-m (144-ft) double dome is capped with a finial.*

**★ Marble Screen**
*The filigree screen daintily carved from a single block of marble was meant to veil the area around the royal tombs.*

**Four minarets**, each 40 m (131 ft) high and crowned by a *chhatri*, frame the tomb, highlighting the perfect symmetry of the complex.

**Plinth**

**River Yamuna**

**★ Tomb Chamber**
*Mumtaz Mahal's cenotaph, raised on a platform, is placed next to Shah Jahan's. The actual graves, in a dark crypt below, are closed to the public.*

**STAR FEATURES**

★ Marble Screen

★ Tomb Chamber

★ Pietra Dura

**The Charbagh**
was irrigated
by the water
of the River
Jamuna.

**Main
entrance**

**The Lotus Pool**
*Named after its lotus-shaped fountain spouts, the
pool reflects the tomb. Almost every visitor is
photographed sitting on the marble bench here.*

**Pishtaq**
*Recessed arches
provide depth while
their inlaid panels
reflect the changing
light to give the tomb
a mystical aura.*

**★ Pietra Dura**
*Inspired by the paradise garden,
intricately carved floral designs
inlaid with precious stones embellish
the austere white marble surface to
give it the look of a bejewelled casket.*

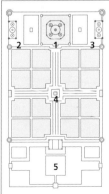

**TAJ MAHAL**

**1** Main Tomb
**2** *Masjid* (mosque)
**3** *Mehmankhana*
(guesthouse)
**4** *Charbagh*
**5** Gateway

**Calligraphic Panels**
*The size of the Koranic verses
increases as the arch gets higher,
creating the subtle optical illusion
of a uniformly flowing script.*

**KEY**

☐ Central illustration

☐ *Charbagh*

# Decorative Elements of the Taj

**Stylized floral motif**

IT IS WIDELY BELIEVED that the Taj Mahal was designed to represent an earthly replica of one of the houses of paradise. Its impeccable marble facing, embellished by a remarkable use of exquisite surface design, is a splendid showcase for the refined aesthetic that reached its height during Shah Jahan's reign. Described as "one of the most elegant and harmonious buildings in the world", the Taj indeed manifests the wealth and luxury of Mughal art as seen in architecture and garden design, painting, jewellery, calligraphy, textiles, carpet-weaving and furniture.

**Detail of the marble screen with an inlaid chrysanthemum**

## PIETRA DURA

The Mughals were great naturalists who believed that flowers were the "symbols of the divine realm". In the Taj, *pietra dura* has been extensively used to translate naturalistic forms into decorative patterns that complement the majesty of its architecture.

*Flowers such as the tulip, lily, iris, poppy and narcissus were depicted as sprays or arabesque patterns. Stones of varying degrees of colour were used to create the shaded effects.*

**Marble inlay above the mosque's central arch**

**White marble, black slate and yellow, red and grey sandstone are used for decoration**

## PIETRA DURA

The Florentine technique of *pietra dura* is said to have been imported by Jahangir and developed in Agra as *pachikari*. Minute slivers of precious and semi-precious stones, such as carnelian, lapis lazuli, turquoise and malachite, were arranged in complex stylized floral designs into a marble base. Even today, artisans in the old city maintain pattern books containing the intricate motifs used on the Taj and can still re-create 17th-century designs in contemporary pieces.

**A contemporary marble inlaid platter**

**A single flower often had more than 35 variations of carnelian**

## CARVED RELIEF WORK

Decorative panels of flowering plants, foliage and vases are realistically carved on the lower portions of the walls. While the *pietra dura* adds colour to the pristine white marble these highlight the texture of the polished marble and sandstone surface.

*Floral sprays,* carved in relief on the marble and sandstone dado levels, are framed with pietra dura and stone inlay borders. The profusion of floral motifs in the Taj symbolizes the central paradise theme.

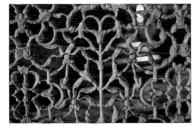

**Jaali patterns** on the octagonal perforated screen surrounding the cenotaphs are a complex combination of the floral and geometric. The filtered light captures the intricate designs and casts mosaic-like shadows on the tombs.

## CALLIGRAPHY

Inlaid calligraphy in black marble was used as a form of ornamentation on undecorated surfaces. The exquisitely detailed panels of inscriptions of Koranic passages, that line the recessed arches like banners, were designed by the Persian calligrapher, Amanat Khan.

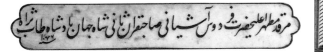

## Exploring the East Bank

THE PICTURESQUE east bank of the Yamuna is dotted with the remains of gardens, palaces, pavilions and the exquisite tomb of **Itimad-ud-Daulah**. North of Itimad-ud-Daulah is **Chini ka Rauza**, (literally, "China tomb" after its tiled exterior) built by Afzal Khan, a poet-scholar from Shiraz who was Shah Jahan's finance minister. This large square structure is Persian in style, and at one time its surface was covered with glazed tiles from Lahore and Multan interspersed with calligraphic panels in graceful Naskh characters. The burial chamber within has painted stucco plaster design that once must have complemented the tiled exterior.

Further upriver is the quiet, tree-shaded **Rambagh** or Aram Bagh ("garden of rest"). This is said to be the first Mughal garden laid out by Babur in 1526 *(see p167)* and his temporary burial place before his body was taken to Kabul to be interred. The spacious walled garden, divided by walkways leading to a raised terrace with open pavilions overlooking the river, was further developed by Nur Jahan.

### Chini ka Rauza
1 km (less than a mile) N of Itimad-ud-Daulah. ◯ *daily.* 🔲

### Rambagh
3 km (2 miles ) N of Itimad-ud-Daulah. ◯ *daily.* 🔲 *free on Fri.*

Riverside pavilion at Rambagh

# Itimad-ud-Daulah's Tomb

A stylized floral motif

LYRICALLY DESCRIBED AS a "jewel box in marble", the small, yet elegant garden tomb of Itimad-ud-Daulah, the "Lord Treasurer" of the Mughal empire, was built over a period of six years from 1622 by his daughter Nur Jahan, Jahangir's favourite wife. This tomb is a brilliant combination of white marble, coloured mosaic, stone inlay and lattice work. Stylistically, too, this is the most innovative 17th-century Mughal building and marks the transition from the robust, red sandstone architecture of Akbar to the sensuous refinement of Shah Jahan's Taj Mahal.

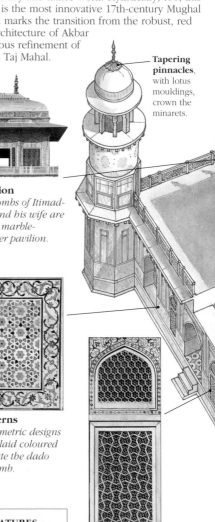

**Tapering pinnacles**, with lotus mouldings, crown the minarets.

**Upper Pavilion**
*The replica tombs of Itimad-ud-Daulah and his wife are placed in the marble-screened upper pavilion.*

**Mosaic Patterns**
*Panels of geometric designs created by inlaid coloured stones decorate the dado level of the tomb.*

---

### STAR FEATURES

★ Pietra Dura

★ Tomb Chamber

★ Marble Screens

---

★ **Marble Screens**
*Perforated marble screens with complex ornamental patterns are carved out of a single slab of marble.*

**The dome** with its canopy-like shape is different from the conventional domes of this period.

### The Tomb
*The square two-storeyed tomb stands in the centre of a charbagh. At the four corners of the low platform are four squat attached minarets.*

**The marble latticed balustrade**

### ★ Tomb Chamber
*The roof has incised, painted and gilded stucco and stalactite patterns. The yellow marble caskets appear to have been carved out of wood.*

### Chhatri
*The open-pillared domed chhatri above the minaret.*

### ★ Pietra Dura
*The polished marble surface is covered with stone inlay, the first time this technique was extensively used in Mughal architecture.*

**Entrance**

### Painted Floral Patterns
*Niches with painted floral bouquets, fruit, trees and wine decanters embellish the interior of the central chamber of the main tomb.*

The entrance to Akbar's mausoleum at Sikandra

## Sikandra ❷

Agra district. 8 km (5 miles) NW of
Agra on NH2. **Road map** D2. 🚗
**Akbar's Mausoleum** 📞 37 1230
(contact for prior permission to go to
the tomb terrace). 🕐 7am–5:15pm
daily. 🎫 free on Fri. 📷 🚻 ♿
🎪 Urs at Akbar's tomb (mid-Oct).

THE MUGHAL EMPEROR, Akbar,
is buried in this small
village on the outskirts of
Agra. Named after Sikander
Lodi, one of the last of the
Delhi sultans (see pp50–51),
this was a pleasant garden
suburb during Agra's golden
age. It is widely believed that
Akbar designed and started
the construction of his own
mausoleum which, after his
death, was modified and
completed by his son and
successor, Jahangir. The result
is this impressive, perfectly
symmetrical complex with the
tomb, located in the centre of
a vast, walled garden.

The main gateway (see p25)
to the south, is a magnificent
red sandstone structure with a
colossal central arch, finished
with an exuberant poly-
chrome mosaic of inlaid white
marble, black slate and
coloured stones. On each
corner of the gateway are
four graceful marble minarets,
considered to be forerunners
of those found later on the
Taj Mahal (see pp154–5).

The garden, where deer
and monkeys frolic, is a
typical charbagh (see p167).
The wide sweep of stone
causeways leading to the
tomb divides the area into
four quadrants, each with its
own fountain and sunken
pond, fruit trees and bushes,
now a derelict tangle.

The main tomb is a distinct
departure from the conventional domed structure of the
tomb of Akbar's father, the
second Mughal emperor,
Humayun, at Delhi (see p83).
The first three storeys of this
majestic, four-tiered composition, comprise red sandstone pavilions.
Above them is an
exquisite marble-
screened terrace
enclosing the
replica tomb,
which is pro-
fusely carved
with floral and
arabesque
designs, Chinese
cloud patterns,
and the 99
names of Allah.
The upper levels are now
closed and permission is
required to view the terrace.

The actual tomb is within
a domed sepulchre in the
heart of the building, illuminated by shafts of light from
an arched window. A low
door at the end of the ramp

**Detail of a panel on the
entrance gateway at Sikandra**

ensures that every visitor
bows his head with respect
on entry. Just outside the
complex is the **Kanch
Mahal**, a double-storeyed red
sandstone mansion with an
ornamented façade and
fretted balconies. Further
down, on Mathura Road, is
**Mariam Zamani's Tomb**,
where one of Akbar's wives is
buried in a square building
set on a high plinth within a
small garden. It was used as
an orphanage by the Church
Missionary Society in 1812. A
church has been constructed
in the compound. Further
along the Agra-Delhi highway
is **Guru-ka-Tal**, a unique
example of the many tanks
constructed by
Jahangir for
collecting rain-
water. Broad
flights of steps
lead down to
the water. The
reservoir is now
part of a guru-
dwara complex
dedicated to the
ninth Sikh guru,
Tegh Bahadur
(see p90).

**ENVIRONS:** About 4 km
(2 miles) south of Sikandra, is
a lifesize red sandstone horse
on the spot where Akbar's
favourite steed supposedly
died. Opposite is the gateway
of **Kachi-ki-Sarai**, a historic
rest house along this route.

---

### THE GRAND TRUNK ROAD

A roadside dhaba

The Grand Trunk Road, Rudyard
Kipling's "stately corridor" that linked
Calcutta in the east with Kabul in the
northwest, was laid out by Sher Shah
Sur (see p84) in the 16th century. In
those days, it resounded with the
movement of armies on campaign,
and in times of peace, with the pomp
and pageantry that accompanied the
Mughal emperors as their court
moved from Agra to Delhi.
This is still one of Asia's great roads
and North India's premier highway.
Some of the ancient shade-giving trees still stand, but the
old caravanserais are now in ruins. Instead, at frequent
intervals along the highway, there are dhabas for long-
distance travellers, especially lorry-drivers, to stop for a
cheap and filling meal of dal and roti, washed down with
glasses of hot tea or cooling lassi, and to snatch a quick
nap on string cots thoughtfully provided by the owner.

Vishram Ghat at Mathura where every evening at sunset oil lamps are floated on the river

# Mathura **❸**

Mathura district 62 km (39 miles) from Agra on NH2.
**Road map** D3. 🏚 *1,950,000*.
🚉 🚌 🚹 *Old Bus Stand, Mathura*.
🎪 *Hariyali Teej (July), Janmashtami (Aug–Sep), Annakut (Sep–Oct), Kansa Vadha (Sep), Holi (Feb–Mar)*.

**M**ATHURA, on the west bank of the Yamuna, is where the story of Krishna begins. A dark, cell-like room in the complex of the rather modern Sri Krishna Janmabhoomi Temple on the periphery of the city, is revered as the birthplace of one of India's most popular gods. Further away, along the riverfront, the city's 25 ghats form a splendid network of temples, pavilions, trees and steps leading to the water. Teeming with colourful shops selling traditional items, such as its delicious *pedas* (milk sweets), this is the heart of the town.

The evening *aarti*, when small oil lamps are floated on the river, is performed at **Vishram Ghat**, where legend says Krishna rested after he killed the tyrant Kamsa. Close by is the **Sati Burj**, a red sandstone pavilion built in the 1570s, and **Kans Qila**, the site of the old fort where Sawai Jai Singh II of Jaipur constructed one of his five observatories *(see pp192–3)*.

The **Jami Masjid**, with its striking tile-work, and a number of other interesting buildings with elaborately carved façades, lie behind the riverfront. A charming oddity is the Roman Catholic Church of the Sacred Heart, built in 1860 in the army cantonment. It combines Western elements with details taken from local temple architecture.

Mathura's ancient history predates the better known legend of Krishna. From about the 5th century BC until the 4th century AD, the city prospered as a major centre of Buddhism. Under the powerful Kushana and Gupta dynasties, it was renowned thoughout the ancient world as North India's cultural capital. During this period the Mathura School of Art flourished *(see pp46–7)*, and superb pieces of sculpture, made from the distinctive local white-flecked red sandstone, were carved by artisans in workshops here and exported to far off places.

The **Government Museum** collection highlights the Mathura School of Art and

**A religious icon from Mathura**

has some exquisite pieces. These include a perfectly preserved Standing Buddha, the famous headless statue of the great Kushana king Kanishka, as well as a huge collection of carved columns, railings and fragments of narrative panels, excavated from nearby archaeological sites, depicting court scenes and religious imagery.

Also on view are artifacts from the other centres of Buddhist art, such as Gandhara (now in Pakistan), showing Graeco-Roman influences after Alexander's invasion of the northwest. There are also sections on terracotta pottery and figurines dating from the 2nd–1st centuries BC, coins and medieval stone, brass and metal objects.

**🏛 Government Museum**
Dampier Nagar. ☎ *(0565) 40 3191*.
🕒 *10:30am–4:30pm Tue–Sun*. ⬤ *Mon & public hols*. 📷 *extra charges*.

**A boat carrying pilgrims along the Yamuna**

# Brindavan ❹

Mathura district. 68 km (42 miles)
N of Agra off NH2. **Road map** D3.
🏯 *475,000.* 🚌 ℹ️ *Old Bus Stand,
Mathura.* 🎭 *Holi (Feb–Mar), Rath ka
Mela (Mar), Hariyali Teej (Jul),
Janmashtami (Aug–Sep).* 🛕 *daily.*

**Pilgrims on the *chaurasi kos ki yatra***

SITUATED ALONG the River
Yamuna, Brindavan
(literally, "forest of fragrant
basil") became an important
pilgrim centre after the early
16th century when Chaitanya
Mahaprabhu, a Vaishnava
saint from Bengal, revived the
Krishna cult. He encouraged
Bengali devotees, especially
widows, to settle here in
ashrams endowed by wealthy
Hindu merchants. However,
the town's mythic origins are
much older, as devout Hindus
believe that the young Lord
Krishna once lived here as a
humble cowherd with his
foster parents. So "his" cows
still have the run of the streets
and his name is continuously
chanted in prayer halls. Stalls
outside temples sell elaborate
flower garlands and milk
sweets called *pedas*, believed
to have been loved by
Krishna. All this gives the
feeling that the people of
Brindavan live in an
enchanted time warp.

This charming phenomenon
is best seen in Brindavan's
numerous temples and ghats,
built by the Hindu kings of
Amber, Bharatpur and Orchha
and by rich merchants. The
edge of the old town has the
historic **Govindeoji Temple**,
originally a seven-storeyed
structure built in 1590 by Raja
Man Singh I of Amber. The
presiding deity is now in
Jaipur *(see p182)*. Across this
temple is the 19th-century **Sri
Ranganathji**, an imposing
Dravidian-style temple with a
gold-plated ritual pillar and a
fascinating museum of temple
treasures. Beyond these, and
within the narrow streets of

# Brajbhumi Driving Tour ❺

DEVOTEES BELIEVE that the area around
Braj is composed of sacred *mandalas*
(circuits) that map the idyllic pastoral
landscape of Krishna's early life. Divided
by the Yamuna, this tour partly follows
the *chaurasi kos ki yatra,* a traditional
pilgrimage of about 300 km (112 miles),
undertaken around Janmashtami.

**Kosi** ⑥
This was the
treasure-house of
Krishna's foster
father, Nand.

↖*DELHI*

**Barsana** ④
With its 17th-century
Ladliji temple, Barsana is
believed to be the home
of Radha.

**Nandgaon** ⑤
Krishna lived here
with foster parents
Nand and Yashoda
after his escape
from Gokul and
the evil Kamsa.

**Govardhan** ③
This pilgrim town has grown
around the hill that legend says
Krishna lifted on his finger to shield
the people of Braj from torrential
rain. Nearby is Kusum Sarovar.

the old town, are the sacred walled groves of Seva Kunj, linked with the Raslila dance of the region *(see p28)*.

The **Shahji Temple** with its spiral columns, lies on the way to Nidhivana where Swami Haridas, the guru of Tansen *(see p174)*, developed the classic musical tradition of Dhrupad in the 16th century. Other notable temples are the **Madan Mohan Temple**, built in 1580 with local red sandstone, on a hill next to the river. A little further, are the popular **Banke Bihari Temple**, which can be approached from the main bazaar street, and the 16th-century **Jugal Kishore Temple**, adjoining the main pilgrim route to the ghats. The **Gopinath** and **Radha Raman** temples are located close to each other near Keshi

*A Vaishanavite sadhu*

*Gopuram of the South Indian-style Ranganathji Temple*

Ghat. The ISKCON Temple and the Brindavan Research Institute, on the outskirts of the town, are recent additions to the town's skyline.

At Holi and Janmashtami *(see pp36–7)*, Brindavan is a riot of colour and dance as people celebrate the god who still enchants them and where his *lila* (divine sport) is still a living presence.

# Deeg ❻

Bharatpur district. 98 km (61 miles) N of Agra on NH2. **Road map** D3. 🛈 *RTDC Hotel Saras, Agra Rd, Bharatpur (05644) 22 542.* 🎉 *Holi (Feb–Mar), Rath ka Mela (Mar).*

ONCE THE CAPITAL of the Jat kings of Bharatpur *(see p166)*, Deeg rose to prominence after the decline of the Mughal empire in the 18th century. Its square fort, a massive edifice, has mud and rubble walls which are buttressed by 12 bastions and a shallow moat. The fortified town outside the fort once had grand mansions, lush gardens and pools, that now lie unkempt and forlorn. Deeg's Raja Suraj Mal and his son, Jawahir Singh, were also builders of lavish pleasure palaces. Of these, the most remarkable is the **Water Palace** *(see pp164–5)*, built in celebration of the monsoon. This was a favourite summer retreat of the Bharatpur Kings.

---

**Radhakund** ②
Said to be Radha's personal bathing pool, it has a special sanctity for her devotees.

**Brindavan** ①
An important pilgrim centre, it is separated from Mathura by the River Yamuna.

### KEY

▬ Tour route

– Roads

≈ Rivers

0 kilometres         5

0 miles         2

## TIPS FOR DRIVERS

**Length:** 105 km (65 miles).
**Stopping-off points:** Brindavan has good hotels and restaurants and is the ideal base for the tour. Both Radhakund and Barsana have UPSTDC tourist bungalows, and Govardhan and Kosi have petrol stations. However, private transport will be a more convenient way to explore this region.

## THE KRISHNA CULT

A peacock feather, a flute and the colour blue announce the presence of Krishna. Named after his dark skin, this most human of gods still haunts the glades and forests along the Yamuna. A naughty child who was passionately fond of milk and butter, Krishna is also the charming flute-player whose flirtatious dalliance with Radha is a metaphor for the complex metaphysics of temporal and spiritual love, widely celebrated in art and literature.

*Sanjhi, Brindavan's paper stencil craft*

# Deeg Water Palace

**Sandstone carving on Singh Pol**

T HE MAGIC OF THE MONSOON and the traditions of music and dance associated with it inspired the Bharatpur kings to build a romantic "water palace" at their summer capital, Deeg. A lyrical composition of sandstone and marble pavilions, gardens and pools, this late 18th-century marvel, built by Raja Suraj Mal, used a number of innovative special effects that simulated monsoon showers, even producing rainbows. The skilful cooling system drew water from a huge reservoir that originally took two days to fill. The coloured fountain-jets are now played only during the Jawahar Mela.

**Nand Bhavan**
*Huge terracotta water pitchers placed inside its innovative double roof insulated its interior against the heat of summer.*

**The main entrance**, Singh Pol, is named after the two lions (*singh*) sculpted on its front arch.

**★ Sawan Pavilion**
*Shaped like an upturned boat, its ingenious water system created a semi-circle of falling water.*

**Gopal Sagar Tank**

**Mughal Marble Swing**
*This was a part of Suraj Mal's war booty, now placed in front of Gopal Bhavan.*

**Bhadon Pavilion**

**★ Gopal Bhavan**
*This elegant complex is flanked by the boat-shaped Sawan-Bhadon pavilions. Its numerous overhanging kiosks and balconies are reflected in Gopal Sagar from which it seems to rise. The interior still retains the original furnishings and objets d'art of this palace.*

### ★ Keshav Bhavan

*Heavy lithic balls were placed on the roof here. When water gushed up the hollow pillars and pipes inside the arches, the balls rolled on the roof to produce "thunder".*

### Lotus Quoins

*Placed at each corner of the plinth, these urns were inspired by Mughal designs.*

**Rup Sagar Tank**

**Kishan Bhavan**

### Suraj Bhavan

*A pillared, secluded pavilion with a splendid view of the* charbagh, *it was part of the zenana enclosure.*

**The roof-level reservoir** had water drawn to it from four wells. Pipes led from holes in its sides to supply the chutes and fountains with a continuous stream of water.

*Charbagh*

## MONSOON ARCHITECTURE

In the dry areas of North India, light and wind direction guided architecture. Underground rooms, water channels, fountains, latticed screens, terrazzo floors and open courtyards were devices to keep homes cool before the advent of electricity. The Sawan-Bhadon pavilions at Deeg, named after the months of the monsoon (July–August), are an architectural style inspired by the rainy season. Built to savour the thunder and rain of the monsoon, such pavilions adorned forts and palaces.

**Coloured water fountains at Deeg**

### STAR FEATURES

★ **Gopal Bhavan**

★ **Sawan Pavilion**

★ **Keshav Bhavan**

## Bharatpur ⑦

Bharatpur district. 55 km (34 miles)
from Agra. **Road map** D3.
🏛 *1,700,000.* ℹ *opp RTDC Hotel
Saras, Agra Rd, (05644) 22 542.* 🚌
⚄ *Jaswant Mela (Oct).*

**The State Museum at Lohagarh Fort, Bharatpur**

**M**OST FAMOUS for its bird
sanctuary, the kingdom
of Bharatpur, on the eastern
edge of Rajasthan, came into
prominence during the
declining years of the Mughal
Empire. It was founded by
the fearless Jats, a community
of landowners. Their most
remarkable leader was Raja
Suraj Mal (r.1724–63) who in
1733, captured and fortified
the city of Bharatpur, thereby
laying the foundations of his
capital. This powerful ruler
defied the reigning Mughal
emperor, stormed Delhi and
Agra and brought home the
massive gates of Agra Fort
and installed them at his own
fort at Deeg's Water Palace
(*see pp164–5*), near Bharatpur. A prolific builder as well,
he used the loot from Mughal
buildings, including a swing
(now in Deeg), to embellish
the forts and palaces he built
throughout his kingdom.

In the centre of the town is
**Lohagarh** ("iron fort") which
withstood repeated attacks by
the Marathas and the British
until it was finally captured
by Lord Lake in 1805. When
built, it was a masterpiece of
construction with massive
double ramparts made of
solid packed mud and rubble
that were surrounded by
impressive moats. Most of the

outermost ramparts have
disintegrated, but the inner
ones are intact and are
distinguished by two towers,
the Jawahar Burj and Fateh
Burj, built to mark successive
Jat victories over the Mughals
and British. The Victory
Column at Jawahar Burj
carries an inscription
with the genealogy
of the Jat kings.
Both its north and
south gates were
part of the loot from
the imperial Mughal
capital at Delhi.

Three palaces
were built in the
fort by the rustic
Jats in a surprisingly
fine mix of Mughal
and Rajput stylistic
detail. The royal apartments,
in Mahal Khas, had unusual
octagonal chambers in the
corners with colourful painted
walls, but these are now the
site of a pharmaceutical
college. The other two

**Figure of Krishna,
State Museum**

palaces were located around
the Katcheri (court) Bagh,
and now house the **State
Museum**, where a rare
collection of 1st- and 2nd-
century stone carvings as
well as terracotta toys from
nearby excavations can be
seen. An interesting
sunken *hamam* is
close by.

In 1818, Bharatpur
became the first
Rajput state to sign
a treaty of alliance
with the British East
India Company. A
later maharaja was
a keen collector of
Rolls Royce cars,
which he converted
for use on tiger and
duck shoots.

🏛 **State Museum**
Near Nehru Park. ☎ *(05644) 28 185.*
○ *10am–5pm.* ● *Fri & public hols.*
🎫 *free on Mon.* 📷 *extra charges.*

## Keoladeo Ghana National Park ⑧

*See pp 168-9.*

## Fatehpur Sikri ⑨

*See pp 170-71.*

## Dholpur ⑩

Dholpur district. 54 km (34 miles) S
of Agra. **Road map** D3. 🏛
*750,000.* ℹ *Bharatpur, (05644) 22
542.* 🚌

**S**ITUATED ON THE BANKS of
the River Chambal, the
small town of Dholpur was
strategically located on the

**The moat and ramparts of Lohagarh**

**The lakeside temples of Machkund**

route from Delhi to the Deccan, making it the target of invading armies. In 1504, Sikandar Lodi (see pp50–51) set up camp here for a month on his march against Gwalior. Some 20 years later, Babur made this a royal domain of his new empire. The ruined Shergarh Fort, said to be 1,000 years old, is in Dholpur and so is a modest 19th-century palace (closed to the public) which can only be seen through an ironwork railing. The palace has a number of art deco rooms covered with European tiles. Dholpur is today associated with the beige-coloured sandstone quarried nearby, used in buildings all over Rajasthan and made famous by Lutyens, who used it for the building of New Delhi (see pp68–9)

**ENVIRONS:** Dholpur town is a convenient base to explore a number of fascinating neighbouring sites. **Machkund** (3 km/2 miles west), has over 100 temples along its lake. Its waters are said to heal all skin diseases. **Damoh**, a popular picnic spot, has 76 waterfalls. **Talab Shahi** (40 km/25 miles) has the remains of Mughal hunting lodges developed by the Jat rulers of Dholpur for their European guests. Off the beaten track is **Jhor** (16km/10 miles), where in 1978, Babur's 400-year-old Lotus Garden was discovered.

## Bari ⓫

Dholpur district. 84 km (68 miles) SW of Agra. **Road map** D4.
🛈 Bharatpur, (05644) 22 542. 🚌

**Shah Jahan's palace gate, Bari**

THE SITE of an old 100-acre garden once so dense that sunlight could not reach the ground, Bari was where Emperor Shah Jahan built a number of pleasure pavilions. Located nearby is the Vana Vihar Ram Sagar Wildlife Reserve, home to crocodiles, sambhar, wild boar and several species of migratory bird. Remains of an old fort built by Feroze Shah Tughlaq (see p97) can also be seen here.

---

## BABUR AND THE PARADISE GARDEN

**The Garden of Fidelity in the Babur Nama**

The concept of the Paradise Garden, the hallmark of Mughal landscape design, was introduced by the first Great Mughal, Babur. Craving for the natural beauty of Ferghana, his homeland in Central Asia, he re-created the Persian paradise garden based on Islamic geometric and metaphysical concepts of design.

The *charbagh* was an enclosed garden divided into four quarters, representing the four quarters of life, by a system of raised walkways, sunken groves and water channels. Water was the central element, for it was regarded by the rulers of Central Asian desert kingdoms as the source of life. The intersecting water channels met at a focal point which contained a pavilion for the emperor, seen as a representative of God on earth.

The Mughals used their gardens as living spaces, and also as settings for their garden tombs (see p27). The Jhor garden of paradise, sometimes referred to as the Lotus Garden, was laid out in 1527, barely a year after Babur invaded India. Three water channels, Babur's hot bath, a tank and a pavilion are all that remain of the original garden, which once covered several acres.

# Keoladeo Ghana National Park ❽

A WORLD HERITAGE SITE regarded as one of the world's most important bird sanctuaries, Keoladeo Ghana derives its name from a Shiva temple (Keoladeo) within a dense *(ghana)* forest . This once-arid scrubland was first developed by the Bharatpur rulers in the mid-18th century by diverting the waters of a nearby irrigation canal to create a private duck reserve. Extravagant shooting parties for viceroys and other royal guests were held here, and horrifying numbers of birds were shot in a single day. Today, the park spreads over 29 sq km (11 sq miles) of wetlands, and attracts a wide variety of migrant and water birds who fly in each winter from places as distant as Siberia. Keoladeo's dry area has a mixed deciduous and scrub vegetation and is home to many mammals such as the nilgai.

**Bharatpur's shallow wetlands hold one of the world's finest heronries**

**Around the Park**
*Expert boatmen navigate the wetlands and point out bird colonies. Bicycles and cycle-rickshaws are also available for touring the forest paths.*

**Dry scrubland** provides good grazing for many species of deer and cattle.

## BIRDS, RESIDENT AND MIGRANT

**The male Sarus crane dances to attract his mate**

The park attracts over 375 bird species belonging to 56 families. Egrets, darter cormorants, grey herons and storks hatch nearly 30,000 chicks every year. The park's most eagerly awaited visitor is the Siberian crane, now an endangered species. Other birds include the peregrine falcon, steppe eagle, garganey teal, snake bird and the white ibis. Among the large variety of storks are the open-bill stork, the painted stork and the black-necked stork, considered to be the world's tallest stork. When standing on coral legs, the bird rises to a height of 2 m (6 ft), with a wing spread of 2.5 m (8 ft). The Sarus crane, a symbol of fertility in Indian mythology, woos its partner for life with an elaborate mating dance.

**Baby cormorants**

Forest Lodge ★

Shanti Kutir

Mrig Tal

Sapan•

Ramnagar

Lala Pyar• ka Kund

NH11

JAIPUR

Chiksana Canal

•Aghapur

**KEY**

| | |
|---|---|
| ▬ | Main road |
| = | Minor road |
| ˉ ˈ | Park boundary |
| · · | Walk/cycle trail |
| | Marshland |
| ☀ | Viewpoint |
| | Jetty |
| | Boating area |
| | Police station |
| | Temple |

BHARATPUR CITY

**Painted Storks**
*Between July and October, the trees become nesting sites for nearly 5,000 pairs of these birds named after their colourful beaks and plumage which is "painted" with black bands.*

• Jatoli

AGRA

NH11

0 kilometres 1

0 miles 1

**Turtle**
*Other living species include turtles, otters, foxes and reptiles such as the rock python.*

**Nilgai (Blue Bull)**
*The largest of all Asiatic antelopes, these avid crop grazers are protected against hunting because of their resemblance to the holy cow. Their broad backs offer comfortable resting places to birds.*

• Ghasola

Kadam Kunj

oladeo mple lan ovar

thon oint

Hans Sarovar

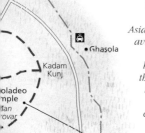

**Siberian Crane**
*The subcontinent's only winter habitat for this rare bird, Keoladeo was visited by a lone pair in 1999. Poachers on the 6,400 km (3,977 miles) route have decimated their migrant flocks.*

Koladahar

• Bahnera

Chiksana Canal

Naswaria

• Darapur

**A stone plaque** near the temple records figures of past bird shoots.

**Nesting**
*With the arrival of the monsoon (late June), thousands of birds set up nesting colonies. As many as 60 noisy nests on one tree may be seen during this season.*

# Fatehpur Sikri ❾

**Fretwork *jaali***

**B**UILT BY AKBAR in 1571 in honour of the famous Sufi saint, Salim Chishti *(see pp220–21)*, Fatehpur Sikri was the Mughal capital for 14 years. An example of a Mughal walled city with defined private and public areas and imposing gateways, its architecture, a blend of Hindu and Islamic styles, reflects Akbar's secular vision as well as his style of governance. After the city was abandoned, some say for lack of water, many of its treasures were plundered *(see pp54–5)*. It owes its present state of preservation to the initial efforts of Lord Curzon *(see pp56–7)*, a legendary conservationist.

**Pillar in the Diwan-i-Khas**
*The central axis of Akbar's court, supported by carved brackets, was inspired by Gujarat buildings.*

**Haram S complt**

**Jami Masjid**

**Khwabgah**
*The emperor's private sleeping quarters, this "chamber of dreams" with murals and Persian calligraphy has an ingenious ventilating shaft near his bed.*

**Anoop Talao** or pool is associated with Akbar's legendary court musician Tansen who, it is said, could light oil lamps with the magic of his voice.

**Abdar Khana**

**Entrance**

**★ Turkish Sultana's House**
*The elaborate dado panels and delicately sculpted walls of this ornate sandstone pavilion make the stone seem like wood. It is topped with an unusual stone roof with imitation clay tiles.*

**Diwan-i-Aam**
*This large courtyard with an elaborate pavilion was originally draped with rich tapestries and use for public hearings, receptions and celebrations.*

**★ Panch Mahal**
*A five-storeyed open sandstone pavilion, it overlooks the Pachisi Court, where Akbar's queens savoured the cool evening breezes. Its decorative screens were probably stolen after the city was abandoned.*

**VISITORS' CHECKLIST**

Agra district 47 km (23 miles) W of Agra. **Road map** D3.
**i** UPTDC, 64 Taj Rd, Agra, (0562) 36 0517. ◯ 7am–7pm daily. 🖼 free on Fri. 🎦 🖺

Jodha Bai's Palace    Maryam's House

Birbal's House

**★ Diwan-i-Khas**
*Perhaps a debating chamber, the real function of this unique structure is still unknown.*

**Ankh Michauli**
*Sometimes identified as the treasury, this building has mythical guardian beasts carved on its stone struts. Its name means "blind man's buff".*

**Pachisi Court** is named after a ludo-like game played here by the ladies of the harem.

**STAR FEATURES**

★ Diwan-i-Khas

★ Panch Mahal

★ Turkish Sultana's House

**PLAN OF FATEHPUR SIKRI**

Fatehpur Sikri's royal complex contains the private and public spaces of Akbar's court, which included the harem and the treasury. The adjoining sacred complex containing the Jami Masjid, Salim Chishti's tomb and the Buland Darwaza, are separated from the royal quarters by the Badshahi Darwaza, an exclusive royal gateway.

**KEY**

☐ Area illustrated above

☐ Other buildings

☐ Sacred complex (Jami Masjid)

# Exploring Fatehpur Sikri

**Detail of a carved panel**

THE PRINCIPAL BUILDINGS of the imperial palace complex, clustered on a series of terraces along the sandstone ridge, formed the core of Akbar's city. Stylistically, they marked the absorption of Gujarat into the Mughal Empire and reveal a successful synthesis of pre-Islamic Hindu and Jain architecture (as in the carved brackets) with the elegant domes and arches of Islamic buildings. The concentric terraces clearly divide the public spaces from the private royal quarters. The buildings, mostly in Akbar's favourite red sandstone, were quarried from the ridge on which they stand.

**Stone "tusks" at the Hiran Minar**

**Aerial view of Fatehpur Sikri**

EVEN TODAY, the access to the city that was Akbar's capital is provided by a straight road he built, then lined with exotic bazaars. It leads visitors through the Agra Gate to the triple-arched **Naubat Khana**, where the emperor's entry used to be announced by a roll of drums. The imperial palace complex is entered from the west through the Naubat Khana and opens into the spacious cloistered courtyard of the **Diwan-i-Aam**, where Akbar gave public audiences. A passage behind it leads into the so-called "inner citadel" which contains the **Diwan-i-Khas**, **Khwabgah**, **Anoop Talao**, the **Turkish Sultana's House**, the treasuries and the **Abdar Khana** where water and fruit for the royal house-hold were stored. In the great courtyard in front of the Diwan-i-Khas is the **Pachisi Court**, named after the open space in the centre which was

created to resemble the board of a traditional game similar to ludo. Legend has it that the emperor, seated on a platform, played *pachisi* here with the ladies of his harem.

The **Haram Sara**, or harem complex, was a maze of interconnected buildings beyond Maryam's House or **Sunehra Makan** ("golden house"), named after its rich frescoes and gilding. The massive and austere exterior of the harem leads to **Jodha Bai's Palace**, a large inner courtyard, surrounded by pavilions decorated with azure glazed tiles on the roof. A screened viaduct, presumably for privacy, connected the palace to the **Hawa Mahal** facing a small formal garden. The **Nagina Masjid**, adjoining the garden, was the royal ladies' private mosque. The two-storeyed pavilion popularly said to be

**Birbal's House**, situated to the east of Jodha Bai's palace, has spectacular carving on the exterior and interior of its unusual layout. Beyond this lies a large colonnaded enclosure surrounded by cells, meant probably for the servants of the harem, and the royal stables.

The **Hathi Pol** and **Sangin Burj**, the original gateways to the harem, lead to the outer-most periphery of the palace complex. This was laid out in concentric circles around the inner citadel and is made up of ancillary structures, such as the caravanserais, the domed *hamams* and waterworks. The **Hiran Minar** ("deer tower"), believed to be a memorial to Akbar's favourite elephant, was probably an *akash deep* ("heavenly light") with lamps suspended from stone "tusks" to guide visitors.

**Entrance to Birbal's House**

# Jami Masjid

**An inlaid panel**

THIS GRAND OPEN mosque towers over the city of Fatehpur Sikri and was the model for several Mughal mosques. Flanked by arched cloisters, its vast *namazgah* has monumental gates to the east and south. However, the spiritual focus of the complex is the tomb and hermitage of the Sufi mystic, Salim Chishti, as popular today as it was in the days of its Mughal patrons.

**Tomb of Sheikh Salim Chishti**
*Exquisite marble serpentine brackets and almost transparent screens surround the inner tomb which has a mother-of-pearl canopy inlaid with sandalwood.*

**Hujra**
*Symmetrically flanking the main mosque, this pair of identical cloistered prayer rooms has flat-roofed pillared galleries that run round the complex.*

**Badshahi Darwaza**
*Akbar used the steep steps of this royal gateway to enter the complex. The view of the sacred mosque directly across, greeted his entry.*

**Corridors**

**Buland Darwaza**
*Erected by Akbar, the huge 54 m (177 ft) gateway later inspired other lofty gates. Young boys dive from its ramparts into the pool below to fish for coins.*

## MAKING A WISH IN CHISHTI'S TOMB

Ever since Akbar's childlessness was ended by the remarkable prediction of Salim Chishti in 1568, the saint's tomb has become the haunt of those in search of a miracle. The *dargah*, lavishly endowed by both Akbar and his son Jahangir, attracts crowds of supplicants who make a wish, tie a small cotton thread on the screen around the tomb, and go back confident that the saint will make it come true.

**A thread tied to a screen in Chishti's tomb**

The strikingly ornamental façade of Gwalior Fort

## Gwalior ⑫

Gwalior district. 118km (73 miles) S of Agra on NH3. **Road map** D4. 🏯 1,500,000. 🚉 Platform 1, Railway Station (0751) 54 0777. 🚌 🚆 🎻 Tansen Music Festival (Oct–Nov).

THIS ROYAL SEAT of the Scindias is dominated by a massive hill **fort**. The interior owes some of its finest features to the Tomar musician-king, Man Singh (r.1486–1517). Near the ornate Hindola Gate, one of three gateways located near the old city, is the romantic Gujari Mahal (1510) built by Man Singh for his tribal wife, the beautiful Mrignayani, and it now houses the outstanding **Archaeological Museum**. His main palace, the Man

**Frieze in Gwalior fort**

Mandir, with an amazing variety of ornamental glazed tile patterns, is considered the most remarkable example of an early Hindu palace. In the city below the fort, the 19th-century Italian palazzo-style **Jai Vilas Palace** houses the Scindia Museum. Famous for a magnificent crystal staircase and furniture, its vast Durbar Hall has Venetian chandeliers that weigh three tons. A silver model train, laden with brandy and cigars, once used to serve guests at the spectacular royal feasts held here.

Other notable sights are the tombs of Tansen and Muhammad Ghaus, as well as early temples such as Teli ka Mandir *(see p24)* and the Sas-Bahu ka Mandir.

🏯 **Gwalior Fort**
⏱ 8am–6pm daily.

Son et Lumière daily 🎫
🏛 **Archaeological Museum**
⏱ 10am–5pm Tue–Sun. ● Mon & public hols. 🎫
🏯 **Jai Vilas Palace**
S of Fort. ⏱ 9:30am–5pm Tue–Sun.
● public hols. 🎫 🚫

**Datia Palace**

## Datia ⑬

Datia district. 187 km (116 miles) S of Agra. **Road map** D4. 🏯 380,000. 🚉 UPTDC, Hotel Veerangana, Shivpuri Rd, Jhansi (0517) 42 402. 🚌

THE MAIN FOCUS of this ghostly town is the five-storeyed Datia Palace, an outstanding building of great structural complexity. Built by the Bundela king Bir Singh Deo in 1620, its sinister underground chambers still exude an eerie ambience. The finely painted royal apartments within the main courtyard are connected to the galleries around them by double-storeyed bridges.

Another important building is the later Rajgarh Palace, which has a fine view of the entire walled town.

---

### GWALIOR GHARANA OF MUSIC

**Akbar, Tansen and Guru Ramdas**

The Gwalior Gharana is one of the oldest schools of North Indian classical music. Its greatest achievement was the adaptation of folk music into the orthodox Dhrupad mode, a contribution of Raja Man Singh and Mrignayani, whose tribal music wove a spell on the king. This form was given lively expression by Gwalior-born Tansen, Akbar's court musician, who developed a range of exciting new *ragas (see p28)*.

# A Tour of Bundelkhand ⑭

GWALIOR AND THE ADJOINING REGION of Bundelkhand, named after the Bundela Rajputs, make up a culturally distinctive area in Central India. Innumerable forts and monuments situated in a boulder-strewn landscape of great beauty still echo with stories of the valour and pageantry of the Bundela Rajput courts, and warriors such as the Rani of Jhansi. The area's glorious history and refined cultural traditions are reflected in the architectural treasures of Gwalior, the magical, medieval capital of Orchha, and the hilltop temples of Sonagiri.

**Gwalior** ①
The capital city of many great dynasties since its origins in the 1st century AD, Gwalior is the most splendid of the "gateways" to the Bundelkhand region.

**Pawaya** ②
The remains of an ancient fort can be seen in this capital of the Nag kings (3rd century AD) from the highway at Dabra

**Sonagiri** ③
This impeccably maintained complex of 77 Jain temples is approached through a thriving pilgrim settlement.

**Datia** ④
This erstwhile Bundela capital surrounded by numerous small lakes, has scenically located palaces on hillocks.

## KEY

▪ Tour route

〓 Other roads

≈ Rivers

| 0 kilometres | 20 |
|---|---|
| 0 miles | 10 |

**Orchha** ⑥
The temples, cenotaphs and tiered palaces here are perfect examples of Bundelkhand architecture (see pp176–7).

**Jhansi** ⑤
Best known for its impressive fort and the heroic Rani Laxmi Bai, who died leading her troops in the 1857 Indian Mutiny.

## TIPS FOR DRIVERS

**Length:** 120 km (75 miles).
**Stopping-off points:** Gwalior, Sonagiri, Datia, Jhansi, Taragram, Orchha. After Gwalior, there is a petrol pump at Dabra on NH3. Accommodation in the form of state tourism hotel and guesthouses is available at Gwalior, Jhansi and Orchha. Local buses run between the major stops.

**Taragram** ⑦
Its fascinating handmade paper factory is an interesting experimental centre aimed at upgrading local craftsmanship.

The 16th-century Chaturbhuj
Temple at Orchha

## Orchha ⑭

Tikamgarh district. 238 km (148 miles)
S of Agra. **Road map** E5. ⓘ *MPTDC,
Sheesh Mahal.* 🎭 *Ramnavami
(Mar–Apr), Dussehra (Sep–Oct).*

ORCHHA is dramatically
positioned on a rocky
island, enclosed by a loop of
the River Betwa. Founded in
1531, it was the capital of the
Bundela kings until 1738,
when it was abandoned in
favour of Tikamgarh.

Crumbling palaces,
pavilions, *hamams*, walls and
gates connected to the town
with an impressive 14-arched
causeway, are all that remain
today. Three main palaces,
**Raj Mahal** (1560), **Jahangiri
Mahal** (1626) and **Rai
Praveen Mahal** are massed
symmetrically together. Rai
Praveen Mahal was named
after a royal paramour and
Jahangiri Mahal after the
Mughal prince who spent a
mere night here.

There are three beautiful
temples in the old town, the
Ram Raja, the Chaturbhuj and
the Laxminarayan. A unique
blend of fort and temple
styles, the **Chaturbhuj
Temple**, dedicated to Vishnu,
has huge arcaded halls for
massed singing and a soaring
spire towering over the area.

Lying along the Kanchana
ghat of the Betwa are 14
hauntingly beautiful *chhatris*
of the Orchha rulers. Along
with the many *sati* pillars in
Jahangiri Mahal's museum,
these are reminders of
Orchha's feudal past when
*sati* queens jumped into their
husband's funeral pyres.

# Jahangiri Mahal

**Flower motif
in turquoise
stone**

NAMED AFTER the Mughal emperor
Jahangir who spent one night here
with his Bundela ally Bir Singh Deo, this
is an excellent example of Rajput Bundela
architecture. The many-layered palace has
132 chambers off and above the central
courtyard and an almost equal number of
subterranean rooms. The square sandstone palace is extravagantly embellished
with lapis lazuli tiles, graceful *chhatris* and ornate *jaali*
screens. The palace also has a modest museum.

**Chhatris**
*These give a delicate and
airy feel to the roofline of
the palace.*

**Carved niches** line
the outer walls.

**Entrance**

★ **Entrance Gateway**
*The impressively fringed entry
gate, flanked by stone elephants,
offers a good view of River Betwa.*

**STAR SIGHTS**

★ **Entrance Gateway**

★ **Screened Corridor**

## VISITORS' CHECKLIST

Palace Complex ☐ 8am–6pm
daily. ● public hols. ⓘ MPTDC,
Sheesh Mahal. 🖼 ☑ 🍴 📷
🚻 **Museum** ☐ 10am–6pm.

### ★ Screened Corridor

*A screened corridor runs round the fourth
level which has eight pavilions with lavishly
painted interiors, separated by courts.*

#### Glazed Tilework

*Geometric lapis motifs decorate the
outer façade at the upper levels.*

**Jahangir's
bedroom**

**Fortified bastions**
protect the palace.

**The central courtyard** can
be viewed from each part
of the palace and has a
small museum in a set of
rooms that run along it.

## PLAN OF ORCHHA

The fortified town of Orchha
encloses three major palaces
and ruined ancillary structures.

**1** Jahangiri Mahal
**2** Sheesh Mahal
**3** Raja Mahal
**4** Rai Praveen Mahal
**5** *Hamam*
**6** Stable

### KEY

☐ Area illustrated above

# JAIPUR AND ENVIRONS

THE JAIPUR REGION *of Rajasthan lies on the eastern fringes of the Thar Desert, a semi-arid land cut southwest to northeast by the craggy Aravalli Hills. Studded by hilltop and jungle forts, its valleys and plains glitter with palaces and pavilions, pleasure gardens and temples. Once ruled by proud Rajput princes, this territory is still sustained by memories of a feudal past that is kept alive by its splendid architectural remains and deep-rooted traditional culture.*

At the end of the 11th century, the Kachhawahas of Jaipur established their kingdom at Amber. In the region around it lay other Rajput kingdoms – the Chauhan stronghold of Ajmer that would soon fall to Muslim forces, and the massive Rathore jungle fort of Ranthambhore, which would later become a Mughal preserve. By the 18th century the fierce feudal lords of Shekhawati would become vassals of Amber-Jaipur, while Jat kings would rule over Bharatpur, the only non-Rajput kingdom in the area.

The early Rajput states engaged in bitter internecine clan wars, but with the rise of the Delhi sultans *(see pp50–51),* their energies were directed at keeping their lands safe from the marauding Muslim troops. Finally, under the Mughal emperor Akbar, military and matrimonial alliances paved the way for peace in the region. The result was a cultural and social synthesis which produced some outstanding art and architecture. The British also followed this policy of appeasement and offered the princes military protection in return for their loyalty. The rule of the princely states ended when, after Independence, they were incorporated into the modern Indian state of Rajasthan, with Jaipur as the administrative capital.

But despite democracy, the Rajput feudal tradition, with its code of loyalty to the local chieftain, and immense pride in their past, remains alive. This is perhaps what has preserved the extraordinary culture of the region, so that for many it still remains the romantic land of forts, palaces and kings it was in medieval times.

The sacred ghats at Pushkar attract crowds of devotees during Kartik Purnima in October–November

◁ Jaipur's signature building, the fanciful Hawa Mahal or "Palace of Winds"

# Exploring Jaipur and Environs

THIS HISTORICALLY RICH TERRITORY is centred around the old capital of Amber and the "newer" city of Jaipur with its palace, observatory, temples and bazaars and impressive modern buildings. To Jaipur's north are the attractive Samode palace and Shekhawati areas, while to its northeast is the wooded area of the Aravallis, where Alwar, a former princely state, and the Sariska National Park are situated. To the southwest, past the textile towns of Sanganer and Bagru, are the religious sites of Ajmer and Pushkar. Southeast of Jaipur lies Chaksu, a pilgrim centre, and the important medieval kingdom of Tonk, beyond which is the spectacular tiger sanctuary of Ranthambhore, nestling beneath the grand ramparts of a historic medieval fort.

**A roadside tea stall**

## KEY

| | |
|---|---|
| ■ | Major road |
| | Minor road |
| | River |
| ☀ | Viewpoint |

| | |
|---|---|
| 0 kilometres | 30 |
| 0 miles | 25 |

**Pushkar holds the world's largest cattle fair in October**

*Bikaner*

**SHEKHAWATI** ⑬ NH11

**SAMODE**

**CHOMU** ⑪

*Luni*

**MAKRANA** ⑮

**SAMBHAR SALT LAKE** ⑭

**JAIPUR**

**BAGRU** ④

**SANGA**

**PUSHKAR** ⑯ **KISHANGARH**

⑰ ⑱ **AJMER**

NH8

**BEAWAR**

*Udaipur*

**TON** ⑳

*Kota*

## SEE ALSO

- **Where to Stay** pp243–7
- **Where to Eat** pp261–3

## GETTING AROUND

Jaipur's airport is at Sanganer *(see p204)*, and two superfast trains (the Pink City Express and Shatabdi Express) connect the city to Delhi. Air-conditioned luxury coaches from Delhi to Jaipur are run by Rajasthan Tourism. The rest of the region is best explored by road. The Palace on Wheels *(see p295)*, a luxury rail tour through the region, is for the well-heeled tourist who wishes to savour the trip through the desert in royal comfort.

**A sacred tank at Galta**

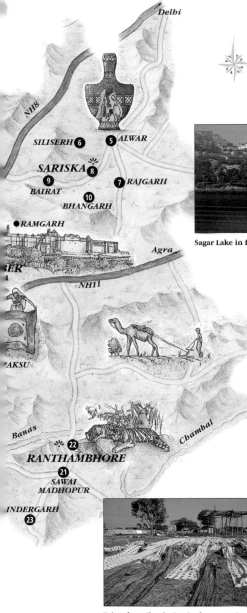

**Sagar Lake in front of Amber Fort**

## SIGHTS AT A GLANCE

**Printed textiles drying in the sun at Sanganer**

# Jaipur ●

**Stone guardian at Hawa Mahal**

**A** LABYRINTH OF fascinating bazaars, opulent palaces and historic sights, Jaipur offers a chance to see the medieval alongside the modern. On its colourful streets camels jostle for space with motorbikes, and turbaned village elders rub shoulders with youngsters in blue jeans. Often called the Pink City because its prominent buildings are washed with this colour, Jaipur's old walled area has the City Palace Museum, a medieval astronomical observatory and bazaars that sell everything from precious jewellery to camel skin shoes. Recent additions include a multi-arts centre, yet the city's focal point is still the myriad-windowed pink Hawa Mahal, the Palace of Winds.

**Govind Dev Temple, dedicated to Krishna**

## 🏛 City Palace Museum
*See pp188–91.*

## 🔱 Govind Dev Temple
Jaleb Chowk, behind City Palace.
⏱ *5–11am, 6–8pm daily.* 🎉 *Holi (Mar), Janmashtami (Jul–Aug), Annakut (Oct–Nov).*
The presiding deity of this unusual temple is the flute-playing Krishna (also known as Govind Dev). This image, originally from the Govindeoji Temple in Brindavan *(see p162)*, was brought to Amber in the late 17th century to save it from the iconoclastic zeal of Aurangzeb. It is believed that this temple was once a garden pavilion called Suraj Mahal where Sawai Jai Singh II lived while his dream-city Jaipur was being built. Legend has it that one night, the king awoke from his sleep to find himself in the presence of Krishna who demanded that his *devasthan*

("divine residence") be returned to him. Jai Singh then moved to the Chandra Mahal, at the opposite end of the garden, and installed the image as the guardian deity of Jaipur's rulers. Devotees are allowed only a brief glimpse of their god seven times a day, and on special festivals such as Janmashtami *(see p39)*.

## 🌺 Jai Niwas Bagh
⏱ *6am–10pm daily.*
Just behind the temple is the 18th-century Jai Niwas Bagh, planned as a private leisure

ground for the ladies of the royal household. Inspired by the classic Mughal *charbagh*, it has features such as water channels, fountains and neat flower-beds. Towards the north is the **Badal Mahal**, a five-arched hunting pavilion on the banks of the Talkatora. Its ceilings still bear faint traces of the cloud *(badal)* pattern in blue and white.

Railway station

MIRZA  ISMAIL  ROAD

ASHOK  MARG

SARDAR PATEL ROAD

BHAGWANDAS ROAD

MAHAVIR MARG

*Raj Mahal Palace*

CHANDPOL BAZAAR

KISHANPOL

INDIRA BAZAAR

NE

Nahar Fo

Statue Circle & Birla Planetarium

SANSAR CHANDRA ROAD

RAMSINGH ROAD

0 metres          500

0 yards          500

*Rambagh Palace*

Jawahar K & Sangane

**A view of the walled city of Jaipur**

### Talkatora

N of Jai Niwas Bagh. daily.

The Talkatora is an artificial tank that existed before Jaipur was built. This may have been one of the reasons why this site was chosen for the new city. When excavated, it was surrounded on three sides by a lake known as Rajamal ka Talab, making it look like a *tal-katora*, literally a "bowl in a lake". Sawai Jai Singh II was particularly fond of this rather secluded spot and used to breed crocodiles here. The original lake was later filled in and developed as a residential area.

### Chaugan Stadium

Brahmpuri. *5am–8pm daily.*

This large open area near the City Palace derives its name from *chaugan*, an ancient Persian form of polo played with a curved stick. In the past, this area was used for festival processions, wrestling matches, as well as elephant and lion fights. The maharajas and nobility watched from the pavilions of Chini ki Burj (which still retains some of the old blue and white tilework), Moti Burj, Chatar ki Burj and Shyam ki Burj, all located here. *Chaugan* is not played any more, but the stadium is the venue for the famous Elephant Festival held at the time of Holi *(see p38)*.

**VISITORS' CHECKLIST**

261 km (162 miles) from Delhi on NH8. *2,000,000.* *Sanganer.* *Sindhi Camp.* *RTDC, Hotel Swagatam Complex (0141) 20 2761. Paryatan Bhavan, MI Rd (0141) 37 0180.* *Mon–Sat.* *Gangaur (Mar–Apr), Elephant Festival (Feb–Mar), Teej (Jul-Aug), Kite Flying (mid-Jan).*

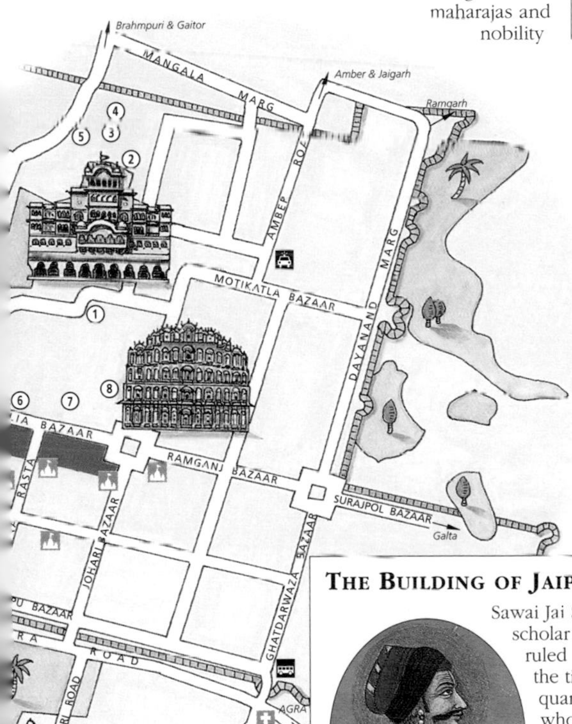
Brahmpuri & Gaitor
MANGALA MARG
Amber & Jaigarh
Ramgarh
AMBER ROAD
MOTIKATLA BAZAAR
DAYANAND MARG
RAMGANJ BAZAAR
SURAJPOL BAZAAR
Galta
JOHARI BAZAAR
GHATDARWAZA BAZAAR
ROAD
AGRA
Sisodia Bagh
NH8 BYPASS
MOTI DOONGRI ROAD
Museum of Indology & Moti Doongri
1
2
3
4
5
6
7
8

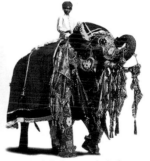

**Caparisoned elephant at a festival**

**KEY**

- Street-by-Street *See pp182–3*
- Bus stand
- Tourist information
- Post office
- Police
- Temple
- Church

### THE BUILDING OF JAIPUR

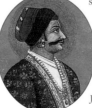

**Sawai Jai Singh II (r.1700–43)**

Sawai Jai Singh II, a brilliant statesman, scholar and patron of the arts who ruled for 40 years, was awarded the title of "Sawai" ("one-and-a-quarter"), a metaphor for one who is extraordinary, by Mughal emperor Aurangzeb when he was just 11 years old. Along with a talented Bengali scholar and engineer, Vidyadhar Chakravarty, Jai Singh supervised the building of a new capital south of Amber and named it Jaipur ("city of victory"). Work started in 1727 and took six years to complete. Surrounded by a crenellated wall pierced by seven gates, Jaipur is one of North India's finest examples of a planned urban city. Its grid of nine rectangular sectors, believed to represent the nine cosmic divisions of the universe, is actually based on a geometric and pragmatic plan with a system of main streets, intersected by spacious market squares. Jai Singh encouraged traders and artists to settle here, giving tax incentives to merchants to ensure its economic prosperity.

# Street-by-Street: Around Badi Chaupar

THE BADI CHAUPAR ("large square") is at one end of the colourful Tripolia Bazaar. There have been few changes to the original 18th-century plan of streets and squares. Narrow pedestrian lanes branch out of the main streets where artisans fashion puppets, silver jewellery, and other local crafts in tiny workshops. Behind are the *havelis* of eminent citizens, some used as schools, shops and offices. The area is a hub of activity, rich with pungent smells and vibrant colours, with temple bells adding to the cacophony of street sounds.

**Gangaur Festival**
*A colourful procession of bullock carts mark Gangaur festivities.*

**Ishwar Lat**
*Ishwari Singh built this tower in 1749 to commemorate his victory over his stepbrother, Madho Singh I.*

★ **Jantar Mantar**
*Jai Singh II's observatory of astronomical instruments looks like a set of futuristic sculptures (see pp192–3).*

City Palace

Tripolia Gate

TRIPOLIA

Chandpol

**Choti Chaupar** ("small square") leads to Kishanpol Bazaar, famous for its shops selling rose-, saffron-, almond- and vetiver-flavoured sherbets.

KISHANPOL BAZAAR

NATANIYON KA RASTA

MANIHARON KA RASTA

Maharaja Arts College

**Flower Sellers**
*Marigolds and other flowers made into garlands, sell briskly as offerings to beloved deities in temples and roadside shrines.*

**Lac Bangles**
*Maniharon ka Rasta is full of tiny workshops of lac bangle-makers.*

**★ Hawa Mahal**
*An unfamiliar rear view of the Hawa Mahal, seen from the City Palace.*

**★ Johari Bazaar**
*Vegetable sellers sit at one end of this street where the big gem dealers also have their offices and shops.*

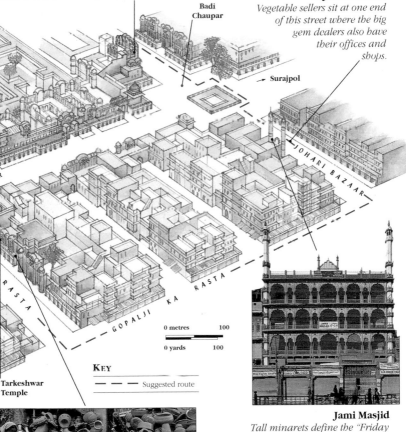

**Badi Chaupar**

→ **Surajpol**

JOHARI BAZAAR

GOPALJI KA RASTA

KA RASTA

AURA RASTA

ZAAR

| 0 metres | 100 |
|---|---|
| 0 yards | 100 |

**KEY**

— — — Suggested route

**Tarkeshwar Temple**

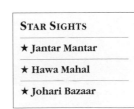

**Jami Masjid**
*Tall minarets define the "Friday Mosque", its three storeys fronted by an arched screen.*

**Pottery Shop**
*Large terracotta urns, pots of all sizes, bells, statues, foot-scrapers and oil lamps made by traditional craftsmen are sold here.*

**STAR SIGHTS**

★ Jantar Mantar

★ Hawa Mahal

★ Johari Bazaar

## 🕌 Hawa Mahal

Sireh Deori Bazaar. ☎ *(0141) 66 8862.* ⏲ *9am–4:30pm.* ● *Holi & public hols.* ▨ ⭘ *extra charges.* ▨

A whimsical addition to Rajasthan's rich architectural vocabulary, the fanciful Hawa Mahal or "Palace of Winds" was erected in 1799 by the aesthete Sawai Pratap Singh (r.1778–1803). Its ornate façade has become an icon for the city, a tiered baroque-like composition of projecting windows and balconies with perforated screens. Though five storeys high it is just one room deep, with walls no thicker than 20 cm (8 inches). Built of lime and mortar and painted pink, this structure was so designed to enable the purdahed ladies of the harem to watch unnoticed the colourful street scenes and state processions on Sireh Deori Bazaar below. Visitors are permitted to climb up the winding ramp to the top.

Pratap Singh was a poet, composer and patron of the arts. A devotee of Krishna, he dedicated the Hawa Mahal to him, and many believe that when seen from afar, the building looks like the *mukut* (crown) that often adorns Lord Krishna's head.

A gateway towards the west leads into the complex and to

**Façade of Hawa Mahal**

the administrative offices and **archaeological museum**.

## 🏛 Archaeological Museum

Tripolia Bazaar. ⏲ *9am–5pm.* ● *Fri & public hols.*

## 🕌 Tripolia Bazaar

To the south of the City Palace is one of the walled city's busiest streets and bazaars. The shops here mainly sell an enormous range of metal goods and kitchenware. The pavements outside the shops attractively display utensils in brass, copper, aluminium and

**Detail of a painted gate**

steel as well as crowbars, chisels and other assorted hardware. Sometimes, handicrafts, plastic and paper products, such as the traditional red cloth-bound *bahi khathas* (account books) still used by merchants and moneylenders, are also available. At Badi Chaupar, towards the end of the street, are flower-sellers with baskets full of fragrant roses, marigolds, tube-roses and jasmine, and shops selling silver jewellery, hand-embroidered *jootis* (slippers) and feather-light cotton quilts.

In the centre of this lively commercial artery stands the majestic Tripolia ("triple-arched") Gate. Constructed in 1734, this was once the main entrance to the palace and on festive occasions, crowds watched the royal entourage of the maharaja and his nobles *(thakurs)*, clad in ceremonial robes, seated on elephants and horses pass through this impressive gate. Today, its use is confined to members of the royal family and their special guests and a guard on duty reminds visitors that this is not a public thoroughfare.

A short distance from Tripolia Gate, towards the east, is the well-maintained **Nawab Saheb ki Haveli**, named after Nawab Faiz Ali Khan, Ram Singh II's *(see p194)* prime minister. This 18th-century mansion was once the residence of Vidyadhar Chakravarty, who is believed to have chosen this site to supervise the building of the new city of Jaipur. Its enclosed terrace offers some marvellous views of the city. Other *havelis* of eminent citizens can be seen in the narrow alleys off the main street. Some of these gracious old buildings are still occupied by descendants of the original owners, others have been rented out to schools, shops and offices.

## 🕌 Nawab Saheb ki Haveli

⏲ *10am–6pm daily.* ▨

**A view of Tripolia Gate with Ishwari Singh's victory tower seen in the distance**

# Jewellery

WHETHER IT BE the fabulous emeralds and rubies sported by former maharajas and their queens or the splendid silver and bone ornaments worn by peasants, jewellery is an integral part of Rajasthani culture. Even camels, horses and elephants have specially designed anklets and necklaces. Jaipur is one of the largest ornament-making centres in India, and *meenakari* (enamelling) and *kundankari* are two traditional techniques for which it is most famous. In the 16th century, Man Singh I *(see p49),* influenced by the prevailing fashions of the Mughal court, brought the first five Sikh enamel workers from Lahore to his state. Since then, generations of highly skilled jewellers have lived and worked here. Jaipur caters to every taste, from chunky silver ornaments to elegant designs intricately set in gold with precious stones.

**A *kundankari* pendant**

**A jewelled trinket box** *with a kundankari lid, the lower portion of this box is worked in fine meenakari and has traditional floral patterns in red, blue, green and white.*

**Sarpech**, *the cypress-shaped turban ornament, was a fashion statement introduced by the Mughal emperors in the early 17th century to display their finest gems. Rajput rulers, impressed by Mughal flamboyance, sported dazzling ornaments like this piece of enamelled gold set with emeralds, rubies, diamonds and sapphires with a pearl drop*

**The skill of setting stones** *can be seen in the crowded alleys of Haldiyon ka Raasta, Jadiyon ka Raasta and Gopalji ka Raasta. An inherited art, the trade of jewellery is in the hands of artisans' guilds.*

**Meenakari** *embellishes the obverse side of kundan jewellery, for the Rajasthani love of adornment decrees that even the non-visible back of a piece of jewellery, which touches the wearer's skin, must be as beautiful as the front.*

**Kundankari** *uses a highly refined gold as the base, which is then inlaid with lac and set with precious and semi-precious stones to provide the colour and design. Purified gold wire outlines the design and also conceals the lac background.*

**Jaipur** *is now a centre of lapidary, specializing in the cutting of emeralds and diamonds that come from Africa, South America, and parts of India. Gem-cutters learn their skill by cutting garnets.*

# City Palace Museum

**Jaipur's coat-of-arms**

OCCUPYING THE HEART of Jai Singh II's city, the City Palace has been home to the rulers of Jaipur since the first half of the 18th century. The sprawling complex is a superb blend of Rajput and Mughal architecture, with open, airy Mughal-style public buildings leading to private apartments. The opulence and exquisite craftsmanship is a tribute both to the wealth of the former maharajas and their lavish patronage of the arts. Today, part of the complex is open to the public as the Maharaja Sawai Man Singh II Museum, popularly known as the City Palace Museum, but the beautiful Chandra Mahal remains the residence of the erstwhile maharaja.

★ **Pritam Chowk**
*The "Court of the Beloved" has four delicately painted doorways representing the seasons.*

**Sileh Khana**
*The erstwhile armoury houses the museum's collection of weapons, some lavishly decorated, and is considered among the finest in India.*

**Crafts demonstration area**

★ **Mubarak Mahal**
*This sandstone "Welcome Palace" was built in 1900 by Madho Singh II to receive guests, hence the name. It is now the costume and textile gallery.*

★ **Rajendra Pol**
*Flanking the gateway are two huge elephants, each carved from a single block of marble.*

**STAR FEATURES**

★ **Pritam Chowk**

★ **Mubarak Mahal**

★ **Rajendra Pol**

★ **Silver Urns**

### Chandra Mahal

*Each floor of this seven-storeyed palace is extravagantly decorated and has a specific name according to its function. The palace is closed to the public.*

**Riddhi-Siddhi Pol**

### ★ Silver Urns

*Two giant silver urns in the Diwan-i-Khas, listed in the Guinness Book as the largest silver objects in the world, carried sacred Ganges water for Madho Singh II's visit to London in 1901.*

**Shops**

**Transport gallery**

**Entrance**     **Ticket counter**

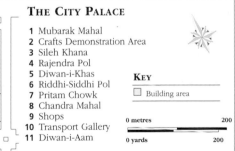

### Diwan-i-Aam

*In the Art Gallery is this "golden throne" (Takth-e-Rawan) on which the maharaja sat when he appeared in public. It was either put on an elephant's back or carried by palanquin bearers.*

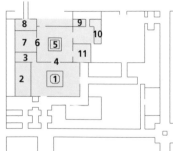

### THE CITY PALACE

1 Mubarak Mahal
2 Crafts Demonstration Area
3 Sileh Khana
4 Rajendra Pol
5 Diwan-i-Khas
6 Riddhi-Siddhi Pol
7 Pritam Chowk
8 Chandra Mahal
9 Shops
10 Transport Gallery
11 Diwan-i-Aam

**KEY**

☐ Building area

0 metres               200

0 yards                200

# Exploring the City Palace Museum

THE MAHARAJA SAWAI MAN SINGH II Museum provides a splendid introduction to the arts and crafts and the courtly pomp and ceremony of Jaipur in the old days. In their long reign, which spanned almost a thousand years, the Kachhawaha rulers amassed a fabulous collection of treasures – rare manuscripts, miniature paintings, carpets, textiles, costumes and weaponry, palanquins and chariots. These are some of the royal and historical memorabilia displayed here. Initially a private collection open only to select visitors and dignitaries, in 1959 it was formally declared a state museum that is open to the public.

Jahangir's archery ring

A detail of a gold-embroidered skirt belonging to one of the queens

## TEXTILES AND COSTUMES GALLERY

A GLITTERING COLLECTION of textiles and costumes from the royal *toshakhana* is displayed on the first floor of **Mubarak Mahal**. On view are rich, gorgeous brocades, known as *kimkhabs*, from Surat, Aurangabad and Varanasi, exquisitely embroidered and handloom-woven shawls from Kashmir, embroidered silks, embossed velvets and light, gossamer muslins typical of Dhaka (today in Bangladesh), which collectively represent India's great textile tradition. The expert and refined craftsmanship that existed in Jaipur almost three centuries ago is visible in the wide variety of hand blockprinted textiles from nearby Sanganer and tie-and-dye *(bandhini)* pieces specially produced by the printers and dyers from the palace workshops. Equally breathtaking is the

**A tissue *ghaghara*, early 20th century**

incredible range of well-preserved royal garments. Dazzling gathered skirts and long, flowing veils *(odhnis)*, decorated with delicate *zari* (gold thread embroidery) and *gota* (gold or silver frill), worn by the ladies of the court, vie for attention with the brocaded robes, waist-bands *(patkas)*, pyjamas and turbans that comprised the male attire. The most striking of these royal robes is the enormous pale pink *atamsukh* ("comfort of the soul") of Sawai Madho Singh I (r.1750–68), who was 2 m (7 ft) tall and 1.23 m (4 ft) in girth, and weighed about 230 kg (500 lbs)! This long, quilted cloak-like robe, worn usually by men in winter, is embossed with gold work.

Other exhibits include a range of royal paraphernalia including rich tent hangings, curtains, carriage and dish covers dating back to the 17th century. Among these is a rare gold brocaded velvet throne cover bearing seal marks that date to 1605, and an intricately woven gold and silk circular *thal-posh* (dish-cover).

The lattice screens that run round the balcony here once enabled royal ladies to view the hall without being seen.

## ART GALLERY

THE DIWAN-I-AAM or Sabha Niwas, built on a raised, pillared platform, was once used by the maharajas for formal durbars, ceremonies and receptions. This has now been converted into an art gallery, displaying some of the museum's greatest treasures. Exhibits include an excellent collection of 17th-century Mughal and Indo-Persian floral carpets, woven in Lahore, Herat and Agra during the reign of Emperor Shah Jahan. Also displayed here are the maharajas' valuable and fine collection of miniatures from the late Mughal, Rajput and Deccani courts, depicting both religious and secular themes. Some of the treasures include *Krishna Playing Holi* (Amber-Jaipur, 1737), *Lord Krishna's Cosmic Dance* (Jaipur, late 18th century), *Allah-Wirdi Khan with Attendants in a Garden* (Deccan, early 18th century), *Madho Singh I on a Boat* (Jaipur, 18th century) and *Nari Kunjar* (Jaipur, 18th century), an unusual compostion of female figures entwined imaginatively to

**One of the rare Mughal miniatures in the Art Gallery**

create an elephant. There is also a large selection of *Ragamala* and *Baramasa* sets depicting the seasons, as well as some superb paintings from Kishangarh *(see p215)* by Nihal Chand.

This gallery also has rare palm leaf manuscripts and books bound with painted wood covers, and scrolls of religious texts. Of particular interest are the two priceless Persian manuscripts of the Hindu epics, the *Ramayana* and the *Mahabharata*. The latter, known as *Razmnama*, was specially prepared, at huge cost, for Emperor Akbar by Abu'l Fazl, his biographer, and profusely illustrated by his court painters. Sadly, this unique manuscript is never displayed. Sawai Jai Singh II's large personal collection of astronomical books in Arabic, Persian, Latin and Sanskrit, which formed the basis for his study and understanding of the movement of the planets, is also kept in the art gallery.

Other interesting items are an ivory howdah, a silver mobile throne and a selection of old cameras and black and white prints dating to the reign of Ram Singh II (1835–80), a versatile ruler and passionate photographer.

Manuscript of the *Geet Govinda* in the Art Gallery

## ARMS GALLERY

THIS GALLERY known as the Sileh Khana is located near the Mubarak Mahal. Some of the exhibits, displayed under exuberantly painted ceilings, are reputed to be the finest examples of weapons used in medieval India and are a tribute to the Rajput warrior's worship of arms. Whether specially commissioned, or acquired by the maharajas, the weapons in the royal armoury were both lethal and exquisitely crafted. On view are a range of swords, daggers and *katars*, a two-sided blade with a grip handle. Some are of green or white jade and are carved, while others are studded with jewels. Hilts are engraved with hunting

**Diamond-studded dagger with pistols**

**Emperor Akbar's helmet**

scenes, images of gods and goddesses, or topped with the heads of exotic birds and animals. Among the swords on display is one belonging to Raja Man Singh I (r.1590–1619) weighing about 5 kg (11 lbs). Another, made by Abdullah Islahani, bears the emblem of the Shah of Persia. There are two swords of Jahangir and Shah Jahan and also Akbar's gold-encrusted helmet, shaped like a turban. A fascinating section displays gunpowder containers, some made of ivory, others decorated with mother-of-pearl inlay on shell.

The gallery's collection of horrors contains such gut-wrenching exhibits as a lotus-shaped steel mace belonging to Jai Singh I. When rammed into the enemy's stomach, it would spring into a deadly fan of sharp spikes and disembowel the victim.

## TRANSPORT GALLERY

A COMPARATIVELY recent addition is the Transport Gallery situated near the Art Gallery. It exhibits a selection of palanquins, chariots, *ikkas*, buggies and carriages from the old Buggi Khana which fell into disuse after the motor car became popular with the maharajas. Don't miss the gigantic Indra Vamaa carriage, which used to be pulled by four elephants. Until they were installed here, they were used only for ceremonial occasions. Now they conjure up some of the pomp of a bygone era.

**Fragment of a 16th-century Persian carpet**

# Jantar Mantar

**Kantivrita Yantra**

O F THE FIVE OBSERVATORIES built by Sawai Jai Singh II, the one in Jaipur is the largest and best preserved; the others are in Delhi *(see p77)*, Ujjain, Mathura and Varanasi. A keen astronomer himself, Jai Singh was aware of the latest astronomical studies in the world, and was most inspired by the work of Mirza Ulugh Beg, the astronomer-king of Samarkand. Built between 1728 and 1734, this observatory resembles a giant sculptural composition of 16 instruments and has been described as "the most realistic and logical landscape in stone". Some of the instruments are still used to forecast how hot the summer months will be, the expected date of arrival, duration and intensity of the monsoon, and the possibility of floods and famine.

**Narivalaya Yantra**
*Inclined at 27°, these represent the two hemispheres and are sundials that calculate time by following the solar cycle.*

**Laghu Samrat Yantra**
*This "small sundial" is constructed on Latitude 27° North (Jaipur's latitude) and calculates Jaipur's local time up to an accuracy of 20 seconds.*

**Unnatansha Yantra** was used to determine the positions of stars and planets at any time of day or night.

**City Palace Museum**

**Entrance**

**Chakra Yantra**
*A brass tube passes through the centre of two circular metal instruments through which the angle of stars and planets from the equator can be observed.*

**★ Ram Yantra**
*Vertical columns support an equal number of horizontal slabs in two identical stone structures that comprise this instrument. The readings from these determine the celestial arc from horizon to zenith as well as the altitude of the sun.*

**Jantar Mantar**
*The complex of stone and metal instruments was repaired with the addition of marble inlay by Madho Singh II in 1901.*

**★ Samrat Yantra**
*Jai Singh believed that gigantic instruments would give more accurate results. This 23-m (75-ft) high sundial forecasts the crop prospects for the year.*

Hawa Mahal

**Rashivalaya Yantra**
*This is composed of 12 pieces, each of which represents a sign of the zodiac and so faces a different angle and constellation. This yantra, used by astrologers to make accurate horoscopes, is only available here.*

**★ Jai Prakash Yantra**
*Two sunken hemispheres map out the heavens. This instrument is believed by some historians to have been invented by Jai Singh himself to verify the accuracy of all the others in the observatory.*

**STAR FEATURES**

★ Ram Yantra

★ Samrat Yantra

★ Jai Prakash Yantra

# South of the Walled City

*Jaali* detail

By THE END OF THE 19TH CENTURY, Jaipur had spread far beyond the boundaries established by Sawai Jai Singh II. Much of the area outside the walled city was developed by the enlightened ruler, Sawai Ram Singh II (r.1835–80). This competent administrator also modernized the city by adding many civic amenities such as good roads, street lighting and running water. As Jaipur expanded, it incorporated the pleasure palaces and hunting lodges existing on its outskirts. The still-gracious city we see today is a harmonious blend of the old and the new.

**The Indo-Saracenic style Government Central Museum (Albert Hall)**

## 🏛 Government Central Museum

Ram Niwas Bagh. 🔲 *(0141) 56 5124.*
🔲 *10am–4:30pm Sat–Thur.*
🔲 *Fri & public hols.* 🔲 *free on Mon.*
Designed by Sir Samuel Swinton Jacob, Albert Hall or the Government Central Museum was commissioned by Sawai Ram Singh II to honour the visit of Albert, the Prince of Wales, in 1876. Swinton Jacob had perfected the Indo-Saracenic style of architecture *(see p25)*, a hybrid form that combined modern European with traditional Indian elements to create a highly ornamental style used for many public buildings during the Raj.

This grand multi-layered building, with its domes, parapets and balustrades, is located in the centre of the Ram Niwas Gardens. Its ground floor displays decorative shields and embossed salvers in Jaipur's famed metalware, life-sized models of rural scenes, good examples of Jaipur's glazed pottery, and even an Egyptian mummy. A 30-ft (9-m) long *phad* (painted cloth scroll), depicts the life of Pabuji, a 14th-century Rajasthani folk hero. The first floor has a fine collection of Mughal and Rajput miniature paintings.

The museum's greatest treasure, one of the world's largest Persian garden carpets (1632) housed in the Durbar Hall, can be seen on request.

## 🏛 Museum of Indology

Nilambara, Prachaya Vidya Path, 24 Gangwal Park. 🔲 *(0141) 60 7455.*
🔲 *10am–5pm, daily.* 🔲 🔲 🔲
The large mansion of the reputed scholar, Acharya RC Sharma "Vyakul", is now home to a privately owned museum that displays his unusual personal collection. Among the exhibits are impressive displays of maps and coins, manuscripts, textiles and jewellery, fossils, gems and clocks. The museum's

charm, however, lies in its idiosyncrasies, such as a map of India painted on a grain of rice, a copy of Rajasthan's oldest newspaper (1856), and letters written, incredibly, on a single strand of hair.

## 🏛 Moti Doongri

Jawaharlal Nehru Marg.
🔲 *to the public.*
Moti Doongri owes its florid exterior to Sawai Man Singh II who converted the old fort of Shankargarh into a palace, and added turrets in the style of a Scottish castle. In 1940 he married the beautiful Princess Gayatri Devi of Cooch Behar, and this palace with its modernized interior became the venue for glittering parties hosted by the glamorous couple for their wide circle of friends. After his death in 1970, the maharani, by then a Member of Parliament, lived here for some years to keep in touch with her constituency. The palace, a private property, is perched on a low hillock, with only its ramparts and the tall spire of an ancient Shiva temple visible from the road.

At the foot of Moti Doongri is the white marble **Lakshmi Narayan Temple**. This generously endowed building was erected in 1979 on a piece of land sold by the Jaipur royal family for a token sum to the Birlas, an important industrial family. Though the sale was disputed and created a huge uproar in the local press, the temple is now a popular place of worship, admired for its carvings.

**Lakshmi Narayan Temple, a white marble addition to the Pink City**

**The luxurious interior of Rambagh Palace**

### ♨ Statue Circle
Bhagwan Das Rd.
This popular landmark is a traffic roundabout, circling an imposing white marble statue of Sawai Jai Singh II, commissioned by the Sawai Jai Singh Benevolent Trust. It was installed in 1968 and is now a lunch-time recreational spot for office workers and for evening joggers.

Facing the statue to the left is the **Birla Planetarium**. The complex comprises two modern buildings: the science museum with an auditorium, and the planetarium. The main entrance of the building is a replica of Amber Fort's Ganesh Pol *(see pp200–201)*. Exhibitions and sales of Rajasthani handicrafts are held here periodically.

### 🏛 Birla Planetarium
Statue Circle, Prithviraj Rd.
◯ *10am–8pm daily.* 【 *(0141) 38 1594.* 📷 🚫

### ♨ Rambagh Palace
Bhawani Singh Rd. 【 *(0141) 38 1919.* 🍽 *open to non-residents.*
The Rambagh Palace, now a splendid hotel, has had a colourful past. From its modest origins in 1835 as a small, four-roomed garden pavilion for Ram Singh II's wet nurse, it was used as a hunting lodge after she died in 1856. Later, when Ram Singh II's son, Madho Singh II returned from England, he transformed it with the help of Swinton Jacob into a royal

playground with squash and tennis courts, a polo field and indoor swimming pool. In 1933 it was selected as the official residence of Madho Singh's adopted son and heir, Man Singh II, who invited Hammonds of London to re-do the interiors, adding an exotic red and gold Chinese room, black marble bathrooms and fabulous Lalique crystal chandeliers, fountains and an illuminated dining table. Surrounded by fairy-tale gardens, this was the perfect setting for Man Singh and his lovely wife. Rambagh became the official residence of the Head of State of the new Rajasthan Union in 1949, and a hotel in 1957.

**Statue of Sawai Jai Singh II**

### ♨ Raj Mahal Palace
Sardar Patel Marg. 【 *(0141) 38 1757.* 🍽 *open to non-residents.*
Now a grand heritage hotel, this pleasant 18th-century palace, less opulent than the Rambagh Palace, occupies a

special place in the history of Jaipur. Built in 1729 for Man Singh I's favourite queen, Chandra Kumari Ranawatji, it was used as a summer resort by the ladies of the court. In 1821, it was then declared the official home of the British Resident in Jaipur. However, the most glamorous and memorable phase of its colourful history dates to the time when Man Singh II and Gayatri Devi moved here from Rambagh Palace in 1956. Among the celebrities they entertained were Prince Philip, a polo player like Man Singh, and Jackie Kennedy.

**Jawahar Kala Kendra**

### 🏛 Jawahar Kala Kendra
Jawaharlal Nehru Marg. 【 *(0141) 51 0501.* ◯ *10am–5pm.* 📷 🚻
Designed by Indian architect Charles Correa in 1993, this remarkable building offers tribute to contemporary Indian design. Imaginatively patterned after the famous grid system of the city, each of the nine squares or courts houses a *mahal* named after a planet. Each *mahal* displays selected exhibits of textiles, handicrafts and weaponry, while in the centre there is a grand open air plaza where performances of traditional Rajasthani music and dance are held.

---

### POLO – THE GAME OF KINGS

Polo, said to be Central Asian in origin, was brought to India by the Muslim conquerors. Its requirement of superior cavalry skills made it a popular sport among Rajput royalty and the army. Man Singh II was a dashing polo player and formed the Jaipur polo team and club in the 1930s. Ironically, he died in England in 1970, playing the game he loved so well. Jaipur is still a well-known venue, and international celebrities such as Prince Philip and Prince Charles have played polo here.

**Playing polo requires skill and speed**

# Beyond Jaipur: East

**Wall painting**

ENCLOSING A NARROW VALLEY, a parallel range of hills runs along Jaipur's eastern periphery from Sanganer in the south up to Amber and beyond. This combination of rocky terrain and thickly wooded slopes provided an attractive environment for the rulers and nobility who built temples, garden pavilions and palaces here for themselves. The area is also known for its wildlife, particularly monkeys, after whom the valley is fittingly named the Valley of Monkeys.

**One of Galta's sacred tanks**

### 🛕 Galta

10 km (6 miles) E of Jaipur on Agra Rd.

The picturesque Galta gorge plunges down the hillside to join the Jaipur-Agra road. A great sage, called Galav, is supposed to have lived and performed penance here. Deep within the gorge is Galta Kund, an 18th-century religious site with two main temples dedicated to Ram and Vishnu; the Achariyon ki Haveli; and a number of smaller shrines and now derelict buildings. High on the ridge is the Surya Temple. At different levels are seven sacred tanks, fed throughout the year by natural spring water flowing from a rock resembling a cow's mouth. The water is said to have curative powers. The two *baradaris* on either side of the complex have fairly well preserved frescoes depicting legends from Krishna's life, including a ceiling profusely painted with gorgeous lotus blooms. From the summit there are spectacular views of Jaipur, but do beware of monkeys in search of food.

### 🌺 Sisodia Rani ka Bagh

Purana Ghat. 6 km (4 miles) E of Jaipur on Agra Rd. ☎ (0141) 64 0594. ⭕ 8am–6pm daily. 📷

This terraced garden was laid out in the 18th century for Sawai Jai Singh II's second wife, a Sisodia princess from Udaipur. The marriage was one of convenience to foster better relations between the two powerful princely states, and one of the conditions was that the new queen's son would succeed to the Jaipur throne. To escape the ensuing and inevitable palace intrigues, the queen decided to shift to a more private home outside the walled city.

Her little double-storeyed palace is surrounded by beautiful gardens artfully planted with fragrant bushes of jasmine, where peacocks dance amid the spray of fountains and gurgling water channels. The interiors are decorated with lively murals depicting episodes from Krishna's life, hunting scenes and polo matches, mythical beasts and heroic events. Not

surprisingly, this enchanting place has become a popular location for Indian films.

**ENVIRONS:** Opposite Sisodia Rani ka Bagh is **Vidyadhar ka Bagh**, a small and once beautiful 18th-century garden dedicated to the courtier traditionally credited with designing Jaipur *(see p183).*

### 🛕 Ghat ke Balaji

1 km (4 miles) N of Sisodia Rani ka Bagh towards Galta.

Behind Sisodia gardens a double flight of steps ends in a pair of tall gateways leading to a small temple dedicated to the monkey-god Hanuman (also known as Balaji). This endearing deity is cherished by the local people who treat him with tender care, and in winter wrap his image in a muffler and quilt to keep him warm. The monkeys that inhabit the area are equally well looked after. Every evening at 4pm, a charming ritual takes place when, to the call of the priests, hordes of silver grey langurs with black faces and long tails descend on the temple for a meal specially cooked for them. Then, swishing their tails, they head back to the valley that bears their name.

### 🛕 Ghat ki Guni

6 km (4 miles) E of Jaipur on Agra Rd.

In the 18th and 19th centuries the ministers and dignitaries of the Jaipur court created a tranquil summer retreat in this valley, when the area would bustle with the constant to and fro of aristocracy. Now, the deserted *havelis*, temples

**Sisodia Rani ka Bagh was laid out as a formal Mughal *charbagh***

**Elegant *chhatris* of deserted buildings line the Ghat ki Guni road**

and bathing ghats are all that remain of this once exclusive resort. On either side of the road today, are dense rows of niched façades perforated by tiny windows and arched *chhatris*, elegant eaves and domes, while among the ruins and winding alleys, a number of tea-stalls and little shops selling trinkets and souvenirs have sprung up.

### ♨ Ramgarh

40 km (25 miles) E of Jaipur.
Ramgarh, on the banks of a man-made lake, is the site of one of the earliest fortresses of the Kachhawahas. It was built by the dynasty's founder, Duleh Rai (r.1093–1135), after he defeated the local Meenas by attacking them on a Diwali night when they were for-bidden to carry weapons. A temple dedicated to the goddess Jamvai Mata, whose divine intervention is said to have led to his victory, was also constructed by him. This temple is visited by thousands of devotees all through the year. The lake itself was created in the late 19th century when Sir Samuel Swinton Jacob planned the con-struction of a dam across the Banganga River, and was, until recently, Jaipur's main source of drinking water. On its northern bank is Ramgarh Lodge, an elegant French villa-style hunting lodge built in 1931 for the Jaipur royal family, and now a pleasing heritage hotel. Ramgarh is a tranquil retreat for those who wish to escape from the city. Its Polo Club is among one of the best in the country for polo lovers.

**The man-made Ramgarh Lake**

## HANUMAN – THE MONKEY GOD

**Hanuman statue**

A much loved figure in the pantheon of Hindu gods *(see pp22–3)*, Hanuman appears wherever Rama is worshipped. In the *Ramayana (see p37)*, this loyal trooper and his monkey army play a crucial role in the defeat of Ravana and the rescue of Sita. To this day, warriors, acrobats and wrestlers regard him as their patron deity. The cult of Hanuman as a martial god and protector is so widespread that even a simple stone daubed with orange vermilion paste *(sindur)* signals his presence.

Yet, he has another more loveable side which widens the circle of his devotees. They believe this fearless warrior, who set Lanka afire and decimated Ravana's army, is ignorant of his own miraculous powers. Not only can he cure disease and exorcise evil spirits; he can cure infertility because his celibacy gives him that power. Others believe he also knows the secrets of yoga and the finer points of music and Sanskrit grammar. By combining the might of a martial god with the endearing qualities of the monkey he resembles, Hanuman becomes a link between warrior princes and simple peasants.

# Beyond Jaipur: North

TOWERING ABOVE JAIPUR are the two dramatic fortresses of Nahargarh and Jaigarh that guard the approach from the north to both Amber and the new capital of Jaipur. Today, they recall a bygone age when warrior clans fought for supremacy. The surrounding rocky terrain also has the remains of fortified walls, temples and shrines, *havelis* and the ornate

**Mural motif**  marble cenotaphs of the Kachhawaha kings.

## 🏯 Nahargarh

9 km (5 miles) NW of Jaipur on Amber Rd. 📞 *(0141) 32 0538.* 🕐 *9am–4:30pm daily.* ● *public hols.* 📷 🚻 ⚟

The forbidding hill-top fort of Nahargarh ("tiger fort") stands in what was once a densely forested area. The fierce Meena tribe ruled this region until they were defeated by the Kachhawahas. Legend says that this was the site of the cenotaph of Nahar Singh, a martyred Rathore warrior, and when Sawai Jai Singh II ordered that its fortifications be strengthened to defend the newly-built Jaipur, the warrior's spirit resisted all construction until a priest performed tantric rites. Successive rulers further expanded the fort. Madho Singh II added a lavish palace called Madhavendra Bhavan for his nine queens. Laid out in a maze of terraces and courtyards, it has a cool, airy upper chamber from which the ladies of the court could view the city. Its walls and pillars are an outstanding example of *arayish*, a plaster-work technique that is hand-polished with a piece of agate to produce a marble finish.

## 🏯 Pundarik ki Haveli

Shastri Chowk, Brahmpuri. 📞 *(0141) 32 1534.* 🕐 *8am–5:30pm daily.* 🚻 ⊘

Lying to the east of Nahargarh, on the way to Gaitor, is the Brahmpuri area where the grand *havelis* of the pundits and scholars of the Jaipur court once stood. One mansion was the residence of Pandit Ratnakar Pundarik, a Brahmin courtier during the reign of Sawai Jai Singh II who, it is said, conducted the *puja* that appeased the spirit of Nahar Singh. Fortunately, this *haveli* has survived the ravages of time and is partly occupied. A portion is now a protected monument to preserve the superb frescoes decorating the walls and ceilings of the living rooms. These lively paintings depict gods and goddesses, courtly scenes and festival processions. One also portrays life on the different floors of the seven-storeyed Chandra Mahal *(see pp188–9)*.

## 🏯 Gaitor

Brahmpuri. 🕐 *9am–4:30pm.* ● *public hols.*

The marble cenotaphs of the Kachhawaha kings are enclosed in a walled garden just below Nahargarh Fort. Sawai Jai Singh II chose this to be the new cremation site after Amber was abandoned *(see p203)*. Ornate, carved pillars support the marble *chhatris* erected over the platforms where the maharajas were cremated. One of the most impressive cenotaphs is that of Jai Singh II himself. It has 20 marble pillars, carved with mythological scenes and

**Maharani ki Chhatri**

One of the exquisite, well preserved murals at Pundarik ki Haveli

**The picturesque Jal Mahal seemingly afloat in the monsoon**

topped by a white marble dome. Another is that of Sawai Ram Singh II, whose stone pillars and dome panels are carved with images of Hindu deities and scenes from Krishna's life. There is another sandstone and marble *chhatri* in memory of Madho Singh II. The most recent cenotaph was erected in 1997 in memory of Jagat Singh, the only son of Sawai Man Singh II and Gayatri Devi.

**ENVIRONS**: The *chhatris* of the official wives of the Jaipur kings are located in a separate enclosure called **Maharani ki Chhatri**, outside the Jorawar Singh Gate of the walled city, on the road to Amber. Set in a pleasant garden, the complex with its cupolas and carved pillars was restored in 1995.

### ♜ Maharani ki Chhatri
Amber Rd. ☐ *9am–4:30pm daily.*
● *public hols.* 🎫

### ♜ Jal Mahal
Amber Rd, opp Trident Hotel.
☐ *restricted entry.*
During the monsoon when water fills the Man Sagar, the Jal Mahal or "water palace" rises like a mirage from the calm waters of the lake. Built in the mid-18th century by Madho Singh I, it was based on the Lake Palace at Udaipur where the king spent his childhood. Later it was used as a lodge for duck shooting parties, and even today, a large number of waterbirds can be sighted here. A terrace garden is enclosed by arched passages, and at each corner is a semi-octagonal tower capped by an elegant cupola.

**ENVIRONS**: Sawai Jai Singh II performed a number of Vedic *yagnas* on the western banks of Man Sagar. Dating to that period are traces of a **Yagna Stambha** ("pillar") where he performed a horse sacrifice, and the **Kala Hanumanji**, a temple dedicated to the well-known monkey god.

To the north of Jal Mahal is the splendidly restored **Kanak Vrindavan Temple** dedicated to Krishna where the image of Govind Dev *(see p182)* was lodged before it was taken to the City Palace. This picturesque complex with its well-landscaped gardens, fountains and pavilions makes a popular picnic spot.

### ♜ Jaigarh
Amber Rd. ⒸⒸⒸ *(0141) 63 0848.*
☐ *9am–5pm daily.* ● *public hols.* 🎫
Legendary Jaigarh, the "victory fort", watches over the old capital of Amber, its great, crenellated outer walls delineating the edge of a sharp ridge for 3 km (2 miles)

from north to south. Located within the fort is one of the world's few surviving cannon foundries. Its most prized possession is the monumental Jai Van, cast in 1726 and believed to be the world's largest cannon on wheels. Its 6-m (20-ft) long barrel has fine carvings of elephants, birds and flowers. Ironically, despite its impressive size, the cannon remained a work of art and was never fired.

An interesting sight is the massive Diva Burj, a tower on whose uppermost seventh storey a huge oil lamp would be lit on the king's birthday and during Diwali, until the top two storeys were struck down by lightning. The fort has two temples and a large palace complex built over 200 years by different rulers. Located here are the Subhat Niwas (audience hall), the profusely painted Aram Mandir (an airy pleasure pavilion), the residential Laxmi Niwas with baths, and a small theatre for music, dance and puppet shows. The fort's intricate system of collecting and storing rainwater in huge tanks located in the courtyard is unique. Legend has it that Man Singh I's vast treasure, amassed during his military campaigns, was hidden within these tanks. In 1976, the government carried out a massive but unsuccessful hunt, even to the extent of draining the water tanks to locate this legendary trove.

**The famous Jai Van**

**The ramparts of Jaigarh Fort are a feat of military engineering**

# Amber Fort ②

**Detail of door at Shila Devi**

T HE FORT PALACE OF AMBER WAS the Kachhawaha citadel until 1727, when their capital moved to Jaipur. Successive rulers continued to come here on all important occasions to seek the blessings of the family deity, Shila Devi. The citadel was established in 1592 by Man Singh I on the remains of an old 11th-century fort, but it was the various buildings added by Jai Singh I (r.1621–67) that constitute its magnificent centrepiece.

**Elephant ride on the cobbled pathway to the fort**

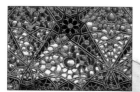

**★ Sheesh Mahal**
*The flame of a single candle, reflected in the tiny mirrors embedded in this chamber, transforms it into a starlit sky.*

**Aram Bagh,** the pleasure garden.

**Jas Mandir**
*This hall of private audience has latticed windows, a floral ceiling of elegant alabaster relief work and glass inlay. A marble screen here overlooks the Maota Lake and wafts in cool air.*

**Jai Mandir**

**Location of Amber Fort**
*Protected by Jaigarh Fort, the massive ramparts of Amber Fort follow the contours of a natural ridge.*

---

**STAR FEATURES**

★ **Sheesh Mahal**

★ **Ganesh Pol**

★ **Shila Devi Temple**

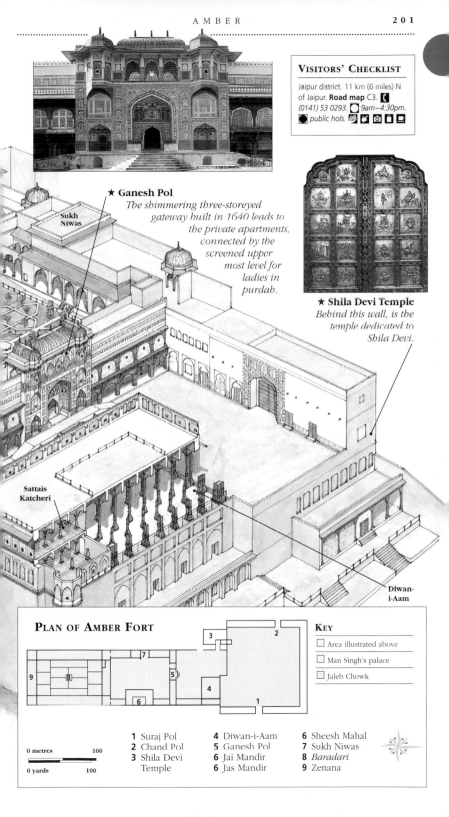

**VISITORS' CHECKLIST**

Jaipur district. 11 km (6 miles) N
of Jaipur. **Road map** C3.
(0141) 53 0293. ☐ 9am–4:30pm.
⬤ public hols. 🎨 🎫 📷 🚻 🏪

★ **Ganesh Pol**
*The shimmering three-storeyed
gateway built in 1640 leads to
the private apartments,
connected by the
screened upper
most level for
ladies in
purdah.*

**Sukh
Niwas**

★ **Shila Devi Temple**
*Behind this wall, is the
temple dedicated to
Shila Devi.*

**Sattais
Katcheri**

**Diwan-
i-Aam**

---

**PLAN OF AMBER FORT**

**KEY**

☐ Area illustrated above

☐ Man Singh's palace

☐ Jaleb Chowk

| | |
|---|---|
| **1** Suraj Pol | **4** Diwan-i-Aam |
| **2** Chand Pol | **5** Ganesh Pol |
| **3** Shila Devi | **6** Jai Mandir |
| Temple | **6** Jas Mandir |

| | |
|---|---|
| **6** Sheesh Mahal |
| **7** Sukh Niwas |
| **8** *Baradari* |
| **9** Zenana |

0 metres        100

0 yards         100

# Exploring Amber (the Old Capital)

**Painting detail on Ganesh Pol**

CROWNING THE CREST of a hill, Amber Fort and its ramparts offer a panoramic view of Maota Lake, two exquisite formal gardens, and the historic old town at the base of the hill, dotted with the remains of an older capital before it shifted to the precincts of the fort. Some of the old *havelis* and numerous temples here are remarkably well-preserved, while stepwells and lakes point to the existence of a self sufficient township where even the great Mughal emperor Akbar stopped on his annual pilgrimage to Ajmer.

The magnificent **Ganesh Pol** is the gateway to three private palaces built around a Mughal-style garden *(see p167)*, **Aram Bagh**. Each of these pleasure-palaces has some special feature. Sukh Niwas has doors carved from fragrant sandalwood, and water cascades over marble chutes to cool the interior. The marble Jai Mandir, at the other end of the garden, has the superb **Sheesh Mahal** studded with mirrors. The adjoining **Jas Mandir** has a marble screen across its eastern façade that overlooks the Maota Lake.

The lake, which provided water to the fort, is surrounded by two exquisite gardens. The **Kesar Kyari Bagh** has star-shaped flower beds once planted with saffron *(kesar)* flowers, while **Dilaram Bagh**, built in 1568 as a resting place for Emperor Akbar on his way to Ajmer, is a clever pun on the name of its architect, Dilaram ("heart's ease"). A small archaeological museum is located near Dilaram Bagh.

The furthermost end of the fort, which was also its oldest section, was converted into the **Zenana** ("women's quarters") by Man Singh I to house his 12 wives and concubines. The apartments bear the distinct stamp of Mughal zenana architecture, with screens and covered balconies for the protection and purdah of the royal ladies. Faint traces of frescoes are still visible on the walls. In the centre of the courtyard is a colonnaded pavilion called the **Baradari**.

**Sattais Katcheri, where the revenue records were written**

## The Fort Complex

The main entrance to the historic Amber Fort is through the imposing **Suraj Pol** ("sun gate"), so called because it faces the direction of the rising sun, the Kachhawaha family emblem. This gate leads into a huge flagged courtyard, **Jaleb Chowk**, literally, "the square where elephants and horses are tethered". Originally the fort's parade ground, its central area is surrounded on three sides by guard rooms, now souvenir and refreshment shops. A flight of steps leads to the **Shila Devi Temple**, which contains the image of the Kachhawaha family deity, a stone *(shila)* goddess Kali, brought here by Man Singh I from Bengal in 1604. The temple has ornately carved silver doors presented by the second wife of the last maharaja in 1939, silver oil lamps and grand pillars of green marble carved to look like banana trees.

The next courtyard has the **Diwan-i-Aam**, the space for public audience. Near it are 27 *(sattais)* airy colonnades, called the **Sattais Katcheri**, where scribes once sat to record revenue petitions.

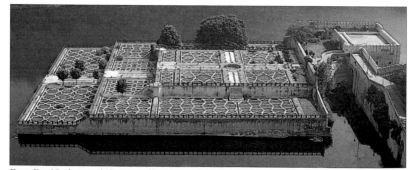

**Kesar Kyari Bagh, named after rare saffron flowers once planted in its star-shaped flower beds**

Bharmal ki Chhatri, the old cenotaphs of the Kachhawaha rulers

## The Township

The **Chand Pol** ("moon gate"), directly opposite Suraj Pol, leads to the old town outside the fort. The **Narsimha Temple**, built in the early 15th century by the Kachhawaha king Narsingh Dev, is the first of many on this route. The temple itself is only a small part of a derelict palace complex which was the site of past coronations before the Amber rulers abandoned it for the fort.

East of this lies the beautiful **Jagat Shiromani Temple**, erected in the early 17th century by Man Singh I in memory of his eldest son, Jagat Singh. A remarkable *toran* (carved lintel) adorns the doorway of the temple which has images of Vishnu, Radha and Krishna. Legend says that in the 16th century, the saint-poetess Mira Bai, famous for her devotion to Lord Krishna, brought an image of Krishna with her from Chittaurgarh, her home in southern Rajasthan.

Moving further east is the **Sanghi Jutharam Temple** which at one time had a beautiful 12-sided well, a small garden and several chambers. It is now protected by the Archaeological Survey of India (ASI). To its northeast lies the **Ambikeshwar Mahadev Temple**, dedicated

**Marble carving in Narsimha Temple**

to a manifestation of Shiva. One of the oldest temples here, it now stands 3 m (10 ft) below ground level and is said to be slowly sinking.

North of the Ambikeshwar Temple is **Panna Mian ka Kund**, built in the 17th century by a eunuch Panna Mian, a leading figure at the court of Raja Jai Singh I. From here, there is a cobbled path winding eastwards past further ruins and out through **Kheri Gate**, one of the old gates of Amber, leading to a popular picnic spot called **Sagar**, with its two terraced lakes. These were once important sources of water supply during times of siege. Located in a depression formed by the surrounding hills, just behind Jaigarh Fort, the site still bears traces of an elaborate water transport system in which elephants were used to carry water up to the fort.

These monuments lie to the west of the main Jaipur-Delhi highway that cuts across the town. The main market and the Amber bus stand are also located along this road, which is

now almost entirely occupied by tiny wayside eateries and souvenir shops. Further along this road, to the north, stands the **Akbari Mosque**, built by Emperor Akbar in 1569 at one of the spots where he stopped to pray on his way to Ajmer *(see pp218–19)*. The basic structure of the mosque is intact even though it has been often repaired.

Further westwards down this road is **Bharmal ki Chhatri**, a walled enclosure containing a group of memorials. This was the old cremation site for the rulers of Amber until a new spot was established at Gaitor *(see pp198–9)* after the capital moved from Amber to Jaipur.

**Steps criss-cross down to the water in the partly restored Panna Mian ka Kund**

Marble statue of a Jain *tirthankara* at Sanganer's Sanghiji Temple

# Sanganer ❸

Jaipur district. 16 km (10 miles) SW of Jaipur. **Road map** C3. ✕ 🚌 *daily.*

TWO ORNATE triple-arched gateways lead into Sanganer, a colourful town renowned for its blockprinted cotton textiles. According to local lore this tradition of blockprinting goes back to the 16th century when Sanga, one of the 18 sons of Prithviraj, the Kachhawaha ruler of Amber, re-established the town. Printers from nearby villages were asked to migrate to this new settlement to develop a range of textiles for the Jaipur court. It was Sanganer's river with its mineral powers of fixing the colours of the dyes that gave this printing village its fame and wealth. Today, the town resounds with the thud of printing, as craftsmen work in their sheds amidst bolts of cloth, dye-soaked pads and wooden blocks. Most of the printers and dyers in the town belong to a guild with retail outlets that sell reasonably priced fabric, tailored linen and accessories.

Sanganer is also a centre of handmade paper, a spin-off from textile printing, and Jaipur's famous Blue Pottery (*see p266*). Raja Man Singh I of Amber (*see p49*) set up the first workshops here to

**Frieze at Sanghiji Temple**

produce this special type of hand-painted pottery inspired by Persian and Chinese blue and white tiles so popular at the Mughal court.

Tucked away in the old walled town is an impressive 11th-century Jain temple. The **Sanghiji Temple** was probably built by a Jain trader with additional donations from the town's other wealthy merchants. Like other Jain temples found elsewhere in Rajasthan, this too is lavishly decorated with ornate stone carvings that include images of all the 24 Jain *tirthankaras* (saints) and a beautiful statue of Mahavira, the founder of Jainism, in the innermost sanctuary.

Sanganer is now a busy suburb of Jaipur city and the location of its airport.

# Bagru ❹

Jaipur district. 32 km (20 miles) SW of Jaipur past Sanganer on Ajmer Rd. **Road map** C3. 🚌 🏠 *daily.*

THE SMALL VILLAGE of Bagru is yet another traditional textile printing centre. Unlike the refined prints of Sanganer, Bagru's are bolder and more earthy, with a limited colour palette of red and black. The indigo, yellow and green that we see today are later additions. The origins of blockprinting in Bagru are again obscure. It is said that about 300 years ago, the first few printing families were brought to this village by the then *thakur* of Bagru, an important fiefdom of the Jaipur kings. Over time, more printers settled here, lured by state patronage as well as the abundant supply of water, so essential for printing.

Bagru's printers (*chhipas*) supplied the fabric that was used by the local farming communities as both stitched and unstitched garments. As the demand for blockprinted textiles increased, their clientele became more varied and their range of products more diversified. Yet, in many ways, little has changed and this is one of the few places to see the printing process at work. Craftsmen still follow the traditional methods of resist-printing, blockprinting and bleaching, and though the use of synthetic dyes has crept in, some colours, such as black and yellow, are still extracted from vegetable and mineral matter.

**Faded wall paintings outside the palace at Bagru**

# Blockprinted Textiles

DELICATE FLOWERS and foliage, paisleys, birds and animals on a white background are Sanganer's special imprint. Handed down from father to son, these motifs were inspired by the flower studies of miniature paintings *(see pp30–31)* and Mughal *pietra dura* motifs *(see pp156–7)*. Blockprinting can be seen in the workshops of the city's Chhipa Mohalla, where each stage of this ancient technique, from

**An intricate paisley motif**

chiselling intricate patterns on wooden blocks, to dyeing the fabric in huge copper vats on wood-fed fires, and printing, is all done by hand. In the more complex designs, a single motif may use up to ten different colours with as many blocks, each with a different design. In the final stage, swathes of printed cloth are spread on riverbanks or hung on huge frames to dry under the sky.

*Sanganeri motifs of stylized flowers* (phool) *and leaves* (buti) *in soft colours re-create a field of dainty flowers.*

**Textile printing** *is done with wooden blocks. These are dipped in dye to print the cloth stretched across a low stool. Earlier, colours were extracted from vegetable and mineral matter. Pomegranate rinds, saffron, madder root, turmeric and the indigo plant were some natural sources. Chemicals have now replaced natural dyes.*

**Wooden printing blocks** *are carved by hand with popular design motifs. The traditional designs have been enlivened by input from Indian fashion designers.*

**Bagru's** *floral, figurative and geometric motifs are printed on a coarse cotton cloth that is made into blouses and gathered skirts worn by local women. However, in recent years, these earthy prints have become popular in urban centres too.*

## HANDMADE PAPER

The Kagazi Mohalla, the colony of papermakers, recycles scraps of cloth and silk thread to produce an impressive range of decorative and functional paper products. Fabric is first converted into pulp and then flattened on a wire mesh. The thin sheets of paper are finally peeled off and hung up to dry. These craftsmen jealously preserve their trade secrets and seldom marry outsiders.

**Sheets of handmade paper hung to dry**

# Alwar ⑤

**Gate of Fateh Jang's Tomb**

SITUATED between Mughal and Rajput territories, Alwar's place in history was manipulated by its rulers who made shrewd alliances to gain political leverage. Alwar's growth as a vassal state of the Kachhawaha kings to a significant Rajput state came about after Pratap Singh captured the fort of Bala Qila in 1775. Later, as the British cultivated it as a friendly base in Rajputana, there followed a burst of architectural extravagance that went along with a lavish round of tiger shoots as its rulers tried to rival the glittering lifestyle of their cousins in Jaipur. Today, Alwar is a dusty provincial town with some remarkable monuments, mostly visited by tourists on their way to the Sariska National Park.

**From the *Gulistan*, an 18th-century Mughal manuscript**

### 🏛 City Palace
Near Collectorate. ◯ 10am–4:30pm.
A stunning profusion of architectural features marks this palace, with Rajput *bangaldar* eaves and elegant *chhatris* alongside Mughal floral tracery and *jaalis*. Built in 1793, the District Collectorate and Police Headquarters now occupy most of the palace, so it is best viewed from the large central courtyard. A stairway flanked by two marble kiosks leads from here to the gorgeous Durbar Hall and Sheesh Mahal, to see which special permission is needed.

A door on the right of the courtyard leads to the **City Palace Museum**, spread over three halls of the upper storey. These contain some treasures of the erstwhile rulers, such as their famed collection of Mughal and Rajput paintings of the Alwar, Jaipur and Mughal schools. The 7,000 rare manuscripts in Persian, Arabic,

**Dagger, City Palace Museum**

Urdu and Sanskrit include an illuminated Koran, a version of the rare and precious *Gulistan* of the great Persian poet Sa'adi, as well as the *Babur Nama* or "Memoirs of Babur" (1530). The awesome armoury display includes the swords of Mohammed Ghori, Akbar and Aurangzeb, and a macabre coil called *nagphas*, used for strangling enemies. The first room contains a silver dining table with dividers through which moving metal shoals of swimming fish can be seen. Behind the palace, across a magnificent *kund* is the cenotaph of Maharaja Bakhtawar Singh (r.1790–1815). It is locally known as **Moosi Maharani ki Chhatri** after his mistress who performed *sati* here when he died. One of Rajasthan's most elegant monuments, blending brown sandstone and white marble, its carved pavilion has domed arches with exquisite

floral tracery, and ceilings adorned with fading gold leaf paintings of mythological characters and courtly scenes.

### 🏛 City Palace Museum
◯ 10am–4:30pm. ● Fri & public hols. 🈺 🚫

### 🛕 Moosi Maharani ki Chhatri
◯ 10am–4:30pm. ● Fri & public hols. 🈺 **Shoes not allowed**.

### 🛕 Bala Qila
◯ daily. Written permission is needed from the office of the Superintendent of Police, City Palace.
Perched on a steep hill above the city, easily accessible by car, the Bala Qila was originally a 10th-century mud fort. Several additions were made to it by the Jats and Mughals (Babur is said to have spent a night here) until it was finally captured in 1775 by Pratap Singh of Alwar. Now a police wireless station, its sprawling complex was defended by 66 large and small towers. The frescoed palace within, the Nikumbh Mahal, was named after its first occupants, the Nikumbh Rajputs. The entire city can be seen from the fort's extensive ramparts, which give an idea of its scale and of the engineering skills that went into its building. Also visible are the ruins of Salim Mahal, named after Jahangir (Salim), who was exiled here after he plotted to kill Abu'l Fazl, Akbar's official biographer and one of the "nine gems" of his court.

**The elegant marble pavilion at Moosi Maharani ki Chhatri**

A stone aqueduct brought water from Siliserh to the Company Bagh

**VISITORS' CHECKLIST**

Alwar district. 150 km (93 miles)
NE of Jaipur. **Road map** C3.
👥 *2,300,000.* 🚉 *Nehru Marg.*
🚌 *Manu Marg.* ℹ️ *TRC, near
Railway Station, Alwar (0144) 21
868; Paryatan Bhavan, MI Road,
Jaipur (0141) 37 0180.* 🚹 *daily.*
🎭 *Jagannathji Fair (Mar–Apr),
Laldas Mela (May), Sawan Teej
(Jul–Aug), Diwali (Oct–Nov).*

### 🌸 Company Bagh

Vivekanand Marg. 🕐 *6am–6pm.*
A lovely garden when it was
laid out in 1868, the Company
Bagh is now a shadow of its
former self. It was originally
named after Alwar's British
ally and protector, the East
India Company. Later, it was
christened Purjan Vihar by
Maharaja Jai Singh. An enchanting greenhouse here is
named "Simla", because it
reminded the maharaja of the
British summer capital in
North India. A three-km (two-
mile) long aqueduct, made of
solid stone masonry, brought
water from a reservoir at
Siliserh to this garden.

### 🏛 Fateh Jang's Tomb

Near Railway Station.
🕐 *9:30am–4:30pm.*
The tomb of Fateh Jang, one
of Shah Jahan's ministers, is a
five-storeyed monument,
constructed in 1647. Dominated by an enormous dome, its
walls and ceiling have raised
plaster reliefs, and fine calligraphic inscriptions can be
seen on the first floor. A
school now occupies the
tomb's compound.

**ENVIRONS:** To the north of
Alwar, located at the edge of
Vijay Sagar Lake is the 105-
roomed **Vijay Mandir
Palace**, built to look like an

anchored ship by Jai Singh
(r.1892–1937). A great builder
of palaces, the eccentric Jai
Singh had the famous 100-
roomed Moti Doongri palace-
fortress to the south of the
Company Bagh blown up
because it offended his
sensibilities. Vijay Mandir was
his last official residence and
he lived here for many years.
The former ruling family still
occupies it and reserves the
right of admission to it.
Alwar is full of apocryphal
stories of Jai Singh's strange
tastes. His Bugatti cars were
"buried" after he tired of
them, and he once ordered a
custom-made gold Lancaster
car that resembled the King of
England's coronation coach,
minus the horses!

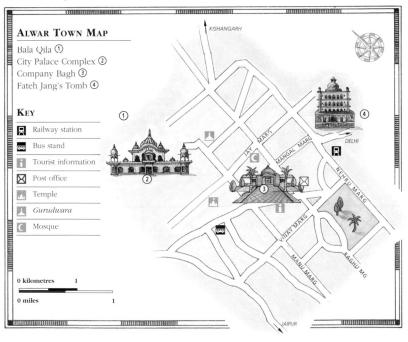

### ALWAR TOWN MAP

Bala Qila ①
City Palace Complex ②
Company Bagh ③
Fateh Jang's Tomb ④

### KEY

🚉 Railway station
🚌 Bus stand
ℹ️ Tourist information
✉️ Post office
🛕 Temple
🛐 *Gurudwara*
☪️ Mosque

0 kilometres          1

0 miles                1

## Siliserh ❻

Alwar district. 13 km (8 miles) SW of
Alwar. **Road map** C3. 🛈 *TRC, near
Railway Station, Alwar (0144)
21 868.* 🚉

Rajgarh Fort, once the capital of the Alwar kings

THIS ENCHANTING SPOT is
midway between Alwar
and Sariska National Park *(see
pp210–11)*. The 10.5 sq km
(4 sq miles) Siliserh Lake, in a
valley bounded in by low
forested hills, is still the main
reservoir supplying water to
Alwar and the surrounding
area. Perched on a hillock
overlooking the lake is the
water palace built in the mid-
19th century by the king of
Alwar, Vinay Singh, for his
beautiful wife, a local village
girl, so that she could be near
her family home. This once-
grand palace is now a hotel
and an ideal place for a quiet
getaway, as the only sounds
one hears are those made by
cormorants, ducks and other
waterbirds. Pathways lead up
the foothills and around the
lake where the remains of old
cenotaphs still stand. From
the palace's open terrace
there are wonderful views of
the sun setting over the lake.

## Rajgarh ❼

Alwar district. 35 km (22 miles) S of
Alwar. **Road map** C3. 🛈 *TRC, near
Railway Station, Alwar (0144)
21 868.* 🚉

OVERLOOKING a picturesque
valley with green fields
and citrus groves is the grand
hilltop fort of Rajgarh, the old
capital of the Alwar rulers.
Built by the founder of the
dynasty, Pratap Singh, in the
mid-18th century, its status as
the capital was brief, and in
1775, when Pratap Singh
captured Bala Qila *(see p206)*,
the court moved to Alwar.
The fort, however, with its
once beautiful Sheesh Mahal,
frescoed walls and secret
passages, was maintained as a
summer residence, but over
time, it fell into disuse until
finally it was abandoned. The
town, too, at the foot of the
hill, wears a desolate look.

## Sariska National Park ❽

*See pp210–11.*

## Bairat ❾

Alwar district. 64 km (40 miles) SW of
Alwar. **Road map** C3. 🛈 *TRC, near
Railway Station, Alwar (0144)
21 868.* 🚉

NOWHERE IS THE AGE and
majesty of the Aravalli
Hills as apparent in the region
as it is at Bairat. The striking
topography of giant rocks,
variously textured and
shaped, provides a dramatic
backdrop for an excavated,
ancient archaeological site
that dates back to the 3rd
century BC. One of the cities
along the main north-south
trade route, this was a major
Buddhist centre. A rock edict
of Emperor Ashoka (273–232
BC) was found here, and at
one end of the village, off a
dirt track, high on a hillock
locally known as Bijak ki
Pahadi, are the remnants of a
Buddhist monastery and
circular temple. It is believed
to be India's oldest free-
standing structure. Historians
have identified it as a *chaitya*
hall or chapel which was
once supported by 26
octagonal wooden columns.

**Siliserh Palace built on a hillock overlooking the lake**

Bairat's history, however, goes back to the time of the *Mahabharata* (around the 9th century BC), when this land formed part of a kingdom comprising much of eastern Rajasthan, and was ruled by King Virat from his capital of Viratnagar (present Bairat). It was here that the Pandavas *(see p141)* spent the 13th year of their exile. Locals believe that one of the Pandava brothers, the mighty Bhim, lived at **Bhim ki Doongri** ("Bhim's hillock"), and that Arjuna created the River Banganga when he struck an arrow into the earth. King Virat joined the Pandavas in the battle at Kurukshetra, and his daughter married Arjuna's son, Abhimanyu.

On the other side of town, near the rock edict, is an early 17th-century garden mansion dating to Jahangir's reign. Within the compound is a Jain temple, and just outside is the charming 16th-century hunting lodge where Akbar camped on his way to Ajmer. Locally known as the Chhatri, it was built on a raised platform, with five well-sculpted pavilions.

Remains of the circular temple dating to the Buddhist period, Bairat

## Bhangarh ⑩

Alwar district. 56 km (35 miles) S of Sariska via Thana Gazi. **Road map** C3. 🛈 *TRC, near Railway Station, Alwar (0144) 21 868.* 🚌

A BUMPY RIDE from Sariska will take you to the abandoned city of Bhangarh, a fascinating site said to be a clan citadel before Amber. Local legend says that the place was deserted when cursed by an evil magician, and many of its structures were transported to the new capital, Ajabgarh. Built in the early 17th century by Madho Singh, the younger brother of Amber's Raja Man Singh I *(see p49)*, Bhangarh, also known as the "City of Ten Thousand Homes", exemplifies the hierarchy of traditional town planning.

A stone colonnaded pathway lined with market kiosks, stables or residences leads to the inner sanctum at the foot of the hills where a ruined palace, derisively called Randiyon ka Mahal ("palace of the prostitutes") remains, overlooking the Someshwar Temple, still in use. Three other temples dot the sprawling site, of which the Mangala Devi Temple, with a corbelled dome and finely carved exterior, is by far the most imposing.

**ENVIRONS:** On the road to Bhangarh is Ajabgarh, built by Madho Singh's grandson as a new settlement for the people of Bhangarh, by erecting a wall to separate the two cities. Part of the old town is under water, but a fort and some ruins may still be seen.

Carved bracket from the Mangala Devi Temple, Bhangarh

## THE PANDAVAS IN EXILE

The Great Epic, the *Mahabharata (see p141)*, describes how, after losing the Pandava kingdom and wife Draupadi to the wicked Kauravas at a game of dice, Prince Yudhishthira, along with his brothers, Bhim, Arjuna, Nakul and Sahdev, were banished to 13 years of exile. The last year was the most crucial and had to be spent in complete anonymity for, if recognized, it meant another 12 years of exile. Forced to accept these rigid terms, the Pandavas roamed the country, spending their 13th year in disguise at the court of King Virat. The story of the Pandavas, their exile and the final battle are important components of the land's folklore, while sites such as Kurukshetra *(see p140)*, associated with their adventures, are venerated pilgrim spots.

The five Pandava brothers, from a popular TV serial

# Sariska National Park

**Silk cotton in bloom**

**D**ESIGNATED A TIGER RESERVE under Project Tiger (*see p223*) in 1979, the park sprawls over 800 sq km (308 sq miles) with a core area of 480 sq km (185 sq miles). The Aravallis branch out at Sariska, forming low plateaux and valleys that harbour a wide spectrum of wildlife in the dry jungles. Formerly the private hunting ground of Alwar State, Sariska owes a debt to the strict game and protection laws laid down by its conservation-conscious rulers, which preserved its natural habitat and wildlife. A 17th-century fortress and several ancient temple ruins, such as the Pandupol Temple, also lie within the park.

**Langur Monkeys**
*These black-faced primates with long tails are known as Hanuman langurs.*

**Sariska Palace**
*A turn-of-the-century hunting lodge of the Alwar rulers, this splendid palace, now a luxury hotel, has a collection of vintage photographs of past hunts, and period furnishings.*

JAIPUR

Thanaghazi

Bandipul

Sariska

Bha

Karn

**Entrance**

Udainath   Kankwadi

Kaligha

Teh

**Endangered Species**
*Forest guides who keep track of where a tiger was last seen can lead you to spot this elusive predator.*

**Water Holes**
*To combat the chronic shortage of water in the region, the Forest Department has laid out a series of water holes at Pandupol, Bandipol, Slopka, Kalighati and Talvriksha. These make good vantage points to view wildlife, especially at sunset, when herds of animals flock to them to quench their thirst.*

### Flora

*The dry deciduous forests of Sariska come to life during the brief spring and early summer when the flowering* dhak *(Butea monosperma) and laburnum bloom. The date palm begins to bear fruit, while berries, locally known as* kair *(Capparis decidua) appear on the bushes.*

ALWAR

### Jackal

*Jackals and hyenas often lead trackers to a tiger kill. Along with panthers and jungle cats, these carnivores feed on the many species of deer, nilgai or blue bull, wild boar and porcupine in the forest. Tiger sightings are however, rare in Sariska.*

0 kilometres    5

0 miles    2

Jpol

Umri

ka

### Chital

*The gentle chital or spotted deer, like the sambhar, is commonly seen at the park's water holes, or resting under the trees. The other deer species, the* chowsingha *(four-horned antelope), is specific to Sariska and can be seen around Pandupol.*

### Grey Partridge

*The hides at Kalighati and Slopka are ideal for observing the park's birdlife, such as the crested serpent eagle, the great Indian horned owl, woodpeckers, kingfishers and partridge.*

# Chomu ⓫

Jaipur district. 32 km (20 miles) NW of
Jaipur. **Road map** C3. 🅷 *Govt
Hostel, MI Rd, Jaipur (0141) 37 0181.*
🚌 *daily.*

THE SMALL TOWN of Chomu
links Jaipur with the
Shekhawati region. Traces of
a grander past are visible in
its once impressive fort,
handsome *havelis* and stepwells. But Chomu's charm lies
in its rural ambience, where
bullocks and camels plough
the fields, and the unique
four-pillared well is the main
source of water. In the
market, tractor spare parts
and tubewell pump-sets vie
for attention with hand-carts
spilling over with mounds of
cucumbers and *ber (Zizyphus
mauritiana)*, a berry for
which the region is famous.

# Samode ⓬

Jaipur district. 42 km (26 miles) NW of
Jaipur. **Road map** C3. 🅷 *Govt
Hostel, MI Road, Jaipur (0141) 37
0181.* 🚌 *daily.* 🎭 *Gangaur festival
(Mar–Apr).*

SAMODE'S romantic palace,
immortalized in films such
as *The Far Pavilions*, is the
main reason why this minor
Rajput hamlet is now a

The fairy tale Samode Palace, a luxurious retreat set amidst rugged hills

luxurious tourist destination.
Erected in the late 19th
century by a powerful noble
of the Jaipur state, this jewel-
like palace nestles among the
hills below an older hill fort.

A flight of stairs leads up to
a massive gateway and into
the palace. Its simple exterior
is highly deceptive for, surrounding the vast central
courtyard, are spacious rooms
on three levels. Of these, the
chambers on the uppermost
level are the most opulent.
The Durbar Hall, Sheesh
Mahal and Sultan Mahal are
embellished all over with
dazzling mirrorwork and
elaborate murals that depict
courtly life, hunting scenes
and religious themes, along
with floral and geometric

motifs. The murals represent
the best of the Jaipur style
and are said to rival those at
Jaipur's Chandra Mahal *(see
pp188–9)* and Tonk's Sunehri
Kothi *(see p222)*. However,
entrance is restricted since it
is now a luxury hotel.

A short distance away is
Samode Bagh where the more
adventurous can stay in one
of the 50 deluxe tents pitched
in the formal garden. Other
points of interest are the
abandoned old fort at the end
of a strenuous walk up 376
steps, and the quaint little
village where a wide variety
of local handicrafts such as
colourful hand-woven
*dhurries*, tie-and-dye fabric,
lac bangles and *jootis*
(slippers) are available.

---

## THE PAINTED HAVELIS OF SHEKHAWATI

In the many little towns of Shekhawati are the ancestral
homes of some of India's leading industrialist families, such
as the Birlas, Dalmias and Goenkas. These sprawling, old
*havelis* with their exuberantly frescoed walls *(see p27)* were

The entrance to Biyani
Haveli, Sikar

built between late 18th to early
20th centuries by the local
Marwari merchants who had
migrated to the port-cities of
Bombay and Calcutta to seek
their fortunes. Their interaction
with the British and exposure to

A "pop art" view of Rajput
chieftains

modern urban and industrial trends influenced their lifestyles,
and their homes reflected the new ideas they brought back with
them, as well as their new-found wealth and social status.

The style and content of the Shekhawati frescoes are a telling
comment on the urbanization of a traditional genre. The local
artists still followed the one-dimensional realism of traditional
Indian painting *(see pp30–31)*, but juxtaposed among the gods,
goddesses and martial heroes are images from a changing world.
In their celebration of contemporary "pop" themes, the frescoes
of British ladies, top-hatted gentlemen, brass bands and soldiers,
trains, motor cars, aeroplanes, gramophones and telephones,
symbolize the emerging industrial society of the late 19th century.

# A Tour of Shekhawati ⑬

NORTHEAST OF JAIPUR, situated along the old camel caravan trade route, lies Shekhawati, or the "garden of Shekha", named after Rao Shekha, a fiercely independent ruler who consolidated the region in the 15th century. Today, it is known as Rajasthan's most famous open air museum. A network of excellent roads through semi-arid scrubland connects most towns and villages where the painted *havelis* of India's leading merchant families stand today in ghostly splendour.

**Gods and goddesses frolic on the wall of Biyani Haveli, Sikar**

**Mandawa** ④
The fort-palace is now a charming hotel and a convenient base from which to visit the neighbouring towns.

**Dundlod** ⑤
Its fort-palace and two splendid Goenka *havelis* are worth a visit.

**Fatehpur** ③
This picturesque mid-15th century town is best known for the Singhania, Goenka and Jalan *havelis*.

## KEY

| | |
|---|---|
| ▬ | Tour route |
| ═ | Roads |
| ≋ | Rivers |

*Mukundgarh*

*JHUNJHUNU*

0 kilometres 20
0 miles 10

**Lachhmangarh** ②
This 19th-century town is based on Jaipur's grid plan. The Char Chowk ("four coutyards") Haveli, owned by the Ganeriwala family, is said to be the grandest in the region.

**Nawalgarh** ⑥
The Poddar and the Aath ("eight") *havelis* are renowned for their frescoes.

*NAGAUR*

*JAIPUR*

## TIPS FOR DRIVERS

**Length:** *111 km (69 miles).*
**Stopping-off points:** *Mandawa, Dundlod, Mukundgarh, Fatehpur and Nawalgarh have good hotels. Petrol pumps are at regular intervals on the main road. Apart from NH11, the lesser roads towards Jhunjhunu are poor, but there are roadside eateries at intervals selling mineral water, hot and cold drinks and snacks.*

**Sikar** ①
Sikar's charm lies in its *havelis*, bazaars and rural ambience.

# Sambhar Salt Lake ⑭

Jaipur district. 70 km (44 miles) NE of Ajmer. **Road map** B3. 🚌 🚉
*Sambhrai Mata Mela (Oct).*

Sambhar Lake is among the six important sites in India designated by the World Wide Fund for Nature (WWF) as a wetland of international importance. This vast inland saline lake spreads over an area of roughly 230 sq km (89 sq miles) and is fed by five rivers. During November and December, several species of migratory bird, especially flamingoes, can be seen here. A number of local legends are connected with the lake's origin, and a Shiva temple and two sacred tanks dedicated to mythological princesses are an indication of the lake's antiquity. The place, however, came into prominence after it was noticed by Babur in the 16th century. Since then, it has been a major source of salt for the country. One of the reasons for this is that after a good monsoon, the water level can rise by up to 3 ft (1 m), but over winter, the lake turns brackish due to capillary action caused by evaporation, drawing up salt from underground deposits. The little township that has grown around the lake survives on the extraction and packaging of salt. Men, women and even children can be seen working away at the countless trenches and mounds that are spread across the ghostly-white terrain. This has now become a highly commercial business, and though only one state-owned company has the monopoly, there has been an unprecedented growth in the numbers of private manufacturers. Many *bunds* (small dams) have been illegally constructed in the catchment area to retain rainwater for small-scale operations. This has affected not only the flow of water into the lake but has also put a considerable strain on its ecosystem.

**Flamingoes in flight over Sambhar Lake**

# Makrana ⑮

Nagaur district. 80 km (50 miles) N of Ajmer. **Road map** B3. 🚶 *67,000.*
ℹ️ *Khadim Hotel, Ajmer.* 🏠 *daily.*

Great slabs of hewn marble indicate that Makrana is a highly commercial stone-quarrying centre. The quarries stretch over a distance of

**Marble quarrying at Makrana**

20 km (12 miles) and produce the highly-prized luminous white marble that was used to build the Taj Mahal (*see pp154–5*). Quarrying began several centuries ago, and traditional open-pit methods are still used to excavate the stone. The demand for good quality marble has not lessened, and nearly 50,000 tons are mined annually and transported throughout the country. The town is also a good place to pick up gifts and souvenirs. Many small workshops have sprung up where artisans carve statues, pillars, vases, lamps and other objects for local sale and export. Objects are also sent to Agra where marble inlayers re-create the same delicate floral patterns as seen in the Taj Mahal (*see pp156–7*).

**Salt packaging at Sambhar Salt Lake**

**Phool Mahal Palace in a picturesque setting**

# Kishangarh

Ajmer district. 30 km (19 miles) NE of Ajmer on NH 8. **Road map** B4. 22,000. Khadim Hotel, Ajmer.

OF ALL RAJPUTANA'S princely states, this was the smallest. It was established in the early 17th century by Kishan Singh, a Rathore prince from Jodhpur, on lands near Ajmer. The king's sister was one of Jahangir's wives (*see pp52–3*), a privilege that gave him a special status at the Mughal court. An obvious outcome of this proximity was that the Kishangarh kings tried to emulate the cultured lifestyle of the Mughal emperors, and when the arts lost imperial patronage under the leadership of the austere

Aurangzeb, this tiny state became a haven for several migrant miniature painters.

The old city is certainly worth exploring as it remains much as it was in the past. The narrow streets are lined with *havelis*, some of which have been converted into shops, and on the pavements

**Roopangarh Fort**

are vendors selling all kinds of merchandise, including the red chillies for which the region is famous. The **Phool Mahal**, a privately-owned palace now a heritage hotel, has an idyllic setting on the banks of a lake that attracts a variety of waterbirds. Shady balconies, courtyard gardens and brass doors flanked by paintings hint at its past glory.

**Phool Mahal**
(01463) 47 405.

**ENVIRONS:** The 17th-century Roopangarh Fort, 25 km (15 miles) from Kishangarh, was once the capital of the state. Among the riches of this splendid heritage hotel is a rare collection of the famous Kishangarh miniatures.

## THE KISHANGARH SCHOOL (1735–70)

In the mid-17th century, many miniature painters left the imperial atelier and moved to the Rajput, Central Indian and Punjab hill states, where each court evolved its own distinct regional style. Kishangarh's School of Painting flourished under the reign of Raja Sawant Singh (r.1748–64) who was a mystic, poet and Krishna devotee. His talented court painter, Nihal Chand, immortalized the love story of the king and his court singer in lyrical, romantic paintings where they are portrayed as Radha and Krishna. They are often surrounded by animals and birds, also in pairs, celebrating the union of the gods. The most famous painting is the portrait of Bani Thani, as the court singer was known. She is depicted in profile with a sharp nose and very elongated eyes and tapering wrist and fingers. This highly stylized form of portraiture became the hallmark of the Kishangarh School.

**Portrait of Bani Thani**

# Street-by-Street: Pushkar ⑰

**A turtle shrine**

**A** PEACEFUL PILGRIM TOWN of lakes and 400 temples, Pushkar derives its name from *pushpa* (flower) and *kar* (hand) after a legend that says that its lakes were created from the petals that fell from the divine hands of Brahma, the Creator *(see pp22–3)*. Today, life revolves around its lakeside ghats, temples and vibrant, colourful bazaars, and it is this harmonious mix of the spiritual and commercial that draws people to Pushkar.

**Villagers at the Fair**
*Hundreds of thousands of people, camels and cattle attend the annual fair, said to be the largest in Asia.*

**Dhanna Bhagat Temple**

**Residential area**

SADAR BAZAAR

| 0 metres | | 100 |
|---|---|---|
| 0 yards | | 100 |

← **To Savitri Temple**

PARIKRAMA MARG

**★ Brahma Temple**
*This is one of the few temples in India dedicated to Brahma who, as myth says, was cursed by his wife Savitri when, in her absence, he invited Gayatri, a tribal girl, to take her place in an important ritual.*

**Badi Ganeshji Temple**

**Parshuram Temple**

**KEY**

– – – Suggested route

**STAR SIGHTS**

★ **Brahma Temple**

★ **Ghats**

**Pushkar Lake**
*A view of the sacred lake at Pushkar. The Savitri Temple stands on top of the distant hill. Across the lake, on a hill, is the Gayatri Temple.*

### Rangaji Temple

*This temple is conspicuous for its South Indian style of architecture. Its* gopuram *(pagoda), intricately carved with over 360 images of deities, towers over the area.*

**Women at Sadar Bazaar**

**Camel race at the Pushkar fair**

### Pushkar Mela

In the Hindu month of Kartik (Oct–Nov), ten days after Diwali, this quiet town and its environs come alive as the much-anticipated annual cattle fair gets going. Temporary tents and campsites suddenly appear to accommodate the thousands of pilgrims, tourists and villagers who come here with herds of cattle, horses and camels to participate in this spectacular event. Pushkar has always been the region's main cattle market for local herdsmen and farmers buying and selling camels and indigenous breeds of cattle. Over the years, this trade in livestock has increased in volume to become what is said to be Asia's largest cattle fair.

In the vast, specially-built amphitheatre on the outskirts of the town, numerous camel, horse and donkey races and contests take place amid lusty cheers from a huge audience. A festive funfair atmosphere prevails over Pushkar during the two-week duration. Giant-wheels and open air theatres offer amusement, while food stalls do a brisk trade, as do the shops that sell a fascinating variety of goods. In the evenings, people huddle round campfires, listening to the haunting strains of Rajasthani folk ballads. The fair reaches a crescendo on the night of the full moon *(purnima)*, when pilgrims take a dip in the holy lake and, at dusk, during the beautiful *deepdan* ceremony, hundreds of clay lamps on leaf boats are lit and set afloat in a magical tableau.

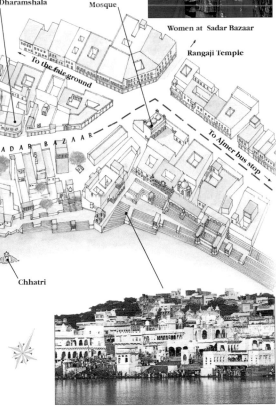

**Digambar Jain Dharamshala**

**Mosque**

To the fair ground

**Rangaji Temple**

To Ajmer bus stop

**Chhatri**

### ★ Ghats

*Pushkar has 52 ghats. Devout Hindus make at least one pilgrimage to Pushkar and bathe at the holy ghats to wash away their sins and thereby earn themselves a place in heaven.*

# Ajmer ⑱

**Calligraphy, Adhai Din ka Jhonpra**

Famous throughout the subcontinent as the holiest Muslim pilgrim centre after Mecca, Ajmer's prominence in history is connected to the *dargah* of a Sufi saint, Khwaja Moinuddin Chishti. The Mughals made Ajmer the provincial capital of their territories in Rajputana, and it was here that Sir Thomas Roe, the first British ambassador, presented his credentials to Jahangir in 1615. Although the *dargah* is still its most important landmark, Ajmer is also known for its proximity to another famous pilgrim centre, Pushkar. The town is framed by undulating hillocks dotted with interesting ruins. The picturesque environs of Anasagar Lake with charming pavilions, are popular with picnickers.

## 🛕 Taragarh Fort

⏰ 9:30am–4:30pm.

This rugged, sprawling 7th-century "Star Fort" occupies the summit of Beetli Hill. A series of five gateways lead into this once-impregnable citadel, said to be the earliest hill fort in the country. Many ruined buildings lie within it, among which are a mosque, still in use, and the shrine of Miran Sayyid Hussain, a 12th-century governor of the fort. The later structures were added by the British whose troops occupied the fort in the 19th century.

## 🕌 Dargah Sharif

See pp220–21.

## ⛪ Adhai Din ka Jhonpra

N of Dargah Sharif, Nalla Bazaar. ⏰ 9:30am–4:30pm.

This impressive complex of pillared cloisters is all that remains of a mosque built around AD 1200 by the Slave king, Qutbuddin Aibak. Some say that the mosque's name, which means "a hut of two-and-a-half days", indicates the time taken to build it.

**The Dargah Sharif dome rises above the surrounding houses**

However, it is more likely that it refers to the duration of a religious fair held during the Urs in the 18th century. Like the Quwwat-ul-Islam mosque at Delhi's Qutb complex *(see p112)*, also built at the same time, pillars and fragments from nearby Hindu and Jain temples were used for its construction. The mosque

itself, said to have been built over a demolished Jain college, stands on a plaform cut out of the hillside, with ten shallow domes supported by 124 columns. The glory of the structure is an exquisite seven-arched screen in front of the many-pillared hall. Each arch is different from the next, and every column is ornamented with delicate engravings and calligraphic inscriptions in both Kufic and Tughra (early Arabic scripts). The sheer exuberance of decoration and ingenious use of materials led Cunningham, the first Director-General of the Archaeological Survey of India, to describe it as "one of the noblest buildings the world has produced".

## 🏛 Rajputana Museum

Near bus stand. 📞 (0145) 62 0637. ⏰ 9:30am–4:30pm daily. ⬤ public hols. ♿

Akbar's fort and palace, in the heart of the old city, has had a chequered history. The first seat of Mughal power in Rajasthan, it was later used by the British as an arsenal. Finally, on the orders of the Viceroy Lord Curzon, the fort was converted into a museum in 1908. Its varied collection highlights the sculpture and other antiquities gathered from sites all over Rajasthan. The most impressive exhibits are the sculptures dating from the 4th to 12th century, of which the most remarkable are the four-armed Vishnu seated on Garuda, and a door-frame from the ancient site of Baghera, depicting the ten *avatars* of Vishnu. Other important displays include antique coins, inscriptions, copper plates, paintings and weapons.

**The exuberantly decorated seven-arched screen at the Adhai Din ka Jhonpra**

The Aravalli Range picturesquely frames the Anasagar Lake

### VISITORS' CHECKLIST

Ajmer district. 135 kilometres
(112 miles SW of Jaipur). **Road
map** B4. 1,735,000.
RTDC Hotel Khadim (0145)
52 426. Near Hotel Khadim.
Station Rd. Sanganer.
Urs (Oct–Nov).

### Nasiyan Temple

Anok Chowk, Seth Moolchand Soni
Marg. *summer: 8am–5pm;
winter: 8:30am–5pm daily.*
Built in the 19th century, the
"Red Temple" in the heart of
Ajmer, is a typical example of
a Jain religious building. Just
behind the main temple
(closed to non-Jains) is the
double-storeyed Svarna
Nagari Hall. It is elaborately
decorated with coloured glass
mosaics, and large gilded
wooden figures re-create
scenes from Jain mythology,
such as the birth and life of
Rishabhdeva, the first Jain
*tirthankar* (saint)

### Anasagar Lake

Circular Rd. *7am–10pm.*
This tranquil lake to the north
of the city is named after
Anaji (r.1135–50), the
grandfather of Prithviraj
Chauhan. Charmed by
its scenic beauty,
Jahangir laid out a
garden, Daulat Bagh,
and Shah Jahan built
the marble pleasure
pavilions.
  Overlooking this
popular picnic spot,
is a grand colonial
building, now the Circuit
House, where the British
Resident once lived.

### Mayo College

*Can visit with Principal's permission.*
Set up in 1875 by Lord Mayo
as an "Eton of the East" for
Rajput princes, the school's
main building, designed by
Charles Mant, is a jewel of
Indo-Saracenic architecture
*(see p25)*. Its early
students were allowed to
live in their individual
"houses" with English
private tutors and
family retainers. Some,
such as the prince of
Alwar, would ride to
school after vacations
on an elephant. After
1947, commoners
were allowed entry,

**Lord Mayo**

and today, along with its girls'
section, Mayo is rated as one
of India's best public schools.

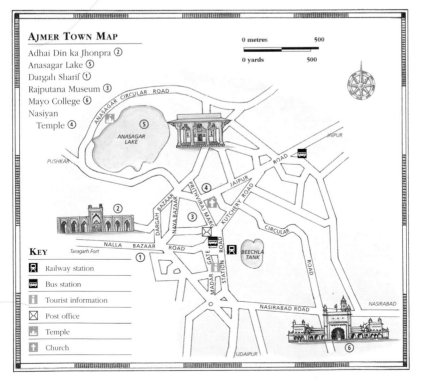

**AJMER TOWN MAP**

Adhai Din ka Jhonpra ②
Anasagar Lake ⑤
Dargah Sharif ①
Rajputana Museum ③
Mayo College ⑥
Nasiyan
  Temple ④

0 metres        500
0 yards         500

**KEY**

| | |
|---|---|
| 🚉 | Railway station |
| 🚌 | Bus station |
| ℹ️ | Tourist information |
| ✉️ | Post office |
| 🛕 | Temple |
| ✝️ | Church |

# Dargah Sharif

**A**REVERED Muslim pilgrim centre since the 12th century, the Dargah Sharif contains the tomb of the famous Sufi saint Khwaja Moinuddin Chishti (1143–1236), popularly called Garib Nawaz, or "protector of the poor". Reputed to possess miraculous powers, people of every faith flock to his *dargah* to seek favours and blessings. It is said that the saint entered his cell to pray in seclusion until his death on the sixth day. Each year, six days in the seventh lunar month (October) are marked as his Urs (death anniversary) celebrations. Over the years, the saint's royal devotees built grand extensions to the tomb, so that today the *dargah* complex, teeming with pilgrims and tourists, is virtually a township in itself.

**Shahjahani Gate**

★ **Mehfil Khana**
*Built in 1888 by the Nizam of Hyderabad, the richest Indian of the time, all-night qawwalis are held here.*

★ **Shahjahani Masjid**
*Shah Jahan built this marble mosque. The Mughals made many such generous endowments.*

**Qawwali Singers**
*Qawwalis (see p28), always sung by a group, are specially composed to sing the saint's praises in front of his tomb.*

★ **Mazar Sharif**
*Chishti's tomb, begun during the saint's lifetime by Iltutmish, was completed in the 16th century by Humayun. Later Mughal princes added to it. A marble dome surmounts the simple brick tomb, enclosed by a silver railing and a marble lattice screen.*

**Ibadat Khana,**
**(prayer hall)**

| STAR FEATURES |
| --- |
| ★ Mazar Sharif |
| ★ Shahjahani Masjid |
| ★ Mehfil Khana |

### Akbar's Mosque
*Akbar, Chishti's most illustrious devotee, walked from Agra to Ajmer twice: once for enabling his conquest of Chittor, and again after the birth of his heir, Prince Salim, the future Jahangir.*

**VISITORS' CHECKLIST**

Ajmer district. 141 km (87 miles) SW of Jaipur. **Road map** B4.
🛈 *RTDC, Hotel Khadim (0145) 52 426.* ◻ *daily.*
📅 *Urs (Oct–Nov).* 🗓

### Pilgrims
*People of every faith come to seek favours and bring flowers and chadors as thanksgiving offerings.*

**Nizam Gate**

**Dargah Bazaar**

**Shahjahani Gate**

### Buland Darwaza
*This imposing entrance doorway was erected by one of the Khilji rulers. A flag is hoisted over its ramparts to mark the start of the Urs ceremony held each October.*

### Dargah Bazaar
*The long road that lies outside the Nizam Gate, the main entrance to the complex, is the location of a bustling market. Colourful stalls and kiosks sell baskets of rose petals as well as chadors for devotees to offer at the dargah.*

### Degs
*Two enormous* degs *(iron cauldrons), one nearly 10 ft (3 m) in diameter, are used during the Urs for cooking a special rice pudding,* tabarrukh. *After they have been emptied, professional divers "loot" the* degs *by jumping in and scooping out the dregs.*

A 15th-century manuscript, Arabic and Persian Research Institute, Tonk

## Chaksu ⑲

Jaipur district. 43 km (27 miles) S of Jaipur on NH12. **Road map** C4.
🚶17,000. 🚌 🏛 Shitala Ashtami (Mar–Apr).

THIS SLEEPY LITTLE village on the road from Jaipur towards Sawai Madhopur is known for its small white temple dedicated to Shitala Mata, the goddess who wards off disease, especially small-pox. A hundred steps lead up to the shrine, around which devotees gather for a gossip after propitiating the deity. Shitala Mata is much venerated in parts of rural Rajasthan where diseases are still fatal. Every year in March or April, a fair is held here, which attracts a large number of pilgrims. Food is cooked a day before Ashtami, the eighth and most auspicious day after the new moon, and offered cold to the goddess to ensure her protection.

## Tonk ⑳

Tonk district. 96 km (60 miles) S of Jaipur on NH12. **Road map** C4.
🚶111,000. 🚌 🏛 daily 10am–7:30pm. 🏛 Id (Feb–Mar).

THE SMALL PRINCIPALITY of Tonk, the only Muslim kingdom in Rajasthan, was created by the British in the early 19th century to appease the powerful Pathan warlord, Amir Khan. The legacy of its nawabs is evident throughout the old city. They constructed the imposing Jami Masjid for worship, as well as a number of fine painted mansions of which the **Sunehri Kothi** ("golden mansion"), built in 1824 by Amir Khan in the old palace complex, is the most spectacular. Magnificent enamelled mirrorwork and gilded stucco cover the walls and ceilings of its jewel-like interior, the windows are fitted with stained-glass and the floors beautifully painted.

The old city also has many Raj-style bungalows that were once the homes of the British Resident and his entourage.

The nawabs were dedicated patrons of art and literature. In the late 19th century, the third ruler established a grand centre of Islamic art, now known as the **Maulana Abul Kalam Azad Arabic and Persian Research Institute**. Its collection of rare Arabic and Persian manuscripts includes several illuminated Korans, such as Aurangzeb's *Alamgiri Koran Sharif* and the *Koran-e-Kamal,* prepared on the orders of Shah Jahan. There are also translations of the epics, the *Ramayana* and the *Mahabharata* inscribed in exquisite Persian and also Arabic calligraphy.

🏛 **Sunehri Kothi**
◯ Under renovation. Enquire at Tourist Reception Centre, Jaipur.
🏛 **MAKA Arabic and Persian Research Institute**
Near new bus stand. ◯ 10am–5pm.
⬤ Sun. 📞 (01432) 42 389.

## Sawai Madhopur ㉑

Sawai Madhopur district. 172 km (107 miles) SE of Jaipur. **Road map** C4. 🚶151,000. 🚆 🚌 🏛 Mon–Sat.
🏛 Shivaratri (Feb), Ganesha Chaturthi (Aug–Sep).

AN IMPORTANT railway junction and entry point to the Ranthambhore National Park, Sawai Madhopur is named after its founder Sawai Madho Singh I (r.1750–68). The historic 10th-century

A cart stands outside a village hut on the outskirts of Sawai Madhopur

**A rooftop view of the distant Indergarh Fort**

Ranthambhore Fort (now in the park), a prized trophy on the main route to Central India, was the scene of many terrible battles between its Rajput chieftains and the invading armies from Delhi and Agra. The fort was attacked by Alauddin Khilji *(see pp50–51)* and later by Akbar in 1569. This battle has been glorified in Mughal miniatures and bards have sung about the heroic deeds of its Rajput defenders. The fort was eventually handed over to the Amber kings *(see pp200–203)*. This jungle fort, despite its ruined state, looks daunting. Its massive gateways, ramparts and bastions make entry a tricky affair. Within it is an 8th-century temple dedicated to Ganesha, whose priest receives sacks of letters, sometimes addressed simply to "Shri Ganesha, Ranthambhore", especially during the marriage season, in order to invoke the deity's blessings. Clumps of grass tied together by newlyweds for luck are also seen along the way to the fort temple.

**ENVIRONS:** About 37 km (24 miles) west of Sawai Madhopur, is the sprawling **Uniara Palace**. Further towards Tonk, past **Hathi Bhata**, a life-sized elephant carved out of a single rock, is the picturesque **Kakod Fort**. East of Sawai Madhopur, is the vast **Mansarovar Lake**.

# Ranthambhore National Park ㉒

*See pp224–5.*

# Indergarh ㉓

Kota district. 52 km (33 miles) S of Sawai Madhopur. **Road map** C4. **Indergarh Fort** ☐ *8am–5pm daily, on request to the caretaker who lives below the fort. Donation optional.*

THIS SMALL TOWN, founded by Raja Indrasal in 1605, lies huddled beneath the ramparts of a picturesque hill fort which is clearly visible from the flat rooftops of houses where, in summer, people sleep at night. Though dilapidated, some fort areas still bear traces of exquisite murals depicting court scenes and legends. Indergarh's two main temples, one dedicated to Bijasan Mata (a form of Durga) and the other to Kuanwalji (Lord Shiva), are popular places of worship for pilgrims.

## TALE OF THE TIGER

The tiger plays a major role in Indian myth as a symbol of supreme power, kingship and manhood. In Puranic legend it is Durga, the fearsome goddess with ten arms, who rides a tiger and defeats the invincible buffalo-headed demon, Mahishasura. Yet, for all its aura of strength and power the tiger is a vulnerable creature today.

**Durga riding a tiger, detail of a miniature painting**

Statistics claim that at the turn of the 20th century India's tiger population was about 40,000, but by 1972, the figure had dropped to roughly 1,800. This was when a special Task Force of the Indian Board for Wildlife constituted Project Tiger to address the alarming issue of dwindling tiger populations across the country. In the first year of Project Tiger, nine wildlife sanctuaries were declared tiger reserves, one of them being Ranthambhore.

There are now 25 reserves, and the number of tigers has grown substantially, though persistent habitat destruction, illegal poaching and trading of tiger parts for medicinal and other derivatives in many Far Eastern countries continue to threaten the life of this supreme predator.

# Ranthambhore National Park ㉒

**Park sign**

**Rajbagh**
*Ruined pavilions stand on the banks of Rajbagh Talao, one of the three lakes in the park.*

THIS PARK LIES IN the shadow of the Aravalli and Vindhya mountain ranges and covers a core area of 400 sq km (155 sq miles). Its razor-sharp ridges, deep boulder-filled gorges, lakes and jungle are the habitat of carnivores such as the caracal, panther, jackal and hyena, species of deer, and a rich variety of resident and migratory birds. The most famous resident, however, is the endangered tiger, and it is fairly common to catch glimpses of this fascinating animal by day or night. Like other parks in the region, this was originally the Jaipur state's hunting grounds and became a Project Tiger Reserve in 1973.

**Ranthambhore Fort**
*The park derives its name from this great Rajput jungle fort that is 1,000 years old and stands at a height of 215 m (705 ft).*

**Sambar Stag**
*Large herds of sambar are seen around the lakes, wallowing in the water, swimming and feeding on aquatic plants, unperturbed by jeeps and visitors.*

JAIPUR

TONK

Sawai Madhopur

MUMBAI

Nalghati Valley

Milak Talao
Padam Talao
Rajbagh Talao
Ranthambhore Fort
Jogi Mahal
La
Lahapur
Man Sarovar

**Banyan Tree**
*India's second-largest banyan tree (Ficus bengalensis) lies in the grounds of Jogi Mahal. Its several spreading branches are all supported by roots.*

0 kilometres     5

0 miles     2

**Tiger**
*Sitings of the park's
main predator are a
matter of chance, but
traces of its activities
are equally exciting.*

## VISITORS' CHECKLIST

Sawai Madhopur district. 180 km
(112 miles) SE of Jaipur. **Road
map** C4. 🚂 *Sawai Madhopur.*
🛈 *RTDC Hotel Vinayak, Sawai
Madhopur (07462) 21 333.*
◯ *Oct–Jun: 7–10am & 3–6pm.*
● *Jul–Sep.* 🖼 ✓ 📷 📫 *The
Dastkari Kendra, opp Kutalpura
village on way to Kundera.*
📞 *(07462) 52 009.*
**No walking** *only jeeps hired
from Project Tiger, office of the
Forest Dept, Sawai Madhopur
are allowed inside the park.*
📞 *(07462) 20 223.*

**Indian Roller Bird**
*This is one of the
many bird species
found in the park. The
others include birds of
prey such as the
crested serpent eagle
and Bonelli's eagle,
and many species of
pigeons, flycatchers,
storks and waterbirds.*

**Marsh Crocodiles**
*Muggers, or marsh crocodiles, are commonly seen
submerged in water or basking on the shores of
the lakes. Ungulates are their main prey species,
and sometimes one can glimpse a crocodile
dragging the carcass of a deer into the water. The
monitor lizard and python are some of the other
reptiles found in the park.*

**Sloth Bear**
*This shaggy
bear with short
hind legs and a
long muzzle emerges
at dusk to feed.
During the day
it shelters in the
rocky outcrops
and is difficult
to sight.*

Banas

Semli
Valley

karda

Galai Sagar

Khandhar
Fort

pur

Khatola

### KEY

━━ Major road

── Railway

▬ Park border

⚶ Viewpoint

• ▪ Trails

⋔ Archaeological sight, ruin

🛈 Information centre

# TRAVELLERS' NEEDS

# WHERE TO STAY

POPULARLY KNOWN AS the Golden Triangle, the Delhi, Agra and Jaipur region receives the largest number of tourists in India, so this area is well-equiped with places to stay. The choice of accommodation ranges from up-market luxury hotels run by international or leading Indian chains, to small guesthouses and youth hostels. In addition, there are state-run tourist hotels in several towns, with comfortable board and lodging at reasonable rates. On the more exotic

**Palace doorman**

side are the grand old palaces and *havelis* of the Jaipur region which re-create the lavish lifestyles of former rulers and aristocracy (*see pp232–3*). For the budget traveller, on the other hand, there is a choice of ashrams and small guesthouses, sometimes with extremely basic facilities. Tented accommodation is as yet rare, as is self-catering. Rooms are usually cheaper during the off-season (Apr–Sep). For more information on places to stay in this region, refer to the detailed listings on pages 234–47.

## HOTEL CHAINS, GRADING AND FACILITIES

AT THE TOP END of the range are the five-star deluxe hotels which provide luxurious accommodation for the international visitor. Many of these are part of national chains, such as the **Ashok Group**, or of international groups such as the **Sheraton** and **Radisson** (*see p231*). Below them are the four- and three-star hotels, guesthouses and tourist lodges, some of which may offer additional facilities, such as a pool or tennis court. International television channels are now shown on most hotel room sets. In Agra and Jaipur, palaces, bungalows and *havelis* have been converted into heritage hotels, which carry the flavour of erstwhile grandeur

and graciousness. Except in some of the lower priced hotels, the bathrooms, even in older properties, are in Western style. Room service, safe deposits and daily laundry are standard in more expensive places. The reception desk can advise on tours, and large hotels have travel agencies on the premises.

**Traditional huts, Desert Resort, Mandawa**

## LUXURY HOTELS

INDIA'S TOP LUXURY hotels match the best in the world in their elegance, professional services, and wide range of facilities. Architecturally, many of them have cleverly combined traditional Indian and modern

**Five-star hotel logo**

design, while their interiors are sumptuously decorated with the best of Indian crafts and textiles. The hotels run by the large international and national chains are fully air-conditioned and offer a wide range of conveniences such as a resident doctor, shopping arcades and patisseries, banqueting halls, a 24-hour coffee shop, bars and gourmet restaurants. For the business traveller there are business and conference centres equipped with computers for personal use with facilities for access to the Internet. Desk jacks and modems are provided for personal computers and laptops. Additional facilities include beauty parlours and fitness centres, swimming pools and tennis courts. The front desk can often make bookings for golf and other activities. Some hotels even have a regular palmist, tarot card reader or astrologer.

**Agra's Mughal Sheraton is renowned for its innovative architecture**

◁ **Vegetables temptingly stacked in a roadside stall**

## HERITAGE HOTELS

SEVERAL PALACES and stately homes, particularly in Rajasthan, have been restored and converted into hotels. These come under the banner of **Heritage Hotels Association of India**. A private agency, **WelcomHeritage** (see p231) specializes in booking accommodation to these hotels which have been classified as Grand, Classic and Ordinary, and are priced accordingly. However, most travel agents can also make bookings at these places.

## MIDDLE-RANGE HOTELS

THESE ARE four- and three-star establishments that may lack the stylish decor, slickness and range of facilities of five-star hotels. Though smaller in size they are always comfortable, clean and well-serviced. The rooms are generally air-conditioned with attached baths that have hot and cold running water. Some are surrounded by extensive gardens and may even have cafés and business centres.

**Logo of the Welcomgroup chain**

## BUDGET HOTELS AND TOURIST LODGES

BUDGET HOTELS are usually found in the older sections of cities, near the railway and bus stations. The accommodation is mostly simple and varies from very basic to homely guesthouses. Ceiling fans, mosquito nets and private, Indian- or Western-style bathrooms are generally provided. The rates in Delhi are higher than the rest of the region.

The wide network of tourist "bungalows" or lodges established by state tourism departments and the national India Tourism Development Corporation's (ITDC) Ashok Group (see p297) make travelling to lesser-known places easier. The rates are reasonable, and there is a choice of dormitories as well as double rooms with attached bathrooms.

## GUESTHOUSES

THE TERM "GUESTHOUSE" can be a misnomer. Both mid-range and budget hotels can have "guesthouse" appended to their name, and so the prices and the services can vary enormously. If you opt for a lower priced one, do make it a point to inspect the room before checking in, especially the bathroom, which will probably contain an Indian-style toilet. The better guesthouses all have air-conditioning and attached baths with Western toilets. In Jaipur, some families have converted all or part of their large *havelis* to guesthouses, providing meals on order.

*A **dharamshala** in Haridwar*

## PAYING GUESTS

YOU CAN FIND short-term paying guest accommodation in Delhi through the **Government of India Tourist Office** (see p279) or your travel agent. In Agra, the tourist information counter at the railway station can supply addresses, and in Jaipur, **Rajasthan Tourism (RTDC)** (see p231) has an official and comprehensive list of families under a good Paying Guest Scheme administered by them. **Munjeeta Travel**, based in the United Kingdom (see p231) can organize Homestay Tours across India.

## DHARAMSHALAS AND ASHRAMS

REST HOUSES for pilgrims known as *dharamshalas* are run by a religious trust, but anyone can stay, as in the **International Rest House** in Brindavan, or **Ramakrishna Mission** and **Sri Aurobindo Ashram** in Delhi (see p231), provided the rules of the place are strictly followed. They charge absurdly low rates. In cities, *dharamshalas* in the older sections may have dubious standards of hygiene, and the facilities can amount to a bare room with no bedding, shared with others along with the bathroom. Some temples and ashrams also rent out rooms to guests seeking a religious retreat. The amenities here are basic, though clean, and guests are expected to respect the rules of the community.

**A luxurious deluxe room in a five-star hotel**

## YOUTH HOSTELS

THERE IS A NETWORK of youth hostels across India, including the YMCA (see p281). They offer unbelievably low rates, although the YMCA's are pricier with better facilities and are found only in selected cities. Though it is not necessary to be a member of Youth Hostel International to gain entry, during the busy season, its members do get priority and always get lower rates. Rooms and dormitories are both usually available, and the rules of the hostel must be respected.

## NATIONAL PARKS AND CAMPING SITES

THE NATIONAL PARKS have several places to stay in, but no dedicated camping sites. At the Pushkar fair grounds, Rajasthan Tourism sets up a **Tourist Village** on a large campsite. A few hotels in Rajasthan, such as Samode Bagh or **Sawai Madhopur Lodge** also offer some tent accommodation, and in Uttar Pradesh, apart from private operators, such as **Outdoor Adventures** and **Milestones**, the state government has a river rafting campsite on the River Ganges at Rishikesh.

## PRICES AND DISCOUNTS

RATES VARY between cities, with Delhi being the most expensive, and the small-town hotels being absurdly cheap at times. The five-star

A view of the main swimming pool at the Rajvilas Hotel in Jaipur

luxury and the palace or heritage hotels are at the top end of the scale. Those run by the state tourism development corporations can vary from state to state with Delhi again being the most expensive. Prices at the so-called guesthouses swing from high to low. Most hotels offer discounts during the low season from April to September. This can bring the original rates down by almost 50 per cent at times.

Every October, hotels raise their rates by a nominal percentage. Various taxes are charged, over and above the listed rates, as notified by the government from time to time. Foreigners have to pay cash amounts in foreign currency, usually in dollars or pounds sterling which is about 25 per cent higher than payment in Indian rupees.

**RAJVILĀS**

Logo of an Oberoi luxury hotel

## TAXES

TAXES VARY FROM state to state. A ten per cent luxury tax is levied on the room rate in all five-star hotels. An additional ten per cent expenditure tax on the rack rate is charged on any special rates given by the hotel. Food and beverages carry a tax of 17 per cent on the listed price. A ten per cent service tax is normally included in the bill.

## HIDDEN EXTRAS

SERVICES FOR which you may be charged extra could include bottles of mineral water, breakfast, laundry, extra bedding, telephone calls, e-mails and faxes, the mini bar in your room, and special pay channels on television (you should read the screen or your room service folder before pressing the remote). Hotels usually charge extra for transport to and from the hotel. When telephoning, it is cheaper to use the pay phones in the lobby or at outside STD booths (see p291). At small-town hotels with no running hot water, the hotel will give you a bucket of hot water once a day at a nominal cost.

## BOOKING, CHECKING IN AND OUT

IT IS A GOOD IDEA to make your hotel bookings well in advance, especially for the peak October to March tourist

The Glass House on the Ganges in Rishikesh

season when many confer-
ences and cultural festivals
take place. You can fax or
telephone your requirements,
but do insist that you are sent
a written confirmation.

Check out time is usually at
12 noon, though at smaller
establishments they are not so
particular and calculate by the
day. Before checking out, do
study your bills carefully and
retain all the receipts.

## TOUTS

A T THE AIRPORT or railway
station you may be
besieged by touts *(see p265)*,
many of whom also operate
as taxi and three-wheeler
drivers, who insist on taking
you to hotels where they get
a commission. The best
solution is to have prior
bookings. Failing this, the
counter at the airport or
station will help you find a
place suitable to your needs.
However, if there is no other
option, you should be firm
about how much you are
willing to spend and check
out the tout's commission.
You should also ask for
choices, and when you reach
the hotel, be sure it is
acceptable to you before
dismissing the driver. If touts
continue to pester you, speak
to the nearest policeman.

**Samode Bagh's exquisite tents recreate a royal Mughal ambience**

### FACILITIES FOR CHILDREN

T HE STAFF AT HOTELS are
usually very good with
children. Many hotels will
willingly add an extra bed in
your room for a child for a
small extra charge. Very few
provide baby-sitting services,
and you should check at the
front desk, but usually
parents are expected to look
after their children. Most
hotels do not have any
special facilities for children.

### DISABLED TRAVELLERS

O NLY THE NEWER and fancier
hotels make an effort to
provide ramps, special lifts
and wheelchairs for disabled

travellers. However, you can
always seek the help of the
staff. Many of the older
hotels, especially in Rajasthan,
which are converted from
palaces and private mansions,
have several levels within
them, with no ramp or lifts
for easy movement. Do check
out these facilities before
making your bookings.

### TIPPING

T IPPING is expected even
though there may be a
service charge on bills. The
amounts are at the discretion
of the guest, starting with
Rs10 for car parking attendants, slightly more for a
porter, and ten per cent of the
total bill for waiters.

---

## DIRECTORY

### HOTEL CHAINS

**Ashok Group**
ITDC, Scope Building, 7
Lodi Rd, Delhi.
(011) 436 0303.

**Oberoi Group**
Oberoi Maidens, 7 Sham
Nath Marg, Delhi.
(011) 389 0505.

**Radisson Hotels**
National Highway 8,
Mahipalpur Rd, Delhi.
(011) 612 9191.

**Taj Group**
Taj Mahal
Intercontinental, Apollo
Bunder, Mumbai.
(022) 202 3366.

**Welcomgroup
Maurya Sheraton**
Maurya Sheraton, Sardar
Patel Marg, Delhi.
(011) 611 2233.

### HERITAGE HOTELS

**Heritage Hotels
Association of India**
306, Anukampa Towers,
Church Rd, Jaipur.
(0141) 37 4112.

**WelcomHeritage**
J Block Mkt, Saket, Delhi.
(011) 686 8992.

### PAYING GUEST ACCOMMODATION

**Munjeeta Travel**
12 Cavendish Rd, Woking,
Surrey GU22 OEP, UK.
(01483) 77 3331.

**RTDC, Jaipur**
Govt Hostel, MI Rd.
(0141) 37 0181.
Swagatam Tourist Campus.
(0141) 37 5834.

### DHARAMSHALAS AND ASHRAMS

**International Rest
House**
Shri Krishna-Balaram
Temple, Brindavan.
(0565) 44 478.

**Ramakrishna
Mission**
Ramakrishna Ashram
Marg, Delhi.
(011) 352 7110.

**Sri Aurobindo
Ashram**
Aurobindo Marg, Delhi.
(011) 656 9225.

### NATIONAL PARKS AND CAMPING SITES

**Milestones**
C-426 Chittaranjan Park,
Delhi.
(011) 622 0529.

**Outdoor
Adventures**
S-234 Panchsheel Park,
Delhi.
(011) 622 7485.

**Sawai Madhopur
Lodge**
National Park Rd, Sawai
Madhopur.
(07462) 20 541.

**Tourist Village
(RTDC)**
Pushkar.
(0145) 72 074.

# Heritage Hotels

THE TERM "heritage hotel" is given to some palaces and *havelis* that have been discreetly modernized to meet the needs of international travellers and run as high-class hotels. Fitted with modern plumbing and air-conditioning and with facilities such as swimming pools and tennis courts, such hotels take care that their history, architecture and innate elegance are suitably highlighted. The interiors display old sepia photographs, memorabilia and exquisite furniture tended by a caring staff, often old family retainers. The high tariffs of such hotels are compensated by their special ambience.

**Castle Mandawa, Mandawa**
*This mid-18th century fortress is now a charming heritage hotel and ideal base to explore the painted havelis of Shekhawati. Live entertainment by Rajasthani folk dancers and musicians and camel rides are some of its attractions (see p246).*

**Samode Palace, Samode**
*All the grandeur of royal Rajasthan is visible in this opulent painted palace. Its magnificent Durbar Hall and Sheesh Mahal are now reception areas where guests can dine (see p247).*

JAIPUR AND ENVIRONS

**Hotel Pushkar Palace, Pushkar**
*The lake-side palace, once the property of the Maharaja of Kishangarh, is now a popular hotel in this temple town. Its location is ideal for views of the bathing ghats, the rugged Aravalli Hills and the town's 400 temples (see p247).*

**Narain Niwas Palace, Jaipur**
*Surrounded by sprawling gardens and mango orchards, this traditional palace was built in 1928 (see p245).*

**Neemrana Fort Palace, Neemrana**
*Built in 1464, this fort was one of India's first heritage hotels. Meticulously restored to re-create the original plan and architecture; its interior is an eclectic blend of traditional design and its modern interpretations (see p246).*

0 kilometres 100

0 miles 50

DELHI

**The Hill Fort, Kesroli**
*This seven-turreted fort is believed to be 600 years old. Built on top of a small hillock, it commands a splendid view from its high ramparts and is a perfect base from which to visit neighbouring sites and sanctuaries (see p243).*

AGRA AND AROUND

**Laxmi Vilas Palace, Bharatpur**
Located near the Keoladeo National Park, the palace was built in 1899 for the women of the royal family. The architecture is a mix of Mughal and Rajput styles. Spacious airy rooms are furnished with period furniture and the courtyards are decorated with colourful frescoes *(see p241)*.

**Sawai Madhopur Lodge, Sawai Madhopur**
A colonial building furnished in the 1930s style, on the outskirts of the Ranthambhore National Park, this was a hunting lodge of the Maharaja of Jaipur *(see p247)*.

**Usha Kiran Palace, Gwalior**
*The Maharaja of Gwalior's official guesthouse is now a pleasant hotel with an old-world charm (see p241).*

# Choosing a Hotel

Most of the hotels in this guide, listed according to region, have been included because of their location, the excellence of their service, facilities offered and value for money. Map references refer to the Delhi Street Finder maps on pages 124–131. Colour-coded thumb tabs show the regions covered on each page. For restaurant listings see pages 256–263.

## Delhi

| Hotel | Credit Cards | Swimming Pool | Western Bathrooms | Coffee Shop | Garden/Terrace |
|---|---|---|---|---|---|
| **New Delhi:** *Indraprastha.* **Map** 5 A1. Rs Rs<br>19 Ashok Rd. *(011) 334 4511.* FAX *(011) 336 8153.*<br>Basic facilities, good rates, at walking distance from the city centre, this is a popular budget hotel for the intrepid traveller. ***Rooms:*** *450.* | | | | ● | |
| **New Delhi:** *Prince Polonia.* **Map** 1 B3. Rs Rs<br>2325/26 Tilak Gali, Paharganj. *(011) 351 1930.* FAX *(011) 355 7646.*<br>@ *polinter@del3.vsnl.net.in* Friendly, clean and cosy, this hotel provides a cheap option for low-budget travellers. Its convenient location near the railway station is an added advantage. 24 TV ***Rooms:*** *27.* *21.* | AE | ● | ■ | | |
| **New Delhi:** *YMCA Tourist Hostel.* **Map** 1 B5. Rs Rs<br>Jai Singh Rd. *(011) 336 1915.* FAX *(011) 374 6035.* @ *ymcth@ndf.vsnl.net.in*<br>Reasonable rates, plain but comfortable rooms, and good access to the commercial heart of the city. 24 TV ***Rooms:*** *112.* *80.* | AE DC MC V | ● | ■ | ● | ■ |
| **New Delhi:** *YWCA of Delhi.* **Map** 1 B5. Rs Rs<br>Blue Triangle Family Hostel, Ashok Rd. *(011) 336 0133.* FAX *(011) 336 0202.*<br>A homely atmosphere, very popular with budget travellers and students. The hostel has both rooms and dormitories. ***Rooms:*** *40.* *20.* | | | ■ | | |
| **New Delhi:** *Janpath.* **Map** 5 A1. Rs Rs Rs<br>Janpath. *(011) 334 0070.* FAX *(011) 334 7038.*<br>This well-run hotel is located on a popular shopping avenue and near several travel and car rental agencies. 24 TV ***Rooms:*** *200.* *200.* | AE DC MC V | | ■ | ● | |
| **New Delhi:** *Marina.* **Map** 1 C4. Rs Rs Rs<br>G–59 Connaught Place. *(011) 332 4658.* FAX *(011) 332 8609.*<br>@ *marina@nde.vsnl.net.in* This unassuming hotel with high-ceilinged, old-fashioned rooms offers basic facilities. 24 TV ***Rooms:*** *100.* *100.* | AE DC MC V | | ■ | ● | |
| **New Delhi:** *Nirula's.* **Map** 1 C4. Rs Rs Rs<br>L Block, Connaught Place. *(011) 332 2419.* FAX *(011) 332 4669.*<br>@ *delhihotel@nirula.com* A clean and compact hotel, it has an excellent Chinese restaurant *(see p256).* 24 ***Rooms:*** *29.* *29.* | DC MC V | | ■ | ● | |
| **New Delhi:** *Yorks.* **Map** 1 C4. Rs Rs Rs<br>K–10 Connaught Circus. *(011) 332 3769.* FAX *(011) 335 2419.*<br>Simple rooms and essential services. A reasonably priced city centre hotel with a restaurant. TV ***Rooms:*** *27.* *27.* | AE DC MC V | | ■ | | |
| **New Delhi:** *Ambassador.* **Map** 5 B3. Rs Rs Rs Rs<br>Sujan Singh Park, Subramaniam Bharati Marg. *(011) 463 2600.* FAX *(011) 463 2252.*<br>@ *ambassadorhotel@vsnl.com* Integrated with an old and gracious residential complex, the hotel has been refurbished and upgraded and has an excellent South Indian restaurant. 24 TV ***Rooms:*** *88.* *88.* | AE DC MC V | | ■ | ● | ■ |
| **New Delhi:** *Centre Point.* **Map** 1 C5. Rs Rs Rs Rs<br>Kasturba Gandhi Marg. *(011) 335 4304.* FAX *(011) 332 9138.*<br>@ *hefadmis@nda.vsnl.net.in* A renovated old colonial bungalow, this is a compact hotel close to the city centre. 24 TV ***Rooms:*** *50.* *50.* | AE DC MC V JCB | | ■ | ● | ■ |
| **New Delhi:** *Connaught.* **Map** 1 B4. Rs Rs Rs Rs<br>37 Shahid Bhagat Singh Marg. *(011) 336 4225.* FAX *(011) 334 0757.*<br>@ *PROMINENT.HOTELS@gems.vsnl.net.in* Unremarkable, but an ideal place to stay if you need a central location. 24 TV ***Rooms:*** *80.* *80.* | AE DC MC V | | ■ | ● | |
| **New Delhi:** *Hotel Kanishka.* **Map** 5 A1. Rs Rs Rs Rs<br>19 Ashok Rd. *(011) 334 4422.* FAX *(011) 336 8242.*<br>Several tourist offices are on the premises of this comfortable high-rise hotel in the heart of Lutyens's Delhi. 24 TV ***Rooms:*** *315.* *315.* | AE DC MC V | ● | ■ | ● | ■ |

**Price categories** for a standard double room per night including tax and service charges but not including breakfast:

(Rs) under 550 rupees
(Rs)(Rs) 550–1,200 rupees
(Rs)(Rs)(Rs) 1,200–3,000 rupees
(Rs)(Rs)(Rs)(Rs) 3,000–6,000 rupees
(Rs)(Rs)(Rs)(Rs)(Rs) over 6,000 rupees

**CREDIT CARDS**
Indicates which credit cards are accepted: *AE* American Express; *DC* Diners Club; *MC* Master Card/Access; *V* Visa; *JCB* Japanese Credit Bureau.
**WESTERN BATHROOMS**
Indicates sit-down, flush toilets; showers and/or baths. Others have squat toilets and bucket-and-mug baths.
**COFFEE SHOP**
Hotels with coffee shop.
**GARDEN/TERRACE**
Hotels with a garden, courtyard or terrace.

| | CREDIT CARDS | SWIMMING POOL | WESTERN BATHROOMS | COFFEE SHOP | GARDEN/TERRACE |
|---|---|---|---|---|---|
| **NEW DELHI:** *Claridges.* Map 5 A3. (Rs)(Rs)(Rs)(Rs)<br>Aurangzeb Rd. (011) 301 0211. FAX (011) 301 0625. @ claridges.hotel@gems.vsnl.net.in<br>This large mansion-like hotel with charm and character is located next to the historic Lodi Gardens. It also has tennis courts, good restaurants and an irresistible bakery. ❚❚ ❚ ❚ 24 TV 🔓 *Rooms: 162.* ▤ 162. | AE<br>DC<br>MC<br>V | ● | ▦ | ● | ▦ |
| **NEW DELHI:** *Hans Plaza.* Map 2 D5. (Rs)(Rs)(Rs)(Rs)<br>Barakhamba Rd. (011) 331 6861. FAX (011) 331 4830.@ hansotel@nde.vsnl.net.in<br>A mid-range hotel with modern conference facilities located in an area that has many business offices and banks. A floor here offers extra amenities at a higher charge. ❚❚ ❚ 24 TV 🔓 *Rooms: 70.* ▤ 70. | AE<br>DC<br>MC<br>V | | ▦ | ● | ▦ |
| **NEW DELHI:** *Imperial Hotel.* Map 1 C5. (Rs)(Rs)(Rs)(Rs)(Rs)<br>Janpath. (011) 334 1234. FAX (011) 334 2255. @ hotel@imperialindia.com<br>One of Delhi's institutions, this colonial-style luxurious hotel enviably located at walking distance from a row of fascinating shops, proudly preserves its Raj ambience. ❚❚ ❚ 24 TV 🔓 *Rooms: 265.* ▤ 265. | AE<br>DC<br>MC<br>V<br>JCB | ● | ▦ | ● | ▦ |
| **NEW DELHI:** *Inter-Continental.* Map 2 D5. (Rs)(Rs)(Rs)(Rs)(Rs)<br>Barakhamba Ave, Connaught Place. (011) 332 0101. FAX (011) 332 5335.<br>@ buscentr@nda.vsnl.net.in A popular luxury hotel close to the city centre. Adjacent to the World Trade Centre, its location is an advantage for the business traveller. ❚❚ ❚ ❚ 24 TV 🔓 *Rooms: 445.* ▤ 445. | AE<br>DC<br>MC<br>V | ● | ▦ | ● | ▦ |
| **NEW DELHI:** *Le Meridien.* Map 5 A1. (Rs)(Rs)(Rs)(Rs)(Rs)<br>Windsor Place, Janpath. (011) 371 0101. FAX (011) 371 4545. @ meridien@vsnl.com<br>A magnificent atrium hotel, it includes book shops and boutiques encircling the central space, and excellent restaurants including one cantilevered on the topmost level. ❚❚ ❚ ❚ 24 TV 🔓 *Rooms: 355.* ▤ 355. | AE<br>DC<br>MC<br>V | ● | ▦ | ● | |
| **NEW DELHI:** *The Oberoi.* Map 6 D4. (Rs)(Rs)(Rs)(Rs)(Rs)<br>Dr Zakir Hussain Rd. (011) 436 3030. FAX (011) 436 0484.<br>@ reservations@oberoidel.com Definitely the most exclusive establishment in the city. Speciality restaurants and an enviable executive centre appeal to up-market visitors. ❚❚ ❚ ❚ 24 TV 🔓 *Rooms: 290.* ▤ 290. | AE<br>DC<br>MC<br>V<br>JCB | ● | ▦ | ● | ▦ |
| **NEW DELHI:** *The Park.* Map 1 C5. (Rs)(Rs)(Rs)(Rs)(Rs)<br>Parliament St. (011) 373 3737. FAX (011) 373 2025. @ theresi@nda.vsnl.net.in<br>In the heart of busy Connaught Place, this luxurious hotel has a popular disco with live jazz on fixed days of the week. It also hosts interesting talks and programmes. ❚❚ ❚ ❚ 24 TV 🔓 *Rooms: 224.* ▤ 224. | AE<br>DC<br>MC<br>V | ● | ▦ | ● | ▦ |
| **NEW DELHI:** *Taj Mahal.* Map 5 B3. (Rs)(Rs)(Rs)(Rs)(Rs)<br>Mansingh Rd. (011) 302 6162. FAX (011) 302 7299. @ tajmahal@giasdl01.vsnl.net.in<br>Situated along a leafy avenue, this beautiful hotel combines traditional decor with modern facilities, superb restaurants and a sumptuous handicrafts and book shop. ❚❚ ❚ ❚ 24 TV 🔓 *Rooms: 300.* ▤ 300. | AE<br>DC<br>MC<br>V | ● | ▦ | ● | ▦ |
| **NIZAMUDDIN:** *Jukasso Inn.* Map 6 D3. (Rs)(Rs)(Rs)<br>50 Sundar Nagar. (011) 469 0308. FAX (011) 469 4402.<br>Very popular with a business clientele, this converted residence in one of New Delhi's more affluent localities is next door to a market known for its antique shops. 24 TV *Rooms: 50.* ▤ 50. | AE<br>DC<br>MC<br>V | | ▦ | | |
| **NIZAMUDDIN:** *La Sagrita Tourist Home.* Map 6 D3. (Rs)(Rs)(Rs)<br>14 Sundar Nagar. (011) 460 1249. FAX (011) 463 6956.<br>Located in a peaceful residential area, this is a comfortable up-market guesthouse with a warm, friendly atmosphere. 24 TV *Rooms: 19.* ▤ 19. | AE<br>DC<br>MC<br>V | | ▦ | | ▦ |
| **NIZAMUDDIN:** *Maharani Guest House.* Map 6 D3. (Rs)(Rs)(Rs)<br>3 Sundar Nagar. (011) 469 3128. FAX (011) 462 4562.<br>Another residence converted into an elegant guesthouse. The staff are extremely courteous and helpful. 24 TV *Rooms: 24.* ▤ 24. | AE<br>DC<br>MC<br>V | | ▦ | | ▦ |

**Price categories** for a standard double room per night including tax and service charges but not including breakfast.

- (Rs) under 550 rupees
- (Rs)(Rs) 550–1,200 rupees
- (Rs)(Rs)(Rs) 1,200–3,000 rupees
- (Rs)(Rs)(Rs)(Rs) 3,000–6,000 rupees
- (Rs)(Rs)(Rs)(Rs)(Rs) over 6,000 rupees

**CREDIT CARDS**
Indicates which credit cards are accepted: *AE* American Express; *DC* Diners Club; *MC* Master Card/Access; *V* Visa; *JCB* Japanese Credit Bureau.
**WESTERN BATHROOMS**
Indicates sit-down, flush toilets; showers and/or baths. Others have squat toilets and bucket-and-mug baths.
**COFFEE SHOP**
Hotels with coffee shop.
**GARDEN/TERRACE**
Hotels with a garden, courtyard or terrace.

| | CREDIT CARDS | SWIMMING POOL | WESTERN BATHROOMS | COFFEE SHOP | GARDEN/TERRACE |
|---|---|---|---|---|---|
| **OLD DELHI:** *Broadway.* **Map** 2 E3. (Rs)(Rs)(Rs)<br>Asaf Ali Rd. (011) 327 3821. FAX (011) 326 9966.<br>This old hotel has easy access to both Old and New Delhi and is upgraded with modern facilities. A restaurant with delectable Kashmiri cuisine is on the premises. **Rooms:** 32. 32. | AE DC MC V | | ■ | | |
| **FURTHER AFIELD (NORTH):** *Oberoi Maidens.* (Rs)(Rs)(Rs)(Rs)<br>Sham Nath Marg. (011) 397 5464. FAX (011) 398 0771. @ bsparmar@tomdel.com<br>Close to Delhi University and the picturesque Ridge, this early 20th-century hotel has the elegant ambience of the Raj days when Edwin Lutyens first stayed here. **Rooms:** 54. 54. | AE DC MC V | ● | ■ | ● | ● |
| **FURTHER AFIELD (WEST):** *Diplomat.* (Rs)(Rs)(Rs)(Rs)<br>Sardar Patel Marg, Diplomatic Enclave. (011) 301 0204. FAX (011) 301 8605.<br>@ diplomat@nda.vsnl.net.in The advantage of staying in this stylish, well-managed and friendly hotel is that it is conveniently located near some important embassies. **Rooms:** 25. 25. | AE DC MC V | | ■ | ● | ● |
| **FURTHER AFIELD (WEST):** *Ashok Hotel.* (Rs)(Rs)(Rs)(Rs)(Rs)<br>Chanakyapuri. (011) 611 0101. FAX (011) 687 3216.<br>@ ashoknewdelhi@gems.vsnl.net.in A classic example of early modern Indian design, this majestic government-run hotel has grand suites and a wonderful shopping arcade. **Rooms:** 564. 564. | AE DC MC V | ● | ■ | ● | ● |
| **FURTHER AFIELD (WEST):** *Centaur.* (Rs)(Rs)(Rs)(Rs)(Rs)<br>IG International Airport. (011) 565 2223. FAX (011) 565 2256.<br>@ centaur@ndf.vsnl.net.in Since it is close to the airport, this modern hotel is popular with transit passengers. **Rooms:** 372. 372. | AE DC MC V | ● | ■ | ● | ● |
| **FURTHER AFIELD (WEST):** *Taj Palace.* (Rs)(Rs)(Rs)(Rs)(Rs)<br>Sardar Patel Marg, Diplomatic Enclave. (011) 611 0202. FAX (011) 611 0808.<br>@ palace.delhi@tajhotels.com Grand and imposing, this is a stylish member of the Taj Group, popular with the rich and famous for its speciality restaurants *(see p258).* **Rooms:** 420. 420. | AE DC MC V | ● | ■ | ● | ● |
| **FURTHER AFIELD (WEST):** *Welcomgroup Maurya Sheraton.* (Rs)(Rs)(Rs)(Rs)(Rs)<br>Sardar Patel Marg, Diplomatic Enclave. (011) 611 2233. FAX (011) 611 3333.<br>@ guest@cyber-club.com A plush, top-of-the-market hotel complete with a yoga centre, library, and a superb restaurant by the poolside renowned for its barbequed fare *(see p258).* **Rooms:** 440. 440. | AE DC MC V | ● | ■ | ● | ● |
| **FURTHER AFIELD (SOUTH):** *Lodhi Hotel.* (Rs)(Rs)(Rs)<br>Lala Lajpat Rai Marg. (011) 436 2422. FAX (011) 436 0883.<br>Despite its small rooms, this is a popular hotel. On its premises is one of Delhi's best South Indian restaurants. **Rooms:** 205. 205. | AE DC MC V | | ■ | ● | |
| **FURTHER AFIELD (SOUTH):** *Manor Country Hotel.* (Rs)(Rs)(Rs)(Rs)<br>Friends Colony West. (011) 692 5151. FAX (011) 684 0481.<br>@ manordel@ndf.vsnl.net.in Perhaps the most elegantly designed boutique hotel in the city, its location in one of the oldest and quietest residential colonies is an added advantage. **Rooms:** 18. 18. | AE MC V | | ■ | | |
| **FURTHER AFIELD (SOUTH):** *Qutab Hotel.* (Rs)(Rs)(Rs)(Rs)<br>Off Aurobindo Marg. (011) 652 1010. FAX (011) 696 0828.<br>A good base to explore important historic sites as well as some unusual examples of modern Indian architecture in the adjacent Jawaharlal Nehru University and institutional area. **Rooms:** 92. 92. | AE DC MC V | ● | ■ | ● | |
| **FURTHER AFIELD (SOUTH):** *Grand Hyatt.* (Rs)(Rs)(Rs)(Rs)(Rs)<br>Vasant Kunj, Phase II. (011) 612 1234. FAX (011) 689 5891.<br>@ info@hyattdelhi.com This impressive Millennium hotel ushers in the highest standards of international hotel technology along with the warmth of personalized services. **Rooms:** 390. 390. | AE DC MC V | ● | ■ | ● | |

**FURTHER AFIELD (SOUTH):** *Hyatt Regency.* ⓇⓈⓇⓈⓇⓈⓇⓈ
Bhikaji Cama Place, Ring Rd. **☎** *(011) 679 1234.* **FAX** *(011) 679 1122.*
**@** hyatt@del2.vsnl.net.in Very much in the five star tradition, this grand
hotel is near a busy commercial complex and is well known for its
popular bar. **🍴 🍸 🛏 24 📺 🛗** *Rooms: 518.* **▤** *510.*
AE DC MC V

**FURTHER AFIELD (SOUTH):** *Park Royal.* ⓇⓈⓇⓈⓇⓈⓇⓈ
Nehru Place. **☎** *(011) 622 3344.* **FAX** *(011) 622 4288.* **@** reservations@parkroyal.com.in
The hotel is in the heart of a buzzing South Delhi business area.
Excellent tea and coffee is served in the lobby, while conferences are
hosted with professional ease. **🍴 🍸 🛏 24 📺 🛗** *Rooms: 215.* **▤** *215.*
AE DC MC V

**FURTHER AFIELD (SOUTH):** *Radisson Hotel.* ⓇⓈⓇⓈⓇⓈⓇⓈ
National Highway 8, Mahipalpur Rd. **☎** *(011) 612 9191.* **FAX** *(011) 612 9090.*
**@** raddel@del2.vsnl.net.in Ideal for travellers who want to stay near the
airport. Part of an international chain, this hotel has many speciality
restaurants *(see p259).* **🍴 🍸 🛏 24 📺 🛗** *Rooms: 256.* **▤** *256.*
AE DC MC V

**FURTHER AFIELD (SOUTH):** *Surya.* ⓇⓈⓇⓈⓇⓈⓇⓈⓇⓈ
New Friends Colony. **☎** *(011) 683 5070* **FAX** *(011) 683 7758.*
**@** suryahot@ndf.vsnl.net.in One of the Best Western-USA chain hotels, the
Surya has easy access to several boutiques, shops and popular mid-range
restaurants in its neighbourhood. **🍴 🍸 🛏 24 📺 🛗** *Rooms: 236.* **▤** *236.*
AE DC MC V JCB

**FURTHER AFIELD (SOUTH):** *Vasant Continental.* ⓇⓈⓇⓈⓇⓈⓇⓈⓇⓈ
Vasant Vihar. **☎** *(011) 614 8800.* **FAX** *(011) 614 8900.* **@** hvc@del3.vsnl.net.in
A luxury hotel close to an up-market residential area, it is also near a
modern multiplex cinema and a lively market area that has good eateries
and shops. **🍴 🛏 24 📺 🛗** *Rooms: 134.* **▤** *134.*
AE DC MC V

**FURTHER AFIELD (SOUTH OF DELHI):** *Heritage Village.* ⓇⓈⓇⓈⓇⓈ
Manesar, Gurgaon. **☎** *(0124) (Dial 91 from Delhi) 37 3090.* **FAX** *(0124) 37 2272.*
Less than a 40 minute drive from the international airport on the Jaipur
highway, this hotel has an ethnic ambience and is in the vicinity of the
new Classic Golf Resort. **🍴 🛏 24 📺** *Rooms: 82.* **▤** *82.*
AE DC MC V

**FURTHER AFIELD (SOUTH OF DELHI):** *Bristol.* ⓇⓈⓇⓈⓇⓈⓇⓈ
Sikandarpur, Gurgaon. **☎** *(0124) (Dial 91 from Delhi) 35 6030.* **FAX** *(0124) 35 7834.*
**@** sales@thehotelbristol.com Respectably turned out, the hotel is a
convenient base for visitors whose interests are focused in this fast
expanding part of the region. **🍴 🍸 🛏 24 📺 🛗** *Rooms: 85.* **▤** *85.*
AE DC MC V

**FURTHER AFIELD (SOUTH OF DELHI):** *Ibrahim Kothi.* ⓇⓈⓇⓈⓇⓈⓇⓈ
Distt Pataudi, Haryana. **☎** For reservations: (011) 301 3549. **FAX** (011) 618 6833.
An elegant palatial establishment belonging to the Pataudi nawabs of
cricketing fame, this is an excellent place to take time off for a few days
of pampering and self indulgence. *Rooms: 10.*

## NORTH OF DELHI

**HARIDWAR:** *Himgiri.* ⓇⓈⓇⓈ
Devpura Chowk. **☎** *(0133) 42 4506.*
Specially designed for pilgrims, the rooms offered here are cheap, cool
and comfortable. **📺** *Rooms: 18* **▤** *14.*

**HARIDWAR:** *Jayaram Ashram.* ⓇⓈⓇⓈ
Near Birla Ghat. **☎** No telephone.
One of the nicer *dharamshalas* to stay in Haridwar. The throwaway rates
include basic meals. However, only very few rooms are furnished with
attached bathrooms. *Rooms: 500.*

**HARIDWAR:** *Rahi Motel (UPSTDC).* ⓇⓈⓇⓈ
Near Bus Stand, Station Rd. **☎** *(0133) 42 6430.*
A modern bungalow with a pleasant garden and attentive staff. It also
houses the regional office of UP Tourism. **🍴** *Rooms: 20.* **▤** *8.*

**HARIDWAR:** *Teerth.* ⓇⓈⓇⓈ
Subhash Ghat, Bara Bazaar. **☎** *(0133) 42 5311.*
Though in a crowded area, each room has a balcony with a good view
of the river and Har-ki-Pauri, the main ghat. **🍴 24 📺** *Rooms: 36.* **▤** *10.*

**HARIDWAR:** *Classic International.* ⓇⓈⓇⓈⓇⓈ
Jwalapur Rd. **☎** *(0133) 42 8005.* **FAX** *(0133) 42 0374.* **@** classic@nde.vsnl.net.in
A basic but comfortable hotel. The in-house restaurant offers good
vegetarian food. **🍴 🛏 24 📺** *Rooms: 44.* **▤** *44.*
AE DC MC V

**Price categories** for a standard double room per night including tax and service charges but not including breakfast:

Ⓡ under 550 rupees
ⓇⓇ 550–1,200 rupees
ⓇⓇⓇ 1,200–3,000 rupees
ⓇⓇⓇⓇ 3,000–6,000 rupees
ⓇⓇⓇⓇⓇ over 6,000 rupees

**CREDIT CARDS**
Indicates which credit cards are accepted: *AE* American Express; *DC* Diners Club; *MC* Master Card/Access; *V* Visa; *JCB* Japanese Credit Bureau.

**WESTERN BATHROOMS**
Indicates sit-down, flush toilets; showers and/or baths. Others have squat toilets and bucket-and-mug baths.

**COFFEE SHOP**
Hotels with coffee shop.

**GARDEN/TERRACE**
Hotels with a garden, courtyard or terrace.

| | CREDIT CARDS | SWIMMING POOL | WESTERN BATHROOMS | COFFEE SHOP | GARDEN/TERRACE |
|---|---|---|---|---|---|
| **HARIDWAR:** *Sagar Ganga Resorts.* ⓇⓇⓇ <br> Mayapur, Niranjini Akhara Rd. ☎ *(0133) 42 8478.* <br> This exclusive property once belonged to the Nepal royal family, and has large rooms and an Art Deco ambience. It is situated on the banks of the river with its own private ghat. ⏹ 24 TV *Rooms: 6.* ▤ *4.* | AE | | ■ | ● | ■ |
| **HARIDWAR:** *Suvidha Deluxe.* ⓇⓇⓇ <br> Subhas Ghat, Sravan Nath Nagar. ☎ *(0133) 42 7243.* <br> A centrally-located new hotel with an unmistakable small-town air, this is essentially a clean, no-frills establishment. ⏹ 24 TV *Rooms: 28.* ▤ *14.* | AE | | ■ | ● | ■ |
| **KURUKSHETRA:** *Neelkanthi Krishna Dham Yatri Niwas.* ⓇⓇ <br> Distt Kurukshetra, Haryana. ☎ *(0121) 21 615.* <br> This simple and good value tourism department hotel has a central open courtyard with rooms and dormitories around it. For those in search of quiet, there are meditation halls within the complex. ⏹ *Rooms: 30.* ▤ *6.* | | | | | |
| **MEERUT:** *Naveen Deluxe.* ⓇⓇⓇ <br> Abu Lane. ☎ *(0121) 66 1029.* FAX *(0121) 66 4111.* <br> The hotel's main advantage is its proximity to the railway station, bus stand and the main business centre. ⏹ 24 TV ▣ *Rooms: 24.* ▤ *24.* | MC V | | ■ | | |
| **MEERUT:** *Rajmahal.* ⓇⓇⓇ <br> 187 Abu Lane. ☎ *(0121) 66 1779.* FAX *(0121) 66 6266.* <br> Easily accessible, this hotel has clean and comfortable rooms and is popular with business travellers. ⏹ 24 TV ▣ *Rooms: 35.* ▤ *35.* | AE DC MC V | | ■ | ● | |
| **PANIPAT:** *Gold.* ⓇⓇ <br> Grand Trunk Rd. ☎ *(01742) 60 012.* FAX *(01742) 60 011.* <br> Situated along the national highway running through the city centre, this is a cheaper option for business visitors. ⏹ TV *Rooms: 30.* ▤ *30.* | | | | | |
| **PANIPAT:** *Skylark.* ⓇⓇ <br> Skylark Tourist Complex. ☎ *(01742) 41 051.* <br> This pleasant motel is run by Haryana Tourism which has an established reputation for good service and hospitality. ⏹ 24 TV ▣ *Rooms: 19.* ▤ *16.* | | | | | |
| **RISHIKESH:** *Bhandari Swiss Cottage.* Ⓡ <br> Tapovan. ☎ *(0135) 43 2676.* <br> An old and quaint establishment with great charm and character. The accommodation includes tents. *Rooms: 10.* | | | | | |
| **RISHIKESH:** *GMVN Tourist Bungalow.* Ⓡ <br> Muni-ki-Reti. ☎ *(0135) 43 0373.* <br> Pleasant and roomy with cottages set in a quiet garden, it is located at a short distance from the city centre. It is advisable to book rooms in advance in this popular hotel. ⏹ TV *Rooms: 48.* ▤ *2.* | | | ■ | | |
| **RISHIKESH:** *High Bank Peasants Cottage.* Ⓡ <br> Tapovan. ☎ *(0135) 43 1167.* FAX *(0135) 43 1654.* @ *himalayas@vsnl.com* <br> This cosy little place is attractively located high above the Ganges and has a pretty flower and vegetable garden. Good discounts are given for stays extending over a week. *Rooms: 4.* | | | ■ | | ■ |
| **RISHIKESH:** *New Bhandari Swiss Cottage.* Ⓡ <br> Tapovan. ☎ No telephone. <br> The main attraction here is the in-house bakery which offers fresh breads, delicious muffins and pies every morning. ⏹ *Rooms: 18.* | | | ■ | | |
| **RISHIKESH:** *Shikhar.* Ⓡ <br> Tapovan, Laxman Jhula Rd. ☎ *(0135) 43 3817.* <br> An attractive, cosy place, its charming restaurant extends into the garden where tables are placed under colourful umbrellas. ⏹ 24 TV *Rooms: 20.* | | | ■ | | ■ |

**RISHIKESH:** *Tourist Rest House (GMVN).*  (Rs)
Near Natraj Cinema, Haridwar Bypass Rd. ( *(0135) 43 3002.* FAX *(0135) 43 0372.*
Fairly well managed by the government, the grounds around this hotel
are its main attraction. A cheap place to stay, the rooms with attached
baths are priced higher than the rest. **Rooms: 50.** 2.

**RISHIKESH:** *Yog Niketan and Ashram.*  (Rs)
Shivanand Nagar, Muni-ki-Reti. ( *(0135) 43 0227.*
If you are serious about meditation and *hatha* yoga classes, this is the
place to choose. Rates are minimal, but if you plan to stay for more than
a week, you will have to pay in advance. **Rooms: 100.**

**RISHIKESH:** *Ganga Kinare.*  (Rs)(Rs)
16 Veerabhadra Rd. ( *(0135) 43 1658.* FAX *(0135) 43 5243.*  AE DC MC V
This riverside hotel has a panoramic view of the hills. It offers free
meditation classes, has its own rowing boats, and an in-house travel desk
can arrange treks and white-water rafting. **24 Rooms: 38.** 38.

**RISHIKESH:** *The Glass House on the Ganges.*  (Rs)(Rs)(Rs)
23rd Milestone, Rishikesh-Badrinath Rd. ( For reservation: *(011) 461 6145.*
Set in a litchi orchard with a garden of tropical plants, butterflies and rare
birds, this exclusive resort has a private sand beach. **Rooms: 12.**

**RISHIKESH:** *Mandakini.*  (Rs)(Rs)(Rs)
63 Haridwar Rd. ( *(0135) 43 0781.* FAX *(0135) 43 1081.*  AE DC MC V
Great views of the Ganges and surrounding mountain ranges come with
this rather modish hotel. The amenities are meant to suit tourists who
want comfort as well as peace. **24 Rooms: 31** 31.

**SAHARANPUR:** *Classic International.*  (Rs)(Rs)
Dehradun Rd. ( *(0132) 72 3451.* FAX *(0132) 72 3605.*  AE
A kitsch hotel in the centre of the town, popular with business visitors to
this famous centre of wood-carving because of its location near the
railway station and bus stand. **24 Rooms: 24.** 12.

## AGRA AND AROUND

**AGRA:** *New Bakshi's House.*  (Rs)
5 Laxman Nagar. ( *(0562) 30 2176.* FAX *(0562) 30 1448.*
If looking for the experience of living with an Indian family, then this is
the place for you, though the rates are higher than other paying guest
accommodation elsewhere. Book in advance. **Rooms: 14** 4.

**AGRA:** *Tourist Bungalow (UPSTDC).*  (Rs)
Raja ki Mandi, Delhi Gate. ( *(0562) 35 0120* FAX *(0562) 35 1720.*
A small, clean and cheerful hotel with a pleasant courtyard. An added
bonus is its thoughtful staff. **24 Rooms: 27.** 27.

**AGRA:** *Amar Yatri Niwas.*  (Rs)(Rs)
Tourist Complex Area, Fatehabad Rd. ( *(0562) 33 3800.* FAX *(0562) 33 0299.*  AE MC V
Though the decor is slightly garish, the hotel is popular, and has a range
of rooms equipped with essential facilities. **Rooms: 33.** 33.

**AGRA:** *Lauries Hotel.*  (Rs)(Rs)
Mahatma Gandhi Rd. ( *(0562) 36 4536.* FAX *(0562) 26 8045.*  AE MC V
One of Agra's oldest hotels, its non-airconditioned rooms keep the rates
low. It also offers camping facilities. **24 Rooms: 28.**

**AGRA:** *Mayur Tourist Complex.*  (Rs)(Rs)
Fatehabad Rd. ( *(0562) 33 2302.* FAX *(0562) 33 2907.*  AE DC MC V
A mid-range, well-managed hotel with cottages set within an extensive
lawn. Very popular and often full, it has a good restaurant with an
efficient and courteous staff. **TV Rooms: 30.** 30.

**AGRA:** *Taj Kheema.*  (Rs)(Rs)
Eastern Gate, Taj Mahal. ( *(0562) 33 0140.* FAX *(0562) 23 0001.*
A small government-run hotel near the Taj with simple, good value
standard rooms. Photographers will appreciate the superb views of the
monument from the raised garden. **24 Rooms: 6.** 2.

**AGRA:** *Agra Ashok Hotel (ITDC).*  (Rs)(Rs)(Rs)
6-B The Mall. ( *(0562) 36 1223.* FAX *(0562) 36 1620.*  AE DC MC V
Located close to the railway station, this well-managed hotel, in the
standard tradition of all ITDC hotels, has comfortable rooms and a
friendly staff. **24 TV Rooms: 55.** 55.

*For key to symbols see back flap*

**Price categories** for a standard double room per night including tax and service charges but not including breakfast:

(Rs) under 550 rupees
(Rs)(Rs) 550–1,200 rupees
(Rs)(Rs)(Rs) 1,200–3,000 rupees
(Rs)(Rs)(Rs)(Rs) 3,000–6,000 rupees
(Rs)(Rs)(Rs)(Rs)(Rs) over 6,000 rupees

**CREDIT CARDS**
Indicates which credit cards are accepted: *AE* American Express; *DC* Diners Club; *MC* Master Card/Access; *V* Visa; *JCB* Japanese Credit Bureau.

**WESTERN BATHROOMS**
Indicates sit-down, flush toilets; showers and/or baths. Others have squat toilets and bucket-and-mug baths.

**COFFEE SHOP**
Hotels with coffee shop.

**GARDEN/TERRACE**
Hotels with a garden, courtyard or terrace.

---

**AGRA:** *Clarks Shiraz.*   (Rs)(Rs)(Rs)
Agra Cantt, 54 Taj Rd. [ (0562) 36 1421. FAX (0562) 36 1428.
Pleasantly located amidst extensive gardens, this was India's first 5-star hotel and has recently been given an attractive face lift. The rooms have beautiful views of the Taj. **11 Y 11 24 TV 5** *Rooms: 237.* 237.
*Credit cards:* AE DC MC V
*Swimming Pool* ● *Western Bathrooms* ● *Coffee Shop* ● *Garden/Terrace* ●

**AGRA:** *Holiday Inn.*   (Rs)(Rs)(Rs)(Rs)
Sanjay Place Commercial Complex. [ (0562) 35 7642. FAX (0562) 35 7625.
@ hinnagra@nde.vsnl.net.in A new hotel owned by a well-known international chain, it is sensitively designed and serviced in the best traditions of Indian hospitality. **11 Y 11 24 TV 5** *Rooms: 237.* 237.
*Credit cards:* AE DC MC V
*Swimming Pool* ● *Western Bathrooms* ● *Garden/Terrace* ●

**AGRA:** *Howard Park Plaza International.*   (Rs)(Rs)(Rs)(Rs)
Taj Ganj, Fatehabad Rd. [ (0562) 33 1870. FAX (0562) 33 0408.
@ hhpi@nde.vsnl.net.in A modern and very elegant hotel with a rooftop viewing gallery. The hotel's cuisine is renowned, especially that of the Indian poolside restaurant. **11 Y 11 24 TV 5** *Rooms: 83.* 83.
*Credit cards:* AE DC MC V
*Swimming Pool* ● *Western Bathrooms* ● *Coffee Shop* ● *Garden/Terrace* ●

**AGRA:** *Jaypee Palace Hotels.*   (Rs)(Rs)(Rs)(Rs)
Fatehabad Rd. [ (0562) 33 0800. FAX (0562) 33 0850. @ jaypeeag@nde.vsnl.net.in
Comfortable rooms set around a series of impressive terraced courts in 25 acres of lush, landscaped gardens and ponds make this an attractive place for a longer stay. **11 Y 11 24 TV 5** *Rooms: 350.* 350.
*Credit cards:* AE DC MC V
*Swimming Pool* ● *Western Bathrooms* ● *Coffee Shop* ● *Garden/Terrace* ●

**AGRA:** *Mansingh Palace.*   (Rs)(Rs)(Rs)(Rs)
Fatehabad Rd. [ (0562) 33 1771. FAX (0562) 33 0202. @ mansingh.agra@mailcity.com
This luxurious hotel, named after a famous Rajput king, has a few rooms overlooking the Taj. The bar, jacuzzi, and swimming pool with a water slide are special attractions. **11 Y 24 TV 5** *Rooms: 100.* 100.
*Credit cards:* AE DC MC V
*Swimming Pool* ● *Western Bathrooms* ●

**AGRA:** *Taj View.*   (Rs)(Rs)(Rs)(Rs)
Taj Ganj, Fatehabad Rd. [ (0562) 33 1841. FAX (0562) 33 1860. @ tjagra@nde.vsnl.net.in
Only 1 km away from the Taj this magnificent hotel nestles amongst acres of landscaped gardens. **11 11 24 TV 5** *Rooms: 100.* 100.
*Credit cards:* AE DC MC V
*Swimming Pool* ● *Western Bathrooms* ● *Coffee Shop* ● *Garden/Terrace* ●

**AGRA:** *The Trident.*   (Rs)(Rs)(Rs)(Rs)
Tajnagri Scheme, Fatehabad Rd. [ (0562) 33 1818. FAX (0562 ) 33 1827.
Run by the Oberoi group, the hotel's impressive decor is inspired by the Mughal style. Considered to be one of Agra's best, expect to find the highest standards here. **11 Y 11 24 TV 5** *Rooms: 143.* 143.
*Credit cards:* AE DC V
*Swimming Pool* ● *Western Bathrooms* ● *Coffee Shop* ● *Garden/Terrace* ●

**AGRA:** *Welcomgroup Mughal Sheraton.*   (Rs)(Rs)(Rs)(Rs)
Taj Ganj. [ (0562) 33 1701. FAX (0562) 33 1730. @ mughal@welcomgroup.com
The architecture of this hotel is a fitting tribute to the great Mughal builders. Gloriously landscaped and lavishly furnished, this is one of India's finest hotels. **11 Y 11 24 TV 5** *Rooms: 285.* 285.
*Credit cards:* AE DC MC V
*Swimming Pool* ● *Western Bathrooms* ● *Coffee Shop* ● *Garden/Terrace* ●

**BHARATPUR:** *Hotel Saras (RTDC).*   (Rs)
Agra Rd. [ (05644) 23 700. FAX (05644) 24 021.
A government-run tourist hotel, its main advantage is that it is at walking distance from the Keoladeo National Park. **11 24 TV 5** *Rooms: 30.* 30.
*Western Bathrooms* ● *Coffee Shop* ● *Garden/Terrace* ●

**BHARATPUR:** *Eagle's Nest.*   (Rs)(Rs)
Agra Rd. [ (05644) 25 144. FAX (05644) 23 170.
This is one of several little guesthouses located in close proximity to the bird sanctuary. Very friendly and welcoming, the hospitality makes up for the lack of sophistication. **11 24 TV 5** *Rooms: 11.*
*Western Bathrooms* ● *Coffee Shop* ● *Garden/Terrace* ●

**BHARATPUR:** *Bharatpur Forest Lodge (ITDC).*   (Rs)(Rs)(Rs)
Keoladeo National Park. [ (05644) 22 760. FAX (05644) 22 864.
This beautifully sited hotel right inside the sanctuary, though comparatively expensive, is the best place to stay in. Its restaurant is open to non-residents. **11 TV** *Rooms: 17.* 17.
*Credit cards:* AE DC MC V
*Western Bathrooms* ● *Coffee Shop* ●

**BHARATPUR:** *Chandra Mahal Haveli.*
Peharsar, Naqbai Tehsil, Jaipur-Agra Rd. ( (05644) 43 238.
A heritage hotel at a short distance from Bharatpur town, it is surrounded
by brilliant yellow mustard fields in winter. An ideal resting place after a
long day's outing. **Rooms:** 16. 4.

AE

**BHARATPUR:** *Laxmi Vilas Palace.*
Kakaji ki Kothi, Agra Rd. ( (05644) 23 523. FAX (05644) 25 259.
An eclectic and lively fusion of Rajput and Mughal architecture. Palatial
rooms, royal hospitality and gourmet cuisine. TV **Rooms:** 30. 30.

AE
MC
V

**BRINDAVAN:** *Sri Krishna Balaram International Guest House.*
Raman Reti. ( (0565) 44 2670. FAX (0565) 44 4600. @ ramamani@nde.vsnl.net.in
Only members of the ISKCON Society or their guests may stay here. The
guesthouse charges no fee but accepts donations. **Rooms:** 44.

**BRINDAVAN:** *Bhaktivedanta Ashrama & MVT Guest House.*
Raman Reti. ( (0565) 44 3400. FAX (0565) 44 2952. @ mvt@com.bbt.se
Definitely the nicest place to stay in Brindavan. Well designed and
meticulously clean. 24 **Rooms:** 29. 8.

**BRINDAVAN:** *Geet Govind Tourist Complex.*
Nandanvan, Raman Reti. ( (0565) 44 2517. FAX (0565) 442 2645.
An agreeable place in peaceful surroundings, its clean and comfortable
rooms offer a restful stay. TV **Rooms:** 10.

**BRINDAVAN:** *Sri Banke Bihari Guest House.*
Ahir Pada, Sri Banke Bihari Temple Rd. ( (0565) 44 3530.
An adequate guesthouse, and with a copy of the *Bhagavad Gita* in each
room, appropriate for visitors to this temple town. 24 TV **Rooms:** 8. 6.

AE
MC

**DEEG:** *Midway Hotel (RTDC).*
Distt Bharatpur. ( (05641) 21 000.
A tiny guesthouse located close to the bus stand, this government hotel is
at walking distance from Deeg Palace. 24 **Rooms:** 3.

**FATEHPUR SIKRI:** *The Archaeological Survey Dak Bungalow.*
The Mall. ( (0562) 33 0140. FAX (0562) 101 1049.
This spacious old colonial-style resthouse adjoining the historic complex
can be booked only through the ASI office. Meals are cooked on request
by the staff. *Rooms:* 5.

**FATEHPUR SIKRI:** *Gulistan Tourist Complex.*
Agra Rd. ( (05613) 88 2490. FAX (05613) 88 2840.
Surprisingly attractive for a small-town hotel run by the government, it is
close to the local bus stand. 24 TV **Rooms:** 24. 8.

**GWALIOR:** *Regency Resort.*
Malanpur. ( (075394) 83 320. FAX (075394) 83 452.
If you are agreeable to staying slightly away from the city, you will not
be disappointed by this hotel, located in an open area near a beautiful
lake with boating facilities. 24 TV **Rooms:** 15. 15.

AE
DC
MC
V

**GWALIOR:** *Shelter.*
Padav, Near Indian Airlines Office. ( (0751) 32 6209. FAX (0751) 32 6212.
A newish hotel, typical of many small towns, it is close to all major
tourist sites as well as the railway station. It also offers assistance with
travel bookings and a 24-hour taxi service. 24 TV **Rooms:** 42. 38.

AE
DC
MC
V

**GWALIOR:** *Tansen Gwalior (MPSTDC).*
6-A Gandhi Rd, Civil Lines. ( (0751) 34 0370. FAX (0751) 34 0371.
Pleasantly located, the hotel is popular with business travellers. Advance
booking is strongly recommended. 24 TV **Rooms:** 36. 24.

AE
MC

**GWALIOR:** *Gwalior Regency.*
Link Rd. ( (0751) 34 0670. FAX (0751) 34 3520.
A well-appointed hotel in the centre of town with rooms ranging from
good-value "economy" to "super deluxe". It has a discotheque and an
excellent restaurant. 24 TV **Rooms:** 51. 51.

AE
DC
MC
V

**GWALIOR:** *Welcomgroup Usha Kiran Palace.*
Jayendraganj, Lashkar. ( (0751) 32 3993. FAX (0751) 32 1103.
Newly refurbished, this glamorous and luxurious hotel was once the
maharaja's guesthouse. Snooker, croquet and badminton facilities are
available on the premises. 24 TV **Rooms:** 28. 28.

AE
DC
MC
V

**Price categories** for a standard double room per night including tax and service charges but not including breakfast:

Rs under 550 rupees
Rs Rs 550–1,200 rupees
Rs Rs Rs 1,200–3,000 rupees
Rs Rs Rs Rs 3,000–6,000 rupees
Rs Rs Rs Rs Rs over 6,000 rupees

**CREDIT CARDS**
Indicates which credit cards are accepted: *AE* American Express; *DC* Diners Club; *MC* Master Card/Access; *V* Visa; *JCB* Japanese Credit Bureau.

**WESTERN BATHROOMS**
Indicates sit-down, flush toilets; showers and/or baths. Others have squat toilets and bucket-and-mug baths.

**COFFEE SHOP**
Hotels with a coffee shop.

**GARDEN/TERRACE**
Hotels with a garden, courtyard or terrace.

| | Price | CREDIT CARDS | SWIMMING POOL | WESTERN BATHROOMS | COFFEE SHOP | GARDEN/TERRACE |
|---|---|---|---|---|---|---|
| **JHANSI:** *Sita.*<br>Post Box No 84, Civil Lines, Shivpuri Rd. ☏ *(0517) 44 2956.* FAX *(0517) 44 4691.* Located opposite the railway station, this is probably the most comfortable hotel in town. It also has a good restaurant and offers foreign exchange facilities. 🍴 24 TV 🛗 *Rooms: 29.* 🛏 *23.* | Rs Rs | MC V | | ▪ | ● | ▪ |
| **JHANSI:** *Veerangana (UPSTDC).*<br>Civil Lines, Shivpuri Rd. ☏ *(0517) 44 2402.* This spartan, government-run hotel with a pleasant lawn includes dormitories at rock-bottom rates. Beer is available. 🍴 *Rooms: 20.* 🛏 *4.* | Rs Rs | | | ▪ | | ▪ |
| **MATHURA:** *International Guest House.*<br>Sri Krishna Janm Bhoomi. ☏ *(0565) 40 5888.* Popular and often fully occupied because of its cheap rates. The in-house restaurant serves only vegetarian food. 🍴 *Rooms: 45.* | Rs | | | | | ▪ |
| **MATHURA:** *Surya International.*<br>Bagh Bahadur, Station Rd. ☏ *(0565) 40 9344.* This clean hotel is a quiet oasis in an otherwise busy area. It provides guides and vehicles for sightseeing. 🍴 24 TV *Rooms: 19.* 🛏 *7.* | Rs | | | ▪ | | ▪ |
| **MATHURA:** *Agra Hotel.*<br>Bengali Ghat. ☏ *(0565) 40 3318.* Overlooking the river, this small but clean 70-year-old hotel offers all essential facilities. 🍴 *Rooms: 15.* 🛏 *3.* | Rs Rs | AE DC MC V | | ▪ | | |
| **MATHURA:** *Mukund Palace.*<br>Sonkh Adda, Junction Rd. ☏ *(0565) 41 0316.* FAX *(0565) 41 1312.* Not an exceptional place, this modest hotel is nevertheless well-located and quite spacious. 🍴 24 TV *Rooms: 29.* 🛏 *23.* | Rs Rs | MC V | | ▪ | | |
| **MATHURA:** *Mukund Vihar Inn.*<br>Opp Petrol Pump, Masani Rd. ☏ *(0565) 40 6999.* Spacious lawns cradle this homely motel. However, their cafeteria opens only in the evenings. 🍴 *Rooms: 7.* 🛏 *2.* | Rs Rs | | | ▪ | | ▪ |
| **MATHURA:** *Best Western Radha Ashok.*<br>P O Chhatikara, Masani Bypass Rd. ☏ *(0565) 40 5557.* FAX *(0565) 40 9557.* The most ritzy hotel in Mathura, run by a reputable hotel group, it is popular with an international clientele. 🍴 🛎 24 TV 🛗 *Rooms: 25.* 🛏 *25.* | Rs Rs Rs | AE DC MC V JCB | ● | ▪ | ● | ▪ |
| **MATHURA:** *Madhuvan.*<br>Krishna Nagar. ☏ *(0565) 42 0064.* FAX *(0565) 42 0684.* One of the fancier hotels in town, visitors are attracted here by its swimming pool, health centre and live performances of Indian classical music in the evenings. 🍴 TV 🛗 *Rooms: 28.* 🛏 *28.* | Rs Rs Rs | AE DC MC V | ● | ▪ | ● | ▪ |
| **MATHURA:** *Mansarovar Palace.*<br>State Bank Crossing. ☏ *(0565) 40 8686.* FAX *(0565) 40 1611.* The façade may be a poor imitation of a traditional gateway, but this is a well-maintained hotel with friendly services. 🍴 24 TV *Rooms: 31.* 🛏 *21.* | Rs Rs Rs | AE MC DC V | | ▪ | | ▪ |
| **ORCHHA:** *Betwa Cottages (MPSTDC).*<br>Orchha, Distt Tikamgarh. ☏ *(07680) 52 618.* Individual cottages are charmingly set in a garden near the banks of the River Betwa. The complex is walking distance from the superb Orchha cenotaphs. Its serene environment is recommended. 🍴 *Rooms: 10.* 🛏 *6.* | Rs Rs | | | ▪ | | ▪ |
| **ORCHHA:** *The Orchha Resort.*<br>Kanchanaghat, Distt Tikamgarh. ☏ *(0517) 45 2759.* FAX *(0517) 44 9817.* This garish resort is a discordant presence in this serene town, but is popular with tourist groups as it is one of the few options available and offers standard comforts. 🍴 🛎 24 TV *Rooms: 34.* 🛏 *34.* | Rs Rs Rs | MC V | ● | ▪ | | |

**ORCHHA:** *Sheesh Mahal (MPSTDC).*
Orchha, Distt Tikamgarh. [ (07680) 52 624.
A later wing of the historic Jahangiri Mahal (built in 1626) this is now a
charming state-run hotel. The rooms, redolent with history, offer visitors
a romantic ambience. 11 Y 5 *Rooms: 8.* 目 *1.*

## JAIPUR AND ENVIRONS

**AJMER:** *Prithviraj.*
Opp Patel Stadium, Jaipur Rd. [ (0145) 43 2297. @ hotel.prithviraj@usa.net
Clad in marble, this hotel may have the air of a nouveau riche house, but
it offers excellent rates for budget travellers. 24 TV *Rooms: 25.*

**AJMER:** *Fort Baghera.*
P O & Vill Baghera. [ (01467) 81 231.
A stopover in this historic 17th-century fort on the Ajmer-Sawai
Madhopur bus route offers a chance to savour some folk music and
dances. You can also boat on the Varah Sagar Lake. 11 24 *Rooms: 5.*

**AJMER:** *Khadim (RTDC).*
Near bus stand, Savitri Girls College Rd. [ (0145) 62 7490.
A standard state tourism hotel, well kept, with dormitories and facilities
to arrange air and rail tickets. 11 24 *Rooms: 66.* 目 *30.*

**AJMER:** *Merwara Estate (Tikam Niwas).*
Daulat Bagh, Mahavir Circle. [ (0145) 42 0691. FAX (0145) 42 0261.
Built on a hillock in 1887 in the colonial style, with painted ceilings,
Italian marble floors and Belgian etched glasswork, this is a pleasant
hotel overlooking the Anasagar Lake. 11 24 TV 5 *Rooms: 18.* 目 *18.*

**AJMER:** *Mansingh Palace.*
Near Anasagar, Vaishali Nagar, Circular Rd. [ (0145) 42 5702. FAX (0145) 42 5858
@ mansingh.ajmer@mailcity.com In spite of its wonderful location near the
lake and its good facilities, the services could be more sophisticated to
justify the hotel's comparatively high rates. 11 24 TV 5 *Rooms: 54.* 目 *54.* — AE DC MC V

**ALWAR:** *Alwar Hotel.*
26 Manu Marg. [ (0144) 33 6184. FAX (0144) 33 2250.
Economical, with basic facilities, the hotel is clean and quiet with
comfortable, good-sized rooms. 11 TV *Rooms: 10.* 目 *7.* — V

**ALWAR:** *Meenal (RTDC).*
Near Circuit House, Bhavani Tope. [ (0144) 22 852.
This tourism department hotel is located away from the crowded parts of
the city, surrounded by trees. It offers reasonable and basic facilities
without many frills. 11 *Rooms: 6.* 目 *2.*

**ALWAR:** *Aravalli.*
1 CEB, Near Railway Station. [ (0144) 33 2883. FAX (0144) 33 2011.
Though small, this is without doubt the best place to stay in Alwar. The
hotel is equipped with most facilities. The owners are very friendly, and
offer help to organize treks and tours. 11 Y 24 TV 5 *Rooms: 70.* 目 *32.* — MC V

**ALWAR:** *Hill Fort Kesroli.*
Vill Kesroli, Near M I A. [ For reservation: (011) 461 6145. FAX (011) 462 1112.
For the sheer thrill of dining on its ramparts, a stopover in this 600-year-
old, seven-turreted hotel is highly recommended. *Rooms: 22.* — MC V

**DUNDLOD:** *Dundlod Fort.*
Dundlod, Distt Jhunjhunu-Shekhawati. [ & FAX (01594) 52 519.
An 18th-century heritage hotel with lots of atmosphere. A royal welcome
with folk music, camels and garlands can be arranged on request, and
you could not ask for a more gracious host. 24 5 *Rooms: 45.* — AE MC V

**FATEHPUR:** *Hotel Haveli (RTDC).*
1 km S of Fatehpur on NH 11, Distt Sikar. [ (01571) 20 293.
For those who wish to spend a few days in the Shekhawati area, this
clean, reasonably-priced old-fashioned place offers both air-cooled rooms
and dormitories. Meals are available. *Rooms: 25.*

**JAIPUR:** *Bissau Palace Hotel.*
Outside Chand Pol. [ (0141) 30 4371. FAX (0141) 30 4628.
A charming heritage hotel, this oasis in the heart of the Pink City has
lawn tennis courts, and a fascinating collection of rare books, old silver
and armour. 11 24 TV 5 *Rooms: 40.* 目 *40.* — AE MC V

For key to symbols see back flap

**Price categories** for a standard double room per night including tax and service charges but not including breakfast:

Rs under 550 rupees
Rs Rs 550–1,200 rupees
Rs Rs Rs 1,200–3,000 rupees
Rs Rs Rs Rs 3,000–6,000 rupees
Rs Rs Rs Rs Rs over 6,000 rupees

**CREDIT CARDS**
Indicates which credit cards are accepted: *AE* American Express; *DC* Diners Club; *MC* Master Card/Access; *V* Visa; *JCB* Japanese Credit Bureau.

**WESTERN BATHROOMS**
Indicates sit-down, flush toilets; showers and/or baths. Others have squat toilets and bucket-and-mug baths.

**COFFEE SHOP**
Hotels with coffee shop.

**GARDEN/TERRACE**
Hotels with a garden, courtyard or terrace.

| | Credit Cards | Swimming Pool | Western Bathrooms | Coffee Shop | Garden/Terrace |
|---|---|---|---|---|---|
| **JAIPUR:** *Diggi Palace.* Diggi House, Sawai Mansigh Rd. (0141) 37 3091. FAX (0141) 37 0359. This is a small and attractive *haveli*-turned-guesthouse. Unlike some converted family homes, the modest charges here may suit the budget traveller in search of traditional hospitality. Rooms: 44. 12. (Rs)(Rs) | AE DC MC V | | ● | ● | ● |
| **JAIPUR:** *L M B Hotel.* Johari Bazaar. (0141) 56 5844. FAX (0141) 56 2176. With small well-kept rooms, the hotel's main attraction is its location above a famous vegetarian restaurant in the centre of one of Jaipur's most popular bazaars. Rooms: 33. 33. (Rs)(Rs) | AE DC MC V | | ● | ● | ● |
| **JAIPUR:** *Achrol Lodge.* Civil Lines, Jacob Rd. (0141) 38 2154. FAX (0141) 38 4477. A palatial old mansion surrounded by trees, and dancing peacocks in the monsoon, its collection of antique furniture, portraits and books add to the ambience. You may camp on the lawns. Rooms: 8. 8. (Rs)(Rs)(Rs) | AE DC V | | ● | ● | ● |
| **JAIPUR:** *Alsisar Haveli.* Sansar Chandra Rd. (0141) 36 8290. FAX (0141) 36 4652. This 19th-century *haveli* has retained its medieval look with large courtyards, arched corridors and a huge garden in front. The rooms are well furnished and serviced. Rooms: 30. 30. (Rs)(Rs)(Rs) | MC V | ● | ● | | ● |
| **JAIPUR:** *Jaipur Ashok (ITDC).* Jai Singh Circle, Bani Park. (0141) 20 4491. FAX (0141) 20 2099. The tourism department manages this well-designed hotel located near the railway station. Set in a landscaped garden, it is well-appointed with most modern facilities. Rooms: 99. 99. (Rs)(Rs)(Rs) | AE DC MC V | ● | ● | ● | ● |
| **JAIPUR:** *Karauli House.* Sodala, New Sanganer Rd. (0141) 21 1532. FAX (0141) 21 0512. Another old family house in the region that has now been converted to a small guesthouse, this privately-run establishment offers a warm and homely atmosphere. Rooms: 6. 6. (Rs)(Rs)(Rs) | | ● | ● | ● | ● |
| **JAIPUR:** *Khasa Kothi.* Mirza Ismail Rd. (0141) 37 5151. Literally a "special mansion" built in the colonial style, it was a state guesthouse 100 years ago. Centrally located, it is well-appointed with large rooms surrounded by cool lawns. Rooms: 36. (Rs)(Rs)(Rs) | | ● | ● | ● | ● |
| **JAIPUR:** *Royal Castle Kanota.* Kanota Bagh, Narain Singh Rd. (0141) 56 1291. FAX (0141) 56 1045. Built in 1872, this fortified castle is private and exclusive. Well worth a stay if only to see its unique library and armoury. Rooms: 12. (Rs)(Rs)(Rs) | AE MC V | | ● | | ● |
| **JAIPUR:** *Chokhi Dhani.* 19 km from Ajmeri Gate on Tonk Rd. (0141) 58 3534. FAX (0141) 38 1888. More like a resort, this eye-catching place, designed to look like a village complex, is one of Jaipur's attractions. Equipped with most resort facilities you can easily spend a few lazy days here. Rooms: 39. (Rs)(Rs)(Rs)(Rs) | | ● | ● | ● | ● |
| **JAIPUR:** *Clarks Amer.* Jawaharlal Nehru Marg. (0141) 55 0616. FAX (0141) 55 0013. If you want to stay closer to the airport or would like to explore the textile town of Sanganer at leisure, this is a conveniently located hotel, pleasant and well-managed. Rooms: 202. 202. (Rs)(Rs)(Rs)(Rs) | AE MC V | ● | ● | ● | ● |
| **JAIPUR:** *Holiday Inn Jaipur.* Amber Rd. (0141) 63 5000. FAX (0141) 63 5608. On the town's outskirts en route to Amber, this fine hotel has views of the beautiful Nahargarh Fort. Rooms: 72. 72. (Rs)(Rs)(Rs)(Rs) | AE DC MC V | ● | ● | ● | ● |

**JAIPUR:** *Jai Mahal Palace.* ⓇⓈⓇⓈⓇⓈ
Civil Lines, Jacob Rd. 📞 *(0141) 37 1616.* FAX *(0141) 36 5237.*
Designed by Sir Swinton Jacob, the building is now a luxurious and elegant hotel. Its attractions include antique furniture and a solar-heated pool. 🍴 🛉 24 TV 🛠 *Rooms: 102.* 🖥 *102.*
AE DC MC V

**JAIPUR:** *Mansingh Palace.* ⓇⓈⓇⓈⓇⓈ
Sansar Chandra Rd. 📞 *(0141) 37 8771.* FAX *(0141) 37 7582.*
@ *mansingh.jaipur@mailcity.com* Well-equipped with modern conveniences, this hotel has a wonderful feeling of space with large windows looking out of lavishly decorated rooms. 🍴 🛉 24 TV 🛠 *Rooms: 92.* 🖥 *92.*
AE DC MC V

**JAIPUR:** *Mansingh Towers.* ⓇⓈⓇⓈⓇⓈ
Sansar Chandra Rd. 📞 *(0141) 37 8771.* FAX *(0141) 36 0453.*
@ *mansinghtower.jaipur@mailcity.com* This is the elegant and well-appointed new wing of the Mansingh Palace. 🍴 🛉 24 TV 🛠 *Rooms: 54.* 🖥 *54.*
AE MC V

**JAIPUR:** *Narain Niwas Palace Hotel.* ⓇⓈⓇⓈⓇⓈⓇⓈ
Kanota Bagh, Narain Singh Rd. 📞 *(0141) 56 1291* FAX *(0141) 56 1045.*
@ *kanota@jp1.dot.net.in* Built in 1928, this was the royal Kanota family's country residence. It is surrounded by mango orchards and its traditional interior has been carefully preserved. 🍴 24 TV *Rooms: 38.* 🖥 *38.*
AE DC MC V

**JAIPUR:** *Raj Mahal Palace.* ⓇⓈⓇⓈⓇⓈ
Sardar Patel Marg, C–Scheme. 📞 *(0141) 38 1625.* FAX *(0141) 38 1887.*
Among the rich and famous who have stayed here were Prince Philip and Jacqueline Kennedy. The rooms are standard sized but luxurious; the restaurant good 🍴 24 TV 🛠 *Rooms: 11.* 🖥 *12.*
AE DC MC V

**JAIPUR:** *Ramgarh Lodge.* ⓇⓈⓇⓈⓇⓈ
Ramgarh Lake, Ramgarh. 📞 *(01426) 52 217.* FAX *(01426) 52 079.*
Try to stay in a suite overlooking the glorious Ramgarh Lake in this former royal hunting lodge. Though ideal for polo lovers, there are facilities for tennis, squash and boating. 🍴 🛉 24 TV 🛠 *Rooms: 18.* 🖥 *18.*
AE DC MC V

**JAIPUR:** *Samode Haveli.* ⓇⓈⓇⓈⓇⓈⓇⓈ
Ganga Pol. 📞 *(0141) 63 2370.*
Built in phases over 200 years, this gracious mansion offers traditional Rajasthani folk dances and cuisine. Some rooms, with original wall paintings and mirrorwork, are stunning. 🍴 TV 🛠 *Rooms: 20.* 🖥 *20.*
AE MC V

**JAIPUR:** *Trident.* ⓇⓈⓇⓈⓇⓈⓇⓈ
Opp Jal Mahal, Amer Rd. 📞 *(0141) 63 0101.* FAX *(0141 63 0303.*
@ *sgoel@jp.com* One of the Trident group of hotels, it has expected high standards of service and decor, but without doubt its most attractive quality is its location directly opposite the Jal Mahal. 🍴 24 TV 🛠 *Rooms: 138.* 🖥 *138.*
AE DC MC V

**JAIPUR:** *Rajvilas Hotel.* ⓇⓈⓇⓈⓇⓈⓇⓈⓇⓈ
Goner Rd. 📞 *(0141) 64 0101.* FAX *(0141) 64 0202.*
A spectacular Oberoi chain boutique hotel with impeccable services. Set in 32 ha of beautiful gardens, each room, luxury tent, and villa with a private pool is superbly crafted. 🍴 🛉 24 TV 🛠 *Rooms: 72.* 🖥 *72.*
AE DC MC V

**JAIPUR:** *Rambagh Palace.* ⓇⓈⓇⓈⓇⓈⓇⓈⓇⓈ
Bhawani Singh Rd. 📞 *(0141) 38 1919.* FAX *(0141) 38 1098.* @ *rambagh@jpl.vsnl.net.in*
This sumptuous palace-hotel is an all-time favourite, as its interior still retains much of the original and splendid decor from the time it was the home of the Jaipur royal family. 🍴 🛉 24 TV 🛠 *Rooms: 106.* 🖥 *106.*
AE DC MC V

**JAIPUR:** *Welcomgroup Rajputana Sheraton.* ⓇⓈⓇⓈⓇⓈⓇⓈⓇⓈ
Palace Rd. 📞 *(0141) 36 0011.* FAX *(0141) 36 7848.* @ *rajputana@welcomgroup.com*
A large, elegantly designed hotel, with consistently high standards of service. Various cultural programmes held in the evenings add to its attractions. 🍴 🛉 24 TV 🛠 *Rooms: 216.* 🖥 *216.*
AE DC MC V

**JHUNJHUNU:** *Shiv Shekhawati Hotel.* ⓇⓈⓇⓈ
Distt Shekhawati. 📞 *(01592) 32 651.*
A well-kept clean, *haveli*-style lodge, whose interesting owner is a fund of knowledge about the history and architecture of the Shekhawati area, and is happy to share this information with his guests. *Rooms: 18.* 🖥 *7.*

**JHUNJHUNU:** *Hotel Jamuna Resort.* ⓇⓈⓇⓈ
Distt Shekhawati. 📞 *(01592) 32 871.*
Run by the owner of Shiv Shekhawati, the swimming pool and outdoor dining area here is open to non-residents. *Rooms: 4.* 🖥 *1.*

For key to symbols see back flap

**Price categories** for a standard double room per night including tax and service charges but not including breakfast:

Rs under 550 rupees
Rs Rs 550–1,200 rupees
Rs Rs Rs 1,200–3,000 rupees
Rs Rs Rs Rs 3,000–6,000 rupees
Rs Rs Rs Rs Rs over 6,000 rupees

**CREDIT CARDS**
Indicates which credit cards are accepted: *AE* American Express; *DC* Diners Club; *MC* Master Card/Access; *V* Visa; *JCB* Japanese Credit Bureau.
**WESTERN BATHROOMS**
Indicates sit-down, flush toilets; showers and/or baths. Others have squat toilets and bucket-and-mug baths.
**COFFEE SHOP**
Hotels with coffee shop.
**GARDEN/TERRACE**
Hotels with a garden, courtyard or terrace.

| | CREDIT CARDS | SWIMMING POOL | WESTERN BATHROOMS | COFFEE SHOP | GARDEN/TERRACE |
|---|---|---|---|---|---|
| **KISHANGARH:** *Phool Mahal Palace.* Rs Rs Rs <br> Distt Ajmer. (01463) 47 405. FAX (01463) 42 001. Beautifully situated on the banks of the lake, this recently restored heritage property is reason enough to opt for an overnight stay in this otherwise modest town. ▮ 24 TV ▮ *Rooms: 27.* ▤ 27. | AE V | ● | ▨ | | ▨ |
| **KISHANGARH:** *Roopangarh Fort.* Rs Rs Rs <br> Roopangarh, Distt Ajmer. (01497) 20 217. FAX (01463) 42 001. @ tis@giasdl01.vsnl.net.in This captivating fortress-turned-hotel is ideally situated for excursions. It also organizes camel or horse safaris, trips for birdwatching, and tours of craft centres. ▮ 24 TV ▮ *Rooms: 20.* ▤ 4. | | | ▨ | ● | ▨ |
| **MANDAWA:** *Castle Mandawa.* Rs Rs Rs Rs <br> Mandawa, Distt Jhunjhunu. (01592) 23 124. FAX (01592) 23 171. One of the oldest and most popular heritage hotels in the region, restored with evocative private and public spaces. Its excellent services try to emulate the famed Rajasthani courtly style. *Rooms: 74.* ▤ 74. | AE MC V | | ▨ | | ▨ |
| **MANDAWA:** *The Desert Resort.* Rs Rs Rs Rs <br> Distt Jhunjhunu. (01592) 23 245. A quaint, comfortable resort designed to look like a traditional village, this is an ideal take-off point from Mandawa into the desert. *Rooms: 59.* | AE MC V | ● | ▨ | | ▨ |
| **MUKUNDGARH:** *Mukundgarh Fort.* Rs Rs <br> Distt Jhunjhunu. (01594) 52 396. FAX (01594) 52 395. Located in the heart of the Shekhawati area, this heritage hotel has an interesting bar, but could well do with a face-lift. *Rooms: 46.* | AE DC MC V | | ▨ | | ▨ |
| **NAWALGARH:** *Apni Dhani.* Rs Rs <br> Jhunjhunu Rd, Nawalgarh, Distt Jhunjhunu. (01594) 22 239. FAX (01594) 24 061. @ rcjangid@yahoo.com One of the best guides in the region, the owner of this "eco-conscious" resort offers imaginatively-designed thatched mud huts, equipped with baths and solar panel heating. ▮ *Rooms: 7.* | | | ▨ | | ▨ |
| **NAWALGARH:** *Roop Niwas Palace.* Rs Rs Rs <br> P O & Vill Nawalgarh, Distt Jhunjhunu. (01594) 22 008. FAX (01594) 23 388. This heritage hotel is a charming blend of European and Rajput style architecture. Well-mannered staff add to its gracious atmosphere. Horse and camel tours are a regular feature. ▮ 24 *Rooms: 35.* | AE | ● | ▨ | | ▨ |
| **NEEMRANA:** *Neemrana Fort Palace.* Rs Rs Rs Rs <br> Post Neemrana, Distt Alwar. (01494) 6006. FAX (01494) 6005. @ sales@neemrana.com Great hospitality awaits you in this vast, imaginatively restored fort palace. The luxury, personal attention and, in season, the live music, are highly recommended. ▮ *Rooms: 40.* ▤ 22. | AE MC V | | ▨ | | ▨ |
| **PUSHKAR:** *Peacock Holiday Resort.* Rs <br> Panchkund Rd, Distt Ajmer. (0145) 72 093. FAX (0145) 72 516. @ peacock@datainfosys.net A large shady courtyard adds to the tranquil atmosphere of this temple town hotel. The rooms have attached baths. Special prices are offered during the Pushkar Mela. ▮ *Rooms: 15.* ▤ 8. | MC V | ● | ▨ | | ▨ |
| **PUSHKAR:** *Tourist Village (RTDC).* Rs <br> Fair Grounds, Distt Ajmer. For reservations: (0141) 20 2586. FAX (0141) 20 1045. During the annual camel fair, the government sets up a tented village with about 300 single and double tents at different price ranges that include meals. A few huts are open all year round. ▮ *Rooms: 30.* | MC V | | ▨ | | ▨ |
| **PUSHKAR:** *Sarovar (RTDC).* Rs Rs <br> Pushkar, Distt Ajmer. (0145) 72 040. Located near the Pushkar Palace, this state tourism hotel has both rooms and dormitories. It is one of the few places that can organize camel, horse and jeep safaris. ▮ ▮ *Rooms: 38.* | MC V | | ▨ | | ▨ |

**PUSHKAR:** *Pushkar Palace.*  (Rs)(Rs)(Rs)  MC V
Pushkar Lake, Distt Ajmer. ( (0145) 72 001. FAX (0145) 72 226.
Beautifully located on the banks of Pushkar Lake, this 400-year-old palace hotel commands a panoramic view of the town. During the annual camel fair, tented lodging is available. ▮▮ 24 TV **Rooms:** 36. 目 36.

**PUSHKAR:** *Pushkar Resorts.*  (Rs)(Rs)(Rs)  AE MC V
Vill Ganhera, Motisar Rd. ( (0145) 72 017. FAX (0145) 72 946. @ pushres@ndf.vsnl.net.in
Clusters of luxury cottages with private lawn space re-create an oasis. An added attraction is the town's only bar. ▮▮ 24 TV ▮ **Rooms:** 40 目 40.

**SAMODE:** *Samode Bagh.*  (Rs)(Rs)(Rs)(Rs)  AE MC V
Vill Fathepura, Bansa, Distt Jaipur. ( (0141) 63 2407. FAX (0141) 60 2370.
Associated with the Samode Palace hotel, the Bagh has luxury tents with attached baths situated in an idyllic garden which spreads over 20 ha. It offers the ambience of a royal desert camp. **Tents:** 50.

**SAMODE:** *Samode Palace.*  (Rs)(Rs)(Rs)(Rs)  AE MC V
Distt Jaipur. ( (0141) 63 2370, (0141) 63 2407.
A stay in this 400-year-old palatial heritage hotel with exquisite interiors and modern facilities offers the chance to savour a royal lifestyle. This is one of the region's finest heritage hotels. ▮▮ 24 TV ▮ **Rooms:** 35. 目 35.

**SARISKA:** *Tiger Den (RTDC).*  (Rs)(Rs)
Alwar-Jaipur Rd, Distt Alwar. ( (0144) 41 342.
Adjacent to the Sariska sanctuary, this is the only cheap option for visitors to the park. The dormitories, rooms and services have fairly acceptable standards of comfort and efficiency. ▮▮ 24 **Rooms:** 36. 目 10.

**SARISKA:** *Sariska Palace.*  (Rs)(Rs)(Rs)  AE DC MC V
Sariska, Distt Alwar. ( (0144 ) 41 322. FAX (0144) 41 323. @ sariska@del2.vsnl.net.in
After a tiring day out in the sanctuary, the palatial comforts of this former royal hunting lodge are most welcome. Folk songs, dances and a campfire are offered in the evenings. ▮▮ 24 TV **Rooms:** 49.

**SAWAI MADHOPUR:** *Ankur Resorts.*  (Rs)(Rs)
Ranthambhore Rd. ( (07462) 20 792. FAX (07462) 20 697.
The rooms and independent cottages of this tranquil resort are located around three spacious lawns. Barbeque nights and folk performances are regular features in season. **Rooms:** 27

**SAWAI MADHOPUR:** *Castle Jhoomar Baori (RTDC).*  (Rs)(Rs)
Ranthambhore Rd. ( (07462) 20 495.
This charming old royal jungle lodge has superb views of the countryside and is rich in atmosphere. You can even hear tigers roar at night in the nearby sanctuary. Very much in demand, so book ahead. **Rooms:** 12.

**SAWAI MADHOPUR:** *Ranthambhore Regency.*  (Rs)(Rs)
Ranthambhore Rd. ( (07462) 21 176. FAX (07462) 22 299
A comparatively new hotel, it offers decent rooms and food for surprisingly good rates. **Rooms:** 20. 目 4.

**SAWAI MADHOPUR:** *Ranthambhore Bagh.*  (Rs)(Rs)(Rs)
Ranthambhore Rd. ( (07462) 22 879. FAX (07462) 22 879.
This interesting wildlife resort offers a range of accommodation from dormitories to Swiss luxury tents. It has also devised several outdoor activities to entertain visitors. **Rooms:** 22.

**SAWAI MADHOPUR:** *Sawai Madhopur Lodge.*  (Rs)(Rs)(Rs)(Rs)
Ranthambhore Rd. ( (07462) 20 541. FAX (07462) 20 718. @ smlodge@jp1.dot.net.in
This 1930's lodge of the Jaipur maharaja is far superior to the rest in town, combining modern comforts with classic style. Several recreational facilities are available on the premises. TV **Rooms:** 35. 目 29.

**SILISERH:** *Lake Palace (RTDC).*  (Rs)
Siliserh, Distt Alwar. ( (0144) 86 322.
Overlooking the lake, this fairytale palace is best for a quiet retreat, with the promise of glorious sunsets over the tranquil lake waters. Activities include boating, long walks and birdwatching. **Rooms:** 10. 目 5.

**UNIARA:** *Sardar Fort Uniara.*  (Rs)
Tonk-Uniara Highway, Distt Tonk. ( For reservations: (0141) 39 7462.
Rooms in the sprawling old Uniara palace en route to Sawai Madhopur have been made habitable again by sons of the former raja. The fort's peaceful and evocative atmosphere is recommended. **Rooms:** 3.

For key to symbols see back flap

# WHERE TO EAT

THE UNIQUE FLAVOURS of Indian food depend heavily on the imaginative blend of spices and use of fresh ingredients. Once, seasonal fruits and vegetables dictated menus in restaurants, so the standard restaurant offered a choice of Mughlai preparations and a sprinkling of colonial fare, such as roast lamb with mint sauce, fried fish and vegetables *au gratin*. Today, eating habits, especially in Delhi, have become much more sophisticated, and most Indians, when they dine out, prefer food that is quite different from what is

Chief chef of a five-star Delhi hotel

cooked at home. The search for new culinary experiences has led to the proliferation of excellent speciality restaurants, fast food and pizza parlours to satisfy all tastes. These newer, fancier, and more cosmopolitan establishments have added to the eating-out scene, but good Indian food, such as succulent kababs, rich aromatic curries, or even the simple dal and *roti* served at *dhabas* still remain popular. The listings of restaurants on pages 256–63 are organized by area to help you choose where and what kind of food you wish to eat.

The stylish Polo Bar at Rambagh Palace Hotel, Jaipur

## RESTAURANTS

THERE IS A WIDE choice of places to eat in Delhi from snack bars in markets to speciality restaurants in luxury hotels. Every commercial area has a large number of eateries starting with mobile vans which offer low priced sandwiches, burgers and Indian-style Chinese chowmein and soups. South Indian eating places are widespread and good value for money with a wide choice of dishes. Others specialize in the North Indian barbecued and tandoori meats and fish. Most places, however, offer standard Indian breads and curries. Many of the American fast food giants, such as Pizza Hut, McDonalds and KFC, have already made their appearance in the bigger

Sign of an Indian restaurant

cities, and are hot favourites with both children and an older crowd. Agra and Jaipur also have a wide range of restaurants, though good Continental food is found mainly in the five-star hotels. Here, too, you will find the tempting lunch buffet where you can feast in luxury.

Most restaurants are open from 11am to midnight. It is a good idea to book in advance for the popular gourmet places. Late hour or early meals are best had at the 24-hour coffee shops at hotels.

## SPECIALITY RESTAURANTS

UP-MARKET restaurants specializing in authentic foods from different parts of the world have become very popular, particularly in Delhi where you have a choice of

cuisines, from China and Thailand, Japan, Mexico or Italy, prepared by chefs from these countries. Most of these restaurants tend to be in the luxury hotels, though a few independent ones have been opened in places like the Hauz Khas Village in Delhi. Prices may be a bit steep, but the food and stylish decor are worth it. Afghan and Middle Eastern, Kashmiri as well as Tibetan food are also found in selected places.

For Indian specialities, most of the good hotels in the Jaipur region make it a point to include traditional Rajput dishes on the menu, while in Delhi and Agra, almost all places will treat you to a delicious Mughal, Kayasth or Punjabi meal prepared from recipes handed down through generations of cooks.

Barbecued foods are a speciality at Bukhara, Maurya Sheraton

**Breakfast on the ramparts of Kesroli Fort**

## COFFEE SHOPS

ALL THE BIGGER HOTELS have 24-hour coffee shops where you can get snacks and even light meals. At busy market places, there are coffee shop-like cafés that are open from 10am to midnight offering a menu of refreshments and simple multi-cuisine dishes that may range from Indian to Indian-style Continental and Chinese. The quality of cooking is average. It is safer to stick to the more common dishes, and to avoid fish and prawns here.

## ROADSIDE AND MARKET FOOD STALLS

IF YOU ARE adventurous, the roadside food stalls or *dhabas* offer a typically Indian meal with a choice of a couple of basic curries, more often than not vegetarian, and *rotis* hot from the fire. However, do remember that the dishes are made to suit an Indian palate that prefers hot spicy food, and when ordering, insist that your meal is made with a minimum of spices. It is also advisable to eat at stalls which appear to have a rapid turnover as the food will be freshly cooked. For health precautions see page 286.

You could also try the Indian-style savoury- and sweet-shops. The choice of sweets is overwhelming; syrupy at times, but delicious. The snacks are often deep-fried such as potato and flour fingerlings, or a variety of spiced nuts. Indian-style Chinese fried chowmein is a great favourite in these places. Indian cities are fast becoming tourist savvy, with market food stalls offering a greater variety of Western-style soups, salads, as well as bakery products, and with the menus almost always in English.

## VEGETARIANS

THERE IS A superb tradition of vegetarian cooking in India. Most of the roadside food stalls are strictly vegetarian, and all three cities have good vegetarian restaurants, which include the ubiquitous South Indian cateries that also offer vegetarian *thalis*. Some of them display a sign that says: "Cooked in pure ghee", or "Cooked in ghee made from cow's milk" which is meant to reassure hardcore vegetarians.

**A special salad buffet**

## WINE AND DRINKS

THERE ARE STRICT restrictions on serving alcohol in the Delhi, Agra, Jaipur region, and only some restaurants and hotels with a liquor permit are allowed to serve alcoholic drinks, though there are liquor shops in all cities. A few places are licensed to serve only beer. Most larger hotels have their own bars and serve both "Indian Made Foreign Liquor" (whisky, rum, gin, vodka and beer), as well as many foreign brands, at a price. Indian wines are few, but some excellent foreign wines are available. Drinking your own liquor in a restaurant is not permitted. The 1st and 7th of each month, national holidays and notified election days are "dry days".

## PRICES AND TIPPING

PRICES ARE fixed everywhere, even at the roadside stalls. At luxury hotels the rates are high and there will be added taxes, but eating at most restaurants and coffee shops in the city is generally affordable, and at the roadside stalls, it is positively cheap. The prices are always listed on the menu and you should check that the figures are right on your bill. Waiters do expect to be tipped, and ten per cent of the bill is appropriate.

**A roadside tea stall in Rajasthan**

# What to Eat

THE FOOD of the Delhi, Agra and Jaipur region is a hybrid cuisine which has grown out of several traditions, techniques and flavours. Its chief influences are the classic Mughal cuisine born in the imperial kitchens, and the vegetarian food of the orthodox Bania (mercantile) community. The British Raj added its own culinary influences, which helped popularize the ubiquitous "Indian curry" in the West. Today, the piquant flavours of cuisine from all over India are on offer together with a range of South Asian and European dishes in top-end restaurants.

**Idli *and* dosa**, *the popular South Indian steamed rice cakes and crisp pancakes, served with coconut chutney and a spicy lentil curry are a national breakfast favourite.*

**Aloo-poori**, *a potato curry eaten with puffed deep-fried bread (poori) makes a good breakfast or lunch dish.*

***Stuffed* paranthas** *are pan-fried breads stuffed with vegetables or mince, eaten with yoghurt and pickles.*

**Nihari**, *a breakfast stew of shank meat and bone marrow, traditionally slow cooked all night on embers.*

**Soups**, *a later addition to Indian cuisine, include the favourite Anglo-Indian Mulligatawny, and Shorba, literally the stock of meat or vegetables flavoured with spices.*

**Mulligatawny, a dal and meat soup with tamarind**

***Shorba*, a meat, tomato or vegetable broth**

## TANDOORI PLATTER

The *tandoor*, a clay oven from Central Asia, has generated a kind of barbecued cuisine now popular all over the world. Meats, fish and vegetables are marinated in yoghurt and spices and grilled on skewers.

**Cauliflower (gobbi)**

**Leg of lamb (raan)**

**Seekh kabab**

**Vegetable rings**

**Cottage cheese (paneer)**

**Vegetarian platter** *has a selection of marinated vegetables grilled on a skewer in the tandoor.*

**Chicken**

**Chicken tikkas**

**Meat and poultry platter**
*offers a mixed grill served with a twist of lemon and onion rings.*

**Punjabi** *specialities include hearty dishes like butter chicken, buttery dal,* sarson ka saag *(cooked mustard leaves),* baingan bharta *(smoked aubergines or eggplants), accompanied by maize flour (makki) rotis.* Lassi *helps digest this meal.*

Dal makhani

Raita

Butter chicken

Paneer bhurji

Kotoo roti

Sarson ka saag

Makki roti

Baingan ka bharta

Saboodana (sago) kheer

Gatta curry

Papad sabzi

Aloo sabzi

The **Navaratris**, *the nine-day fasting period, has given rise to a special vegetarian diet of milk-based products and* rotis *made of water chestnut flour (kotoo).*

Khair sangri

**Rajasthani** *cuisine is robust and highly spiced. Mutton, local vegetable and berry preparations and yoghurt-based curries are eaten either with rice or coarse grain millet (bajra)* rotis *and a variety of chutneys and green salad.*

Kadhi

Lal maas

## DRINKS
The scorching Indian summer inspired cooling drinks (sherbets) made from a variety of fruits, plants and herbs. Believed to have medicinal properties, they are antidotes to sunstroke, and come in a riot of colours.

Custard apple

Mango

*Chikoo* (Sapodilla)

Melon

Fresh lemonade (*nimbu pani*)

Sandalwood (*chandan*) flavoured sherbet

Vetiver (*khus*) sherbet

## FRUIT
India produces many seasonal fruit. Summer brings melons, mangoes and litchis. Winter abounds in apples, grapes, papayas (pawpaws), oranges, bananas, guavas and *chikoos*.

Rooh Afza (a herbal syrup)

Saffron (*kesar*) flavoured *lassi*

Yoghurt drink (*lassi*)

Beer

# The Indian Thali

TRADITIONAL INDIAN MEALS are served in a platter (*thali*) with small bowls (*katoris*) of meat, vegetables and lentils. Pickles, chutneys, a raita (whipped yoghurt) and *papads* are typical accompaniments that enhance the flavour of the main dishes. Many types of unleavened bread are served along with rice, either steamed or as an aromatic *pulao*. The meal is best eaten with the fingers of the right hand, and rounded off with a dessert and *paan*.

### Curry

This Western brand name for meat or vegetables cooked in an onion and tomato or curd based sauce, hardly describes its spicy variations.

**Mutton curry**

**Kadhai murg**

**Korma**

**Dal**

**Rajma**

**Yellow dal**

**Chhole**

### Dal

*A generic name for lentils, India has several variations of this protein-rich dish. Dals are tempered with onions, garlic and ginger or asafoetida and cumin to make them digestible. Rajma (red beans) and chhole (chick peas) are cooked in a similar way.*

**Roti**

**Rice**

**Biryani**

**Pulao**

### Rice

*Although steamed rice may be eaten every day, the biryani (slow-cooked with meat and spices in clay pots) and the vegetarian pulao, a variation, are served on special occasions.*

### Paan

*The betel leaf and nut (supari), silver-coated cloves and cardamoms are traditional digestives eaten after a heavy meal.*

## Vegetables

*Vegetables (sabzi) are usually braised in seasoned oil, most popularly in combination with potatoes, but there are other, more exotic offerings such as jackfruit (kathal) and okra (bhindi), which are cooked with spices and usually with tomatoes.*

**Khumb matar**

**Paneer makhani**

**Malai kofta**

**Bhindi**

**Mixed vegetables**

**Aloo gobhi**

## Accompaniments

*Raitas, salads, chutneys, papads and pickles are served with every meal as savoury accompaniments to complement the rich and spicy flavours of the main dishes.*

**Mint chutney**

**Pickled onions**

**Pickled garlic**

**Raita**

**Green chilli**

**Tamarind sauce**

## Sweets

*Indian sweets are commonly made of milk and elaborately decorated with fine sheets of beaten silver. Sprinkled with rose-water and nuts, they round off the perfect festive meal.*

**Kesari phirni**

**Kulfi kesari falooda**

**Gulab jamun**

**Rasmalai**

## ROTIS

Breads (*rotis*), leavened or unleavened, made of flour, have different textures and names. They are served along with main dishes and help to scoop the food into the mouth.

**Papad**

**Pudina parantha**

**Khasta roti**

**Naan**

**Bakarkhani**

**Ajwain parantha**

# A Glossary of Typical Indian Food

THE ESSENCE OF TRADITIONAL Indian food lies in the infinite variations in the blending and combination of a variety of spices. Chillies need not be used and, in fact, are often regarded as the inputs of a poor cook who uses them to camouflage the lack of subtlety in his seasonings. A typical menu in the region includes meat, lentils, vegetables and tandoori dishes, accompanied by rice and *rotis*. Street food is extremely popular with locals, and consists of savoury snacks, eaten through the day.

*Jamuns,* a monsoon fruit

*Rogan josh,* a meat dish

## SNACKS

Sweet and savoury snacks are an important part of the Indian diet.

**Aloo tikki**
Stuffed potato cutlet cooked on a griddle.

**Chaat**
The most popular items are *papri*, made of fritters, chickpeas, potatoes, yoghurt and spicy sauces; and *gol-guppas*, puffed flour crisps filled with cumin spiced water and chickpeas.

**Jalebi**
Crisp golden coils of flour batter dipped in a rose-flavoured syrup.

**Pakora**
Vegetables or cottage cheese fried in gramflour batter.

**Skewered tikkas**

The *chaat-wallah* has a variety of savouries served in mouth-watering combinations

**Samosa**
Deep-fried pastry triangles filled with spiced potatoes and peas.

## TANDOORI FOOD

The *tandoor* is a clay oven that looks like an upturned pot with a coal fire. Skewered meats and vegetables are barbecued in it, and *rotis* are baked on its inner walls.

**Kababs**
*Seekh* kababs are flavoured minced lamb skewered in a long, tubular shape. Chicken variations include the *reshmi* and *tangri* kababs. For the vegetarian, a *seekh* kabab made of spiced vegetables has been created.

**Raan**
Leg of lamb cooked in yoghurt and spices.

**Tandoori murg**
A whole chicken (*murg*) marinated in yoghurt and specially flavoured spices.

**Tandoori salad**
Lightly marinated and grilled vegetables, such as cauliflower, potatoes, onions, okra and capsicum.

**Tikkas**
Marinated and char-grilled small chunks of chicken, mutton, fish and cottage cheese. The *burra* kabab is meat with bone from the rib, prepared in the same way.

## MAIN NON-VEGETARIAN DISHES

Often spicy and rich, these are among the most delicious examples of Indian cuisine.

**Bhuna gosht**
A dry meat curry, stir-fried slowly till tender.

**Butter chicken**
Tandoori chicken with a tomato and butter sauce.

**Kadhai murg**
A succulent chicken curry stir-fried in a wok.

**Lal maas**
A Rajasthani mutton dish cooked with red chillies. A variation is *safed maas*, a "white" curry with almonds and cashewnuts.

**Mutton** or **chicken korma**
Braised meat or chicken cooked on a slow fire with yoghurt and spices.

**Rogan josh**
Cubes of mutton cooked with red chillies and spices.

**Saag gosht**
Meat cooked with spinach.

*Curry leaves and masur dal*

*Red chilli*

## VEGETARIAN DISHES

Traditionally, only seasonal vegetables (*sabzi*) were used, limiting the choice of dishes.

**Aloo gobhi**
Potatoes (*aloo*) cooked with cauliflower (*gobhi*) and ginger.

**Aloo methi**
Browned potatoes and fenugreek (*methi*) leaves.

**Baingan ka bharta**
Smoked aubergine puréed with onions and tomatoes.

**Bhindi piaz**
Okra and onions (seasonal).

**Dum aloo**
Potatoes with yoghurt and spices cooked over low heat.

**Gatta curry**
Gramflour dumplings in a delicate, aromatic sauce.

A streetside restaurant specializing in *paranthas*

## Kadhi
Fried gramflour dumplings cooked in a yoghurt and gramflour-thickened sauce.
## Khair sangri
Small local berries cooked with spinach-like leaves.
## Khumb matar curry
A mushroom and pea curry.
## Malai kofta
Cottage cheese dumplings in a thick tomato gravy.
## Masala baingan
Stuffed aubergines (eggplants) braised in oil.
## Paneer
*Paneer* (cottage cheese), an all time favourite, is cooked in a variety of combinations. *Palak paneer* is with spinach, and *matar paneer* with peas.
## Paneer makhani
Cottage cheese in a tomato and butter sauce.
## Sarson ka saag
Mustard leaves cooked in milk and served in a puréed form with butter.

### LENTILS

*Chola Bhatura*

Dal, a lentil curry, is the staple meal. *Masur* and *moong* are two varieties.
## Chola bhatura
Chickpeas thickly coated with a spicy sauce eaten with a puffed, deep-fried bread.
## Dal makhani
Unhulled dal cooked in cream and butter.
## Rajma curry
A red kidney-bean curry.
## Sambhar
A South Indian speciality made with *arhar* dal and a special curry powder.

### BREADS

Common breads cooked on a griddle are the chapati, paper-thin *roomali roti* and *parantha*. *Pooris* are deep fried, while tandoori breads include the tandoori and *khastha roti* and *naan*.

### RICE

Biryanis and *pulaos* are eaten with raitas (whipped yoghurt mixed with onions, tomatoes, coriander and green chillies), and a wide range of pickles and chutneys.
## Biryani
Mutton or chicken korma is layered with rice, cooked on a slow charcoal fire, and flavoured with saffron.
## Navratan pulao
Rice cooked with nine types of vegetables.
## Yakhni pulao
Rice and mutton cooked in stock flavoured with aniseed and whole spices.

### SWEETS

Sweets are mainly milk-based.
## Gajar ka halwa
Grated carrots cooked in milk and sugar and browned with pistachios and almonds.
## Gulab jamun
Deep-fried milk and flour dumplings in a thick syrup.
## Kulfi
Hand-churned ice-cream flavoured with pistachios.
## Phirni
A Mughlai riceflour pudding, flavoured with saffron (*kesar*).
## Rabri
Thickened milk and sugar garnished with nuts.
## Rasmalai
A flatter version of the *rasgulla* (*paneer* balls in a thin syrup) in a mildly flavoured creamy sauce.

*Gajar ka Halwa*

### DRINKS

## Elaichi chai
Flavoured cardamom tea.
## Lassi
Whipped yoghurt shake.
## Nimbu pani
Fresh, sweetened or salted lime juice with water or soda.
## Panna
Peeled raw mango boiled, puréed, and mixed in water with salt, sugar and cumin.
## Sherbet
A flavoured sweet drink.

### PAAN

Betel leaf packed with areca nut, lime (*catechu*) paste, and other ingredients such as cardamoms and cloves.

**Paan**, a good digestive, can be made to suit individual tastes

# Choosing a Restaurant

T HE RESTAURANTS in this guide have been selected to suit a wide price range and many are in recommended hotels. Chosen for their exceptional food, good value, and convenient or interesting location, they are listed region-wise. Map references refer to the Delhi Street Finder maps on pages 124–131. Colour-coded thumb tabs show the areas covered on each page.

| | CREDIT CARDS | REGIONAL SPECIALITIES | PURE VEGETARIAN | WESTERN DISHES | OUTDOOR TABLES |
|---|---|---|---|---|---|
| **DELHI** | | | | | |
| **NEW DELHI:** *Triveni Tea Terrace*. **Map** 2 D5. ⓡ<br>Triveni Kala Sangam, Tansen Marg. ◖ *(011) 371 8833.*<br>An ideal place if you wish to enjoy an inexpensive alfresco lunch under<br>flowering creepers in the heart of Delhi's cultural centre. ◌ *B, L.* | | | | | ■ |
| **NEW DELHI:** *Berco's*. **Map** 1 C4. ⓡⓡ<br>E–8 Connaught Place. ◖ *(011) 331 8134.*<br>Good for a quick and inexpensive Indian or Chinese meal in a busy<br>shopping area, this restaurant is packed to capacity at lunchtime. Crispy<br>honey chicken and lamb are a speciality. 目 ◌ *L, D.* | AE<br>DC<br>MC<br>V | | | | |
| **NEW DELHI:** *Coconut Grove*. **Map** 5 A1. ⓡⓡ<br>Indraprastha Hotel, 19 Ashok Rd. ◖ *(011) 334 4511.*<br>The menu has a varied selection of vegetarian and non-vegetarian South<br>Indian cuisine. The buttermilk is recommended, as is *meen pappas*, a<br>light, mildly spiced fresh fish curry from Kerala. 目 ◌ *L, D.* | AE<br>DC<br>MC<br>V | ● | | | |
| **NEW DELHI:** *Dasaprakash*. **Map** 5 B3. ⓡⓡ<br>Ambassador Hotel, Sujan Singh Park. ◖ *(011) 469 4966.*<br>An old-fashioned restaurant, this is one of a chain that specializes in a<br>range of popular South Indian dishes. 目 ◌ *L, D.* | AE<br>DC<br>MC<br>V | ● | ■ | | |
| **NEW DELHI:** *Have More*. **Map** 5 B3. ⓡⓡ<br>11–12 Pandara Rd Market. ◖ *(011) 338 7070.*<br>For those who wish to savour a hearty meal of North Indian food served<br>Punjabi style, this is one of many such Delhi eateries. Located in an<br>unassuming small market that comes alive in the evenings. 目 ◌ *L, D.* | AE<br>DC<br>MC<br>V | ● | | | |
| **NEW DELHI:** *Kwality*. **Map** 1 C5. ⓡⓡ<br>Regal Building, Connaught Place. ◖ *(011) 373 2310.*<br>The *channa bhatooras* (spicy chickpeas and deep-fried puffed bread) is<br>an all-time Punjabi favourite in this well-known restaurant. Its central<br>location makes it a good meeting place for shoppers. 目 ◌ *L, D.* | AE<br>DC<br>MC<br>V | ● | | | |
| **NEW DELHI:** *Chinese Room*. **Map** 1 C4. ⓡⓡⓡ<br>Nirula's Hotel, L Block, Connaught Circus. ◖ *(011) 332 2419.*<br>The slightly dated Oriental decor here belongs to the early sixties when<br>Nirula's introduced Chinese food to Delhi. Outpaced since by more<br>accomplished restaurants, it still has a charming ambience. 目 ◌ *L, D.* | DC<br>MC<br>V | | | | |
| **NEW DELHI:** *Gaylords*. **Map** 1 C5. ⓡⓡⓡ<br>Regal Building, Connaught Place. ◖ *(011) 336 0717.*<br>Known for its cold coffee with ice cream, a central location makes this<br>restaurant a popular meeting place at lunchtime. 目 ▮ ◌ *L, D.* | AE<br>DC<br>MC<br>V | | | ● | |
| **NEW DELHI:** *The Rampur Kitchen*. **Map** 5 B3. ⓡⓡⓡ<br>Khan Market. ◖ *(011) 463 1222.*<br>This cheerful little eatery with speciality food from the princely state of<br>Rampur makes a great place to stop for a lunch between shopping and<br>browsing in Khan Market. 目 ◌ *L, D.* | AE<br>DC<br>MC<br>V | ● | | | |
| **NEW DELHI:** *Tamura*. **Map** 1 C5. ⓡⓡⓡ<br>Chanakyapuri, Nehru Park. ◖ *(011) 611 0552.*<br>Homesick Japanese visitors flock here to savour tempura and sushi. A<br>wide range of fish, prawns, pork and beef preparations are also on offer.<br>The tempura lunch box is a speciality. 目 ▮ ◌ *L, D.* | AE<br>MC<br>DC<br>V | | | | |
| **NEW DELHI:** *Dhaba*. **Map** 5 A3. ⓡⓡⓡⓡ<br>Claridges, 12 Aurangzeb Rd. ◖ *(011) 301 0211.*<br>Inspired by the popular roadside eateries that line North India's highways,<br>Dhaba offers a range of fresh and spicy food. 目 ▮ ▮ ◌ *L, D.* | AE<br>MC<br>DC<br>V | ● | | | |

**Price categories** for a meal for one, including tax and service charges but not alcohol:

Rs under 100 rupees
Rs Rs 100–200 rupees
Rs Rs Rs 200–400 rupees
Rs Rs Rs Rs 400–700 rupees
Rs Rs Rs Rs Rs over 700 rupees

**CREDIT CARDS**
Indicates that major credit cards are accepted.
**REGIONAL SPECIALITIES**
Specialized cuisine is served from regions of India, such as Rajasthan, Gujarat or South India.
**PURE VEGETARIAN**
Restaurant serving only vegetarian food.
**WESTERN DISHES**
French, Italian or other Western fare is on the menu.
**OUTDOOR TABLES**
Tables for eating outdoors, often with a good view.

| | CREDIT CARDS | REGIONAL SPECIALITIES | PURE VEGETARIAN | WESTERN DISHES | OUTDOOR TABLES |
|---|---|---|---|---|---|
| **NEW DELHI:** *The Garden Party.* **Map** 1 C5. Rs Rs Rs<br>Imperial Hotel, Janpath. (011) 334 1234.<br>Overlooking the palm-fringed lawns of the elegant Imperial, this 24-hour restaurant has an open, cheery atmosphere and serves a special "memsahib-style" tea accompanied by iced cakes. ▤ � ▥ ○ *B, L, D.* | AE DC MC V | ● | | ● | ■ |
| **NEW DELHI:** *Baan Thai.* **Map** 6 D4. Rs Rs Rs Rs Rs<br>The Oberoi, Dr Zakir Hussain Marg. (011) 436 3030.<br>The authentic Thai food in this top-notch restaurant is served with great style. Guests have an interesting choice of Western or traditional Thai floor-seating arrangements. ▤ ▥ ▥ ○ *L, D.* | AE DC MC V | | | | |
| **NEW DELHI:** *Baluchi.* **Map** 2 D5. Rs Rs Rs Rs Rs<br>Hotel Inter-Continental, Barakhamba Ave. (011) 332 0101.<br>A fashionable restaurant that specializes in delectable tandoori fare (charcoal grills in a clay oven) from the North-West Frontier region. Live music is played every evening. ▤ ▥ ▥ ○ *L, D.* | AE DC MC V | ● | | | |
| **NEW DELHI:** *The Blue Elephant.* **Map** 2 D5. Rs Rs Rs Rs Rs<br>Hotel Inter-Continental, Barakhamba Ave. (011) 332 0101.<br>Eclectic Thai cooking in an elegant restaurant run by a well known hotel chain that offers many speciality cuisines. The service is efficient and the atmosphere warm and welcoming. ▤ ▥ ▥ ○ *L, D.* | AE DC MC V | | | | |
| **NEW DELHI:** *Captain's Cabin.* **Map** 5 B3. Rs Rs Rs Rs Rs<br>Taj Mahal Hotel, Mansingh Rd. (011) 302 6162.<br>With its nautical ambience, this expensive restaurant specializes in seafood. Added attractions are its bar and a live band. ▤ ▥ ▥ ○ *L, D.* | AE MC DC V | | | ● | |
| **NEW DELHI:** *House of Ming.* **Map** 5 B3. Rs Rs Rs Rs Rs<br>Taj Mahal Hotel, Mansingh Rd. (011) 302 6162.<br>Hailed as the restaurant with the best Chinese cuisine in town. This is now a favourite with those who can afford its expensive cuisine impeccably served in a fashionable setting. ▤ ▥ ▥ ○ *L, D.* | AE MC DC V | | | | |
| **NEW DELHI:** *Kandahar.* **Map** 5 B3. Rs Rs Rs Rs Rs<br>The Oberoi, Dr Zakir Hussain Marg. (011) 436 3030.<br>Famed for its creative and wide selection of traditional Indian and Frontier food, Chef Pankaj prepares delicious meals for both vegetarians and non-vegetarians. Live Indian music in the evenings. ▤ ▥ ▥ ○ *L, D.* | AE DC MC V | ● | | | |
| **NEW DELHI:** *La Rochelle.* **Map** 6 D4. Rs Rs Rs Rs Rs<br>The Oberoi, Dr Zakir Hussain Marg. (011) 436 3030.<br>Continental food is served here in very elegant surroundings. Excellent value lunch buffet with live jazz on Sundays. Superb seafood, delicious salads and cheeses. ▤ ▥ ▥ ○ *L, D.* | AE DC MC V | | | ● | |
| **NEW DELHI:** *Las Meninas.* **Map** 1 C5. Rs Rs Rs Rs Rs<br>The Park, Parliament St. (011) 373 3737.<br>This is the first authentic Spanish restaurant in the region and serves lavish full course meals accompanied by good wines. ▤ ▥ ▥ ○ *D.* | AE DC MC V | | | ● | |
| **NEW DELHI:** *Spice Route.* **Map** 1 C5. Rs Rs Rs Rs Rs<br>Imperial Hotel, Janpath. (011) 334 1234.<br>Its dramatic Asian architectural decor serves as an evocative backdrop to the wide range of spicy cuisine offered here from Kerala to Indonesia. The jumbo prawns here are scrumptious. Book ahead. ▤ ▥ ▥ ○ *L, D.* | AE MC DC V | ● | | | |
| **NIZAMUDDIN:** *Karim's.* **Map** 6 D5. Rs Rs Rs<br>Jha House, Hazrat Nizamuddin West. (011) 463 5458.<br>A branch of the renowned Old Delhi eatery, Karim's offers authentic Muslim cuisine, delectable kababs and "ishtoo" (stew). ▤ ● Mon, Ids and during Ramzan *(see p37)*, only dinner is served. ○ *L, D.* | AE DC MC V | ● | | | |

| | CREDIT CARDS | REGIONAL SPECIALITIES | PURE VEGETARIAN | WESTERN DISHES | OUTDOOR TABLES |
|---|---|---|---|---|---|

**Price categories** for a meal for one, including tax and service charges but not alcohol:

(Rs) under 100 rupees
(Rs)(Rs) 100–200 rupees
(Rs)(Rs)(Rs) 200–400 rupees
(Rs)(Rs)(Rs)(Rs) 400–700 rupees
(Rs)(Rs)(Rs)(Rs)(Rs) over 700 rupees

**CREDIT CARDS**
Indicates that major credit cards are accepted.
**REGIONAL SPECIALITIES**
Specialized cuisine is served from regions of India, such as Rajasthan, Gujarat or South India.
**PURE VEGETARIAN**
Restaurant serving only vegetarian food.
**WESTERN DISHES**
French, Italian or other Western fare is on the menu.
**OUTDOOR TABLES**
Tables for eating outdoors, often with a good view.

**OLD DELHI:** *Chor Bizarre*. **Map** 2 E3.   (Rs)(Rs)
Hotel Broadway, Asaf Ali Rd. **(** *(011) 327 3821.*
This quaint restaurant, decorated with unusual antiques, is famous for its authentic Kashmiri cuisine. 🍴 🍷 🍹 ◯ *L, D.*

| | AE DC MC V | ● | | | |
|---|---|---|---|---|---|

**OLD DELHI:** *Karim's*. **Map** 2 E2.   (Rs)(Rs)(Rs)
Opp Jami Masjid. **(** *(011) 326 4981.*
Located in the heart of a historic area for close to a century, superlative kababs and "ishtoo" (stew) have been their specialities. 🍴 ● Mon, Ids and during Ramzan *(see p37)* , only dinner is served. ◯ *B, L, D.*

| | | ● | | | |
|---|---|---|---|---|---|

**FURTHER AFIELD (WEST):** *Basil & Thyme*. **Map** 4 E4.   (Rs)(Rs)(Rs)(Rs)
Santushti Complex, Chanakyapuri. **(** *(011) 467 4933.*
Light Western food, with special daily menus, makes this charmingly located eatery a popular lunching spot. 🍴 ◯ *L.* ● *Sun.*

| | AE DC MC V | | | ● | |
|---|---|---|---|---|---|

**FURTHER AFIELD (WEST):** *Bukhara*.   (Rs)(Rs)(Rs)(Rs)(Rs)
Maurya Sheraton, Sardar Patel Marg, Diplomatic Enclave. **(** *(011) 611 2233.*
Delhi's most famous restaurant for food from the North-West Frontier offers outstanding barbequed chops, skewered chicken, fish or cream cheese, with a variety of delicious breads. 🍴 🍷 🍹 ◯ *B, L, D.*

| | AE DC MC V | ● | | | |
|---|---|---|---|---|---|

**FURTHER AFIELD (WEST):** *Dum Pukht*.   (Rs)(Rs)(Rs)(Rs)(Rs)
Maurya Sheraton, Sardar Patel Marg, Diplomatic Enclave. **(** *(011) 611 2233.*
Master chef Imtiaz Kureishi's *dum* cuisine, lovingly cooked over a slow fire, produces the best biryanis and kakori kababs in town. Also highly recommended are king prawns with pomegranates. 🍴 🍷 🍹 ◯ *L, D.*

| | AE DC MC V | ● | | | |
|---|---|---|---|---|---|

**FURTHER AFIELD (WEST):** *Jewel of the East*.   (Rs)(Rs)(Rs)(Rs)(Rs)
Ashok Hotel, Chanakyapuri. **(** *(011) 611 0101.*
Exotic Chinese food, including steamed bird's nest with red dates and *ginseng*. The *dim sum* lunch buffets are recommended. 🍴 🍷 🍹 ◯ *L, D.*

| | AE DC MC V | | | | |
|---|---|---|---|---|---|

**FURTHER AFIELD (WEST):** *The Orient Express*.   (Rs)(Rs)(Rs)(Rs)(Rs)
Taj Palace, Sardar Patel Marg, Diplomatic Enclave. **(** *(011) 611 0202.*
Intimate table settings in a "dining compartment" of the legendary Orient Express, where delectable but expensive Western cuisine and wine are stylishly served by attentive waiters. 🍴 🍷 🍹 ◯ *L, D.*

| | AE DC MC V | | | ● | |
|---|---|---|---|---|---|

**FURTHER AFIELD (WEST):** *Tea House of the August Moon*.   (Rs)(Rs)(Rs)(Rs)(Rs)
Taj Palace, Sardar Patel Marg, Diplomatic Enclave. **(** *(011) 611 0202.*
An eclectic mix of great Japanese and Chinese food with delicious starters is served in a dramatic Oriental setting. 🍴 🍷 🍹 ◯ *L, D.*

| | AE DC MC V | | | | |
|---|---|---|---|---|---|

**FURTHER AFIELD (SOUTH):** *Sagar*.   (Rs)(Rs)
Defence Colony Market. **(** *(011) 462 1451.*
The fresh and tasty South Indian food served here is so popular that clients often have to queue up for a table. 🍴 ◯ *B, L, D.*

| | | ● | ▣ | | |
|---|---|---|---|---|---|

**FURTHER AFIELD (SOUTH):** *Farsaan*.   (Rs)(Rs)(Rs)
M-27 Greater Kailash-I. **(** *(011) 646 4318.*
The capital's one and only restaurant for authentic Gujarati food, its pure vegetarian *thalis* come "untainted" by onion and garlic. 🍴 ◯ *L, D.*

| | AE | ● | ▣ | | |
|---|---|---|---|---|---|

**FURTHER AFIELD (SOUTH):** *Flavours*.   (Rs)(Rs)(Rs)
Moolchand Flyover, Bank Complex. **(** *(011) 464 5644.*
This cheerful eatery is run by an Italian who personally rustles up imaginative pastas, salads and dreamy desserts. 🍴 ◯ *L, D.*

| | AE | | | ● | ▣ |
|---|---|---|---|---|---|

**FURTHER AFIELD (SOUTH):** *Park Baluchi*.   (Rs)(Rs)(Rs)
Inside Deer Park, Hauz Khas Village. **(** *(011) 685 9369.*
Enchanting sylvan surroundings add to the taste of succulent roasts and chargrills from traditional recipes of the frontier areas. 🍴 🍷 ◯ *L, D.*

| | AE DC MC V | ● | | | ▣ |
|---|---|---|---|---|---|

**FURTHER AFIELD (SOUTH):** *Sagar Ratna.* (Rs)(Rs)(Rs)
Lodhi Hotel, Lala Lajpat Rai Marg. (011) 436 4442.
An up-market branch of a popular medium-priced restaurant in the New
Delhi area, this serves delicious *dosas, idlis* and vegetarian *thalis* from
South India in a more leisurely style. 目 ◯ *L, D.*
*AE DC MC V*

**FURTHER AFIELD (SOUTH):** *Dehli Ke Aangan.* (Rs)(Rs)(Rs)(Rs)
Hyatt Regency, Bhikaji Cama Place, Ring Rd. (011) 618 1234.
This restaurant offers Old Delhi's superb Kayastha cuisine in a five-star
ambience from a menu devised by the famous Indian chef Jiggs Kalra. A
gourmet kabab brunch is offered on weekends. 目 ▮ ▮ ◯ *L, D.*
*AE DC MC V*

**FURTHER AFIELD (SOUTH):** *La Piazza.* (Rs)(Rs)(Rs)(Rs)
Hyatt Regency, Bhikaji Cama Place, Ring Rd. (011) 618 1234.
This fancy Italian restaurant uses ingredients that are flown in specially
from Italy to be prepared in its open kitchen in full view of its clients. Its
Sunday brunches are very popular. Book in advance. 目 ▮ ▮ ◯ *L, D.*
*AE DC MC V*

**FURTHER AFIELD (SOUTH):** *Spice.* (Rs)(Rs)(Rs)(Rs)
Ambavata Complex, Mehrauli Village, Mehrauli. (011) 652 6872.
Run by two ladies who supervise the great Thai and Indonesian food and
desserts on offer. 目 ● Mon & June. Check on major holidays. ◯ *L, D.*
*AE DC MC V*

**FURTHER AFIELD (SOUTH):** *TK's The Oriental Grill.* (Rs)(Rs)(Rs)(Rs)
Hyatt Regency, Bhikaji Cama Place, Ring Rd. (011) 618 1234.
Famed for its Japanese barbequed delicacies, the special brunch each
Sunday with free champagne is a treat. 目 ▮ ◯ *L, D.*
*AE DC MC V*

**FURTHER AFIELD (SOUTH):** *Village Bistro Restaurant Complex.* (Rs)(Rs)(Rs)(Rs)
Hauz Khas Village, Near Deer Park. (011) 685 3857.
A complex of speciality restaurants overlooking the Hauz Khas Deer
Park 目 ▮ ◯ *L, D.*
*AE DC MC V*

**FURTHER AFIELD (SOUTH):** *Great Kebab Factory.* (Rs)(Rs)(Rs)(Rs)(Rs)
Hotel Radisson, National Highway 8, Mahipalpur. (011) 612 9191.
Nearly 150 types of delicious kababs to please both meat eaters and
vegetarians are served here by attentive waiters. One can eat as much as
one wants at a fixed price. 目 ▮ ◯ *D.*
*AE DC MC V*

**FURTHER AFIELD (SOUTH OF DELHI):** *Zafran.* (Rs)(Rs)(Rs)
The Bristol Hotel, Gurgaon–Faridabad Rd. (91) 35 6030.
The restaurant serves an exotic *samudri badshah* (tandoori lobster) and
tandoori duck to a background of live music. 目 ▮ ◯ *L, D.*
*AE DC MC V*

## NORTH OF DELHI

**HARIDWAR:** *Ahaar.* (Rs)
Upper Rd. No telephone.
A variety of cuisines, such as Punjabi, South Indian and Chinese, are
offered here. The ice-cream parlour also has a variety of flavours. ◯ *L, D.*

**HARIDWAR:** *Bestee.* (Rs)
18 Niranjani Akhara. (0133) 42 0082.
Good breakfasts may be had here, although the restaurant is more
famous for its tasty snacks, milk shakes and seasonal fruit *lassis.* ◯ *L, D.*

**HARIDWAR:** *Chinkara Hills.* (Rs)
Haridwar Rishikesh Rd, Raiwala, Distt Dehradun. (0135) 48 4361.
This tourist stop-off offers quick snacks to tourists en route to Haridwar.
The attraction is the promise of non-vegetarian food and liquor, banned
in Haridwar, that are available here. ◯ *B, L, D.*

**HARIDWAR:** *Mid-way Resorts.* (Rs)
Near Raiwala Railway Bridge, Rishikesh-Haridwar Rd. (0135) 48 4208.
Essentially a tourist stop-off, good for a quick drink and snack. ◯ *B, L, D.*

**HARIDWAR:** *Shivalik.* (Rs)
Station Rd. No telephone.
Specializing in Gujarati food from West India, Indian, Western and the
ubiquitous "Chinese" dishes are also available here. ◯ *B, L, D.*

**RISHIKESH:** *Anjali.* (Rs)
Railway Rd. (01364) 43 1779.
This down-to-earth eatery provides standard Indian fare at very
reasonable prices. 目 ◯ *B, L, D.*

For key to symbols see back flap

**Price categories** for a meal for one, including tax and service charges but not alcohol:

Rs under 100 rupees
RsRs 100–200 rupees
RsRsRs 200–400 rupees
RsRsRsRs 400–700 rupees
RsRsRsRsRs over 700 rupees

**CREDIT CARDS**
Indicates that major credit cards are accepted.
**REGIONAL SPECIALITIES**
Specialized cuisine is served from regions of India, such as Rajasthan, Gujarat or South India.
**PURE VEGETARIAN**
Restaurant serving only vegetarian food.
**WESTERN DISHES**
French, Italian or other Western fare is on the menu.
**OUTDOOR TABLES**
Tables for eating outdoors, often with a good view.

| | CREDIT CARDS | REGIONAL SPECIALITIES | PURE VEGETARIAN | WESTERN DISHES | OUTDOOR TABLES |
|---|---|---|---|---|---|
| **RISHIKESH:** *Chotiwala.*<br>Swarg Ashram, Across Shivanand Jhula. ( (0135) 43 0070.<br>A rooftop restaurant that is part of a popular chain in the region, it prepares delicious *thali* meals for orthodox Hindu pilgrims. ○ *B, L, D.* | Rs | | ■ | | |
| **RISHIKESH:** *Neelam.*<br>Laxman Jhula Rd. ( *No telephone.*<br>Bland Western food, such as soups, macaroni and rice pudding offered here, makes this eatery a change from the usual "pilgrim fare". ○ *B, L, D.* | Rs | | ■ | ● | |
| **ROORKEE:** *Cheetal Grand.*<br>Delhi-Mussoorie Rd, Khatauli. ( (01316) 72 468.<br>This pleasantly landscaped restaurant-cum-hotel, midway between Meerut and Roorkee, serves quick, hot meals courteously. ▤ ○ *B, L, D.* | Rs | | | ● | ■ |
| **AROUND AGRA** | | | | | |
| **AGRA:** *Only Restaurant.*<br>45 Taj Ganj Rd. ( (0562) 36 4333.<br>The reliable if pedestrian Indian, Western and Chinese food served here is accompanied by live Indian music in the evenings. ▤ ○ *L, D.* | Rs | ● | | ● | |
| **AGRA:** *Dasaprakash.*<br>Meher Theatre Complex, Balu Ganj, Gwalior Rd. ( (0562) 26 0269.<br>The restaurant, run by a reputed chain, specializes in hygienically cooked, reasonably priced vegetarian South Indian food. ▤ ○ *B, L, D.* | RsRs | ● | ■ | | |
| **AGRA:** *Kwality Restaurant.*<br>Taj Ganj. ( (0562) 36 7767.<br>As in other Kwality restaurants in India, you are sure of a reliable standard of reasonably priced standard Indian fare. An advantage is the bar next door. ▤ ● Holi & Diwali. Check on major holidays. ○ *L, D.* | RsRs | ● | | | |
| **AGRA:** *Pizza Hut.*<br>8 Handicrafts Nagar, Fatehbad Rd. ( (0562) 33 3049.<br>For those who cannot stay away too long from American fast food, this familiar and popular restaurant is a comforting sight. ▤ ○ *L, D.* | RsRs<br>AE<br>DC<br>MC<br>V | | | ● | |
| **AGRA:** *Zorba The Buddha Osho Restaurant.*<br>E–13 Shopping Arcade, Sadar Bazaar. ( (0562) 36 7767.<br>Run by Osho followers, the "vegetarian delights prepared with meditative consciousness" offered here are cooked hygienically and served in a spiritually stimulating environment. ▤ ● 1 May–5 Jul & Diwali. ○ *L, D.* | RsRs<br>AE<br>MC | ● | ■ | ● | |
| **AGRA:** *Bagh-E-Bahar.*<br>Welcomgroup Mughal Sheraton, Taj Ganj. ( (0562) 33 1701.<br>An attractive restaurant with Continental fare, good and lively Western music at night. ▤ ▯ ○ *B, L, D.* | RsRsRs<br>AE<br>MC<br>DC<br>V | ● | | ● | |
| **AGRA:** *Taj Bano.*<br>Welcomgroup Mughal Sheraton, Taj Ganj. ( (0562) 33 1701.<br>No snacks here, but complete meals from a wide choice of cuisines are accompanied by a live sitar recital at lunch and dinner. ▤ ▯ ○ *B, L, D.* | RsRsRs<br>AE<br>MC<br>DC<br>V | ● | | ● | |
| **BHARATPUR:** *Hotel Pelican.*<br>Near National Park entrance. ( (05644) 24 221.<br>The restaurant in this hotel serves Indian and Western food, and there is a surprising, but modest selection of Israeli dishes. ○ *B, L, D.* | Rs | | | ● | |
| **BHARATPUR:** *Spoonbill.*<br>Behind RTDC Hotel Saras. ( (05644) 23 571.<br>This popular, thatched garden eatery offers Indian and Chinese food, and on winter evenings there is a welcoming campfire. ○ *B, L, D.* | RsRs | | | | ■ |

**BHARATPUR:** *Bharatpur Forest Lodge.*
Inside the National Park. ( *(05644) 22 722.*
Attached to the pleasant hotel inside the park, this state-run restaurant
has sumptuous buffets laid on for hungry birdwatchers. B, L, D.

**BRINDAVAN:** *ISKCON Bhojanalaya.*
Bhakti Vedanta Swami Marg, Raman Reti. ( *(0565) 44 2591.*
A part of the clean and hygienic ISKCON guesthouse, wholesome
vegetarian food at good prices is served here. B, L, D.

**FATEHPUR SIKRI:** *Kallu Hotel.*
Below Buland Darwaza. ( *No telephone.*
The colourful owner, Kallu, is a local institution and amiably presides
over hearty *paranthas* and omelettes, or a spicy meat curry. B, L, D.

**FATEHPUR SIKRI:** *Shere Punjab.*
Bypass Rd. ( *(05619) 2338.*
A little way from the famous archaeological site, this roadside eatery is
the place for a satisfying Punjabi *dhaba*-style meal. B, L, D.

**FATEHPUR SIKRI:** *Gulistan Tourist Complex.*
Fatehpur Sikri Complex. ( *(05619) 88 2490.*
The cheery environs of this government-run garden restaurant enhance
the wide selection of snacks and meals offered here. It is popular with
tourists looking for a convenient stopover point. L, D.

**GWALIOR:** *Volga.*
Jayendraganj, Lashkar. ( *(0751) 32 1092.*
This old Gwalior restaurant lives up to its reputation as one of the best
Indian food places in the city. Diwali & Holi. L, D.

**GWALIOR:** *Dawat*
Opp Gurudwara, M L B Rd ( *(0751) 42 2323.*
A popular venue for business lunches and family dinners, this is the best
place in the city to splurge on fine Mughlai-style cuisine. L, D.

**MATHURA:** *Dalmia Bhojanalaya.*
Sri Krishna Janm Bhoomi. ( *No telephone.*
Tasty vegetarian food is served here in clean surroundings. B, L, D.

**MEERUT:** *Alfa.*
Bombay Bazaar, Meerut Cantt. ( *(0121) 66 0532.*
The garlic and mustard flavoured *tikkas* are recommended. L, D.

**ORCHHA:** *Kaleva.*
The Orchha Resort, Kanchana Ghat, Tikamgarh. ( *(07680) 36 1820.*
Imaginatively designed and conveniently located, this restaurant offers a
choice of both buffet and à la carte meals. B, L, D.
AE MC V

**ORCHHA:** *Sheesh Mahal.*
Orchha, Distt Tikamgarh. ( *(07680) 52 624.*
Located within the Jahangiri Mahal, the fortifying breakfasts and buffet
dinners here are served romantically on the terrace. B, L, D.
AE MC V

## AROUND JAIPUR

**AJMER:** *Bhola Hotel.*
Agra Gate, Subzi.Mandi. ( *(0145) 43 2844.*
The restaurant section of a hotel, this is a good place for vegetarian food,
especially the *thali* which constitutes a complete meal. B, L, D.

**AJMER:** *Honeydew.*
Near KEM Resthouse, Station Rd. ( *(0145) 62 2498.*
Popular with tourists, this fast-food restaurant serves Indian-style burgers
and pizzas and a deliciously cooling banana *lassi.* B, L, D.

**ALWAR:** *Hotel Aravalli.*
Near Railway Station. ( *(0144) 33 2883.*
This restaurant with an attached bar serves standard Indian and Indian-
style Chinese dishes. B, L, D.

**ALWAR:** *Prem Hotel.*
Off Hope Circle. ( *(0144) 21 430.*
An unpretentious vegetarian eatery with reasonably priced snacks, the
speciality here is their inexpensive *thali* meal. B, L, D.

**Price categories** for a meal for one, including tax and service charges but not alcohol:

Rs under 100 rupees
Rs Rs 100–200 rupees
Rs Rs Rs 200–400 rupees
Rs Rs Rs Rs 400–700 rupees
Rs Rs Rs Rs Rs over 700 rupees

**CREDIT CARDS**
Indicates that major credit cards are accepted.
**REGIONAL SPECIALITIES**
Specialized cuisine is served from regions of India, such as Rajasthan, Gujarat or South India.
**PURE VEGETARIAN**
Restaurant serving only vegetarian food.
**WESTERN DISHES**
French, Italian or other Western fare is on the menu.
**OUTDOOR TABLES**
Tables for eating outdoors, often with a good view.

| | | CREDIT CARDS | REGIONAL SPECIALITIES | PURE VEGETARIAN | WESTERN DISHES | OUTDOOR TABLES |
|---|---|---|---|---|---|---|
| **JAIPUR:** *Bake Hut.*<br>Near Niros, Mirza Ismail Rd. (0141) 37 1862.<br>The name says it all: you will find oven-fresh take-away breads, croissants, pastries, doughnuts and other such treats here. *L, D.* | Rs | | | ■ | ● | |
| **JAIPUR:** *Chaitanya Restaurant.*<br>City Centre, Sansar Chandra Rd. (0141) 37 5584.<br>Chinese and Western-style vegetarian dishes with innovative touches are offered here. The restaurant also serves various fast foods and has an attached ice-cream parlour. ▤ ▮ ● Holi & Diwali. *L, D.* | Rs | AE<br>MC<br>V | ● | ■ | ● | |
| **JAIPUR:** *Chanakya.*<br>24-B Mirza Ismail Rd. (0141) 37 6161.<br>Another of Jaipur's North Indian and Western vegetarian cuisine restaurants with a most attentive and efficient staff. *L, D.* | Rs | AE<br>DC<br>MC<br>V | ● | ■ | | |
| **JAIPUR:** *Indian Coffee House.*<br>Mirza Ismail Rd. (0141) 36 2024.<br>The aroma of freshly ground coffee will lead you straight here for the best cup in town. Run by a well-known chain, a modest range of snacks and decent breakfast options are also available. *B, L, D.* | Rs | | | ■ | | |
| **JAIPUR:** *Lassiwala.*<br>Opp Niros, Mirza Ismail Rd. No telephone.<br>You will have to queue up here for the irresistible North Indian *lassi*, a thick, creamy, sweet or salty drink made of curds, variously flavoured and served in terracotta tumblers. *L, D.* | Rs | | | | | |
| **JAIPUR:** *Rajasthan Motel.*<br>Jaipur-Agra Highway, Mahuwa. (07461) 33 210.<br>A highly recommended mid-way stop for the hungry bus or car traveller on the Jaipur-Agra road. *B, L, D.* | Rs | | ● | | ● | |
| **JAIPUR:** *Shiv Oasis.*<br>Delhi-Jaipur National Highway 8, Behror. (01494) 20 718.<br>A limited selection of basic dishes are offered at this mid-way roadside stop on the busy Delhi-Jaipur highway. *B, L, D.* | Rs | | ● | | ● | |
| **JAIPUR:** *Swaad.*<br>B Block, Ganpati Plaza, Mirza Ismail Rd. (0141) 36 0750.<br>The wide menu offers Chinese, Continental and Indian food. There is also a beer bar and a pure vegetarian section in the complex. ▤ *L, D.* | Rs | | | | | |
| **JAIPUR:** *Bhuwaneshwari.*<br>Bissau Palace Hotel, Outside Chand Pol. (0141) 32 0191.<br>Located in a grand palace setting, this restaurant offers authentic Rajasthani delicacies served with style. ▤ *B, L, D.* | Rs Rs | AE<br>DC<br>MC<br>V | ● | | ● | |
| **JAIPUR:** *Copper Chimney.*<br>Opp GPO, Mirza Ismail Rd. (0141) 37 2275.<br>High standards of hygiene and service distinguish this Kwality chain restaurant which has a good selection of traditional and local dishes, such as the spicy *lal maas*, a Rajasthani mutton dish. ▤ *B, L, D.* | Rs Rs | AE<br>DC<br>MC<br>V | ● | | ● | |
| **JAIPUR:** *Golden Dragon.*<br>Hotel Imperial Building, Mirza Ismail Rd. (0141) 37 8651.<br>A pleasant garden restaurant that mainly offers Chinese food, though there is also a selection of Indian and Western dishes. ▤ *L, D.* | Rs Rs | AE<br>DC<br>MC<br>V | ● | | ● | ■ |
| **JAIPUR:** *Gulab Mahal.*<br>Jai Mahal Palace Hotel, Civil Lines. (0141) 37 1616.<br>Elegant service and surroundings. The restaurant is reputed for its Rajasthani *thali* and juicy, garlic flavoured chicken *tikkas*. ▤ *B, L, D.* | Rs Rs | AE<br>DC<br>MC<br>V | ● | | ● | |

**JAIPUR:** *Handi Restaurant.*
Mirza Ismail Rd. (0141) 36 4839.
A tandoori food establishment with stylish variations of barbequed
dishes. Their chicken and *tikkas* are worth trying. L, D.

**JAIPUR:** *Niros.*
Mirza Ismail Rd. (0141) 37 4493.
Crowds swirl in and out of this hugely popular eating place that offers a
selection of Indian, Continental and Chinese food. A great favourite is the
refreshing American ice-cream soda. L, D.

**JAIPUR:** *Laxmi Misthan Bhandar (LMB).*
Johari Bazaar. (0141) 56 5844.
Jaipur's most famous vegetarian restaurant, it also has the largest
selection of Indian sweets made by its traditional *halwais.* B, L, D.

**JAIPUR:** *Nahargarh Fort.*
Nahargarh. (0141) 32 5256.
A good place to enjoy a stunning sunset view of Jaipur city over a
steaming cup of coffee or a cool sundowner. This little restaurant
overlooks the magnificent fort of Nahargarh. L, D.

**JAIPUR:** *Sheesh Mahal.*
Hotel Clarks Amer, Jawaharlal Nehru Marg. (0141) 55 0616.
A stylish restaurant in an elegant hotel, the tandoori chicken here is
highly recommended. L, D.

**JAIPUR:** *Shivir.*
Hotel Mansingh, Sansar Chandra Rd. (0141) 38 7771.
A wonderful view of the city is available from this rooftop restaurant of
the centrally located Mansingh Hotel. There is an excellent range of *thali*
meals along with traditional Rajasthani dishes. L, D.

**NAWALGARH:** *Apani Dhani.*
Jhunjhunu Rd, Nawalgarh, Shekhawati. (015941) 22 239.
In this exceptionally designed Eco Farm you will be served wholesome
vegetarian food made from garden-fresh vegetables organically grown on
the premises, to be eaten in a traditional Indian style. L, D.

**NAWALGARH:** *Roop Niwas Palace.*
1 km from Nawalgarh Fort. (01594) 22 008.
Vegetarian, non-vegetarian and special Rajasthani meals from a fixed
menu are served here. This is a good place to refresh yourself after an
expedition to the Nawalgarh Fort. L, D.

**NEEMRANA:** *Amaltasse.*
Neemrana Fort, Neemrana. (015941) 22 239.
In the enchanting environs of the magnificent Neemrana Heritage Hotel,
this unusual French restaurant offers a gourmet four-course candle-lit
dinner that is worth the drive from Delhi. Book ahead. L, D.

**PUSHKAR:** *Om Shiva.*
Opp State Bank of Bikaner & Jaipur, Mahadev Chowk. (0145) 72 647.
One of the few places in Pushkar that offers an excellent breakfast, a
good buffet meal, and a great view of the temple town. B, L, D.

**PUSHKAR:** *Sun-n-Moon.*
Near Brahma Temple. (0145) 72 883.
This open-air restaurant caters to the foreign traveller with a selected
menu of Western dishes that include a delicious apple pie. B, L, D.

**PUSHKAR:** *Sunset Cafe.*
Hotel Pushkar Inns, Sunset Point. (0145) 72 725.
Its pretty position near the lake shore makes it a good place to enjoy a
light Indian or Western snack, especially at sunset. L, D.

**PUSHKAR:** *Raja Garden Restaurant.*
Near Main Bazaar. (0145) 23 0057.
Located near the bazaar, this restaurant specializes in Western fare and an
inexplicable supply of Marmite! Do try their cheese *naan.* B, L, D.

**PUSHKAR:** *Pushkar Palace.*
Eastern side of Pushkar Lake. (0145) 72 001.
Prices here are relatively high for Pushkar, but the ambience, the buffet
and other meals justify the rates. L, D.

For key to symbols see back flap

# SHOPS AND MARKETS

THE COLOURFUL MARKETS of the region carry a vast and exciting range of handicrafts. The government-run state emporia are well stocked with merchandise at fixed and reasonable rates. Shopping arcades of larger hotels cater to travellers who are hard-pressed for time, though their more sophisticated boutiques are usually pricier. For the more adventurous, there are the street

**Puppet**

stalls and bazaars that offer glimpses of local colour and where bargaining is a way of life. Delhi has some of the region's most elegant shops (see pp118–19), but the charming bazaars of Jaipur and Agra offer visitors a chance to actually observe skilful craftsmen at work. In the smaller towns beyond the main cities, local crafts are often sold in quaint village stores or on the roadside.

**Pavement hawkers in Jaipur**

## OPENING HOURS

MOST SHOPS usually open at 10am and shut down by 7:30pm, though the smaller markets keep longer hours. The government-run emporia close an hour earlier. Markets for fresh produce open at dawn and stay open until late evening, while the temporary bazaars that spring up at different localities on festivals or particular week days gather the crowds until late at night. In Jaipur and Agra, the closing day is Sunday, but in

Delhi, each locality has its own weekly holiday. Shopping centres in the New Delhi area are closed on Sundays, but in South Delhi and Karol Bagh, the closing days are Monday or Tuesday. By law all shops are required to remain closed on the three main national holidays, that is, Republic Day (26 Jan), Independence Day (15 Aug) and Mahatma Gandhi's birthday (Martyr's Day, 2 Oct).

## HOW TO PAY

THE RUPEE is accepted everywhere. The bigger stores accept international credit cards such as VISA, MasterCard, American Express and Diners, and usually display signs prominently inside the shops. But they are still not very common in the smaller shops and towns, and it is always sensible to keep some cash handy when travelling. Traveller's cheques can be encashed at local branches of the State Bank of India (see p288), but again, this facility may not be available in the smaller towns.

**Bright glass and plastic bangles**

## BARGAINING

BARGAINING is an essential part of the shopping experience in India, and at the smaller markets, prices are quoted with the expectation that customers will haggle. Some of the most familiar scenes at all bazaars are those of local shoppers indulging in long and often acrimonious discussions with shopkeepers about price and quality. Most shopkeepers are tourist savvy today and will usually quote a higher price to foreigners. The best way to check out prices is to browse through a fixed-price shop like a government emporium. This will also give you an idea of quality. However, the price you offer to pay should be realistic and not so low that you miss out on a good purchase altogether. If this price is still unacceptable to the shopkeeper, an old and usually very effective bargaining tactic is to walk away feigning indifference.

All the bigger and fancier shops and boutiques, retail outlets of manufacturers and the government emporia have fixed prices with no scope for bargaining. Increasingly, in fact, more shops are tagging their goods with labels that clearly indicate item prices.

**Attractive terracotta pots are incredibly cheap yet durable**

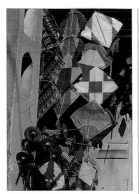

**Paper kite stall in Jaipur**

## RIGHTS AND REFUNDS

BY LAW ALL SHOPS are obliged to give you a receipt or cash memo for all purchases. When buying insist on getting one to which sales tax, generally seven or ten per cent of the total cost, has been added. Often the shopkeeper will say that you can save on the tax if you do not take a receipt, but do insist on one nevertheless. Refunds or the exchange of damaged goods are impossible without one and it is absolutely essential for the more expensive purchases. Bigger shops can be fussy about taking back goods but you can talk to the manager if absolutely necessary.

**Delicately inlaid marble**

If the shop is going to ship your purchases, make sure that you know all the costs involved, including taxes. Also, insist that all the paperwork is done correctly and you have copies of it all. If you wish you can also ship the larger purchases yourself through the international courier services *(see p291)*.

## ANTIQUES

ANTIQUES and art objects that are more than a hundred years old cannot be taken out of the country. If in doubt about your purchases, consult the office of the Archaeological Survey of India *(see p279)*. You should also get a certificate from the shop stating the age of the artifact.

## TOUTS

IN THE LARGER MARKETS that are frequented by tourists, persistent touts can be a problem. Ignore the offers of fantastic bargains because the prices you pay are often suspect. Also beware of polite young men inviting you home for a cup of tea because "home" will be a shop down the lane. Tourist buses will of course stop at their selected shops but you don't have to buy anything from them. Try to shop for expensive things at big shops with price tags on their goods and beware of of shops with "government-approved" boards as these are usually private enterprises.

## BAZAARS

A VISIT to a traditional Indian bazaar is worth the experience much more than the actual shopping. These lively places offer fantastic bargains and a colourful atmosphere. Most bazaars are located in the heart of the old cities, where narrow lanes are lined with rows of shops selling a variety of merchandise from car spare-parts, machinery, cooking utensils and provisions to textiles and jewellery. Vegetables and other fresh produce are sold on the roadside. Most cities also have the weekly bazaars, and rural India has seasonal *haats* that travel from village to village for the local people to shop for everything from

agricultural equipment to clothes to pots and pans. The bazaars in Agra and Jaipur were originally craft guilds and some still specialize in specific local crafts such as textiles, jewellery, marble inlay and leatherwork, where you can watch the craftsmen at work, admire their skills and buy directly from them.

**Bargaining skills are essential at streetside stalls**

## GOVERNMENT EMPORIA

THE CENTRAL GOVERNMENT and the state governments all run shops selling handicrafts and handloom textiles special to their region or state. The prices are fixed and the products genuine. Gangotri, the Uttar Pradesh emporium, stocks crafts from Agra, and Rajasthali, the Rajasthan emporium, concentrates on handicrafts from Jaipur. While Delhi is a centre for emporia from all the states, neither Agra nor Jaipur offer the same range of regional products.

**Roadsides are flooded with colourful, seaonal fruit**

**Anokhi, Jaipur, combines traditional designs with modern-day use**

## SHOPPING IN AGRA

THE EXQUISITE *pietra dura* work on the Taj Mahal is still practised in Agra by descendants of craftsmen who worked on the historic monument. Replicas of the delicate semi-precious stone inlay designs are found on marble and alabaster boxes and bowls, tabletops, chessboards and trays readily available in Agra's bazaars. Large wall panels and ornate sofa backs can be made to order and shipped directly abroad. Plain marble, red sandstone and soapstone items are also popular. Another beautiful craft is *zardozi* embroidery done on silk or velvet with gold and silver thread and sequins to create dress material, bags, jackets and shoes.

Agra is renowned for its shoe industry. The designs are somewhat basic, but the shoes are sturdy and certainly worth their price.

You can also shop for cotton *dhurries* woven in modern or traditional designs.

## NORTH OF DELHI

SMALLER TOWNS near Delhi have their own craft specialities. There are several weaving centres producing pile carpets which are sent to Delhi and other cities to be sold. **Panipat** is famous for its attractive cotton floor coverings and woven home furnishings. In **Saharanpur**, you will find all kinds of woodcarved items in intricate designs and brass inlay work ranging from tables and screens to boxes and ashtrays.

## SHOPPING IN JAIPUR

JAIPUR IS TRULY a shopper's paradise. The range of textiles and handicrafts available here includes an irresistible selection of fabrics (embroidered, blockprinted, tie-and-dyed), as well as ready-made garments. Rolls of colourful quilts in light layered cotton, but surprisingly warm, are piled high on streetside shops, and government emporia and larger shops stock the beautiful Mughal designed woollen carpets that are made in Jaipur. The city is known for its jewellery which ranges from folk designs in silver to the elegant and more pricey gold jewellery in *meenakari* and *kundan* work *(see p187)*.

 **Jaipur blue pottery**

There is also a wide variety of handmade leather goods from *jootis* and bags to saddles and wallets, while in furniture, there is a dazzling choice of carved and painted tables, chairs, screens, wall brackets, candle and lamp stands.

Jaipur was a centre of miniature painting, and artists now sell perfect reproductions at a fraction of the price of originals. Both the religious *pichhwai* and the narrative *phad* cloth paintings make wonderful wall hangings. Blue pottery is another of Jaipur's traditional crafts, using delicate Persian, Turkish and Indian designs on vases, door-knobs and tiles.

## AROUND JAIPUR

BOTH SANGANER and Bagru *(see p204)* are famous for their blockprinted textiles dyed in vegetable colours. In Rajasthan every village has its own artisans. The cobblers produce brightly decorated sandals and bags, potters mould clay into delightful terracotta bowls and plates, and the woodcarver will have wide-eyed puppets hanging on the walls of his workshop. The village markets teem with brightly dressed men and women responding to the cajoling and loud calls of hawkers. Among the traditional metal cooking pots and modern clothes made of synthetic fabric, there are toys and trinkets, lacquer bangles and silver jewellery.

**Weaving a carpet on a traditional pit-loom**

## DIRECTORY

### GOVERNMENT EMPORIA

**Gangotri**
Taj Mahal Complex, Agra.
*(0141) 36 0172.*

**Handloom House**
MI Rd, Jaipur.
*(0141) 36 5331.*

**Khadi Ghar**
MI Rd, Jaipur.
*(0141) 37 3745.*

**Rajasthali**
Govt Hostel, MI Rd, Jaipur.
*(0141) 36 7176.*

**Rajasthan Handloom Project Board**
Chomu House, Jaipur.
*(0141) 36 3907.*

### JEWELLERY

**Koh-i-Noor**
41 MG Rd, Agra.
*(0562) 36 4156.*

**Munshi Ganeshi Lal & Son**
9 MG Rd, Agra.
*(0562) 36 4239.*

**Amrapali**
Tholia Building, MI Rd, Jaipur.
*(0141) 37 5802.*

**Bhuramal Rajmal Surana**
Johari Bazaar, Jaipur.
*(0141) 56 0628.*

**Dwarka's**
H 20 Bhagat Singh Marg, C Scheme, Jaipur.
*(0141) 36 0301.*

**Gem Palace**
MI Rd, Jaipur.
*(0141) 37 4175.*

**Jypore Jewellers**
MI Rd, Jaipur.
*(0141) 37 5913.*

**Silver Mountain**
Chameli Mkt, Jaipur.
*(0141) 37 5913.*

### TEXTILES

**Anokhi**
2 Tilak Marg, Jaipur.
*(0141) 75 0860.*

**Naika**
Tholia Building, MI Rd, Jaipur.
*(0141) 36 2664.*

**Rashid**
Shri Govind Dev Colony, Tal Katora Rd, Jaipur.
*(0141) 31 3237.*

**Shilpi Handicrafts**
Near Siliberi, Sanganer.
*(0141) 73 1106.*

**Soma Shop**
5 Jacob Rd, Civil Lines, Jaipur.
*(0141) 38 3378.*

### EMBROIDERED TEXTILES

**Indian Crafts Gallery**
Fatehabad Rd, Agra.
*(0562) 23 0336.*

**Saurashtra Oriental Arts**
5–6 Jorawar Singh Gate, Amber Rd, Jaipur.
*(0141) 55 2026.*

### CARPETS AND DHURRIES

**Agra Dhurrie Exports**
Gandhi Nagar, Agra
*(0562) 35 2545.*

**Ambika Exports**
Moti Doongri Rd, Jaipur.
*(0141) 60 9821.*

**Ankur Exports**
Opp Rambagh Palace, BS Rd, Jaipur.
*(0141) 51 5553.*

**Shyam Ahuja**
Rambagh Palace, Jaipur.
*(0141) 38 1441.*

**Siddharth Carpet Mfg Co**
Barwara House, Jacob Rd, Jaipur.
*(0141) 38 4981.*

### PAINTINGS AND OBJETS D'ART

**Art Fair**
U2 Chameliwala Mkt, MI Rd, Jaipur.
*(0141) 37 3042.*

**Expo Plus**
Prithviraj Rd, Near Bagria Bhavan, Jaipur.
*(0141) 38 3044.*

**Handicrafts Corner**
Indira Bazaar, Jaipur
*(0141) 31 3696.*

**Ved Pal Sharma Banno**
Chanakya Marg, Subhas Chowk, Jaipur.
*(0141) 60 3450.*

### BLUE POTTERY

**Kripal Singh Shekhawat**
B 18a Siva Marg, Bani Park, Jaipur.
*(0141) 20 1127 (by prior appointment).*

### HANDMADE PAPER

**Salim's Paper**
Gramodyog Rd, Sanganer.
*(0141) 73 0076.*

### BOOKS, TEA AND SPICES

**The Indian Gallery**
Karim Shah Complex, Fatehabad Rd, Agra.
*(0562) 28 2001.*

**Maharaja Exports**
Fatehabad Rd, Agra.
*(0562) 33 4117.*

**Anukamba Mansion**
MI Road, Jaipur.
*(0141) 36 4682.*

**Books Corner**
MI Road, Jaipur.
*(0141) 36 6323.*

**The Book Shop**
Rambagh Palace, Bhawani Singh Rd, Jaipur.
*(0141) 38 1430.*

### SHOES

**Yogi Shoes & Leather Crafts**
Fatehabad Rd, Agra.
*(0562) 33 0029.*

**Bharat Boot House**
Johari Bazaar, Jaipur.
*(0141) 56 4914.*

**Fancy Nagara Shoe Store**
Ramganj Bazaar, Jaipur.
*(0141) 66 3291.*

### MARBLE INLAY

**Ganesi Lal International**
Clarks Shiraz, Agra.
*(0562) 26 4691.*

**Indo Cottage Industres**
6 Fatehabad Rd, Agra.
*(0562) 33 0232.*

**UP Handicrafts Complex**
Fatehabad Road, Agra.
*(0562) 33 1666.*

### BAZAARS

**Agra**
**Johari Bazaar**
Cotton *dhurries*.

**Kinari Bazaar**
Jewellery and *zari* work.

**Nai ki Mandi**
Marble inlay.

**Jaipur**
**Johari Bazaar, Gopalji ka Rasta, Haldiyon ka Rasta**
Jewellery and tie-and-dye textiles.

**Khajanewalon ka Rasta**
Marble carving.

**Kishanpol Bazaar**
Tie-and-dye textiles.

**Maniharon ka Rasta**
Lac bangles.

**Nehru Bazaar**
Embroidered *jootis*.

**Ramganj Bazaar**
Shoes.

# What to Buy

**A bronze monkey**

THE BAZAARS, MARKETS and boutiques of Delhi, Agra and Jaipur showcase the wide range of the region's arts and crafts. In many places there is the joy of watching artisans at work and buying directly from them. The quality can vary, but the range is unbelievable, from exotic, aromatic spices, to ceramics and handicrafts, carpets, textiles and jewellery. There are also elegant contemporary interpretations of traditional design.

**Jewelled and enamelled armband**

### Jewellery

*Antique and jewellery shops stock exquisite pieces of gem-encrusted* kundan *and enamelled* meenakari *jewellery. Also available are the silver ornaments worn by local men and women.*

**Silver anklets, bracelet and armband**

**A pencil holder**

**Hand-crafted cutlery**

### Metal

*Bronze and brass objects of everyday use, such as pots, lamps or boxes, are widely available along with an exciting range of artifacts in silver and other metals created by contemporary designers.*

**A goblet in mixed metal**

**Brass pots (lotas)**

**Silver fan (pankha)**

### Pottery

*Abundant earthenware vessels and toys made by local potters can be seen stacked along the roadside. Commonly found are a sophisticated range of patterned tableware from Khurja, and Jaipur's famous blue pottery.*

**Door-knobs**

**Terracotta votive figure**

**Tiles with floral motifs**

**Jaipur blue pottery jar with lid**

**A folk animal in terracotta**

## Textiles

*Blockprints and silk and cotton woven textiles in a dazzling choice of colours and designs can be bought as yardage or ready-made garments, scarves and saris. Floor coverings are either the thick pile carpets or the colourful cotton dhurries used in Indian homes.*

Pile carpet with floral design

**Window blinds**

Scarves by Abraham & Thakore

**Light-weight cotton quilts**

**Joss sticks (agarbatti)**

## Herbal Products

*Traditional natural remedies have been re-invented to suit the contemporary need for eco-friendly cosmetics, soothing oils and lotions, tea and joss sticks.*

Neem oil

Traditional perfumes (attar)

Soap

Lemon hairwash

**Herbal tea**

## Handicrafts

*Materials such as handmade paper, leather, stone and wood are used to make decorative and functional objects such as shoes, plates, boxes and puppets.*

Handmade paper box

Embroidered slippers

# ENTERTAINMENT

**E**XCEPT FOR DELHI, which offers a wide range of cultural entertainment round the year *(see pp120-21)*, options in most other cities are often restricted to the cultural fare offered by the hotels. Although both Agra and Jaipur have a strong tradition of folk and classical performing arts, these can

**Folk entertainer**

only be seen during the peak season. One reason for this is that most Indians prefer to spend their evenings or holidays with the family. As outings invariably include children, the cinema is a favourite, while religious festivals, which offer free entertainment, are also popular. However, dining out is a rising fad among the urban elite.

## INFORMATION SOURCES

**Y**OUR TRAVEL AGENT is the best source of information on what is happening, where and when. Otherwise, calendars of cultural events are available from the tourist offices and also at hotels. Local newspapers also list daily events and advertise major cultural festivals, such as the Taj Mahotsav *(see p40)*. Small tourist oriented local publications, such as *Jaipur Vision*, available at book shops and hotel receptions, also carry listings of cinemas, restaurants and bars, swimming pools and shops.

## BOOKING TICKETS

**A**LL THE LARGER HOTELS in the region have regular evening performances of classical music and dance in their main restaurants. The dinner cover charge usually includes the performance. But if a show at a theatre or hall is

announced, the tickets are available at the venue and your hotel or travel agent will be able to book them for you.

## CLASSICAL MUSIC AND DANCE

**K**ATHAK and Hindustani music *(see p28)* flourished in this region, patronized first by the Mughal, and later by the regional courts. In an attempt to revive these traditional art forms, classical dance and music festivals are now held regularly in the cities during the peak tourist season sponsored by various cultural organizations. Among auditoria, the **Sur Sadan** in Agra, and in Jaipur, **Ravindra Manch** and **Panghat** are the most popular venues, while on special occasions, well-known dancers also perform before the main deity of the Govind Dev Temple in Jaipur. In Mathura and Brindavan the religious festivals of Holi and Janmashtami also attract classical dancers and singers.

**A Rajasthani folk dancer**

The devotional Sufi qawwali, originally based on the classical *raga* idiom *(see p28)*, is now a popular concert form. However, the best places to hear authentic qawwalis are at the Sufi shrines at Ajmer and Fatehpur Sikri where they are a daily ritual, while during the Urs festivities, special all-night soirées are held.

## FOLK THEATRE, MUSIC AND DANCE

**F**EW AREAS in this region can match the colour and vibrancy of Rajasthan's indigenous folk forms. Sadly, folk theatre and itinerant storytellers like the *phad* bards are fast losing their audiences and can often only be seen in smaller places. Yet, since Jaipur is the capital of the state, some of the best bards and dancers come here to perform at urban centres such as the **Jawahar Kala Kendra**. The *ghumar* dance, performed by women during religious festivals and

**The *bhopa* musicians perform round a campfire**

weddings, and the *kalbelia* or snake dance of a nomadic tribe can be seen at hotel shows. Folk singers, such as the *bhopas*, the Manganiyars or Langas, come regularly to the Pushkar Fair and smaller towns, attracting people with their rich and expressive repertoire of folk ballads.

During the Janmashtami festival (Aug–Sep) the Raslila, an enactment of the story of Lord Krishna, is held in the Brajbhumi area of Brindavan and Mathura *(see p162)*. Local Ramlilas *(see p37)*, are staged all over North India during Dussehra (Oct–Nov). These folk productions, often loud and melodramatic, have a unique vivacity and charm.

## PUPPET SHOWS

PUPPETRY IS a strong folk tradition practised by the Bhatt pastoral community in Rajasthan. String puppets, called *kathputlis,* play out heroic stories of popular folk and legendary characters. The romance of Dhola and Maru, royal lovers who were separated only a few weeks after they were betrothed but finally united, is one of the most popular puppet shows. The riveting performances of these travelling puppeteers is seen at every fair and festival.

## CINEMAS

CINEMA IS still the country's most popular form of entertainment, and even the smallest town has a theatre screening the latest Hindi blockbuster. Jaipur's cinema halls are famous, and the **Raj Mandir**, actually a theatre hall with a flamboyantly kitschy interior, even screens World Cup cricket matches! Indian films are a fantastic mix of action and romance, song and dance, shot in fabulous sets and locales. The films range from the crass to the brilliant.

Dubbing in Hindi of Western mega-hits is the new rage, with films like *Star Wars* and *The World is Not Enough* taking the lead. Though art films have won many international awards, and directors such as Satyajit Ray are considered among the world's best, their films are rarely shown commercially. Nevertheless, a visit to the local cinema will give you an insight into the Indian people's most frequented form of popular entertainment.

**Hollywood mega-hits dubbed in Hindi are hugely popular**

## NIGHTLIFE AND BARS

EXCEPT FOR THE five-star hotels, options for nightlife in Agra and Jaipur are limited. The luxury hotels all have their own bars where there is a good choice of both local and foreign liquors and the atmosphere is pleasant. A few other places in both the cities are licensed to have bars. The choice of spirits is limited but the atmosphere is lively.

---

# SPORTS AND OUTDOOR ACTIVITIES

Previously, only the traditional sports such as cricket and polo provided visitors with opportunities for participating in outdoor activities. But today, the tourism industry offers a vast diversity of choices for specialist holidays. For sports lovers, the main cities, especially Delhi and Jaipur, offer clubs and grounds for golf, tennis, swimming and riding. Those in search of adventure can explore the foothills of the Himalayas and

**After a polo match**

the Aravallis by trekking or rock climbing, while the tumultous mountain streams above Rishikesh are ideal for white-water rafting and kayaking. A camel or horse safari is a good way to experience the haunting beauty of the Rajasthan desert, and wildlife enthusiasts can visit the national parks for tiger-spotting and birdwatching. For those wishing to delve deeper into the mystique of the region, there are centres for yoga and meditation, naturopathy and spiritual studies.

## SPECTATOR SPORTS

Cricket has emerged as the main national sport and, no matter where you travel you will see men and boys batting, bowling and fielding. India hosted the 1996 World Cup, an event that further fuelled the passion for the game and its players, who enjoy a celebrity status equal to film stars. Each year, especially in winter, several international cricket teams come to India, and test matches are played at various cities. The scenic Feroze Shah Kotla ground in Delhi is a major venue. All-night matches are played at the Jawaharlal Nehru Stadium, lit up especially for the occasion. In Jaipur, the Mansingh Stadium is the main cricket playing ground.

Advertisements for national and international matches appear well in advance in all the newspapers, and tickets (usually on sale ten days earlier), are in great demand

even though the more important matches are broadcast on the national network and sports channels.

Indian football is yet to reach international standards, and world-class matches are rarely held in the country. However, passions run high at the Ambedkar Stadium in Delhi where national tournaments are held, and a view from the stands can be a very enjoyable experience on a sunny winter afternoon.

## TENNIS AND SWIMMING

In Delhi, the Lawn Tennis Association maintains some excellent tennis courts. So do some of the city's clubs and sports complexes. In Jaipur, the main tennis courts are at the **Jai Club**, just off Mirza Ismail (MI) Road. Both these cities are venues for the Davis Cup matches, and with India winning the 1999 Wimbledon doubles championship, there is a rapidly growing interest in this international sport.

**A tennis match**

However, because of the scarcity of public tennis courts they are often booked in advance and the best option for a quick game is at your own hotel's tennis court.

Come summer and all clubs, sports centres and five-star hotels in the region open their swimming pools. The most easily accessible to visitors are in the five-star hotels, usually with attached saunas and fitness centres. Non-residents can take temporary membership or pay a fee to use hotel pools.

## GOLF

All major cities have well-maintained golf courses. In Delhi, the oldest and most prestigious course is at the **Delhi Golf Club**, located next to The Oberoi Hotel. This 27-hole course, creatively developed around a cluster of beautiful medieval pavilions, hosts many international

**The Jawaharlal Nehru open air Stadium in New Delhi**

tournaments in the winter season. Military cantonments, both here and at Agra, have their own golf courses. Just outside Delhi, the **Classic Golf Resort** is publicized as a weekend getaway, but is open to golfers through the week. In Jaipur, the Rambagh Palace Hotel has its own golf course and offers golf sets on hire for residents to play on the premises. Most golf clubs offer temporary membership to visitors for a fee.

A golfer tees off beneath the ramparts of Jaipur's Moti Doongri Fort

## RIDING

BOTH DELHI and the Jaipur area have excellent riding clubs which non-members may use for a nominal fee. The **Delhi Riding Club** has a stable full of well-groomed horses for hire. In Shekhawati, the heritage Dunlod Fort *(see p243)* has a polo ground, organizes horse safaris and teaches equestrian skills.

Some hotels in Rajasthan arrange horse safaris for their guests

## POLO

POLO WAS ONCE the preserve of royalty and the army, and the Jaipur maharajas used to personally lead their teams to tournaments abroad. Corporate sponsorship has now revived interest in the game, and a major attraction is the gaiety, pomp and glamour attached to it. Winter is the main polo season in Delhi and Jaipur. Most tournaments in Delhi are played at the polo grounds adjacent to the Race Course on Kamal Ataturk Road, and in Jaipur, matches are played at the **Rajasthan Polo Club** near the Rambagh Palace Hotel.

Ramgarh and Dundlod are major polo centres, where the game is also taught. In March, visitors may see some traditional elephant polo at Jaipur's Chaugan Stadium.

## HELI-TOURISM

HELICOPTER PACKAGE trips are a new departure for the tourism industry in India. Apart from the transport by helicopter, they include lodging, meals and sightseeing. Heli-getaways in the region, organized by **Deccan Aviation** for those who can afford it and are strapped for time, so far include Agra, Jaipur Sariska, and Jaipur-Ranthambhore. From Delhi, World Expeditions India organizes heli-skiing in winter, and also cycling tours.

## JEEP AND DESERT SAFARI

AN ADVENTUROUS WAY to see the countryside is by safari. For wildlife sanctuaries, jeep safaris are common with camping along the way. Camel safaris, organized by travel agents from Jaipur, and

by most heritage hotels especially in Kishangarh *(see p215)*, Mandawa and Nawalgarh *(see p246)*, promise unexpected glimpses of desert life and a first-hand acquaintance with the ship of the desert. Prices vary, depending on the duration of the safari. Camping out in the desert is a romantic experience, especially at night around a campfire with your camel driver relating thrilling stories of desert lovers and villains. Elephant safaris can also be organized for groups through private travel agents.

## CHILDREN'S ACTIVITIES

DELHI OFFERS MUCH to amuse children, beginning with a sprawling Zoo. The Appu Ghar Amusement Park has several roller coasters, water rides and other thrilling games. The **National Science Centre** and the **Nehru Planetarium** organize special shows for children on certain events, such as eclipses. The Rail Museum is also a great hit with children, and offers rides on a special toy train.

Camel safaris provide intimate glimpses of the desert

**Rock climbing**

## CAMPING, TREKKING AND ROCK CLIMBING

THE HIMALAYAN foothills above Rishikesh have ideal locations for camping, trekking and rock climbing. As most of Rajasthan's forts nestle in the craggy slopes of hillsides, they also offer excellent opportunities for rock climbing and exploring the neighbouring countryside. Just beyond South Delhi, near Sohna in Gurgaon, there are many attractive hiking trails. The best source of information on these activities is the **Indian Mountaineering Foundation**, and private operators, such as Milestones and Outdoor Adventures *(see p231)*, who specialize in organizing treks. Most organizers can provide reliable guides, as well as campsite equipment such as tents and sleeping bags, though you may feel more comfortable carrying your own things. The best time for this activity is in the summer months from April to June, and after the monsoon from October to early December, before the weather gets too cold.

## ECOTOURISM

THIS RELATIVELY new concept in tourism, which combines various aspects of nature study along with participation in conservation activities, is steadily gaining

ground in India. There are three main national parks in Rajasthan. Ranthambhore *(see pp224–5)* and Sariska *(see pp210–11)* are known for their tiger populations, while birdwatchers will find many exotic inhabitants at Bharatpur's Keoladeo Ghana *(see pp168–9)*. Tours can be arranged through Rajasthan Tourism. Near Delhi are smaller sanctuaries such as the Sultanpur Sanctuary *(see p116)*. The **World Wide Fund for Nature, India (WWF)**, with its headquarters in Delhi, has an active programme of activities, such as camps, film shows and seminars.

## CULTURAL STUDIES

YOGA AND MEDITATION are taught at ashrams found in most cities. In Delhi, at the **Shivanand Yoga Vedanta Nataraja Centre** there is a good programme all year round. The best centres are, however, found in Rishikesh, where some of the best gurus conduct courses of yoga and Hindu philosophy all year round, and an International Yoga Festival is held here every year *(see p41)*. Naturopathy and ayurveda, two Indian systems that rely on the healing powers of

**Logo of a yoga centre in Rishikesh**

**A yoga asana**

natural foods and herbs, are also practised and taught at many centres, such as the **Ayurveda Kendra Mahesh Yogi Ashram**. In Delhi, the **Kairali Health Resort** specializes in ayurvedic oil massages. Pranic healing, a method that channels positive forces through the *chakras* or energy centres in the body, is taught at the **Aurobindo Centre**. Those who are interested in Buddhist philosophy will find information on this area of study in Tibet House and at the **Toshita Mahayana Meditation Centre**. The **Sadhan Sansthan** can provide details of courses in *vipassana*, an old and efficacious form of meditation, while astrology and palmistry are taught at the Bharatiya Vidya Bhavan. Triveni Kala Sangam *(see p76)* holds short courses in classical singing, dance and painting. Crafts skills can be studied at the Crafts Museum. Some travel agencies have devised special interest tours on subjects such as architecture, traditional crafts and spiritualism, and can draw up itineraries and organize tours to suit individual choices. These agencies have government recognition and are members of international organizations. A "Gourmet Journey through India" is one such tour on the agenda of **Indo Asia Tours** who engage specialists as their consultants.

**Trekking in the Himalayan foothills**

**River rafters relaxing on the banks of the Ganges**

## KAYAKING AND RIVER RAFTING

JUST NORTH OF RISHIKESH, a series of rapids on the Ganges as it rushes down the mountains make for excellent kayaking and river rafting *(see p145)* opportunities. A normal trip stretches over three days as participants are carefully introduced to the intensity of the rapids. The best time for rafting and kayaking is from September to April, when campsites are set up on the pristine beaches along the river both by the Uttar Pradesh State Government

*(see p279)*, and professionally trained private groups, such as Outdoor Adventures *(see p231)* and **Himalayan River Runners**. The complete equipment – tents, rafts, life-saving jackets and helmets are supplied, as well as all meals.

## FISHING

FISHING is permitted in many of the region's rivers and lakes. But you must obtain a licence to do so from the designated local authority on site. In Delhi, the Okhla Barrage, as well as the nearby Suraj-kund and Badkhal lakes are popular with amateur anglers. Further north, where hill streams join the Chandrabhaga and the Ganges, par-ticularly above Haridwar and Rishikesh, the rivers yield a good catch of the local variety of carp and other fish, though rarely, trout.

## WATER SPORTS

RAMGARH LAKE *(see p197)*, near Jaipur where some events of the 1984 Asian Games were held, is being developed by Rajasthan Tourism as a venue for water sports with facilities for parasailing, water-skiing and wind surfing. Currently, you can hire rowing, pedal and motor boats for a ride on the lake. Also, in and around Delhi a number of man-made lakes have facilities for boating and water sports.

**White-water rafting on the River Ganges**

# SURVIVAL
# GUIDE

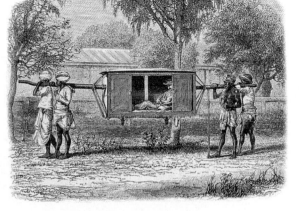

# PRACTICAL INFORMATION

THE COUNTRY'S most popular travel circuit, the three cities of Delhi, Agra and Jaipur, receives the majority of the 2.5 million tourists who visit India annually. Because of this, the range of transport, accommodation and information offered here is among the best in India. The more remote areas are still not equipped to cater to the international traveller who may seek better banking facilities or prefer to pay by credit card. The government-run Department of Tourism (DOT) has

**Logo of the Department of Tourism**

a centrally located office in Delhi and many overseas branches. You can also get the latest and most relevant information at the local state tourist departments of Delhi, Rajasthan and Uttar Pradesh. There are innumerable travel agencies, but it is wise to approach a reputable one when booking accommodation, travel tickets and sightseeing tours. It is also wise to plan and book ahead if you wish to make a visit in the winter months, since this is the peak tourist season.

## WHEN TO GO

THE FINEST WEATHER to travel in North India is from October to March. This season also coincides with an abundance of festivals and cultural events, especially from October to December *(see pp38–41)*. Though it can get quite cold at night in winter (Dec–Jan), the days are crisp and sunny, and the brief spring of February and March is beautiful, with the flowers in full bloom. Try to avoid the summer (Apr–Jun), and rainy season (Jul–Sep) if possible. Summer in North India is unbearably hot, dry and dusty, compounded by power cuts, and during the monsoon, the humidity accentuates the heat, making travelling very uncomfortable. Climate and rainfall charts can be found on pages 38–41.

**Brightly coloured blossoms adorn a Delhi roundabout**

**Donning local attire adds to the fun of a celebration**

◁ **The annual Pushkar camel fair is a riot of colour**

## WHAT TO TAKE

THE CLOTHES you need will depend on the time of year that you visit. At the height of the winter you will need warm clothes – a jacket or a thick pullover, socks and warm trousers, especially during the early mornings and nights, although the days can be much warmer. For autumn and spring, pack light woollens and clothes in natural fibres that are easy to wash. In summer only loose cotton clothes are comfortable. Indian-made ready-to-wear cotton shirts and women's outfits are available everywhere. Choose easy-to-remove footwear as you will have to take off your shoes in places of worship. A first-aid kit is a must *(see p286)*. An umbrella or light raincoat is a good idea, and a powerful torch could be packed for unexpected power cuts.

## ADVANCE BOOKING

SINCE ALL THREE CITIES are both tourist and commercial centres, it is advisable to have confirmed advance bookings for your accommodation and travel, especially during the peak tourist season. Airline tickets are easier to obtain at short notice, but as you can get confirmed train bookings at least two months in advance, it is wise to book ahead for train travel. Hotels and travel agents also book coach tours within Delhi, as well as to Agra and Jaipur as they are within a comfortable distance of each other.

## VISAS AND PASSPORTS

EVERYONE NEEDS a visa to enter India. There are three types of visa for tourists, available from Indian Consular Offices around the world: the 15-day single/ double entry transit visa, the 90-day, or the longer multiple entry visa for six months.

Getting a visa extension beyond 15 days is a complicated procedure. First, you must collect an extension form from the **Ministry of Home Affairs** office, then fill and submit it to the **Foreigners' Regional Registration Office (FRRO)**, who will stamp it. Finally, you must go back to the Ministry of Home Affairs for the actual visa extension.

There are certain places in India that are "Restricted Areas" and for which special permits are required. These include Sikkim, all the Northeastern states, Andaman and Nicobar Islands and Lakshwadweep.

## EMBASSIES AND CONSULATES

Most countries have diplomatic missions in Delhi, but no representation in the other two cities. Consular officials can re-issue passports and help in case of theft, imprisonment, hospitalization or other emergencies. Some embassies have been shortlisted on page 281.

## CUSTOMS INFORMATION

When entering India, visitors are allowed the usual duty-free 950 ml of alcohol and 200 cigarettes. For expensive articles, such as video cameras, jewellery, music systems or laptop computers, you will have to fill in the tourist baggage re-export form, undertaking to take these items back or else pay a fairly heavy duty on them when you leave. Regarding currency, if you are carrying more than $2,500 in cash or traveller's cheques, you are expected to fill in the currency declaration form at the airport, to be attested by a customs official.

Antiques over a hundred years old cannot be taken out of the country. Neither can

**Tourist bargaining with a vendor**

wildlife products, such as animal pelts, shahtoosh shawls or ivory. Consult the **Archaeological Survey of India (ASI)**, or the **Ministry of Environment & Forests** for details of these rules.

## IMMUNIZATION

There are no official immunization requirements unless you travel from designated countries in Africa, South America and Papua New Guinea, in which case you will need a valid vaccination certificate for yellow fever. Vaccination against tetanus, typhoid and hepatitis A and B is a good idea. You can also start a course of anti-malarial tablets before you arrive in India, after consulting a reliable physician about the course.

## INSURANCE AND DRIVING LICENCE

Before arriving in India do take out an insurance policy for medical emergencies and theft. In fact, if you are planning to take part in any adventure activities or sports, medical insurance is a necessity. To drive in India an International Driving Licence is required, which you should get before leaving for India. **The Automobile Association of Upper India (AAUI)** (see p299) can help with a temporary driving licence, but you will have to take a driving test for one.

**Visa stamp**

INMIGRATION I.G.I.A. DELHI
ARR. W-10 (D)
-5 -11- 1998
SIGN...

---

## TOURIST INFORMATION

THE DEPARTMENT of Tourism offices have information on travel throughout India, and its tourism counter in the arrival hall of Delhi's international airport also gives essential information. However, the state tourism departments *(see p279)* will provide more reliable and detailed advice on the three cities. The staff are helpful, with plenty of practical information on sightseeing, travel and accommodation. Tourist brochures and maps are usually distributed free of charge.

**Tourist brochures**

## ADMISSION CHARGES

ADMISSION CHARGES at both government and private museums, palaces and forts are usually nominal. Most places of worship do not charge an admission fee but often have a donation box. For special shows within monuments, such as the *Son et Lumière* at the Red Fort in Delhi *(see pp94–5)*, special tickets have to be bought.

## HOLIDAYS AND OPENING HOURS

ALL BANKS and government offices remain closed on the three national holidays of Republic Day (26 Jan), Independence Day (15 Aug) and Martyr's Day (2 Oct) *(see p39)*, when markets too are closed. Each year a new holiday list is issued by the Indian government, which includes all major religious festivals whose dates change according to the lunar calendar. Certain religious holidays are termed "restricted", so while the office may be open, the required official may be on leave. Monuments and museums normally open from 10am to 6pm, and generally close on Mondays and on government holidays. Shop timings are usually from 10am to 7:30pm. In Delhi, the markets are shut on different days of the week, but in Agra and Jaipur, they are closed on Sundays. Government offices work from Monday to Friday from 9:30am to 6pm, with a half hour lunch break. Senior officials often work overtime.

## GUIDES

ALL TOURIST OFFICES, travel agents and hotels can arrange a certified expert for you at fixed hourly rates. At popular sights amateur guides swarm around tourists hoping to be hired. You should ignore them and look instead for English-speaking guides wearing a metal badge that certifies government tourist department approval.

## BACKPACKERS

FOR STUDENTS and young travellers, each of the three cities has branches of the **Youth Hostels Association of India (YHAI)**. In Delhi, check with the **Vishwa Yuvak Kendra**. There is also a comfortable **YMCA** in Delhi. If you plan to travel by bus and train, you should bring a sturdy backpack that can take rough handling. The safest way to carry money is in a pouch fixed to your belt.

## FACILITIES FOR THE DISABLED

FACILITIES FOR THE disabled are still not well developed in public buildings and places of interest, as ramps or rails are seldom provided. However, airports and all main railway stations do have wheelchairs, ramps and escalators, and porters to carry your luggage. Pavements are difficult to negotiate in a wheelchair as they are often bumpy. Few hotels are equipped for the needs of the disabled traveller. The staff, however, are always helpful.

## TRAVELLING WITH CHILDREN

CHILD-MINDING SERVICES for tourists are rare, but Indians love children so they can accompany parents to most places. However, they must be protected against the fierce sun and drink only mineral water. Most well-known restaurants have food that children may safely eat.

## PLACES OF WORSHIP

THE THREE CITIES have a number of temples, *gurudwaras*, churches, mosques and, in Delhi, a synagogue, holding regular services. Since many are also places of historical or archaeological interest, they are open to foreign tourists. However, certain rules of etiquette *(see pp282–3)* must be observed. Most of these places are open till late in the night, but it is safer, and preferable, to visit them during the day.

**A camel ride is an essential part of the Pushkar experience**

## INDIAN STANDARD TIME AND CALENDAR

IN SPITE OF ITS SIZE, India has only one standard time. India is 5.5 hours ahead of Greenwich Mean Time (GMT), 4.5 hours behind Australian Eastern Standard Time, and 10.5 hours ahead of US Eastern Standard Time.

For all official work, the Western Gregorian calendar is used in India. This avoids the confusion of traditional calendars, which vary between religions and regions. For example, at the Millennium, the official Indian calendar (Saka era), had reached only 1922, whereas the old Hindu calendar, which follows the Samvat era, reads as 2057.

## MEASUREMENTS AND CONVERSION CHART

THE METRIC SYSTEM is that most commonly used all over the country.

**Imperial to Metric**
1 inch = 2.5 centimetres
1 foot = 30 centimetres
1 mile = 1.6 kilometres
1 ounce = 28 grams
1 pound = 454 grams
1 pint = 0.6 litres
1 gallon = 4.5 litres

**Metric to Imperial**
1 centimetre = 0.4 inches
1 metre = 3 feet 3 inches
1 kilometre = 0.6 miles
1 gram = 0.04 ounces
1 kilogram = 2.2 pounds
1 litre = 1.8 pints

**In tourist areas, little photo shops offer film and instant services**

## LANGUAGE

THERE ARE MANY regional languages spoken in India, and in the northern region, both Hindi and English are used as official languages. In the cities, some English is spoken by a wide range of people, especially by those who deal with tourists – taxi drivers, guides – and in hotels, shops and offices. However, it is useful to know a few basic phrases in Hindustani, the colloquial language of the region *(see p320)*. Road signs and numbers are both in English and Hindi.

**A range of plugs**

## ELECTRICITY

THE ELECTRICAL CURRENT is 220-240 volts, 50 Hz. Supply is erratic in summer when power cuts can last for hours, but more reliable in winter. Triple round-pin sockets are the norm, but adaptors for other varieties are available at large markets, as are transformers, needed for some appliances. Do bring along a power surge cable to protect your laptop computer against voltage fluctuations.

## PHOTOGRAPHY

COLOUR CAMERA FILM, easily available at most photo shops, is best bought at large shops. Such shops also have excellent developing and printing facilities and offer quick services. It is courteous to ask permission before photographing people or places of worship. Photographing security sensitive areas is strictly prohibited. Notice boards indicate where photography is not allowed.

*(see p320)*

## DIRECTORY

### USEFUL ADDRESSES

**Youth Hostels/Vishwa Yuvak Kendra**
5 Nyaya Marg, Chanakyapuri, Delhi. **Map** 4 D3.
( (011) 611 6285.
Sanjay Place, MG Rd, Agra.
( (0562) 35 4462.
Bhagwan Das Rd, Jaipur.
( (0141) 51 8330.

**YMCA**
Jai Singh Rd, Delhi.
**Map** 1B5.
( (011) 374 6036.

### EMBASSIES IN DELHI

**Australia**
( (011) 688 8223.

**Ireland**
( (011) 462 6733.

**New Zealand**
( (011) 688 3170.

**South Africa**
( (011) 614 9411.

**United Kingdom**
( (011) 687 2161.

**USA**
( (011) 419 8000.

### PLACES OF WORSHIP

**Baha'i House of Worship**
Kalkaji, Delhi.
( (011) 644 4029.

**Cathedral of the Immaculate Conception**
Wazirpura Rd.
Agra.
( (0562) 35 1318.

**Cathedral Church of the Redemption**
Church Rd, Delhi. **Map** 4 E1.
( (011) 301 53960.

**Judah Hyam Synagogue**
2, Humayun Rd, Delhi.
**Map** 5 B3.
( (011) 463 5500.

**Sacred Heart Cathedral**
Bangla Sahib Rd, Delhi.
**Map** 1 B5.
( (011) 336 3593.

# Etiquette

Friendly and easy-going by nature, Indians consider hospitality intrinsic to their culture and religion. Guests are treated with immense courtesy, and people on the street will go out of their way to help you. If you have any doubts on issues regarding fares, rates or directions, it is better to be patient but firm, rather than arguing or becoming aggressive. As there are diverse religions, castes and social hierarchies in the region, it is safest to address everyone with respect without making allusions to their religious, ethnic or regional group. Public demonstrations of love, such as kissing, are frowned upon. Customs and rules of etiquette still follow traditional Indian norms, except in very Westernized sections of urban society.

Heads should be covered before entering a place of worship

## GREETING PEOPLE

The most common form of Indian greeting is the *namaskar* or *namaste* (pronounced "namastey") when meeting or parting. The palms are pressed together, raised towards the face, and the head is bent slightly forward. Greetings and gestures may vary with religion or regional group. Muslims raise their right hand towards the forehead with the words *adaab* or *salaam aleikum*.

In North India, *"ji"* usually follows the name as a term of respect. On the first meeting, however, it is best to address someone formally with a Mr or Mrs or even Madam before their name. The use of first names is a sign of familiarity. However, the Western handshake is also commonly used, though Indian women still prefer to greet visitors with a *namaskar*.

In many traditional families, it is a polite gesture to touch the feet of elders when greeting them. As a rule, elders are never addressed by their first names. However, a courteous greeting in any form will be acknowledged. Personal questions about subjects which a foreigner may find intrusive, such as one's salary or relationship with one's mother-in-law, are not really considered offensive in Indian society. Seldom seen as an intrusion, they reflect a friendly interest in a new acquaintance.

*Namaskar,* the traditional greeting

## BODY LANGUAGE

Indians tend to shake their heads a lot while talking, and it can be very confusing because sometimes what seems to be a negative shake is actually a sign of agreement. Indians also tend to talk loudly and gesticulate with their hands, giving the impression of being very agitated when they are actually having a perfectly normal conversation.

The head is considered to be the spiritual centre, and an elder will touch the head of a younger person in blessing. The feet are considered the lowliest part of the body, and shoes are treated as unclean. In many traditional Indian homes, you may have to slip them off at the door or before you enter the kitchen. During gatherings where the seating is on the floor, try to sit with your feet crossed or tucked away and not stretched out before you. When food is offered to you, it should be accepted with the right hand.

## PLACES OF WORSHIP

Every major religion of the world is practised in India. The etiquette differs in the places of worship of each religion, but everywhere a simple decorum is expected. If in doubt about what you should do, it is best to observe those around you. Do not disturb people at their prayers by taking photographs or talking loudly. In any case, you should ask permission to take photographs. Clothes should be clean and unrevealing, and the head covered. Women should wear dresses that cover the upper arms and are

A devotee bathing a linga in milk in a Shiva temple

at least mid-calf length, and men should avoid shorts. At most places of worship, shoes are taken off at the door, and you should sit with your feet turned away from the image or the central holy book.

In Hindu temples, it is permissible to offer flowers and incense for worship. Apart from the central deity, the temples often have subsidiary shrines in other parts of the temple precincts. Do not sit or lean against them. Even those in ruins are considered holy. Some Hindu temples do not welcome non-Hindus, but this is rarely the case. However, if stopped at the door, please do not take offence. In mosques and in *gurudwaras*, the head should be covered with a scarf or large handkerchief when you enter, but not with a hat. You should avoid entering a mosque during prayers, and men should stay away from the women's enclosure.

## SUITABLE DRESS

THE INDIAN STYLE of clothing is relatively modest and covers the body well. In small towns, women still prefer the traditional sari or the *salwar-kameez* and seldom wear Western outfits, though very small girls can be seen in skirts or dresses. Delhi has a more cosmopolitan attitude, and in the trendier parts of the city, jeans, short skirts and shorts are common. However, Indian men tend to stare a lot at women, so be prepared for this, whatever you wear. Agra

The *ghunghat* veils a woman's face in traditional communities

and Jaipur are much more conservative cities where short skirts and shorts might well attract unwanted attention.

Do dress a little formally when visiting Indian homes, as Indians like to dress up for occasions. In fact, owning a couple of Indian outfits makes great sense. Ready-made clothes for both men and women are available in most markets at reasonable rates, and are easy and comfortable to wear.

## BARGAINING

BARGAINING is a part of life in India, but do not get aggressive about it. Firmly state what you would like to pay and walk away if the shopkeeper does not agree. Larger shops usually have fixed price tags and do not readily discount.

Wearing shoes is prohibited in religious places

## EATING INDIAN STYLE

MOST INDIAN MEALS are eaten with the fingers to tear the chapati or bread, and to scoop up rice and curry. At best, a spoon may be given to you. It is considered impolite to use your left hand. Most restaurants provide finger bowls at the end of the meal.

## TIPPING

THERE ARE NO FIXED norms for tipping, or *baksheesh*, as it is called. Most restaurants add a service charge to the bill; a ten per cent tip over that is quite adequate. In smaller eateries, the waiter would be happy with less. Hotel staff, porters and most taxi drivers expect to be tipped. So do hairdressers. A small tip given to the person who minds your shoes outside a place of worship will be happily accepted.

The traditional Indian *thali* meal is eaten with the right hand, seated on the floor

## SMOKING AND ALCOHOL

THOUGH CIGARETTE kiosks abound, and pavement sellers even sell one cigarette at a time, in Delhi smoking is officially banned in public places like airports, railway stations and offices (though in practice the ban is often ignored). Only certain restaurants are licensed to serve alcohol, and you are not allowed to drink in parks, buses or trains. Drinking near a place of worship can lead to arrest. It is also considered very offensive.

## BEGGARS

TRAVELLERS CAN FIND beggars difficult to handle as they target foreigners and can be extremely persistent. Tourists who give money to one soon find themselves surrounded by a raucous throng demanding *baksheesh*. Be careful of being pickpocketed in the confusion. Beggars are found in the largest numbers around places of worship as people always give them alms or even food there. But it is best not to encourage them and to walk on till they leave you alone. If necessary, complain to a nearby policeman.

If you do want to help monetarily, your hotel may have a donation box and the staff will be able to suggest a few charitable institutions.

# Personal Security and Health

**Police officer's badge**

THE THREE CITIES of Delhi, Agra and Jaipur are well equipped with an efficient police force and a number of good hospitals. As long as you take a few simple precautions, there is little need to worry. For instance, do not get too friendly with strangers, protect your valuables and do stay and eat only in places that look clean. If you face a difficult situation, take the help of a policeman or file a report at the closest police station.

**Policemen in uniform**

## IN AN EMERGENCY

THE NATIONAL emergency number for police is 100, the fire brigade is 101, and for an ambulance it is 102. Your embassy can also advise you in an emergency. If in need of immediate medical attention, your hotel's doctor-on-call can refer you to a private clinic. Otherwise, all public and most privately owned hospitals and clinics run a 24-hour service for casualty and emergency cases.

## GENERAL PRECAUTIONS

TRAVELLING IN THE region is relatively safe for tourists. Since Delhi, Agra and Jaipur are major tourist centres, there are bound to be touts, beggars and pickpockets who target the tourist. Take simple safety measures, such as wearing a money belt under your shirt in which to keep important documents, such as your passport. Protect your camera and avoid wearing jewellery or carrying large amounts of cash in crowded areas. You can leave your valuables in the hotel safe but insist on a receipt. While shopping, make sure that the shopkeepers make out a bill and process your credit card in front of you. It is also advisable to use a padlock, available at railway stations, during train journeys.

Some shopkeepers lead tourists into believing that goods bought in India can be sold back home at great profit. Unless you can judge a product's authenticity, it is best not to invest your money on such dubious purchases.

A word of caution about dealing with the police. If you find yourself in any trouble, for instance, if you have lost your passport or valuables, you must inform the nearest police station and file an FIR (first information report), but it is also advisable to contact your embassy for advice about the correct procedure.

## NARCOTICS

THE IMAGE OF INDIA as a country that is tolerant of drug use is not true. Possession of all drugs, from hashish to heroin, is banned by law, and penalties for possession, use and trafficking in illegal drugs are strictly enforced. Drug convictions lead to a minimum sentence of ten years without parole or remission. As a precaution, do not leave your luggage unattended or unlocked at public places, and by no means carry anything for strangers or check in their luggage at airports.

## WOMEN TRAVELLERS

WOMEN, both Indian and foreign, face a certain amount of unwanted attention from men in North India, even though "eve-teasing" is a punishable offence. When travelling alone, women can face problems – from being stared at, to more active harassment such as suggestive comments and unwanted body contact on buses and in other crowded places.

Take your cue from Indian women who continue with their independent lifestyles despite such hazards. Avoid wearing clothes that can be thought of as provocative, such as shorts, skimpy dresses and mini skirts at public places, though they can be safely worn inside the hotel. Ignore men lounging at street corners, and if their attention gets offensive, walk towards a policeman. Beware of men who try to draw you into a conversation, and threaten to call the police if they continue to do so.

Avoid moving about alone in quiet places and in the rougher parts of the city. When hiring a car or a taxi, get the hotel to make the booking for you. Hitchhiking is not advisable under any circumstances. A confident attitude, common sense and wariness can help women travellers tackle problems that arise from travelling alone.

**A Delhi police jeep**

**A hospital ambulance**

## LEGAL ASSISTANCE

LEGAL PROBLEMS are very rare for travellers, but if you do find yourself in a legal tangle, immediately contact your embassy *(see p281)*. Always carry your passport and keep a photocopy handy. Do not hand your travel papers over to anyone until your embassy has been informed. Some insurance policies also cover legal costs for certain emergencies such as accidents.

## PUBLIC TOILETS

WAYSIDE PUBLIC TOILETS have poor hygiene. However, though still few in number, those public toilets, known as Sulabh Shauchalayas, located on main city roads are a great civic invention. Attractively designed, they are easy to spot, extremely clean, and charge a very nominal amount for use. They are, however, of the Asian-squat kind and can be difficult to handle. Some restaurants and hotels allow you to use their toilets, but it is best to carry some spare toilet paper as not all public toilets are equipped with it.

**Sign identifying a toilet**

## HOSPITALS AND MEDICAL FACILITIES

DO TAKE comprehensive medical insurance before arriving in India. **MASTA** (Medical Advisory Service for Travellers Abroad) in the UK can give a health update for travellers to India.

In Delhi, there are excellent private hospitals and medical specialists, and though it is crowded like other government hospitals, the renowned **All India Institute of Medical Sciences (AIIMS)**, is a highly advanced hospital and centre of research. Most of the embassies have a list of approved hospitals and clinics as well as the names of the best medical specialists and dental practititiners in town. The local **Indian Red Cross Society** is the safest option for blood transfusions.

**Most markets have several pharmacies like this one**

## PHARMACIES

MOST BIG MARKETS in the three cities have well-stocked pharmacies (or chemist shops, as they are known in India). The pharmacists are often able to advise you on simple remedies. They also stock toiletries, sanitary napkins and tampons, cosmetics, infant food and disposable diapers. If you are taking any special medication, it is advisable to carry the prescriptions, or show the packaging with the generic name if the brand is unfamiliar to the pharmacist. Most pharmacies are open between 9am and 7:30pm. Public hospitals such as AIIMS usually have round-the-clock pharmacies which are also open to non-patients.

**Pavement quacks peddle concoctions of a dubious nature**

## HEAT AND SMOG

SUMMER IN NORTH INDIA is dry and very hot, and the monsoon months that follow are oppressively humid. It takes time to get acclimatized to this weather, so take things at a relaxed pace in the first few days. The best way to beat the heat is to drink lots of fluids at regular intervals, and add a little salt to your food to prevent dehydration. Bathe often and avoid going out in the hottest part of the day, between noon and four o'clock. While walking, try to rest in the shade at regular intervals, for continuous exposure to high temperature can cause heat stroke.

It is advisable to wear light shoes and loose-fitting cottons that cover your arms and legs, as exposed skin can get badly sunburnt. Polyester clothing and covered shoes and socks trap perspiration and can lead to annoying prickly heat and fungal infections. Prickly heat powder is available at most pharmacies. Wear a wide-brimmed hat and sunglasses and use sun-screen to protect your skin.

In the winter, the city air can get quite smoggy. Asthmatic travellers should carry their medication at all times.

## FIRST-AID KIT

MOST FIRST-AID ITEMS are readily available at the pharmacies in the cities, and while going on excursions or day-long trips, it is advisable to carry a basic first-aid kit. This should include any personal medication, aspirin or painkillers for fevers and minor aches and pains, and antiseptic and calamine lotion for cuts and bites, an anti-fungal ointment, plaster and crêpe bandages, scissors, insect repellent and tweezers; antihistamines for allergies, anti-diarrhoea tablets and, water purification tablets; lip

Sugarcane and other juices sold in the open are better avoided

balm, a couple of disposable syringes and a thermometer.

There are some effective herbal remedies, but you should buy only brands recommended by a reliable practitioner or pharmacist.

## MINOR STOMACH UPSETS

DIARRHOEA IS a common stomach disorder among travellers, usually caused by a change of diet, water and climate. Since Indian food is mostly hot and spicy, it can lead to digestive disorders. In such cases, it is best to eat plain boiled food without spices until the attack subsides. Most import-antly, make sure you drink plenty of liquids to replace your body fluids. Avoid tap water and opt for sealed bottles of mineral water, such as Evian or Bisleri, if available. Most known international brands of carbonated drinks are widely available, and are clean and safe, as is fresh coconut water. No matter how tempting the food looks, it is advisable not to eat from streetside food carts. If you do want to eat in a *dhaba*, it is best to go to one that seems popular with the local people. The food there is more likely to be fresh and

**A hand fan**

of a reliable quality. However, it is best to avoid raw salads, cut fruit, cold cuts and fresh juices at wayside eateries.

A good pharmacist will suggest standard diarrhoea medication. In the case of a severe attack, with nausea, cramps and exhaustion, it is best to consult a doctor. You must immediately take oral rehydrating salts (ORS), which are commercially available under the popular Indian brand names of Electral or Electrobion. An effective homemade remedy of half a teaspoon of salt and three teaspoons of sugar mixed in boiled water which has been cooled also helps to keep the body fluids in balance.

## INSECT-BORNE DISEASES

THE SUMMER and monsoon months are the seasons for malaria, though it can occur at any time of the year. Its symptoms include violent shivering followed by high fever and sweating. Caused by a parasite carried in the saliva of the female *Anopheles* mosquito, the incubation period can vary from a few days to several weeks.

Another serious mosquito-borne disease is dengue fever, carried by the *Aëdes egypti* mosquito. The symptoms are similar to malaria and include severe pain in the joints and muscles, and often, rashes. The dengue

**Vicks Vaporub, a decongestant**

mosquito is more active at daytime, unlike others that are active in the dark, between sunset and dawn.

If you are sleeping in a room without air-conditioning, keep the screened windows closed at all times. You can also ask the hotel for a mosquito repellent gadget, as well as a net over your bed. Avoid dark clothing and strong perfumes as these attract mosquitoes. If going outdoors in the evenings, you should wear shoes and clothes that cover your arms and legs, and rub mosquito repellent cream on any part of the skin that is widely exposed.

**Mosquito repellent coil and cream**

If you do experience symptoms of malaria, it is best to seek medical help immediately. You must take courses of preventive anti-malarial drugs before, during and after your trip. For the latest information on malaria medication, call a travel clinic or MASTA (*see p285*) who post details free of charge.

## CUTS AND BITES

INSECT BITES ARE A common problem in the rainy season. Many monuments have huge beehives, so you should carry a good antiseptic ointment and antihistamine that would help in case of wasp and bee stings. Snake bites are rare, but if bitten, tie on a tight crêpe bandage, keep the limb immobile and seek immediate medical help. Clean all cuts with an antiseptic solution and cover with sticky plaster or a light bandage.

**Bottled mineral water**

## FOOD- AND WATER-BORNE DISEASES

TRAVELLERS must guard against two types of severe intestinal infection, known as dysentery. The first,

bacillary dysentery, is accompanied by severe stomach pains, vomiting and fever, but rarely lasts longer than a week. Amoebic dysentery has similar symptoms but takes longer to manifest itself. If not treated with a course of prescription drugs, this can later become a recurring, chronic ailment. The same is true of Giardiasis, a type of chronic diarrhoea, caused by contaminated water.

Some forms of hepatitis, a serious liver ailment, such as Hepatitis A and B, can be prevented with a vaccine. Its symptoms include extreme fatigue, body aches, fever, severe chills and jaundice. The only treatment is plenty of boiled water, rest and a strictly controlled diet.

If you are visiting a site ravaged by floods you must get yourself vaccinated early enough against cholera, a serious disease that can be fatal unless the patient is rushed to hospital for re-hydration and medication.

Typhoid, which has a vaccine, is another gastro-intestinal disease transmitted through contaminated water or food. Early symptoms may seem like flu, but develop into high fever, leading to acute dehydration and weight loss. A doctor should be immediately consulted for the right antibiotics.

Since they are the most common ailments faced by travellers to India, certain common-sense precautions, such as eating only at clean places and drinking mineral water, are the best prevention against gastric infections.

## PEOPLE- AND ANIMAL-BORNE DISEASES

AWARENESS OF sexually transmitted diseases such as HIV, which causes Acquired Immune Deficiency Syndrome

(AIDS), is still low, and screening at blood banks unreliable. In case blood transfusion is required, do contact the **Indian Red Cross Society** (*see p285*).

Meningitis, a severe inflammation of the membranes surrounding the spinal cord and brain, is accompanied by high fever and occasional seizures. Penicillin drugs are effective in combating it, but patients must be rushed to a hospital straight away.

To avoid getting rabies if you are bitten by an animal, clean the wound immediately with an antiseptic solution and seek medical help at once, for treatment involves a course of injections. There is also a vaccination against rabies. Vaccination against tetanus is also essential while travelling. This potentially fatal infection is transmitted through open wounds, and its symptoms include lock-jaw, stiff muscles and fatal convulsions. You should clean the wound and go to a good doctor without delay.

Tuberculosis, commonly transmitted through coughing and close household contact with an infected person, is not a great risk for travellers.

Before an inoculation, buy your own disposable syringe, or insist that a new syringe and needle is unwrapped in front of you. Avoid shaves at dubious barber shops, and insist on a new razor blade. Any procedure using needles, such as tattooing and ear-piercing, is best avoided.

**Streetside food looks attractive but can be difficult to stomach**

# Banking and Local Currency

**Logo of the State Bank of India**

THE THREE CITIES provide accessible banking facilities and also money exchange services, with English speaking staff at all the counters. Delhi has a good selection of international banks with a range of services. Exchange facilities are available at major banks and hotels, travel agencies, the international airport, and registered money changers. Unauthorized dealers and touts might offer enticing rates, but they are illegal operators. Some shops will also give better value for money against purchases in major foreign currencies. Traveller's cheques are the safest way to carry money, but always keep some small change and notes for telephones, transport, tips and purchases.

## BANKS AND BANKING HOURS

THERE ARE MANY BANKS with branches across the country offering services, including international money transfers. Most national banks, such as the **State Bank of India**, have their head offices

**American Express offers banking and money changing facilities**

and several branches in Delhi, as well as in the other cities. The State Bank's counter at the international airport and the **Ashok Hotel** in Delhi (see p231) is the only 24-hour banking service in the city. The latter offers money exchange facilities for all travellers, but there could be long queues and a lot of form filling. Foreign banks have offices in Delhi, though not always in the other two cities. Indian banks with branches abroad and foreign banks with branches in India can also wire money by telex from their various offices.

Banking hours are between 9:30/10am–2pm (Mon–Fri), and 9:30/10am–12 noon (Sat). Banks can be closed on regional and national holidays (see p39), and occasionally they shut down without any notice at all in response to public protests or strikes.

## CHANGING MONEY

MOST HOTELS change money for resident guests, but banks offer the best rates. Visitors staying at government hotels require a receipt to show that they have changed their money in a bank. The State Bank of India, in Agra the **Allahabad Bank**, and the **Rajasthan Bank** in Jaipur are the best places in the region. Agents such as **Thomas Cook** (see p297) and **LKP Merchant Financing Travel** also change money at the official rates, but with higher service charges. Newspapers publish exchange rates for major international currencies. The "black market" in India offers better rates than the official ones, but it is safer to go to authorized dealers.

## CREDIT CARDS

INTERNATIONAL CREDIT cards such as VISA, Master Card, Amex and Diners Club are accepted in the larger shops, hotels and restaurants. Look out for the credit card sticker on shop windows. Cards can also be used to book rail and air tickets. American Express in Delhi gives traveller's cheques in US dollars or pounds sterling. Against some cards you can get a cash advance in rupees at many international banks. But credit card related fraud is on the increase, so keep your cards safely, and insist that receipt vouchers at shops are made out in front of you.

---

## DIRECTORY

### INTERNATIONAL BANKS

**American Express Bank**
Hamilton House,
Connaught Place,
Delhi. **Map** 1 C4.
[ (011) 332 5221.

**ANZ Grindlays**
Mercantile House,
15 Kasturba Gandhi Marg,
Delhi. **Map** 1 C5.
[ (011) 332 0793.

**Citibank**
Jeevan Bharti, Connaught
Place, Delhi. **Map** 1 C5.
[ (011) 371 2484.

**Hongkong and Shanghai Bank**
ECE House, 28 K. Gandhi
Marg, Delhi. **Map** 1 C5.
[ (011) 371 6000.

### INDIAN BANKS

**State Bank of India**
Sansad Marg, Delhi.
**Map** 1 B5.
[ (011) 336 2683.

MG Rd, Agra.
[ (0562) 36.4426.
Tilak Marg, Jaipur.
[ (0141) 38 0421.

### MONEY CHANGERS

**American Express**
Connaught Place,
Delhi. **Map** 1 C4.
[ (011) 332 4119.

**LKP Merchant Financing Pvt Ltd**
M-36 Connaught Place,
Delhi. **Map** 1 C4.
[ (011) 335 2468.

**Allahabad Bank**
Hotel Clarks Shiraz,
54 Taj Rd, Agra Cantt.
[ (0562) 38 1416.

**Thomas Cook**
Jaipur Towers, MI Rd,
Jaipur.
[ (0141) 36 0940.

*The State Bank of India operates a counter at the Ashok Hotel in New Delhi, and at the airport. The two places offer the only 24-hour money changing services in the region.*

## CURRENCY

THE UNIT OF CURRENCY is the rupee (Rs), divided into 100 paisas. Among the coins the most commonly used are the 50 paisa and the one, two and five rupee ones. Currency notes range from Rs10 to the newly minted Rs1,000.

Be careful with the 100 and the 500 rupee notes which are quite similar in colour. Also, be wary of accepting torn or taped notes, as banks and shops are very often reluctant to accept or even change them for you.

## TRAVELLER'S CHEQUES

THE WELL-KNOWN NAMES in traveller's cheques in US dollars or pounds sterling are easy to cash, and can be exchanged at all banks and exchange counters. Banks have the lowest surcharge so they give the best value. They always charge a small fee per cheque, so using large denomination cheques at a time is much more economical. Traveller's cheques give better exchange rates than cash.

**The ATM at Citibank, Connaught Place, New Delhi**

## ATM SERVICES

ALL THE FOREIGN and some Indian banks have ATM (automatic teller machine) counters accepting VISA, Master Card, Amex or Diners Club cards. Instructions are displayed in English, and the cash dispensed is in rupees

**Bank Notes**
*All currency is minted by the Reserve Bank of India. The notes have either Mahatma Gandhi or the Ashoka lions on one side.*

10-rupee note

20-rupee note

50-rupee note

100-rupee note

500-rupee note

**Coins**
*The following silver coins are in circulation, with variations of the Rs1 coin. All bear the national insignia.*

50 paisa     1 rupee     Rs 2     Rs 5

# Communications

**Telephone booth sign**

THE POST and telecommunications systems in India are now fairly sophisticated. In addition to the government network, several reputable international courier agencies have offices here. All the main hotels have business centres, and most markets have shops from which international calls can be made, e-mail and faxes sent and the Internet accessed. A wide range of newspapers and magazines is sold in the three cities and, particularly in Delhi, most international newspapers and magazines are available in bookshops.

**Stamps in five-rupee denomination**

## POSTAL SERVICES

THE INDIAN postal service is efficient and reliable. It offers general or registered mail, parcel, *poste restante,* speed post and courier services. Most post offices are open from Monday to Friday between 10am and 5pm, and on Saturdays, only until 12 noon. The closing time for certain services, such as registered mailing, is usually earlier.

Letters sent *poste restante* are held at the post office for up to a month. In Delhi, the **Foreign Post Office,** and in Agra and Jaipur, the **General Post Office (GPO)** will hold your letters for you, but accessing them may take some time. Letters should be addressed with the surname underlined and in capital letters c/o Poste Restante, followed by the name and place of the post office. American Express also

**A regular post box**

provides this service to its clients, and so does the India Tourist Office at Janpath in Delhi *(see p279).* The procedure for sending parcels is not very simple, so check the details before trying to do so on your own.

In some places your hotel sells stamps and may offer to post letters and smaller parcels for you. Indian letter boxes are colour coded: local letters, green; metropolitan and other cities, red; Quick Mail Service (QMS), yellow.

## FAX AND TELEGRAPH SERVICES

FAX SERVICES are available at main post offices and also at market ISD/STD booths which, though often easier to access, charge more. The business centres of all large hotels have centralized telecommunication services, but these are open for use only to those who are staying there.

## INTERNET AND E-MAIL

THE INTERNET is widely used in Indian cities and most larger hotels offer net access to guests. Privately operated cyber cafés with the latest facilities are more common in Delhi than in the other two cities. Libraries, such as the British Council and United States Information Centre in Delhi, have Internet facilities which can be used for a small payment to browse the web and to use for e-mailing.

## COURIER SERVICES

WHILE IT IS BETTER to ship larger items such as furniture by regular land, sea or air cargo, letters, documents or smaller parcels are better sent through a courier agency, even though it may be more expensive. **Under Postal Service (UPS),** an international courier agency, has a widespread network of branches all over the world. Many shops offer to send purchases by courier, but except for the government emporia and well-known shops, you will be doing so at your own risk. If necessary, send the parcel yourself, even though it may be bothersome.

## TELEVISION AND RADIO

THE STATE-RUN Doordarshan television network has programmes in English and the major regional languages. With the arrival of satellite TV, the choice has become much wider. Cable TV is available almost everywhere, including most hotel rooms. Through it you can watch international channels, such as the BBC World Service, CNN, Discovery, National Geographic and the Hong

**General Post Office or Gole Dak Khana, New Delhi**

Kong-based Star TV network. Star Sports and ESPN are exclusive sports channels whereas Channel V and MTV are the music channels.

India also has a wide radio network, with programmes in English and local languages. It is still the best form of information, especially in the rural areas. FM channels are now available in many cities. You should check the daily papers for interesting television and radio programmes.

**Indian dailies publish a wide range of national and world news**

## NEWSPAPERS AND MAGAZINES

INDIA HAS A WIDE VARIETY of national English language newspapers. Leading papers like *The Times of India* and *The Hindustan Times* make for lively reading with fierce debates, cartoons and good sports coverage. Weekly magazines, such as *India Today* and *Outlook*, provide excellent coverage of local and international news. Readily available monthly magazines, such as *Delhi Diary* and *First City* list restaurants, films, exhibitions and other events in Delhi. Agra and Jaipur also have local newspapers in English and Hindi which give details of current cultural programmes.

## INTERNATIONAL AND LOCAL CALLS

ALL MAJOR HOTELS offer international subscriber dialling (ISD) services. You can also book a trunk call from a private telephone. Most markets also have ISD/STD (subscriber trunk dialling) booths from which local and international calls can be made at cheaper rates than the hotels. Look for the yellow ISD/STD sign above the shop. To make an international call you will need to dial: the international access code, followed by the country code, the area code and the local number. Domestic long-distance calls are made on the STD lines, and the service covers a large part of the country, including villages. STD rates depend on the distance and time of the call. These calls are cheapest between 11pm and 6am Indian time. Local calls can also be made from public STD telephone booths. The latter take new one rupee coins, renewable for every additional three minutes.

**Easy-to-operate public telephone**

## ADDRESSES

THE OLDER SECTIONS of Indian cities are often a maze of lanes and alleyways. Some road signs can be confusing and hard to decipher, and sometimes there may not even be a road sign. If you are lost, a passerby will always help, but the best bet is to get directions from a taxi or auto-rickshaw driver. The newer residential localities are divided into blocks, and the block number usually appears with the house number. So B4/88 Safdarjung Enclave would be: house number 88 in the B4 block of Safdarjung Enclave colony.

**Various services are advertised through large signboards**

## USEFUL DIALLING CODES AND NUMBERS

- To make an inter-city call, dial the STD code of that city and the local number. For Delhi, dial 011; Agra, dial 0562; and for Jaipur, dial 0141.
- To make an international call (ISD), dial 00, the country code, area code and the local number.
- Country codes are: UK 44; France 33; USA & Canada 1; Australia 61; Ireland 353; New Zealand 64; South Africa 27; Japan 81.
- Dial 180 to book a Trunk call in the country, and 186 for international calls.
- For directory assistance dial 197 in Delhi, Agra and Jaipur.
- For morning alarm, dial 116 in Delhi and Jaipur, and 361351 in Agra.

# TRAVEL INFORMATION

MOST INTERNATIONAL VISITORS to India arrive by air, and though road and ferry links are used between India and her neighbours, such as Pakistan, Bangladesh and Sri Lanka, this method of travel can be a complicated one. Travelling within the country, and especially between the three cities of the Golden Triangle is possible by air, train and road. Whatever your mode of transport, you should be prepared for delays and unexpected detours that

The Maharaja, mascot of Air India

may test your patience. The distance between the three cities is less than 250 km (155 miles) and only takes a few hours by road or rail. The state-run Indian Airlines has the widest network of air routes. Private airlines like Sahara and Jet Airways also cover many cities in this region. Indian Railways is one of the world's largest networks, and travelling first class is a good way to see the country. The long-distance luxury coach is another easy option.

**Aeroplanes lined up on the international airport tarmac**

## ARRIVING BY AIR

ALL THE MAJOR international airlines land in India, normally as stopovers on air routes between East and West. The international airports are at Delhi, Bombay (Mumbai), Calcutta (Kolkota), Madras (Chennai), Trivandrum (Thiruvananthapuram) and Goa, from where connecting domestic flights cover the rest of India. A direct flight from London to Delhi takes approximately nine hours. From Delhi there are several connecting flights onwards to Agra and Jaipur.

## AIR FARES

AIR FARES can vary according to the airline and the season. Before buying your ticket, do find out from a few travel agents about special offers or discounted fares. Cheaper fares are offered during the off-peak season, but usually stipulate the route and duration of the journey.

## CUSTOMS

THE GREEN CHANNEL is for those who do not have dutiable goods as listed in the Immigration Certificate. The Red Channel is for passengers with goods that attract customs duty, including money in excess of US$2,500.

## INTERNATIONAL AND DOMESTIC AIRPORTS

THE MAIN AIRPORT in Delhi is called Indira Gandhi (IG) International Airport. It has two terminals: Terminal I for domestic flights, and Terminal II for those coming from abroad. The latter has more facilities, with 24-hour currency exchange counters, left luggage services and an air-conditioned visitors' lounge. Travel agencies located in the arrivals area can help you organize your tour itinerary and onward

**DL1Y 1164**
ALL INDIA TOURIST PERMIT

**Licence plate of a taxi**

bookings, while the hotel counters, also located here, can arrange accommodation in a reliable hotel. Terminal I (domestic) is at Palam, 7 km (4 miles) from Terminal II. If transferring to a domestic flight from an international one (or vice versa), do allow enough time to get between the two terminals (approximately 15 minutes driving time). Airport coaches run hourly between the two during peak hours when most international flights arrive, and offer free transfers.

## GETTING TO AND FROM THE AIRPORT

THE DOMESTIC TERMINAL is 12 km (7 miles), and the international terminal, 19 km (12 miles) southwest of the city centre (Connaught Place). Coaches run regularly between these destinations for a fee of about Rs50. You can also book a pre-paid taxi from a counter outside the arrivals area. The rates of these are fixed – about Rs200 from Terminal II and Rs150 from Terminal I to the city centre. If you are booking your accommodation in advance, do check if your hotel is offering a free pick-up service. The trip from the airports to the city centre can take up to 50 minutes, but if your flight arrives or departs in the early hours of the day, it should certainly take less.

**Passengers in the airport lounge**

## TRAVEL PACKAGES

INDIAN AIRLINES offers two travel packages if paid in US dollars. The "Discover India Fare" for 15 or 21 days is about $500–750, and allows unlimited travel with certain route restrictions. " India Wonder Fare" for about $300 is for seven days of travel in one region. It does not include the Andaman Islands.

## DOMESTIC FLIGHTS

WHILE Indian Airlines offers the largest choice of routes and the most frequent services, the two major private-run airlines, Jet Airways and Sahara Airlines, also connect a wide network of cities. Delhi is connected to all Indian airports, while Agra and Jaipur, an hour's flight from Delhi, offer fewer connections. While all domestic airlines have their own booking offices, tickets can also be booked through travel agents (see p297).

**Air tickets**

## CHECK-IN

INTERNATIONAL FLIGHTS usually ask you to check-in two or three hours ahead of the flight departure time. For most domestic flights, it is normally one hour, except when security checks are more stringent, for places such as Kashmir. There is a restriction on the amount of baggage you can carry with you. Most airlines allow 20 kg per person in the hold and one item of hand baggage, though some international airlines allow two full suitcases plus one item of hand baggage. Excess baggage charges can be high.

## TAX CLEARANCE CERTIFICATE

IF YOU STAY in India for more than 120 days from the date of issue of the visa, you need a tax clearance certificate to leave the country. You should apply for the certificate to the **Income Tax Department** Foreign Section. This is to prove that you have financed your trip with your own foreign exchange and not by working in India. Do keep all documents about travel finance in case they are needed later.

## DEPARTURE TAX

WHEN LEAVING INDIA, you have to pay a Foreign Travel Tax of Rs500, unless already included with your ticket. But if travelling to Pakistan, Nepal, Sri Lanka, Bhutan, Burma (Myanmar), the Maldives or Afghanistan, only Rs150 has to be paid.

| AIRPORT | 📞 INFORMATION | DISTANCE TO CITY CENTRE | AVERAGE JOURNEY TIME |
|---|---|---|---|
| Delhi (IG Domestic) Terminal I | (011) 566 5181 | 12 km (7 miles) | Road: 30 minutes |
| Delhi (IG International) Terminal II | (011) 565 2011 | 19 km (12 miles) | Road: 50 minutes |
| Agra | (0562) 36 1241 | 16 km (10 miles) | Road: 45 minutes |
| Jaipur (Sanganer) | (0141) 72 1519 | 13 km (7 miles) | Road: 30 minutes |

# Travelling by Train

**Indian Railways logo**

Travelling through india by train is a truly unforgettable experience. It can be extremely relaxing or uncomfortable, a lot of fun, or frustrating. But, if you can spare the time, it is the best way of getting to know the Indian people and seeing the countryside. India has a well organized railway network but it is also extremely busy, so plan your train journey carefully and do book your tickets well in advance. There are computerized ticket counters at railway stations, and most travel agents can buy tickets for you. The journey between Agra, Delhi and Jaipur takes only a few hours.

**A modern diesel engine train**

## THE RAILWAY NETWORK

The indian railway network is divided by region and the three cities of Agra, Delhi and Jaipur are served by Northern Railways. Delhi has three major railway stations: Delhi Main, New Delhi and Nizamuddin, so make sure from which station your train will be leaving. Most fast trains for Agra, such as the Shatabdi Express, (New Delhi) and the Taj Express (Nizamuddin) take less than three hours. This makes a day trip to Agra possible. Another Shatabdi Express runs between Delhi and Jaipur and takes about five hours after an early start from New Delhi. The Gangaur Express runs between Agra and Jaipur.

**Train timetable**

## TRAINS AND TIMETABLES

There are three kinds of trains: passenger, express and mail. It is best to take the express trains as they have fewer stops and offer better facilities and services. Avoid passenger trains as they stop at all the small stations, sometimes for long periods, and are always very crowded. The major cities are connected by air-conditioned super-fast trains, such as the Rajdhani and Shatabdi Express, which make minimal stops. Their fares include meals, and the Rajdhani also provides its overnight passengers with bedding. Trains have a first and second class, chair-cars, and two- and three-tiered sleeper coaches. Where these are air-conditioned, the fares will increase. Sleeper coaches are a comfortable option on longer journeys, and save useful daytime hours. Train timings are subject to change; these are listed in the updated railway timetable, *Trains at a Glance,* a handy 100-page guide, available at all major railway stations, and even at some bookshops.

## TRAIN TICKETS AND FARES

Be sure to buy your tickets in advance with reserved seat numbers noted on them. Your hotel travel counter or your agent can arrange this for you. Avoid buying tickets from touts, as this is both illegal and unreliable. Reservation fees are nominal and tickets can be booked six months in advance. An **International Tourist Bureau**, on the first floor of New Delhi Railway Station, meant only for foreigners, is open Mon–Sat, from 7:30am to 5pm. The tickets, payable in US dollars or pounds sterling, get priority reservation and are exempted from reservation fees. Though refundable, the tickets are still subject to any cancellation charges. Other railway booking centres are located at **Nizamuddin** and **Sarojini Nagar**.

## INDRAIL PASS

If you are planning to travel extensively around India, the Indrail Pass is a convenient option, saving on hours of queueing time and also on reservation charges. It offers unlimited travel across the country, either first or second class, from 7 to 90 days. It can be bought in India or abroad, but must be paid for in foreign currency. The pass, however, may work out more expensive than buying tickets for individual trips. Ensure that you have a confirmed seat number for each journey.

**A crowded railway platform**

Railway ticket booking centre at New Delhi Railway Station

## SERVICES

A T THE STATION look for the licensed porters or *coolies* who wear a red shirt and an armband with a metal tag bearing a licence number on it. Note the porter's number because you could lose sight of him in the chaos. The tariff varies according to weight, although Rs10–20 per item is an acceptable rate. You would be wise to settle on a fee at the time of hiring your porter.

Railway waiting rooms are the best place to spend the night if you are unable to go elsewhere. Go to the Upper Class Waiting Rooms. The Rail Yatri Niwas, at New Delhi station, offers

Porters in red are easy to recognize

very basic facilities, but is a convenient and safe night halt. Left luggage facilities, called cloakrooms, are offered at most stations. On a day trip to a city, you can leave heavy bags here for a small charge. Avoid stalls with uncovered food and use the station canteens that are reasonably clean and provide reliable mineral water and hygenically-packed meals.

## ON BOARD

I NDIANS TRAVEL with a lot of luggage and like making friends on a train, so unless you bury yourself in a book, be prepared to spend time talking about yourself! Try to get a window seat or the uppermost sleeper. Toilets are of the Indian and Western kind. Carry your own toilet paper, soap and towel.

### DIRECTORY

#### RAILWAY ENQUIRIES

**Delhi**
General Enquiries:
(011) 131.
Arrivals
North 1331. East 1332. West 1333. South 1334.
Departure
North 1336 . East 1337. West 1338. South 1339.

**Agra**
(0562) 131-35 Cantt.
(0562) 36 4612 City.

**Jaipur**
(0141) 131.

#### RAILWAY BOOKING CENTRES IN DELHI

**International Tourist Bureau**
Map 1 C3.
(011) 373 4164.

**Nizamuddin**
Map 6 E5.
(011) 461 9748.

**Delhi Main Rly Stn**
Map 2 D1.
(011) 396 1859.

**Palace on Wheels**
Bikaner House, Shahjahan Rd.
Map 5 B2.
(011) 338 1884.

**Royal Orient**
Tourism Corporation of Gujarat Limited, Baba Kharak Singh Marg. Map 1 B5.
(011) 373 4015.

## THE ROYAL TRAINS

Insignia of the Jaipur State Railway

Travel like the maharajas in the most luxurious trains in India – the **Palace on Wheels** and the **Royal Orient**. From September to April, the Palace on Wheels operates week-long tours through the finest sights of Rajasthan, covering Jaipur, Udaipur, Jaisalmer, Jodhpur, Bharatpur and Agra. The Royal Orient goes through Rajasthan to Ahmedabad, Gujarat. In opulently furnished coaches re-created to look like the saloons of erstwhile royalty, you will be impeccably served and royally pampered as you travel through former glorious kingdoms.

Royal service in the Palace on Wheels

# Travelling Around by Coach

**Logo of the India Tourism Development Corporation (ITDC)**

A<small>LL THE MAJOR</small> Indian cities are well connected by a network of roads, and the highways linking Delhi, Agra and Jaipur are among the busiest in North India. The advantage of travelling by long-distance coaches over trains is that you have a wider choice of timings and stops. Deluxe coaches run by the state tourist departments are comfortable and run on time. The Transport Ministry-owned buses running throughout the day from city bus depots, though cheaper, can be crowded. Travel agencies and private tour operators have a wide choice of itineraries between the three cities and their surrounding areas.

**Boarding a luxury coach**

**Buses leave regularly for various destinations from the ISBT, Delhi**

## DEPARTMENT OF TOURISM-RUN BUSES

T<small>HIS STATE TOURISM</small> department's and the Indian government's **Ashok Tours & Travels** organize guided tours to and around the three cities. Addresses of state tourism offices are given on page 279. The Government of India Tourist Office in each city

**Delhi Tourism organizes a variety of innovative package tours**

offers the latest information on timings and pick-up points. Buses run by the tourism department are by far the best option; they are clean, uncrowded and comfortable, and make less frequent midway stops than ordinary buses which may be much cheaper. Delivery and pick-up points are usually in the city centres.

The Uttar Pradesh Tourism Department (UPTDC) buses also pick up tourists coming from Delhi to Agra by the Taj Express at the railway station. After the day's city tour, the passengers are dropped back at the station in time to catch the evening train to Delhi.

The best option to go to Jaipur from Delhi is by the Rajasthan Tourism Pink Line which leaves at 1:30pm from Bikaner House *(see p279)*. It is a good idea to buy tickets

**RTDC coach ticket**

in advance though they can also be bought on the spot for all buses. The five-hour journey breaks midway for refreshments. From Jaipur, state tourism buses leave from a stand outside Hotel Sheetal.

## STATE GOVERNMENT-RUN COACHES

T<small>HE TRANSPORT DEPARTMENT</small> of the three states also run buses to these three and other cities of India. The main bus station in Delhi is the **Inter-State Bus Terminus (ISBT)** at Kashmiri Gate. It is a chaotic place, so do arrive early to book your ticket. Then check at the enquiry counter to find the stand where your bus will arrive. Finally, be prepared for a lot of jostling as the passengers push to get to the best seats. Rajasthan state buses leave from Bikaner House. Buses for Agra leave from another bus station at **Sarai Kale Khan (SKK)**, a comparatively less crowded bus stop near Nizamuddin railway station. The trip takes about four hours to Agra and almost five to Jaipur. From Agra and Jaipur, buses leave hourly for the other two cities, at Agra from the **Idgah** bus stand, and at Jaipur, from **Sindhi Camp**.

## PRIVATE TOUR OPERATORS

T<small>OUR BUSES</small> run by private operators and travel agencies leave regularly from Delhi for places in the region during the tourist season. To Agra it is a day's trip, unless

During elections and village fairs buses are loaded with passengers

you take in Fatehpur Sikri and all the Agra sites and also want to shop, in which case it involves at least a night's stopover, as it does for Jaipur. Most hotels and travel agents also organize the night's accommodation at a reasonable place. If you are on a travel agent's tour bus, then a guided tour is usually part of the package and the fare includes a guide as well as the overnight stay at a hotel. Most travel agents have a tie-up with luxury buses that pick up tourists from designated hotels. You can make reservations through your hotel's reception desk or through any of the travel agencies who operate in the region.

### COACH TICKETS AND FARES

Bus OR COACH FARES are much less than train fares and depend on the kind of transport you are taking. There is a good choice – from ordinary to deluxe and deluxe air-conditioned coaches. Ordinary buses are slow,

uncomfortable and usually very crowded. A deluxe bus is good for a trip in winter, but in the hot weather, air-conditioning is the only way to survive long-distance travel. If opting for a deluxe bus, you can book your ticket in advance and can also reserve your seat.

### PACKAGE TOURS

THERE ARE PLACES in and around the three cities within easy travelling distance that should be seen. These include religious sites, places of historical interest and wildlife sanctuaries. State tourism departments have a wide range of itineraries and package tours. These are also offered by private tour operators and agencies who can arrange tours to suit your individual interests. Tourism offices and travel agents who specialize in adventure tours *(see p275)* offer excursion packages that include transport, guides and a few days' stay in these places.

**Logo of the Rajasthan Transport Corporation**

Luxury buses run by Rajasthan Tourism are comfortable and clean

# Travel by Road

**Milestones show distances in kilometres**

DRIVING is a comfortable and leisurely way to travel between the three cities. It gives you the opportunity to do the trip at your own pace and visit places along the way. Hiring a chauffeur-driven car makes sightseeing or shopping within the cities much easier as one is relieved of the stress of negotiating traffic and locating destinations. Cars can be hired from car rental companies, hotel and other taxistands.

**Many international companies offer car rental services in India**

## RENTING A CAR

IF YOU PLAN to bring your own vehicle into India, it will have to be done under a carnet. This means you take it out after your visit or else must pay exorbitant taxes. Alternatively, there is a good choice of international and local car rental companies in Delhi. Among them, **Hertz**, **Europcar** and **Budget** offer both self-driven and chauffeur-driven cars which can be hired through travel counters at larger hotels or from tourist offices. Rates are fixed on a daily rental and minimum mileage basis; with each extra mile carrying an extra cost. Fuel and other running costs are extra and a security deposit is taken in advance to be refunded only if there is no damage to the car when you return it. If you plan to drive yourself, make sure you are carrying your international driving licence. If you fail to do so, you might be able to get a temporary one from the **Automobile**

**Logo of the Automobile Association**

**Association of Upper India (AAUI)**, Delhi, provided you have a passport or a valid driving licence from your own country. You may also be required to take a driving test, though this may not always be the case.

A wiser and more common option is to hire a chauffeur-driven car. It is usually cheaper than hiring a self-drive car and fairly hassle-free. If lucky, you may find a driver who could double up as a guide and an interpreter.

## HIRING A CHAUFFEUR-DRIVEN CAR

UNLESS YOU ARE mentally geared to cope with the not-so-well-maintained Indian roads and driving conditions, you should rent a chauffeur-driven car. The drivers are familiar with Indian traffic rules and you won't have to worry about parking either. Taxis with DLY or DLZ number plates can be hired through travel agents, hotels and some taxistands. They have permits to travel beyond

city limits, and you can insist on getting a driver who is familiar with the city you plan to visit. Certain companies require foreign nationals to pay rentals in foreign currency. But some are willing to accept payment in rupees after negotiating a per kilometre rate payable in cash. Car companies in these cities normally charge a fixed rate for

**Logo of a car rental company**

a minimum of four hours or 40 km (25 miles), or up to 80 km (50 miles) for eight hours. Rates differ according to the type of car and from where you rent it.

## FUEL AND FUEL STATIONS

HIGHWAYS AND main roads pumps at regular intervals, usually closer to a town. Most fuel stations now carry unleaded petrol. All three cities have some fuel stations that are open 24 hours; some on the highways are also open round-the-clock. Most cars run on petrol, though some newer ones are being made with diesel engines. Taxis usually run on diesel, which is about half the price of petrol. It is a good idea to use the fuel station's toilet facilities before the next leg of the journey. City stations often have a telephone booth, but only for local calls.

**Fuel stations are found at regular intervals along the highways**

## ROAD SIGNS AND ROAD MAPS

GOOD MAPS ARE available for the three major cities as well as some of the smaller ones. The placement of road signs is erratic and at times these are not in English. Road names have also changed, particularly in Delhi, from the old English names, to names of well-known Indian or international figures. For Delhi there is the excellent *Eicher City Map*. Agra and Jaipur also have fairly clear state tourism city maps which display the major roads and sights. All are in English.

If you are travelling by road between the three cities, you should acquire a road map of North India from the **AAUI (Automobile Association of Upper India)**. The government **Survey of India** also has a good collection of detailed maps available at their office. Maps also indicate lesser known places and road categories. Road signs will also inform you of approaching motels and eateries on the highway.

## RULES OF THE ROAD

THOUGH THERE ARE established traffic rules, such as lane driving and the discreet use of high-beam lights, traffic can be chaotic on Indian roads. All too frequently, traffic lights do not function, and though major crossings have policemen to guide you, this is more often

DLY and DLZ taxis are cars that travel beyond the city limits

the exception than the rule. Bear in mind that there are numerous types of road users, from pedestrians to cyclists, bullock carts and containers. On the highways, be wary of trucks which muscle in whenever possible. There are also some unwritten rules which should be kept in mind. Few adhere to lane driving, and overtaking, meant to be from the right, is often from the opposite side, with no warning. Crossing red lights is one of the biggest hazards, the cause of most accidents, and horns are used even in "No Horn" areas.

Licence plates should be bold and clear

## PARKING

PARKING CAN BE a serious problem in busy shopping centres and in the commercial complexes of the three cities. With the boom in car production in recent years, parking lots are unable to cope with the number of cars driving in. Private parties are contracted by the state to ensure car safety and facilitate parking for a fee ranging from Rs5 to Rs10. You should keep your key but will have to leave your car in neutral gear so that it can be moved back and forth. Make sure the attendant gives you a receipt and check that you pay no more than the amount that is written on it. In New Delhi, Connaught Place is one of the few places which has a tiered and neatly planned and protected car parking lot.

**Hand-cart prohibited**

**Bullock-cart prohibited**

**No horn please**

**Bicycle crossing**

# Local Transport in the Cities

**Logo of the Delhi
Transport Corporation**

THE CHOICE OF LOCAL transport in the three cities is immensely varied. It ranges from buses and taxis to horse-drawn *tongas* and sputtering auto-rickshaws. All three cities are notorious for their traffic jams, and the narrow lanes of the older sections are best negotiated by the smallest vehicle possible. Here, a cycle-rickshaw is often the smartest option. Parking is a real problem, and in some of the extremely crowded areas, there are stringent car parking rules. Though there is a wide choice of local transport, a taxi or hired car is usually the most comfortable and stress-free way to travel. The drivers often speak some English.

**Taxistands are found in all areas**

## GETTING AROUND

DELHI, AGRA AND JAIPUR are all old cities with historic areas that can be congested. The roads carry vehicles that range from ambling bullock carts to expensive Mercedes Benzes. In between there are others such as bicycles, rickety cycle-rickshaws, horse carriages, three-wheelers, taxis, tempos, buses, trucks and, in Jaipur, carts pulled by benign but doleful looking camels.

**Taxi meter**

Perhaps the best way to move around in these three cities is to hire an auto-rickshaw (also known as scooters or autos), or a taxi. In the crowded older city areas, a cycle-rickshaw is the best option. Almost all deluxe hotels have a travel desk to help you with car or taxi hire. It is advisable to avoid public buses which, though cheap, are crowded, especially during peak traffic hours.

## TAXIS

THE BLACK-AND-YELLOW taxis in Delhi move within the city limits. Unlike other cities, they do cruise the streets, though it is safer to hire one from a taxistand. Large hotels have taxis on their premises, and these are always well-maintained with the meters in good working order. There is usually more than one stand in a locality, and taxis can be summoned by telephone provided you have the name and number of the stand. Another type of taxi, which is licensed to run inter-state, is usually white in colour and has a DLY or DLZ attached to its number. These can be hired through car rental companies, travel agencies and a few taxistands.

In Agra and Jaipur, the only option is the tourist taxi which does not run by the meter, but charges according to distance or by the day, or a pre-fixed rate. Your hotel or travel agent will tell you what the latest rules are for hiring these taxis. Many drivers have a tie-up with certain shops who give them a commission on sales, so you must be firm about where you want to go.

## AUTO-RICKSHAWS

YOU CAN'T MISS THEM on the roads. The three-wheeled, black-and-yellow auto-rickshaws zigzag through the traffic like buzzing bees. They offer a noisy, bumpy ride but are still a better option than buses and a cheaper alternative to taxis. In Delhi, they can carry up to three passengers, but in smaller towns, where they look a little different, they are often jammed with several people and baggage.

**Auto-rickshaw, a
cheaper travelling option**

Auto-rickshaws are useful for travelling short distances or through crowded localities.

## FARES AND METERS

ALL AUTO-RICKSHAWS and taxis in Delhi have meters, but this is not so in Agra and Jaipur where fares should be negotiated in advance. You should insist on paying by the meter in Delhi. Starting at Rs 5 for taxis and Rs 1 for auto-rickshaws, the meters register a fare increase proportionate to the number of kilometres travelled. As rates keep changing according to the

**Different modes of transport jostle in the streets of Jaipur**

**Cycle-rickshaws are convenient for covering short distances in inner city areas**

increase in fuel prices and meters are not always simultaneously calibrated, the drivers of taxis and auto-rickshaws always carry an updated fare chart to enable you to calculate the exact amount from the meter reading. Both day and night fares are given separately on either side of the fare chart. Be sure to check the correct column before you pay. Night fares, from 10pm to 6am, are up to 20 per cent extra. You also have to pay an extra charge for luggage.

At railway stations and the airport, you should look for the pre-paid taxi and auto-rickshaw booths where you will be asked to pay a fixed amount in advance according to the distance you travel. You will be given a receipt, to be handed over to the driver at the end of the journey. Also, do carry smaller notes and small change, as very often, the drivers do not have the correct amount to return. It is not necessary in India to tip the drivers, but if you do, they will gladly accept it.

### RICKSHAWS, TONGAS AND TEMPOS

THE BICYCLE-RICKSHAW is the most common mode of transport in the small towns and congested older sections of Indian cities. A convenient means of covering short distances, these are most commonly seen in the walled

city of Old Delhi. In Agra and Jaipur, these are the most popular means of local transport. Always fix the fare beforehand. In small towns, the rickety horse-drawn carriages called *tongas* and *ikkas* offer a leisurely ride. Tempos are wagons with the rear half fitted with seats. They are not very comfortable, and start a trip only when all seats are occupied.

### BUSES

THE BUS SERVICE in most Indian cities is never adequate for the large numbers who can only afford this means of travel, and so buses are always crowded. You buy the bus ticket from a conductor once you have boarded the bus. However, if a bus is full, it will not stop, and bus stops are usually seen full of waiting commuters. Delhi's bus drivers are notorious for their reckless driving. Even the so-called luxury buses drive at great speed. Avoid the experience even though it is the cheapest way to travel.

### DELHI METRO RAILWAY

DELHI HAS a ring railway, encircling a core area of the city and facilitating connections between some of the outer localities to more central parts of the city. From the year 2004, the tired commuters of Delhi can hope to start using a new Metro or subway system which the city badly needs. It has been planned with underground and overhead railway lines, well integrated with other modes of transport and availability of parking areas.

**Auto-rickshaws like this, called Vikram, ply in smaller cities to the north of Delhi**

**The "new look" Maruti Omni is quickly replacing the old Ambassador taxis in Delhi**

# General Index

# Acknowledgments

Dorling Kindersley would like to thank the following people whose contributions and assistance have made the preparation of this book possible.

**Contributors**

Anuradha Chaturvedi is a consultant on architectural conservation with the Indian National Trust for Art and Cultural Heritage (INTACH).

Dharmendar Kanwar is a well-known travel writer based in Jaipur. She has published several books on the architecture and culture of the region.

Partho Datta teaches Indian history at a college in Delhi University. He is interested in modern urban studies on which he has written several papers.

Premola Ghose is a gifted writer and illustrator of children's books. She is the Programme Officer at the India International Centre, New Delhi.

Ranjana Sengupta is a journalist and author of books on Ajanta and contemporary Indian society. She is currently writing a book on Delhi after 1947.

Subhadra Sengupta is a freelance journalist based in Delhi who writes on travel and tourism for several Indian newspapers and magazines.

**Consultants**

Ajai Shankar is a senior civil servant with the Government of India and is the Director-General of the Archaeological Survey of India (ASI).

Aman Nath has written extensively on the crafts and architecture of Rajasthan. He is involved in the restoration of heritage properties in this region.

Daljeet Kaur is the curator of the Indian miniature paintings section in the National Museum, New Delhi and has written several books and articles on this subject.

Ebba Koch has travelled extensively in the subcontinent and is an internationally acknowledged expert on the art and architecture of the Indo-Islamic and Mughal periods.

Giles Tillotson is Senior Lecturer in South Asian Art at SOAS (University of London), and the author of books on architecture in India during the Mughal, Rajput and British periods.

Jyotindra Jain is the founder-director of the Crafts Museum, New Delhi, and has authored several books on Indian crafts.

Kishore Singh is one of India's leading travel writers and is with the *Business Standard* in Delhi. He has written several books on Rajasthan.

Kumkum Roy is an Associate Professor of Ancient History at the Jawaharlal Nehru University, New Delhi. She writes for several prestigious academic journals.

Martand Singh is one of the country's best-known experts on textiles. He is based in Delhi and is a founding member of the Indian National Trust for Art and Cultural Heritage (INTACH).

Narayani Gupta is a Professor of Modern Indian History at Jamia Millia Islamia in New Delhi. Her book on the history of Delhi is widely regarded as an authoritative text.

RV Smith is a journalist who writes on the history and legends of Delhi. His column, "Quaint Corner", has been a regular feature in *The Statesman* for over 25 years.

Satish Grover heads the Department of Architecture at the School of Planning and Architecture, Delhi. He has written three seminal books on the history of Indian architecture.

Sunil Kumar is an Associate Professor in Medieval Indian History at Delhi University. He has a special interest in the Sultanate period and is currently writing a book on the subject.

Vijayan Kannampilly is a journalist and painter based in Delhi and has a special interest in Indian design and contemporary art.

**Editorial and Design**
Publisher Douglas Amrine
Editorial Director Vivien Crump
Art Director Gillian Allan
Senior Managing Editor Louise Bostock Lang
Production Marie Ingledew

**Map Coordinator**
David Pugh.

**Design and Editorial Assistance**
Ipshita Barua, Kiran Mohan, Nandini Mehta, Priyanka Thakur, Tara Sharma, Vandana Mohindra.

**Cartography Assistance**
Kishorchand Naorem, Shivanand.

**Proof Reader**
Abha Kapoor.

**Indexer**
Bibhu Mohapatra.

**Additional Illustrations**
Aniket Vardhan, Arun P, Mugdha Sethi.

**Additional Photography**
Anal Shah, Anand Naorem, Benu Joshi, Ipshita Barua, Mugdha Sethi.

**DTP Designers**
Jessica Subramanian, Shailesh Sharma.

**Special Assistance**
Dorling Kindersley would like to thank all the regional and local tourist offices in Delhi, Agra and Jaipur for their valuable help. Particular thanks also to: Ajai Shankar, ASI, New Delhi; Dr Daljeet, National Museum, New Delhi; Malaynil Singh, TCI; Delhi School of Planning and Architecture; Siraj Qureshi and RVI Singh in Agra.

**Food Photography**
Dorling Kindersley would like to thank Chef Pankaj Mehra of the Kandahar Restaurant (The Oberoi Hotel, New Delhi) for personally supervising the presentation of the food layouts for the book.

## PHOTOGRAPHY PERMISSIONS
Dorling Kindersley would like to thank the following for their kind permission to photograph their products: Abraham & Thakore, Preeti Paul. The publishers would also like to thank the following for permission to photograph at their establishments: Biotique, New Delhi; City Palace Museum, Jaipur; Crafts Museum, New Delhi; Gem Palace, Jaipur; Mathura Museum, Mathura; Maulana Abul Kalam Azad Arabic & Persian Research Institute, Tonk; The Next Shop, New Delhi; Ogaan, New Delhi.

## PICTURE CREDITS
t = top; tl = top left; tlc = top left centre; tc = top centre; tr = top right; cla = centre left above; ca = centre above; cra = centre right above; cl = centre left; c = centre; cr = centre right; clb = centre left below; cb = centre below; crb = centre right below; bl = bottom left; b = bottom; bc = bottom centre; bcl = bottom centre left; br = bottom right; d = detail.

The publishers are grateful to the following individuals, picture libraries and companies, for permission to reproduce their photographs:

AVINASH PASRICHA: 28cla/clb, 28 & 29c, 29bl, 120b, 292c, 293t; BOBBY KOHLI: 54 & 55c, 55b, 56 & 57c, 57tr; B. R. CHOPRA FILMS: 209b; BRITISH LIBRARY, London: 43b; CRAFTS MUSEUM, New Delhi, Pankaj Shah: 86tr/ca/cb, 87tl/tc/cb; DEAN K BROWN: 78t; DK CLASSIC ASIAN COOK BOOK: 25/tc/crb; DN DUBE: 52bl/b, 53cr, 75bc, 170tr, 171t, 172tr/c.

FOTOMEDIA PICTURE LIBRARY: 9 (inset), 29tr, 52tc, 54clb, 55t, 56cb, 105b, 120c (4 pics), 133 (inset), 295bl; Aditya Arya: 295br; Akhil Bakshi: 21t, 22bcr, 28br/b, 29b, 32clb, 195b, 272t, 289t, 294t/b/bl; Amar Talwar: 60cl, 172b, 251clb, 269b, 296t; Amita Prashar Gupta: 266b; Ashim Ghosh: 21bl, 22bcl, 50b, 58cb, 173b, 271t, 278b, 280b, 281b, 283t, 301t; Ashish Chandola: 168b; Ashish Khokar: 283c, 297t; Ashok Dilwali: 150b, 170tl, 172tl; Ashok Kaul: 61tl, 215b; Bimla Verma: 20tl, 22t, 23cr, 34tr, 49bl, 93b, 141bl, 163b, 268br/bcr; BN Khazanchi: 36c, 37br, 169bc, 272c; BPS Walia: 143br, 270c; Christine Pemberton: 15c, 40cl; Deepak Budhraja: 40b; Dharmendar Kanwar: 266t; E Hanumantha Rao: 18tl/clb/bc, 211trc, 225cb/b; François Gautier: 21b; J Saha: 20b; Jatinder Singh: 20tr; Jitendra Singh: 22bc; Joanna van Gruisen: 18cra/b/bl,19cra/bl, 48cb, 61ca, 210b, 224cl; M Balan: 33bcl, 169b; Manu Bahuguna: 39b, 71b, 91b, 232b/bl, 273t; Marie D' Souza: 33cr, 60t, 180t, 269br; Mathew Titus: 23br; Mohit Satyanand: 274b; MS Oberoi: 22br, 254t; Nagaraja: 211t; Neeraj Mishra: 18cla; Nihal Mathur: 224tr; NP Singh: 32b, 184bl; NPS Jhalla: 268bc; NS Chawla: 27c; Pallava Bagla: 18tr, 19tl/tr/trc, 35cr, 38t, 210tl; Pankaj Sekhsaria: 169trc; Pradeep Das Gupta: 255tc; Pradeep Mandhani: 40cl, 61t, 272b; Prakash Israni: 17tl, 22cl, 35cla, 37b, 163tlc, 173bl, 274t; Prem Kapoor: 37c, 38b, 46t, 60b, 60 & 61c, 61br/b; Raj Salhotra: 32cla; Ravi Kaimal: 17c; RK Wadhwa: 23cra; RS Chundawat: 18crb, 116b, 210tr, 211b; S Nayak: 168c; S Venugopal: 141c; Sanjay Saxena: 32cl, 145c, 185b; Sanjeev Saith: 16b,137b, 275t/b;

Sanjiv Misra: 41t; Shalini Saran: 20c, 28tr, 30cl, 32 & 33c, 37t, 38c, 46br, 49tl, 50 & 51c, 52br, 53br, 54br, 57tl, 63 (inset), 73t/b, 88, 107b, 114t, 147b, 150tt, 152tl, 153b, 173tl, 174b, 216tl, 249b; SK Panda: 19cla; Subhash Bhargava: 17b, 23ca, 36t/b, 39c/bl, 50cb, 54cla, 58t, 144b, 164t/cl/b, 165ca/b, 184t, 192c/bl, 200b, 225t, 228c, 254c, 268cr, 273c/b, 274tr; Sudhir Kasliwal: 48c, 187t/b/bl/cl, 195t, 268tr/trc, 276 & 277; Tarun Chopra. 49br; Thakur Dalip Singh: 33bc; Toby Sinclair: 18br, 19crb/clb, 33bl, 118b, 122, 210cb, 224tl/c/b, 225ca, 270b; TS Satyan: 19br, 76c, 141t, 197b, 228t, 252b (2pics), 255b; V Muthuraman: 226 & 227, 251cb.

FRAZER & HAWS, New Delhi: 118c; FREDRIK & LAURENCE ARVIDSSON: 2 & 3, 14, 66, 89t, 98, 132 & 133, 136, 146, 178, 179b; GANESH SAILI: 101b; HENRY WILSON: 212t, 231t, 232c; ITC HOTEL LTD. WELCOMGROUP: 121t, 228b, 248b, 249c; KAMAL SAHAI: 45tr/cla, 47tl; NATIONAL MUSEUM, New Delhi: 44t/cl/bl, 45b, 46c, 46cb, 46 & 47c, 47b, 50t, 51t/bl, 53tr, 72tl/tr/ca/cl/bl/b, 141br, 167tl; JC Arora: 43t, 54bl, 55bl, 64b, 74tl/tr, 75t; RC Dutta Gupta: 29t, 44cla/clb/br, 44 & 45c, 45tlc/cl/ci, 46b, 47tr/cl, 48t/b, 52t, 54t, 74b, 75c/br; NEEMRANA PALACE HOTELS: 48ca, 49tr, 230b, 233c, 249t; THE OBEROI GROUP OF HOTELS: 229b, 230t; OTTO PFISTER: 168t/bl, 169t/c, 211c, 270t; P ROY 187cr/cb.

PRESS INFORMATION BUREAU: 58 & 59 c, 59cr; SATISH SHARMA: 22 & 23c, 23tl/tc/b, 34bl, 35tl; SYNDICATIONS TODAY: 61cb; TEEN MURTI MEMORIAL LIBRARY: 56bl/br, 57b, 58ca, 59tc/bl/br, 60cb; TEXTILE ART SOCIETY: Benoy K Behl 33tc; THEATRE AND TELEVISION ASSOCIATES: Gopi Gajwani 29br; TULSI: Hemant Mehta 269tl; COURTESY OF THE BOARD OF TRUSTEES OF THE V & A MUSEUM: 52cl/ca/cb.

Works of art have been reproduced with the permission of the following copyright holders: © National Gallery of Modern Art, New Delhi: 30 & 31 (all pictures except 30cl).

## SPECIAL ASSISTANCE IN PHOTOGRAPHY
Ajai Shankar, Director-General, Archaeological Survey of India, New Delhi; Aman Nath; Anjali Sen, Director, National Gallery of Modern Art, New Delhi; Aruna Dhir, The Oberoi Hotel New Delhi; Dr Daljeet Kaur, National Museum, New Delhi; JC Grover, National Museum, New Delhi; Jyotindra Jain, Crafts Museum, New Delhi; OP Jain, Sanskriti Museum; Dr RD Chowdhouri, Director-General, National Museum, New Delhi.

Front endpaper: All special photography except SHALINI SARAN: tr.

Jacket: All special photography except ASHIM GHOSH: back b; FREDRIK & LAURENCE ARVIDSSON: front t/cl/cr/c and spine b; PREM KAPOOR: front bl; TOBY SINCLAIR: front cra.

Every effort has been made to trace the copyright holders, and we apologize for any unintentional omissions. We would be pleased to insert the appropriate acknowledgments in all subsequent editions of this publication.

# Further Reading

**ARCHITECTURE**

*Delhi and its Neighbourhood* Sharma, Y.D., Archaeological Survey of India, Delhi 1982.

*Delhi, the City of Monuments* Dube, D.N. and Ramanathan, J., Timeless Books, New Delhi 1997.

*Fatehpur Sikri* Brand, M. and Lowry, G.D. (eds.), Marg Publications, Mumbai 1987.

*Indian Architecture* Brown, P., (2 vols) D.B. Taraporevala Sons & Co. Pvt. Ltd., Bombay 1964.

*Mughal Architecture* Koch, E., PRESTEL-Verlag, Munich 1991.

*Mughal India* Tillotson, G.H.R., Penguin, London 1991.

*Sacred Architecture* Pereira, J., Islamic Books & Books, New Delhi 1994.

*Stones of Empire* Morris, J., Oxford University Press, Oxford 1983.

*Taj Mahal: The Illumined Tomb* Begley, W.E., Aga Khan Program for Islamic Architecture, Massachussetts 1989.

*The Architecture of India* Grover, S., (2 vols), Vikas Publishing House Pvt. Ltd., New Delhi 1981.

*The Forts of India* Fass, V., Collins, London 1986.

*The History of Architecture in India* Tadgell, C., Phaidon, London 1990.

*The Palaces of India* Fass, V. and Maharaja of Baroda, Collins, London 1980.

*The Penguin Guide to the Monuments of India* (Vol 2) Davies, P., Viking, London 1989.

**CULTURE AND CRAFTS**

*A Second Paradise* Patnaik, N., Sidgwick and Jackson Ltd., London, 1985.

*Catalogue of the Crafts Museum* New Delhi 1982.

*Curry and Bugles* Brennan, J., Penguin, London 1992.

*Dance of the Peacock* Bala Krishnan, U. and Kumar, M.S., India Book House, Mumbai 1999.

*The Essence of Indian Art* Goswamy, B. N., Mapin International, San Francisco 1986.

*Hanklyn-Janklin* Hankin, N., Banyan Books, Delhi 1992.

*Indian Art* Dehejia, V., Phaidon, London 1997.

*Indian Painting* Randhawa, M.S. and Galbraith, J.K., Vakils, Feffer & Simon Limited, Bombay 1982.

*Masterpieces from the National Museum Collection* Gupta, S.P., National Museum, New Delhi 1985.

*Paradise as a Garden* Moynihan, E.B., George Braziller Inc., New York 1979.

*The Arts of India* Birdwood, G.C.M., Nanda Book Service, Delhi 1997.

*The Golden Calm* Kaye, M.M. (ed.), Webb & Bower, Exeter 1980.

*The Painted Walls of Shekhawati* Nath, A. and Wacziarg F., Croom & Helm, London 1982.

*The Splendour of Mathura Art and Museum* Sharma, R.C., DK Printworld (P) Ltd., New Delhi 1994.

**FICTION**

*A Passage to India* Forster, E. M., Penguin, London 1924.

*A Suitable Boy* Seth, V., Viking, New Delhi 1993.

*City of Djinns* Dalrymple, W., Flamingo, London 1994.

*The Raj Quartet* Scott, P., Heinemann, London 1976.

*Train to Pakistan* Singh, K., Ravi Dayal Publisher, Delhi 1988.

**HISTORY**

*A History of India* (Vol 2), Spear, P., Penguin, London 1956.

*A Princess Remembers* Gayatri Devi, Rupa and Co., New Delhi 1995.

*Annals and Antiquities of Rajasthan* Tod, J., Oxford University Press,Oxford 1920.

*Delhi Between Two Empires* Gupta, N., Oxford University Press, Delhi 1981.

*Delhi and its Monuments* Spear, P., Gupta N. and Sykes, L., Oxford University Press, New Delhi 1994.

*Freedom at Midnight* Lapierre, D. and Collins, L., Vikas Publishing House Pvt. Ltd., Delhi 1976.

*India Britannica* Moorhouse, G., Paladin Books, London 1984.

*Indian Mythology* Ions, V., Paul Hamlyn, London 1967.

*Jaipur* Nath, A., India Book House, Mumbai 1993.

*Lives of the Indian Princes* Allen, C. and Dwivedi, S. London 1985.

*Myths and Symbols in Indian Art and Civilization* Zimmer, H., Harper and Brothers, New York 1962.

*Symbols in Art and Religion* Werner, K. (ed.), Motilal Banarsidass Publishers Pvt. Ltd., Delhi 1991.

*The History of India* Dodwell, H. H. (ed.), 6 vols, Cambridge University Press, Cambridge 1934.

*The Great Moghuls* Gascoigne, B., Dorset Press, London 1971.

*The Wonder that was India* Basham, A.L., Rupa and Co., New Delhi 1966.

**NATURE AND WILDLIFE**

*Bharatpur: Bird Paradise* Ewans, M., Lustre Press, New Delhi 1992.

*Book of Indian Animals* Prater, W., Bombay Natural History Society, Bombay 1948.

*Book of Indian Birds* Ali, S., Bombay Natural History Society, Bombay 1941.

*The Garden of Life* Patnaik, N., Doubleday, New York 1993.

*In Danger* Manfredi, P., Ranthambhore Foundation, New Delhi 1997.

*Indian Wildlife* Israel S. and Sinclair T. (eds.), APA Publications, Singapore 1989.

*Nature Watch* Singh, K. and Basu, S., Lustre Press, New Delhi 1990.

*Birds of India* Grewal, B., Local Colour, Hong Kong 2000.

*Tigers: The Secret Life* Thapar, V., Elm Tree Books, London 1989.

# Glossary

## ARCHITECTURE

**ashram**: hermitage
**bagh**: garden
**bangaldar**: curved roof derived from Bengali hut *(see p26)*
**baradari**: pavilion with 12 pillars *(see p196)*
**basti**: settlement *(see p81)*
**charbagh**: quadripartite garden *(see p27)*
**dharamshala**: charitable rest house for pilgrims
**ghar**: house, crypt *(see p114)*
**gali**: lane
**jaali**: carved lattice work on stone screens *(see p25)*
**katra**: side lane *(see p89)*
**khirkee**: window
**kotla**: a citadel or fortified area within a city
**kund**: pool, tank *(see p117)*
**mahal**: palace
**mardana**: men's quarters in a palace
**maqbara**: burial-palace, mausoleum, sepulchre *(see p142)*
**masjid**: mosque
**mehmankhana**: guesthouse
**minar**: freestanding tower
**minaret**: tower in mosque for calling the faithful to prayer
**pol**: gate *(see p183)*
**toshakhana**: state treasury *(see p190)*
**zenana**: women's quarters in a palace

## CRAFT AND CULTURE

**bandhini**: tie-and-dye *(see p86)*
**dholak**: drum *(see p97)*
**Dhrupad**: style of North Indian classical music *(see p28)*
**ganjifa**: set of playing cards *(see p141)*
**gharana**: school of classical music or dance *(see p28)*
**ikat**: tie-and-dye yarn woven in a pattern
**katha**: epic tale *(see p29)*
**matka**: earthenware pot
**mela**: fair, fête
**patachitra**: painted scroll with mythological tales *(see p141)*

**phad**: painted cloth scroll from Rajasthan *(see p194)*
**pichhwai**: cloth painting depicting Krishna lore
**raga**: melodic structure with a fixed sequence of musical notes *(see p28)*
**rasa**: mood; essence *(see p29)*
**shahtoosh**: a fine shawl, now banned, that can pass through a ring. It is woven from the down of the endangered chiru antelope.
**tala**: rhythmic cycle of varying beats *(see p28)*
**thal-posh**: dish cover *(see p190)*

## DRESS

**burqa**: concealing cloak worn by Muslim women
**chador**: ceremonial pall of cloth or flowers placed over a Muslim tomb *(see p82)*
**dhoti**: unstitched garment of Hindu men which covers the lower half of the body
**gota**: gold or silver frill
**jootis**: slippers *(see p186)*
**khadi**: hand-woven, hand-spun cloth popularized by Gandhi *(see pp58–59)*
**lehenga**: flounced skirt *(see p93)*
**mukut**: crown *(see p186)*
**zari**: gold thread

## RELIGION

**aarti**: ritual of Hindu worship
**ahimsa**: non-violence
**amrit**: sacred nectar of the gods *(see p23)*
**Balaji**: one of Hanuman's many names in North India *(see p197)*
**bhajan**: devotional song *(see p28)*
**Chishtiyas**: followers of the 12th century Sufi saint, Moinuddin Chishti *(see p82)*
**dharma**: duty, calling *(see p141)*
**kalasha**: urn *(see p115)*
**lila**: divine sport *(see p163)*
**linga**: phallic emblem of Lord Shiva *(see p86)*
**madrasa**: Islamic theological college

***Mahabharata***: famous Hindu epic *(see p141)*
**namaaz**: ritual prayers of Muslims
**pir**: Muslim saint *(see p82)*
**puja**: ritual prayer *(see pp22)*
***Ramayana***: epic on the legend of Lord Rama
**samadhi**: memorial platform over site of cremation *(see p97)*
**sati**: practice of self-immolation by a widow on her husband's funeral pyre
**Shaivite**: followers of Shiva
**tirthankara**: Jain prophet
***Upanishads***: philosophical texts regarded as sacred scripture, dating to the later Vedic age *(see p20)*
**Vaishnavite**: followers of Vishnu
***Vedas***: texts codifying Aryan beliefs and principles, these were orally transmitted until transcribed into Sanskrit as the *Rig Veda, Sama Veda, Yajur Veda* and *Atharva Veda (see p20)*
**yagna**: vedic rite

## MISCELLANEOUS

**badal**: cloud *(see p182)*
**bahi khatha**: cloth bound account book *(see p186)*
**charpoy**: string cot
**chowkidar**: watchman
**Doctrine of Lapse**: this gave the British the right to take direct control of princely states that did not have an undisputed heir *(see p56)*
**haat**: open-air market
**ikka**: pony trap *(see p191)*
**jheel**: shallow lake
**katar**: two-sided blade
**loo**: hot westerly wind that blows over North India from April to June
**machan**: look-out post
**mohur**: Mughal gold coin
**nawab**: a Muslim prince
**pachisi**: a ludo-like dice game *(see p171)*
**Raj**: the period of British rule in India *(see pp56–57)*
**Satyagraha**: a form of moral protest started by Gandhi *(see pp58–59)*
**thakur**: Hindu chieftain

# Phrase Book

HINDI IS THE NATIONAL LANGUAGE of India and even though it is not the mother tongue of a major proportion of the population, it is spoken widely in this region. All nouns are either masculine or feminine and the adjective agrees with the noun. Most masculine nouns end with –aa (as in rather), most feminine nouns end with –i (as in thin), while all plural nouns end in –e (as in hen). Verb endings also differ if it is a man or woman speaking. In the present tense, a man ends his verbs with –a, a woman ends hers with –i.

## IN AN EMERGENCY

| | |
|---|---|
| Help! | Bachao |
| Stop! | Roko |
| Call a doctor! | Doctor ko bulao |
| Where is the nearest telephone? | Yahan phone kahan hai? |

## COMMUNICATION ESSENTIALS

| | |
|---|---|
| Yes | Haan |
| No | Na/ naheen |
| Thank you | Dhanyavad/Shukria |
| Please | Kripaya/Meharbani se |
| Excuse me/sorry | Kshama karen/Maaf karen |
| Hello/goodbye | Namaste |
| Halt | Rook jao |
| Let's go | Chalo |
| Straight ahead | Seedha |
| Big/Small | Bara/Chhota |
| This/That | Yeh/Voh |
| Near/Far | Paas/Door |
| Way | Raasta |
| Road | Sarak |
| Yesterday | Beeta hua kal |
| Today | Aaj |
| Tomorrow | Aane wala kal |
| Here | Yahaan |
| There | Wahaan |
| What? | Kya? |
| Where? | Kahaan? |
| When? | Kab? |
| Why? | Kyon? |
| How? | Kaise? |
| Up | Upar |
| Down | Neeche |
| More | Aur zyada |
| A little | Thora |
| Before | Pehle |
| Opposite/facing | Saamne |
| Very | Bahut |
| Less | Kam |
| Louder/harder | Zor se |
| Softly/gently | Dheere se |
| Go | Jao |
| Come | Aao |

## USEFUL PHRASES

| | |
|---|---|
| How are you? | Aap kaise hain? |
| What is your name? | Aapka naam kya hai? |
| My name is ... | Mera naam ... hai. |
| Do you speak English? | Angrezi ati hai? |
| I understand | Samajh gaya/gayi |
| I don't understand | Nahin samjha/samjhi |
| What is the time? | Kya baja hai? |
| Where is ...? | ...Kahaan hai? |
| What is this? | Yeh kya hai? |
| Hurry up | Jaldi karo |
| How far is ...? | ... Kitni door hai? |
| I don't know | Pata nahin |
| All right | Achcha/Theek hai |
| Now/instantly | Abhi/Isi waqt |
| Well done! | Shabash! |
| See you | Phir milenge |
| Go away! | Hat jao/Hato |
| I don't want it | Mujhe nahin chahiye |
| Not now | Abhi Nahin |

## USEFUL WORDS

| | |
|---|---|
| Which | Kaun Sa |
| Who | Kaun |
| Hot | Garam |
| Cold | Thanda |
| Good | Achha |
| Bad | Kharaab |
| Enough | Bus/Kafi hai |
| Open | Khula |
| Closed | Bund |
| Left | Baayan |
| Right | Daayan |
| Straight on | Seedha |
| Near | Paas/Nazdeek |
| Quickly | Jaldi |
| Late | Der se |
| Later | Baad mein |
| Entrance | Pravesh |
| Exit | Nikas |
| Behind | Peechhe |
| Full | Bhara |
| Empty | Khali |
| Toilet | Shauchaalaya |
| Free/no charge | Nih shulka, muft |
| Direction | Disha |
| Book | Kitab |
| Magazine | Patrika |
| Newspaper | Akhbaar |

## SHOPPING

| | |
|---|---|
| How much does this cost? | Iska kya daam hai? |
| I would like... | Mujhe ... chahiye. |
| Do you have...? | Kya aap ke paas ... hai? |
| I am just looking | Abhi dekh rahen hain |
| Does it come in other colours? | Yeh dooserey rangon main bhi aata hai kya? |
| This one | Yeh wala |
| That one | Voh wala |
| Black | Kaala |
| Blue | Neela |
| White | Safed |
| Red | Lal |
| Yellow | Peela |
| Green | Hara |
| Brown | Bhura |
| Cheap | Sasta |
| Expensive | Mehanga |
| Tailor | Darzi |

## BARGAINING

| | |
|---|---|
| How much is this? | Yeh kitne ka hai? |
| How much will you take? | Kya loge? |
| That's a little expensive | Yeh to mehanga hai |
| Could you lower the price a bit? | Daam thoda kam kariye |
| How about XX rupee? | XX rupeye lainge? |
| I'll settle for XX rupees. | XX rupeye mein dena hai to dijiye |

## STAYING IN A HOTEL

| | |
|---|---|
| Do you have any vacant rooms? | Aapke hotel mein khali kamre hain kya? |
| What is the charge per night? | Ek raat ka kiraya kya hai? |
| Can I see the room first? | Kya main pehle kamra dekh sakta hoon? |
| Key | Chaabhi |
| Soap | Sabun |
| Towel | Tauliya |
| Hot/cold water | Garam/thanda pani |

## EATING OUT

| | |
|---|---|
| Breakfast | Nashta |
| Food | Khaana |
| Water | Pani |
| Ice | Baraf |
| Tea | Chai |
| Coffee | Kaufi |
| Sugar | Cheeni |
| Salt | Namak |
| Milk | Doodh |
| Yoghurt | Dahi |
| Egg | Anda |
| Fruit | Phal |
| Vegetable | Sabzi |
| Rice | Chaawal |
| Pulse (lentil, split pea etc) | Dal |
| Fixed priced menu | Ek daam menu |
| Is it spicy? | Mirch-masala tez hai kya? |
| Not too spicy, ok? | Mirch-masala kam, theek hai? |
| Knife | Chhuri |
| Fork | Kanta |
| Spoon | Chammach |
| Finish | Khatam |

## NUMBERS

| | |
|---|---|
| 1 | Ek |
| 2 | Do |
| 3 | Teen |
| 4 | Char |
| 5 | Panch |
| 6 | Chhe |
| 7 | Saat |
| 8 | Aath |
| 9 | Nau |
| 10 | Dus |
| 11 | Gyarah |
| 12 | Barah |
| 13 | Terah |
| 14 | Chaudah |
| 15 | Pundrah |
| 16 | Solah |
| 17 | Satrah |
| 18 | Atharah |
| 19 | Unnees |
| 20 | Bees |
| 30 | Tees |
| 40 | Chalees |
| 50 | Pachaas |
| 60 | Saath |
| 70 | Sattar |
| 80 | Assi |
| 90 | Nabbe |
| 100 | Sau |
| 1,000 | Hazar |
| 100,000 | Lakh |
| 10,000,000 | Karod (crore) |

## TIME

| | |
|---|---|
| One minute | Ek minit |
| One hour | Ek ghanta |
| Half an hour | Aadha ghanta |
| Quarter hour | Pauna ghanta |
| Half past one | Derh |
| Half past two | Dhai |
| A day | Ek din |
| A week | Ek haftah |
| Monday | Somwar |
| Tuesday | Mangalwar |
| Wednesday | Budhwar |
| Thursday | Veerwar |
| Friday | Shukrawar |
| Saturday | Shaniwar |
| Sunday | Raviwar |
| Morning | Subah |
| Afternoon | Dopahar |
| Evening | Shaam |
| Night | Raat |

# DORLING KINDERSLEY *TRAVEL GUIDES*

## TITLES AVAILABLE

### THE GUIDES THAT SHOW YOU WHAT OTHERS ONLY TELL YOU

#### COUNTRY GUIDES

AUSTRALIA • CANADA • FRANCE • GREAT BRITAIN
GREECE: ATHENS & THE MAINLAND • THE GREEK ISLANDS
IRELAND • ITALY • MEXICO • PORTUGAL • SCOTLAND
SOUTH AFRICA • SPAIN • THAILAND

#### REGIONAL GUIDES

BARCELONA & CATALONIA • CALIFORNIA
FLORENCE & TUSCANY • FLORIDA • HAWAII
JERUSALEM & THE HOLY LAND • LOIRE VALLEY
MILAN & THE LAKES • NAPLES WITH POMPEII & THE
AMALFI COAST • PROVENCE & THE COTE D'AZUR • SARDINIA
SEVILLE & ANDALUSIA • SICILY • VENICE & THE VENETO
GREAT PLACES TO STAY IN EUROPE

#### CITY GUIDES

AMSTERDAM • BERLIN • BUDAPEST • DUBLIN • ISTANBUL
LISBON • LONDON • MADRID • MOSCOW • NEW YORK
PARIS • PRAGUE • ROME • SAN FRANCISCO
ST PETERSBURG • SYDNEY • VIENNA • WARSAW

#### TRAVEL MAPS

AUSTRALIA • FRANCE • FLORIDA
GREAT BRITAIN & IRELAND • ITALY • SPAIN

### DK TRAVEL GUIDES PHRASE BOOKS

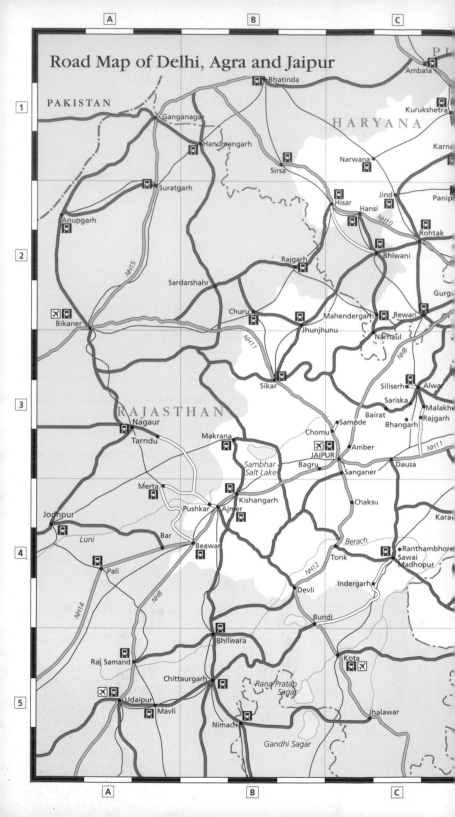

# Road Map of Delhi, Agra and Jaipur